LINUX
KERNEL
PROGRAMMING

3RD EDITION

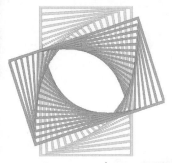

LINUX KERNEL PROGRAMMING

ALGORITHMS AND STRUCTURES OF VERSION 2.4
UPDATED AND EXTENDED 3RD EDITION

MICHAEL BECK, HARALD BÖHME, MIRKO DZIADZKA,

ULRICH KUNITZ, ROBERT MAGNUS, CLAUS SCHRÖTER,

DIRK VERWORNER

an imprint of **Pearson Education**

London • Boston • Indianapolis • New York • Mexico City • Toronto • Sydney • Tokyo • Singapore

Hong Kong • Cape Town • New Delhi • Madrid • Paris • Amsterdam • Munich • Milan • Stockholm

PEARSON EDUCATION LIMITED

Head Office:
Edinburgh Gate
Harlow CM20 2JE
Tel: +44 (0)1279 623623
Fax: +44 (0)1279 431059

London Office:
128 Long Acre
London WC2E 9AN
Tel: +44 (0)20 7447 2000
Fax: +44 (0)20 7447 2170

Website: www.it-minds.com
        www.aw.com/cseng

First published in Great Britain in 2002
English edition © Pearson Education Limited 2002

First published in German as *Linux Kernel-programmierung; Algorithmen und Strukturen der Version 2.46.Auflage*
by Addison-Wesley Verlag, Martin-Kollar-Strasse 10-12, D-81829 München, Germany.

The rights of Michael Beck, Harald Böhme, Mirko Dziadzka, Ulrich Kunitz, Robert Magnus, Claus Schröter,
and Dirk Verworner to be identified as Authors of this Work have been asserted by them in accordance with the
Copyright, Designs and Patents Act 1988.

ISBN 0-201-71975-4

British Library Cataloguing in Publication Data
A CIP catalogue record for this book can be obtained from the British Library

Library of Congress Cataloging in Publication Data
Linux-Kernel-Programmierung. English
Linux kernel programming: algorithms and structures of version 2.4 / Michael Beck... [et
al.].--Updated and extended 3rd ed.
   p cm.
Translation of: Linux-Kernel-Programmierung.
Includes bibliographical references.
ISBN 0-201-71975-4(pbk. : alk.paper)
   1. Linux. 2. Operating systems (Computers) 3. Applications software. I.Beck, Michael.
II. Title.
QA76.76.O63 L54813 2002
005.4'469--dc21

                                                                                    2001056671

The programs in this book and on the CD-ROM have been included for their instructional value. The publisher
does not offer any warranties or representations in respect of their fitness for a particular purpose, nor does the
publisher accept any liability for any loss or damage arising from their use.

10 9 8 7 6 5 4 3 2 1

Designed by Claire Brodmann Book Designs, Lichfield, Staffs
Typeset by Cybertechnics, Sheffield
Printed and bound in Great Britain by Biddles Ltd of Guildford and King's Lynn.

The Publishers' policy is to use paper manufactured from sustainable forests.

CONTENTS

CHAPTER 8 NETWORK IMPLEMENTATION 230

CHAPTER 9 MODULES AND DEBUGGING 261

PREFACE

PREFACE TO THE 3RD EDITION

In a competition at this year's CeBIT, one of the questions was: which LINUX version came before version 0.95? I have to admit that I don't know the answer, but I know for sure that it was not 0.94.

This reminds us of the early days of LINUX, and the creative chaos that surrounded it. At that time it was a challenge for many co-developers of LINUX to understand and modify the sources of an operating system.

Since then, LINUX has not only reached the magical milestone of version 2.4, but also won a solid position in the highly competitive software field. With regard to the challenge of understanding an operating system, nothing has changed, in fact it has become even greater.

Many of the features added since the last milestone version not only embody the very simple functions of an operating system, but more and more functions which provide compatibility with large software products, support new hardware, or improve the performance of the system. Version 2.4 also offers exciting new concepts like IP tables and improved plug-and-play.

As with every new milestone of the LINUX kernel, a kernel book must also be revised to cover the new features. Despite big changes to interfaces and concepts, the book again gives an insight into the workings of LINUX. We hope you will not only enjoy reading it, but also enjoy experimenting with the LINUX kernel.

Michael Beck, Ulrich Kunitz, Harald Böhme,
Robert Magnus, Mirko Dziadzka, Claus Schröter
Berlin/Frankfurt/Furtwangen, 24. 4. 2001

AUTHORS' PREFACE TO THE 1ST EDITION

LINUX has been around for about two years. What started as a programming exercise by the computer science student Linus Torvalds, has become one of the most successful free software projects of today, and gives serious competition to commercial systems. This is the result of the voluntary work of a worldwide programming community connected by the internet, an effective communication medium. The free availability of LINUX has contributed to its quick distribution. Therefore it is hard to estimate the number of LINUX users. In Germany there are more than ten thousand.

We discovered the LINUX system about 18 months ago. One result of this is that that we now have a "correct" UNIX system for our local PCs, without having to put thousands of dollars on the table, which, as students, we didn't have anyway.

The other, perhaps more important, benefit for us, and possibly for the majority of the LINUX community in the world, is the availability of the source code of the LINUX system. It is quite simply fun to root about in the internals of an operating system to try out your own ideas, and out of pure interest to adapt the system to your own wishes. This book is aimed at everybody who thinks the same way, but also at those who simply want to find out how a 32-bit operating system works.

The LINUX kernel has increased in size over time, and one can no longer obtain a good overview. Since the documentation is thin (the only documentation we know of is the outline of the LINUX *Kernel Hackers Guide* [Joh95]), in 1993 we started a LINUX seminar in the summer semester. Everybody involved in LINUX at our workplace, gave an insight into his or her area of interest, knowledge, and experience with "kernel hacking." In the seminar there were often discussions about modeling concepts, implementation variants, and implementation details, which were grasped in various ways. In the context of this seminar we began to write down our knowledge about the LINUX system, to make it simpler for others. This knowledge is revised and represented here.

As the development of LINUX progresses so quickly, we couldn't allow ourselves too much time to write the book. We therefore divided the book into chapters according to the respective area of interest of the authors. Ulrich Kunitz wrote the introduction, the chapter about memory management and the chapter about interprocess communication. Mirko Dziadzka took responsibility for the introduction to the kernel. Harald Böhme, our net expert, surely ought to have written a whole book explaining the network implementation extensively. He could only write an introduction to the matter here. The thankless task of working out the referencing of system calls and explaining system commands was given to Robert Magnus. The other authors split the rest of the chapters between them.

Identifiers from the source code are set in a sanserif font in the text. Parameters are set in an italic serif font. For example:

% make *Argument*

Since not all readers of this book have access to the internet, the enclosed CD contains the Slackware distribution 1.2.0 and German LST distribution 1.7. They allow you to install corresponding startup disks from the CD, which have been produced with the assistance of the MS-DOS programs `GZIP.EXE` and `RAWRITE.EXE`. The authors would like to express their thanks to Patrick J.Volkerding and the LINUX support team, consisting of Ralf Flaxa and Stefan Probst, for the very extensive work that has been put into this book.

The CD contains the LINUX-Kernel version 1.0.9[1] and the sources of the programs explained in Appendix B as well as the sources of the GNU C library and the G ++ library. It also contains texts from the LINUX Documentation Project and the internet RFCs. The files aren't compressed and can be integrated in the directory structure in LINUX using the `mount` command.

The contents of the book correspond to our present knowledge of the LINUX kernel 1.0 but this knowledge is not yet complete. We would be grateful for any corrections, suggestions, notes, and comments.

We can be reached by e-mail at this address: `linux@informatik.hu-berlin.de`

Those who do not have access to e-mail can write to us at:

Linux-Team
Humboldt-Universität zu Berlin
Institut für Informatik
10099 Berlin

LINUS TORVALDS' PREFACE TO THE 1ST EDITION

Creating an operating system has been (and still is) an exciting project, and has been made even more rewarding through the extensive (and almost uniformly positive) feedback from users and developers alike.

One of the problems for people wanting to get to know the kernel internals better has been the lack of documentation, and fledgling kernel hackers have had to resort to reading the actual source code of the system for most of the details. While I think that is still a good idea, I'm happy that there is now more documentation like this which explains the use of LINUX and its internals.

I hope you enjoy LINUX and this book.

Linus Torvalds
Helsinki, 28. 4. 1994

---

1. *Note from the editor* – the CD accompanying this Third Edition contains LINUX kernel version 2.4.4.

ACKNOWLEDGMENTS

This book would not have been possible without the work of several other people. First we would like to thank all the LINUX hackers in the world, and of course Linus Torvalds. A further thank you goes to the Free Software Foundation (also known as GNU). Without GNU software, LINUX would not be what it is today.

We would also like to thank the employees and students at the Institute of Computer Science of the Humboldt-University of Berlin and the Faculty of Computer Science at Furtwangen Technical College who have supported us in our work.

Finally we would like to thank the innumerable copy editors, first of all Ralf Kühnel; the meticulous corrections were a great help to us.

Martin von Löwis also deserves to be mentioned, as he gave constructive criticism and supported us in the implementation of the Windows NT file system for LINUX.

Have a good time reading and working with LINUX!

Michael Beck, Ulrich Kunitz, Harald Böhme,
Robert Magnus, Mirko Dziadzka, Dirk Verworner
Berlin/Furtwangen, 1. 5. 94

1 LINUX – THE OPERATING SYSTEM

LINUX is a freely available UNIX-like operating system. Originally developed only for the PC, it now runs on systems such as Pocket PCs, and is already relatively stable.

LINUX is compatible with the POSIX-1003.1 standard and includes most of the functionality of UNIX System V and BSD. Essential parts of the LINUX kernel with which we will be concerned in this book were written by Linus Torvalds, a Finnish student of computer science. He placed the program source codes under the *GNU Public License*, which means that everyone has the right to use, copy, and modify the programs free of charge.

The first version of the LINUX kernel became available on the internet in 1991. A group of LINUX activists soon formed, who drove the development of this operating system forward. Numerous users test the new versions and help to clear bugs out of the software.

The LINUX software is developed under open and distributed conditions. "Open" means that anyone can become involved if they are able to do so. This requires LINUX activists to be able to communicate quickly, efficiently, and above all, globally. The medium for this is the internet. It is therefore no surprise that many of the developments are the product of gifted students with access to the internet at their universities and colleges. The development systems available to these students tend to be relatively modest and it is no doubt for this reason that LINUX is still the 32-bit operating system that uses the least resources without sacrificing functionality.

As LINUX is distributed under the conditions of the GNU Public License [GPL], the complete source code is available to users. This allows anyone to find out how the system works, and trace and remove any bugs. However, the real attraction for the authors of this book lies in "experimenting" with the system.

Needless to say, LINUX has its drawbacks. It is a "programmer system" like UNIX. Cryptic commands, configurations that are difficult to follow, and documentation that is not always comprehensible make it far from easy to use – and not only for beginners. However, it appears that many users accept this downside to escape the number of limitations (technical as well as financial) found in proprietary systems such as MS-DOS, Windows or commercial UNIX derivates for the PC. Since LINUX first appeared, many books accessible to beginners have been written in addition to the LINUX Document Project [LDP].

LINUX systems are used in software houses, by internet providers, in schools and universities, and in private homes. There are no computer magazines that do not regularly report on this operating system. Considering LINUX simply as a hackers' toy no longer does justice to reality.

Although there are ports to other hardware architectures, most users still run LINUX on Intel 386 or compatible systems. Owing to the wide availability of these systems, there are almost no problems under LINUX with peripheral device drivers. As soon as a new PC expansion board is on the market, some LINUX user will implement a driver from that platform. Since version 2.0 LINUX has also supported multiprocessor systems.

To ensure reasonable performance under LINUX, the PC should have at least 8 Mbytes of RAM, but if the X Window system is being used as the graphical user interface, at least 16 Mbytes are needed. With double this amount, working even becomes fun if you are running several compilers in the background and trying to edit a text in the foreground. However, for special applications such as modem/fax servers or firewalls, 4 Mbytes are sufficient.

In principle, LINUX supports any readily available UNIX software. Thus, object-oriented programs can be written in GNU C++ or graphics can be created under the X Window system. Games such as Tetris will run, as will development systems for graphical user interfaces. With their built-in network support, LINUX computers can be linked into existing networks without problems. This book is (of course) written using LATEX in LINUX.

1.1 MAIN CHARACTERISTICS

LINUX will meet all the demands made nowadays of a modern, UNIX-type operating system.

Multitasking LINUX supports true preemptive multitasking. All processes run entirely independently of each other. No process needs to be concerned with making processor time available to other processes.

Multi-user LINUX allows a number of users to work with the system at the same time. Cards from manufacturers who keep information about the functionality of their hardware secret are the exception to this.

Multiprocessing From version 2.0 upwards, LINUX also runs on multiprocessor architectures. This means that the operating system can distribute several applications (in true parallel fashion) across several processors.

Architecture independence LINUX runs on almost all platforms that are able to process bits and bytes. The supported hardware, from embedded systems to IBM mainframes, is sufficient. This kind of hardware independence is not achieved by any other serious operating system.

Demand load executables Only those parts of a program actually required for execution are loaded into memory. When creating a new process by means of fork(), memory for data is not requested immediately, but the data memory for the data process is used for both processes. If the new process subsequently accesses part of the memory in write mode, this section is copied before being modified. This process is known as *copy-on-write*.

Paging Despite the best efforts to use physical memory efficiently, it may be that the available memory is fully occupied. LINUX then looks for 4 Kbyte pages of memory which can be freed. *Pages* whose contents are already stored on hard disk (for example, program files) are discarded. If one of these pages is subsequently accessed, it has to be reloaded. This procedure is known as paging. It differs from the *swapping* used in older variants of UNIX, where the entire memory for a process is written to disk, which is significantly less efficient.

Dynamic cache for hard disk Users of MS-DOS will be familiar with problems resulting from the need to reserve memory of a fixed size for hard disk cache programs such as SMARTDRIVE. LINUX dynamically adjusts the size of cache memory to suit the current memory usage situation. If no memory is available at a given time, the size of the memory is reduced and new memory provided. Once memory is released, the area of the cache is increased.

Shared libraries are collections of routines needed by a program to work. There are a number of standard libraries used by more than one process at the same time. It therefore makes sense to load the program code for these libraries into memory only once, rather than once for each process. This is made possible by *shared libraries*. As these libraries are only loaded when the process is run, they are also known as dynamically linked libraries. Therefore it is no wonder that in other operating system environments these are known as *dynamic link libraries*.

Support for POSIX 1003.1 standard, in part System V and BSD POSIX 1003.1 defines a minimum interface to a UNIX-type operating system. This standard is now supported by all recent and relatively sophisticated operating systems. LINUX (since version 1.2) has fully supported POSIX 1003.1. There are even LINUX distributions that have gone through the official certification process and therefore have the right to officially call themselves "POSIX compatible." Additional system interfaces for the UNIX System V and BSD developed lines are also implemented.

Various formats for executable files It is naturally desirable to be able to run LINUX programs which run in different system environments. For this reason, emulators for MS-DOS and MS-Windows are currently under development. LINUX can also execute programs for other UNIX systems conforming to the iBCS2 standard. This includes, for example, many commercial programs used under SCO UNIX. Also, in ports to other hardware architectures (for example, Sparc and Alpha), care is taken that the individual "native binaries" can be executed. Thus, there is a wealth of commercial software available to the LINUX user without it having been specially ported to LINUX.

Memory protected mode LINUX uses the processor's memory protection mechanisms to prevent the process from accessing memory allocated to the system kernel or other processes. This is a major contribution to the security of the system. An erroneous program can therefore (theoretically) no longer crash the system.

Support for national keyboards and fonts In LINUX you can use various national keyboards and fonts. Since the Latin1 font defined by the International Organization for Standardization (ISO) contains umlauts, for example, the use of other fonts in Germany is not strictly necessary.

Different file systems LINUX supports a variety of file systems. The most commonly used file system at present is the Second Extended (Ext2) file system. This supports filenames of up to 255 characters and has a number of features making it more secure than conventional UNIX file systems. Other file systems that are implemented are the MS-DOS or Windows 95 partitions, the ISO file system for accessing CD-ROMs and the NFS for accessing the file systems of other manufacturers, and HPFS for accessing the file systems of other UNIX computers present in the network. Less widely spread are the AFF file system for accessing the Amiga Fast File system, the UPS and the Sys V file systems for accessing UNIX file systems of other manufacturers, HPFS for accessing OS/2 partitions, and the Samba file system for accessing systems exported from Windows computers.

Other file systems, such as the Windows NT file system used under Windows NT, are under development and available as beta versions. Journaling file systems, such as the Reiser FS, which are also recommended for commercial systems for their short recovery time, have become widespread. What commercial operating system can offer such a range?

TCP/IP, SLIP and PPP support LINUX can be integrated into local UNIX networks. In principle, all network services, such as the Network File System and Remote Login, can be used. SLIP and PPP support the use of the TCP/IP protocol over serial lines. This means that it is possible to link into the internet via the public telephone network using a high-speed modem.

Embedded LINUX Lately, LINUX has been used more and more for tasks that put emphasis not on user friendliness but on good use of the available resources, for example, the so-called embedded applications, such as industrial controllers, outers, entertainment electronics, and palmtops. In the kernel of version 2.4, some modifications have been carried out that make this application field possible. So, for example, the console can be switched off, and there is a support for commercial flash memory hardware (disk on chip).

1.2   LINUX DISTRIBUTIONS

To install LINUX, the user requires a distribution. This consists of a boot diskette and other diskettes or a CD-ROM. Installation scripts enable even inexperienced users to install systems that can be run. It helps that many software packages are already adapted to LINUX and appropriately configured: this saves a lot of time. Discussions are constantly taking place within the LINUX community on the quality of the various distributions, but these frequently overlook the fact that compiling a distribution of this sort is a very lengthy and complex task.

Internationally, the RedHat, S.u.S.E, Debian, and Slackware distributions are widely used. Which of these distributions is used is a matter of taste. Distributions can be obtained from FTP servers, e-mail systems, public-domain distributors, and some bookshops. Sources of supply can be found by consulting specialist magazines or the LINUX newsgroups in Usenet.

2 COMPILING THE KERNEL

Before we go on to study the inner life of the LINUX kernel in the following chapters, we will first take a look at the source and compiled versions of the kernel.

2.1 WHERE IS EVERYTHING?

As the source codes have grown to a quite considerable size, different parts of the kernel can be found in different directories.

The sources can normally be found under /usr/src/linux. In the following chapters, therefore, the pathnames given are always relative to this directory.

In the ongoing porting to other architectures, the structure of the directory in the single versions of the kernel is always changed.

Architecture-dependent code is held in the subdirectories of arch/. This contains the current directories:

arch/alpha/ for the DEC Alpha architecture,
arch/arm/ for the ARM architecture,
arch/i386/ for the IA-32 architecture,
arch/ia64/ for the IA-64 architecture (Itanium Processor),
arch/m68k/ for the 68000 architecture and compatible processors,
arch/mips/ and arch/mips64 for the MIPS architecture,
arch/parisc/ for the PA RISC architecture,
arch/ppc/ for the PowerPC architecture,
arch/s390/ for the IBM S390 architecture,
arch/sh/ for the SuperH architecture,
arch/sparc/ and
arch/sparc64/ for the port to Sparc workstations.

As LINUX is mainly used on PCs, we will only be considering this architecture in what follows. For the most part, the LINUX kernel is nothing more than a "normal" C program. There are only two real differences: the usual entry function, familiar in C programs as int main(int argc, char *argv[]), is named under LINUX start_kernel (void) and is not given any arguments. In addition, the environment of the "program" does not yet exist. This means that there is a little preparatory work to be done before the first C function is called. The assembler sources which take care of this are held in the directory arch/i386/boot/. They also configure the hardware, so this section is highly machine-specific.

The appropriate assembler routine loads the kernel. It then installs the interrupt service routines, the global descriptor tables, and the interrupt descriptor tables which are only used in the initialization phase. The address line A20 is enabled, and the processor switches to protected mode.

The init/ directory contains all the functions needed to start the kernel. Among the functions held here is start_kernel(), which was mentioned above. Its task is to initialize the kernel correctly, taking account of the boot parameters that are submitted to it. Also, the first process is created without using the system call *fork*, that is, "manually."

The directories kernel/ and arch/i386/kernel/ contain, as their names suggest, the central sections of the kernel. The most important system calls are implemented there. Moreover, the mechanism used by all system calls for the transition to system mode is also defined. Other important sections are time management (system time, timer, etc.), the scheduler, the DMA and interrupt request management, and signal handling.

Memory management sources for the kernel are stored in the directories mm/ and arch/i386/mm/. This takes care of requesting and releasing kernel memory, saving currently unused pages of memory to hard disk (paging), inserting file and memory areas at specified addresses (see the *mmap* system call, Section A.4), and the virtual memory interface.

The virtual file system interface is in the fs/ directory. Some important file systems are *Proc* and *Ext2*. The *Proc* file system is used for system management; *Ext2* is at present "the" standard file system for LINUX.

Every operating system requires drivers for its hardware components. These are held in the drivers/ directory and can be classified into groups according to their subdirectories:

drivers/block/ the device drivers for block-oriented devices (such as hard disks and CD-ROMs),

drivers/cdrom/ the device drivers for proprietary CD-ROM drivers (no SCSI or IDE drivers),

drivers/char/ the character-oriented devices,

drivers/i2c/ a generic I2C driver,

drivers/isdn/ the ISDN drivers,

drivers/net/ the drivers for various network cards,

drivers/pci/ PCI bus access control,

drivers/pnp/ ISA PnP card control,

drivers/sbus/ Sparc S-bus control,

drivers/scsi/ the SCSI interface,

drivers/sound/ the sound card drivers and

drivers/usb/ the driver for the USB subsystem.

There are other subsystems whose drivers can be found here. Some of the drivers listed here are architecture-dependent and would probably belong to the `arch/*/` directory, where the emulation of the FPU is also contained (in `arch/i386/math-emu/`). This only comes into use if no math co-processor is present.

The `ipc/` directory holds the sources for classical interprocess communication (IPC) as per System V. These include semaphores, shared memory, and message queues.

The implementations of various network protocols (TCP, ARP, etc.) and the code for sockets to the UNIX and internet domains have been stored in the `net/` directory. As is usual in other systems, the user can access lower protocol layers (for example, IP and ARP). Because of its complexity, this section has not yet been completed.

Some standard C library functions have been implemented in `lib/`, so that programming in the kernel can use the conventions of programming in C.

The most important directory for programming close to the kernel is `include/`. This holds the kernel-specific header files. The `include/asm-i386/` directory contains the architecture-dependent include files for Intel PCs. To simplify access, the symbolic link `include/asm/` refers to the current architecture directory.

As the header files may change from version to version, it is simpler to set up symbolic links in `/usr/include/` to the two subdirectories `include/linux/` and `include/asm/`.

So, when LINUX kernel sources are changed, the header files are updated automatically.

2.2   COMPILING

In essence, a new kernel is generated in three steps. First, the kernel is configured by:

```
# make config
```

This runs the *Bash* script `scripts/Configure`, which reads in the `arch/i386/config.in` file located in the architecture directory which holds the definitions of the kernel configuration and default assignments, and then queries it to see which components are to be included in the kernel. `arch/i386/config.in` consults the `Config.in` files contained in the directories of the individual subsystems of the kernel. Configuration scripts which are easier to handle can be called with

```
# make menuconfig
```

for a menu-driven installation on the console, or with

```
# make xconfig
```

for a menu-driven installation under X Windows.

During the configuration, the two files `<linux/autoconf.h>` and `.config` are created. The `.config` file controls the sequencing of the compilation, while `<linux/`

autoconf.h> takes care of conditional compilation within the kernel sources. The
.config file is used if configure is called again to determine the default responses to
individual questions. A fresh configuration will thus return the last values as the defaults.
The command

```
# make oldconfig
```

ensures that the default values are accepted without further query. This enables a .config
file to be included in a new version of LINUX so that the kernel is compiled with the same
configuration.

Expansion packages for the kernel will extend the config.in file by entries in
the form of

```
bool 'PC-Speaker and DAC driver support' CONFIG_PCSP
```

so that they can be added to or removed from the configuration. Further facilities for configuring the LINUX kernel are described in the next section but are not required as a rule.

In the second step, the dependencies of the source codes are recalculated. This is done
by means of

```
# make depend
```

and is a purely technical operation. It uses the capability of the GNU C compiler to create
dependencies for the Makefiles. These dependencies are collected in the .depend files in
the individual subdirectories and are subsequently inserted into the Makefiles.

The actual compilation of the kernel now begins, with the simple call:

```
# make
```

After this, the vmlinux file should be found in the uppermost source directory. To create
a bootable LINUX kernel,

```
# make boot
```

must be called. As only a compressed kernel can be booted on PCs, the result of this command is the compressed, bootable LINUX kernel arch/i386/boot/zImage. If an error
message saying that the kernel is too large for a zImage is displayed while the zImage is
being created,

```
# make bzImage
```

is called. Then a further mechanism is implemented which enables the loading of the LINUX
kernel immediately in the memory above the 1MByte of the real mode. The file created is
contained in arch/i386/boot/bzImage.

However, other actions can be initiated using make. For example, the target zdisk not
only generates a kernel but also writes it to a diskette. The target zlilo copies the
generated kernel to /vmlinuz, and the old kernel is renamed /vmlinuz.old. The LINUX

kernel is then installed by means of a call to the LINUX loader (LILO), which must be configured beforehand (see Appendix D.2.4).

For work on sections of the LINUX kernel (for example, writing a new driver) it is not necessary to recompile the complete kernel or check the dependencies. Instead, the call to

```
# make drivers
```

will only cause the sources in the `drivers/` subdirectory, that is, the drivers, to be compiled. If a new linkage to the kernel is also required,

```
# make SUBDIRS=drivers
```

should be called. This approach can also be used for the other subdirectories.

A large number of device drivers and file systems can be created as modules. This can be done using:

```
# make modules
```

Of course, there are also `bzlilo` and `bzdisk` for large LINUX kernels. The modules created by this can be installed by means of

```
# make modules_install. //
```

The installation is carried out in the subdirectories `drivers/`, `fs/`, and `net/` in the `/lib/modules/kernel/version/kernel/` directory.

2.3   ADDITIONAL CONFIGURATION FACILITIES

In special circumstances it may be necessary to change the settings within the sources. Normally, however, one should try not to change the configuration in the kernel sources during runtime.

The following describe the files in the LINUX kernel to which changes can be made.

`Makefile`   This is the only file in which changes cannot be avoided if the user does not have a "Standard PC." The variable

```
ARCH := ...
```

is set to the hardware architecture on which the kernel should run. This is usually done using a script that adopts the architecture of the data of the current system.

Other values for `ARCH` are `alpha`, `sparc`, `m68k`, `arm`, `mips` and `ppc`.

To compile a LINUX kernel for another destination architecture, the path for the corresponding compiler can be set using the variable `CROSS_COMPILE`.

`drivers/char/serial.c`   There is normally no problem with the serial interfaces, as most PCs only possess two of these and by default they use IRQs 4 (`COM1`) and 3 (`COM2`).

If more interfaces are available because of special hardware (for example, internal modem or fax cards), automatic IRQ recognition and support for various special cards (the AST Fourport card and others) can be brought in. An explanation of these and other macros is also given. Most options are also contained in the file `drivers/char/Config.in` and can be set using `make config`.

`drivers/net/Space.c`   This file contains the initial configuration of the network devices. Thus the device structures `eth1_dev`, . . ., which are defined as constants, can be modified.

```
static struct device eth1_dev = {
/* NAME RECVMEM MEM I/O-BASE IRQ FLAGS NEXT_DEV INIT */
"eth1", 0,0, 0,0, ETH_NOPROBE_ADDR , 0, 0,0,0, &eth2_dev,
ethif_probe};
```

Here the I/O address `ETH_NOPROBE_ADDR` means that there is no test for whether this device exists. This can be avoided by entering a zero for an automatic test or the corresponding I/O address. Via the boot parameter

```
ether=irq,port,mem_start,mem_end,name
```

the adjustments can be made after starting up the system.

`include/linux/fs`   In very large networks it may be necessary to manage more than 256 file systems for LINUX computers. However, the number of file systems is restricted to 256 using the `NR_SUPER` preprocessor macro. This restriction can be modified here.

There are many more configuration options for the LINUX kernel. In the following chapters other options will be described, with various examples.

To conclude, we must point out that the modifications to the kernel sources described in this section are not usually necessary and should only be carried out if they are needed.

3 INTRODUCTION TO THE KERNEL

This chapter will focus on the basic structure of the system kernel and the interplay of its main components to provide a foundation for understanding the following chapters. However, before we start, a few more general remarks on the LINUX kernel are in order.

LINUX was not designed on the drawing board but developed in an evolutionary manner, and continues to develop today. Every function of the kernel has been altered and expanded again and again to get rid of bugs and incorporate new features. Anyone who has been personally involved in a major project will know how quickly program code can become impossible to follow and how liable to errors it is. In the face of this, Linus Torvalds, as coordinator of the LINUX project, has managed to keep the kernel organized in a form that is easy to follow and has constantly removed things left over from earlier versions.

Despite this, the LINUX kernel is certainly not in every respect a good model of structured programming. There are "magic numbers" in the program text instead of constant declarations in header files, inline expanded functions instead of function calls, goto instructions in place of a simple break, assembler instructions instead of C code, and many other less than elegant features. Many of these distinctive features of unstructured programming were, however, deliberately included. Large parts of the kernel are time-critical; so the program code is optimized for good runtime behavior rather than easy readability. This distinguishes LINUX from, for example, Minix [Tan90] which was written as a "teaching operating system" and was not designed for everyday use. LINUX, in contrast, is a "real" operating system and, as such, its kernel is structured remarkably well.

The aim of this book is to explain the main functioning of the LINUX kernel. Therefore, the algorithms introduced in this and the next chapters represent a compromise between the original source codes and comprehensible program code, but attention has been paid to making the changes easy to follow.

General architecture Since UNIX came on the scene, the internal structure of operating systems has changed radically. At that time it was revolutionary for most of the kernel to be written in a higher programming language, C. Now it is taken for granted. The present trend is towards a microkernel architecture, such as that of the Mach kernel [Tan86] or the kernel of Windows NT. The UNIX Minix [Tan90] and the Hurd system currently under development are further examples of microkernel-based systems.

The actual kernel provides only the necessary minimum of functionality (interprocess communication and memory management) and can accordingly be implemented in a small and compact form. Building on this microkernel, the remaining functions of the operating system are relocated to autonomous processes, communicating with the microkernel via a well-defined interface. The main advantage of these structures (apart from a certain elegance) is a system structure that is clearly less trouble to maintain. Individual components work independently of each other, cannot affect each other unintentionally, and are easy to replace. The development of new components is simplified.

This in itself results in a drawback to these architectures. The microkernel architectures force defined interfaces to be maintained between the individual components and prevent sophisticated optimizations. In addition, in today's hardware architectures the interprocess communication required inside the microkernel is more extensive than simple function calls. This makes the system slower than traditional monolithic kernels. This slight speed disadvantage is readily accepted since current hardware is generally fast enough and because the advantage of simpler system maintenance reduces development costs.

For the first time, in the past few years some microkernel systems have been created whose performance can be improved using monolithic systems. However, this is still an area of active fundamental research. Microkernel architectures undoubtedly represent the future of operating system development. LINUX, on the other hand, came into being on the "slow" 386 architecture, the lower limit for a reasonable UNIX system. Exploiting all possible ways of optimizing performance to give good run-time behavior was a primary consideration. This is one reason why LINUX was implemented in the classic monolithic kernel architecture. Another reason was undoubtedly the fact that a microkernel architecture depends on careful design of the system. Since LINUX has grown by evolution, starting out from the fun of developing a system, this was simply not possible.

In spite of its monolithic foundation, LINUX is not a chaotic collection of program code. Most components of the kernel are only accessed via accurately defined interfaces. A good example of this is the virtual file system (VFS), which represents an abstract interface to all file-oriented operations. We will be taking a closer look at the VFS in Chapter 6. But the chaos is apparent in the detail. Time-critical points or sections of programs are often written in "hand-optimized" C code, making them difficult to follow. Fortunately, these program sections are quite rare and, as a rule, fairly well annotated.

Looking at the code size of the individual components of the LINUX kernel, one notices that most of them belong to device drivers and similar. On the other hand, the central routines of process and memory management (i.e., the actual kernel in the sense of a microkernel architecture) are relatively small and easily understood, with 13,000 lines of C code in each.

It is possible to separate most device drivers from the kernel. They can be loaded as autonomous, independent modules at runtime as required (see Chapter 9). Thus LINUX successfully tries to make use of the advantages of a microkernel architecture without giving up its original monolithic design.

Processes and tasks As seen by a process running under LINUX, the kernel is a provider of services. Individual processes exist independently alongside each other and cannot affect each other directly. Each process's own area of memory is protected against modification by other processes.

The internal viewpoint of a running LINUX system is a different matter. Only one program – the operating system – is running on the computer, and can access all the resources. The various tasks are carried out by co-routines, that is, every task decides for itself whether and when to pass control to another task.[1] One consequence of this is that an error in the kernel programming can block the entire system. Any task can access all the resources for other tasks and modify them.

Certain parts of a task run in the processor's less privileged user mode. These parts of the task appear from the outside (to someone looking into the kernel) to be processes. From the viewpoint of these processes, true multitasking is taking place. Figure 3.1 should make this clear.

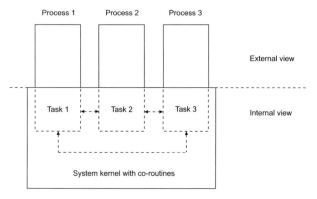

Figure 3.1:   The process seen from outside and inside.

In the following, however, we will not be making any precise distinction between the concepts of task and process, but will use the two words to mean the same thing. However, this simple process model is extended in so far as there can also be threads that exist in the kernel mode only. When a task is running in the privileged system mode, it can take one of a number of states. Figure 3.2 shows the most important of these. The arrows in this diagram show the possible changes of state. The following states are possible:

Running The task is active and running in the non-privileged user mode. In this case the process will go through the program in a perfectly normal way. This state can only be exited via an interrupt or a system call. In Section 3.3 we will see that the system calls are in fact no more than special cases of interrupts. In either case, the processor is switched to the privileged system mode and the appropriate interrupt routine is activated.

---

1   This is also known as cooperative multitasking.

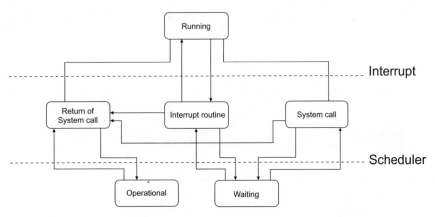

Figure 3.2: Chart of status within a process.

Interrupt routine The interrupt routines become active when the hardware signals an exception condition, which may be new characters input from the keyboard or the clock generator issuing a signal every 10 milliseconds. Further information on interrupt routines is provided in Section 3.2.2.

System call System calls are initiated by software interrupts. Details of these are given in Section 3.3. A system call is able to suspend the task to wait for an event.

Waiting The process is waiting for an external event. Only after this has occurred will it continue its work.

Return from system call This state is automatically adopted after every system call and after some interrupts. At this point checks are made as to whether the scheduler needs to be called and whether there are signals to process. The scheduler can switch the process to the "ready" state and activate another process.

Ready The process is competing for the processor, which is occupied by another process at the present time.

Processes and threads In many modern operating systems a distinction is made between processes and threads. A thread is a sort of independent "strand" in the course of a program which can be processed in parallel with other threads. As opposed to processes, threads work on the same main memory and can therefore influence each other.

LINUX does not make this distinction. In the kernel, only the concept of a task exists which can share resources with other tasks (for example, the same memory). Thus, a task is a generalization of the usual thread concept. More details can be found in Section 3.3.3.

In Section 3.3 we will see that system calls are in fact no more than special cases of interrupts. In both cases the processor is switched to the privileged system mode and the appropriate interrupt routine is activated.

Multiprocessor systems Since version 2.0, LINUX has supported SMP (*symmetric multiprocessing*). While in version 2.0 the implementation was initially still trivial – only one processor at a time could process kernel code – it has now become very complex. Today, several processors can process kernel code at the same time. For this reason, access to all the global data structures of the kernel must be synchronized. In this chapter we have, for the most part, ignored the problems which occur in order to maintain a comprehensible description.

3.1   IMPORTANT DATA STRUCTURES

This chapter describes important data structures in the LINUX kernel. Understanding these structures and how they interact is a necessary foundation for understanding the following chapters.

3.1.1   The task structure

One of the most important concepts in a multitasking system such as LINUX is the task: the data structures and algorithms for process management from the central core of LINUX.

The description of the characteristics of a process is given in the structure `task_struct`, which is explained below. The first components of the structure also are accessed from assembler routines. This access is not made, as it usually is in C, via the names of components, but via their offsets relative to the start of the structure. This means that the start of the task structure must not be modified without checking all the assembler routines and modifying them if necessary first.

```
struct task_struct
{
  volatile long state;
```

`state` contains a code for the current state of the process. If the process is waiting for the CPU to be assigned or if it is running, `state` takes the value `TASK_RUNNING`. If, on the other hand, the process is waiting for certain external events and is therefore idle, `state` takes the value `TASK_INTERRUPTIBLE` or `TASK_UNINTERRUPTIBLE`. The difference between these two values is that in the `TASK_INTERRUPTIBLE` state a task can be reactivated by signals, while in the `TASK_UNINTERRUPTIBLE` state it is typically waiting directly or indirectly for a hardware condition and therefore will not accept any signals. `TASK_STOPPED` describes a process which has been halted, either after receiving an appropriate signal (`SIGSTOP`, `SIGSTP`, `SIGTTIN`, or `SIGTTOU`) or when the process is being monitored by another process using the *ptrace* system call and has passed control to the monitoring process. `TASK_ZOMBIE` describes a process which has been terminated but which must still have its task structure in the process table (see the system calls *_exit* and *wait* in Section 3.3.3). The keyword `volatile` indicates that these components also can be altered asynchronously from interrupt routines.

```
        unsigned long flags;
```

`flags` contains a bit mask of the system status as `PF_ALIGNWARN`, `PF_STARTING`, `PF_EXITING`, `PF_FORKNOEXEC`, `PF_SUPERPRIV`, `PF_DUMPCORE`, `PF_SIGNALED`, `PF_MEMALLOC`, `PF_VFORK`, and `PF_USEDFPU`.

These flags are basically used for the accounting of processes and do not influence the mode of operation of the system.

The `PF_TRACED` status flag available in the older kernels was set in the component

```
unsigned long ptrace;
```

The values `PF_PTRACED` and `PF_TRACESYS` indicate that the process is being monitored by another process with the aid of the system call *ptrace*. Interested readers will find further information on this system in Section 5.4 and Appendix A.

```
int sigpending;
```

The flag `sigpending` is set when signals must be handed over to this process. Further information can be found in Section 3.2.1.

```
mm_segement_t addr_limit;
```

Unlike the older kernels, since version 2.4 tasks (threads) also can be within the kernel. These can access a larger address space than tasks in the user space. `addr_limit` describes the address space, which it is possible to access using the kernel of the task.

```
struct exec_domain *exec_domain;
```

LINUX can run programs from other systems with an i386 base conforming to the iBCS2 standard. As the various iBCS2 systems differ slightly, a description of which UNIX is to be emulated for each process is kept in the `exec_domain` component for the process.

```
long need_resched;
```

`need_resched` is a flag that indicates that a scheduling must be executed. In the kernel version 2.0 this was still a global variable, but for reasons of efficiency it is now located in the task structure of the current task.

In order to work on multiprocessor systems, the whole structure must be protected before simultaneous access can take place. The locking is carried out via the component

```
int lock_depth;
```

This ends the hard-coded part of the task structure. The following components of the task structure give an overview of groups:

```
long counter;
long nice;
unsigned long policy; /* SCHED_FIFO, SCHED_RR, *
                       * SCHED_OTHER */
unsigned long rt_priority;
```

`counter` contains the time in "ticks" (see Section 3.2.5) for which the process can still run before a scheduling has to be executed. The scheduler uses the value in `counter` to select the following process. Thus `counter` represents something like the dynamic priority of a process. `nice` contains the static priority of the process. Up to kernel version 2.2 this component was called `priority`. The scheduling algorithm (see Section 3.2.6) uses `nice` in order to determine a new value for `count`, if necessary.

LINUX supports many scheduling algorithms. In addition to the classical scheduling (SCHED_OTHER) there are now two more real-time scheduling algorithms (SCHED_RR and SCHED_FIFO), described in POSIX.4. Each process can be inserted in one of the scheduling classes. This is recorded in the components `policy` and `rt_priority` along with the real-time priority. More details about this are given in Section 3.2.6.

Signals

```
/* int sigpending */
sigset_t blocked;
struct signal_struct *sig;

struct sigpending pending;
```

`sigpending` contains, as described above, a bit mask of the signals reached for the process, and `blocked`, a bit mask of all signals but the process only processes later, as their processing is blocked at the moment. The component `sig` refers to the corresponding signal handling routines.

LINUX supports the so-called "reliable signals" or "real-time signals" according to POSIX.4. These cannot be managed as normal UNIX signals in a bit field; the kernel has to make sure that a signal sent repeatedly also reaches the receiver repeatedly. LINUX tries to implement this method for traditional signals as well. Therefore, any signal sent to the process is recorded in a pending list. The evaluation of this signal information is described in Section 3.2.1.

Process relations All processes are entered in a doubly linked list with the help of the following two components:

```
struct task_struct *next_task;
struct task_struct *prev_task;
```

The start and end of this list are held in the global variable `init_task`.

In a UNIX system, processes do not exist independently of each other. Every process (except for the process `init_task`) has a parent process, which has created it using the system call *fork()* (see Section 3.3.3 and Appendix A). There are therefore "family relationships" between the processes, which are represented by the following components:

```
struct task_struct *p_opptr;       /* original parent   */
struct task_struct *p_pptr;        /* parent            */
struct task_struct *p_cptr;        /* youngest child    */
struct task_struct *p_ysptr;       /* younger sibling   */
```

```
        struct task_struct *p_osptr;      /* older sibling    */
```

`p_pptr` is a pointer to the parent process's task structure. To enable a process to access all of its child processes, the task structure holds the entry for the last child process created – the *"youngest child"* process. The child processes for the same parent process are similarly linked together as a doubly linked list by `p_ysptr` (*next younger sibling*) and `p_osptr` (*next older sibling*). Figure 3.3 should clarify the "family relationships" between processes.

The scheduler keeps a list of all processes that apply for the processor. It is implemented as a doubly linked list with the help of the component:

```
struct list_head run_list;
```

Memory management The data for each process needed for memory management is collected in their own substructure for reasons of simplicity:

```
  struct mm_struct *mm;
```

The components of this are:

```
        unsigned long start_code, end_code, start_data, end_data;
        unsigned long start_brk, brk,
        unsigned long start_stack,start_mmap;
        unsigned long arg_start, arg_end, env_start, env_end;
        . . .
```

which describe the start and size of the code and data segments of the program currently running. Further information is given in Chapter 4.

Process ID Every process has its own process ID number, `pid`, and is assigned to a process group, `pgrp`, and session, `session`. Every session has a leader process (`leader`). Because in LINUX threads also are created via a custom task, the thread group ID was inserted via `tgid`. Normally, this is the `pid` of the process, from which new threads are begun. In the classical sense, this also is the true PID.

```
        pid_t pid, pgrp, session, tgid;
        int leader;
```

To create access rights, each process has the *user identification* `uid` and the *group identification* `gid`. These are transmitted by the parent process to the child process via the system call *fork* (see Section 3.3.3 and Appendix A). However, for real access control the user has to adopt the effective user identification `euid` and the effective group `egid`. A new feature in LINUX is the component `fsuid`. This is used whenever identification is required by the file system. As a general rule, (`uid == euid`) `&&` (`gid == egid`) and (`fsuid == euid`) `&&` (`fsgid == egid`) are valid.

Exceptions arise for so-called set-UID programs, where the values of `euid` and `fsuid`, or those of `egid` and `fsgid`, are set to the user ID and the group ID for the owner of the executable file. This makes a controlled distribution of privileges possible.

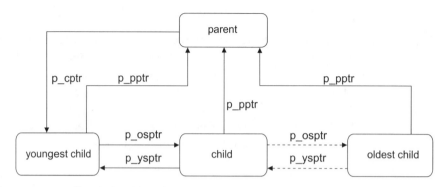

Figure 3.3:   Family relationships of processes.

As a rule, `fsuid` always takes the value of `euid`, and in other UNIX systems or older versions of LINUX the effective user ID `euid` was always used in place of `fsuid`. However, the LINUX *setfsuid* system call allows `fsuid` to be altered without changing `euid`. This means that daemons can limit their rights when accessing the systems with `setfsuid` (to the rights of the user for whom they are providing services), but they will retain their privileges. Similar considerations apply for the component `fsgid` and the system call *setfsgid*.

```
uid_t uid,euid,suid,fsuid;
gid_t gid,egid,sgid,fguid;
```

Like most modern UNIX derivatives, LINUX allows the simultaneous assignment of a process to several user groups. These groups are taken into account during control of access rights to files. Each process can belong to a maximum of **NGROUPS** groups, which are saved in the `groups` components of the task structure.

```
gid_t groups[NGROUPS];
int ngroups;
```

Traditionally, in a UNIX system many actions are left up to the superuser. This is recognized as its effective UID is 0. A process, such as a network connection, can open a privileged port, send a signal to an alien process, or reboot the system using this EUID. This concept of privileges is relatively coarse and in the past it led to many security problems in UNIX systems. LINUX has added the concept "capabilities" to that of "superuser," so that it is possible to grant to a process, for example, the right to open a reserved network port without granting superuser privileges to it. These rights are managed in the components:

```
kernel_cap_t cap_effective;
kernel_cap_t cap_inheritable;
kernel_cap_t cap_permitted;
```

```
        int keep_capabilities:1;
```

and are used in the kernel. A list of the values available for these components can be found in `include/linux/capability.h`. Even if the LINUX kernel is universally switched over to capabilities, these are supported by the management programs and not by the usual file systems. However, an interesting development of safer systems seems possible in the future.

Files The data-specific information is filed in the substructure

```
        struct fs_struct *fs;
```

This also contains the components

```
        atomic_t count;
        int umask;
        struct dentry * root, * pwd;
```

A process can influence the access mode of new files that have to be created via the system call *umask*. The values set with the system call *umask* are stored in the component `umask`. Under UNIX, every process has a current directory `pwd`,[2] which is required for the resolution of relative path names and can be modified with the system call *chdir*. Moreover, each process has its own root directory `root`, used in the resolution of absolute path names. This root directory can only be modified by the superuser (system call *chroot*). As this is seldom used (e.g., anonymous FTP), it is also less well known. `count` is a reference counter, since this structure can be used by several tasks.

A process that opens a file with `open()` or `create()` gets a file descriptor from the kernel for further references to this file. File descriptors are small integer numbers. Under LINUX, the assignment of the file descriptors to the files is carried out via the field `fd` in the substructure

```
        struct files_struct *files;
```

Among other things, it has the following components:

```
        atomic_t count;
        int max_fds;
        struct file ** fd;
        fd_set *close_on_exec;
        fd_set *open_fds;
```

In the field `fd`, file descriptors are used as indices. In this way one can find out the file pointer assigned to the file descriptor, with whose aid it is possible to access the file. `open_fds` is a bit mask of all the file descriptors used.

---

2 The abbreviation pwd in all probabiltity stands for the Unix pwd (print working directory), which outputs the name of the current directory.

The component `close_on_exec` in the substructure includes a bit mask of all the file descriptors that are closed with the system call *exec*. `count` again acts as a reference counter; `max_fds` is the highest number of opened file descriptors for the process.

Timing Various times are measured for each process. Under LINUX, times are always measured in ticks. These ticks are generated by a hardware timer chip every 10 milliseconds and counted by the timer interrupt. In Sections 3.1.6 and 3.2.5 we will be considering timing under LINUX.

`per_cpu_utime[ ]` and `per_cpu_stime[ ]` contain the time needed by the process in user and system mode. In a multiprocessor system, this data is set up for each CPU individually. The sum of these values over all CPUs as well as the sum of the corresponding times of all the child processes are given in the component `times`. The values can be called using the system call *times*.

```
long per_cpu_utime[NR_OF_CPUS];
long per_cpu_stime[NR_OF_CPUS];
struct tms times;
unsigned long start_time;
```

`start_time` contains the time at which the current process was generated.

UNIX supports different process-specific timers. One of these is the system call *alarm*, which ensures that the `SIGALRM` signal is sent to the process after a specific time. Newer UNIX systems also support interval timers (see system calls *setitimer* and *getitimer*, Section A.1).

```
unsigned long it_real_value, it_prof_value, it_virt_value;
unsigned long it_real_incr, it_prof_incr, it_virt_incr;
struct timer_list real_timer;
```

The components `it_real_value`, `it_prof_value` and `it_virt_value` contain the time in ticks, after which the timer will be triggered. The components `it_real_incr`, `it_prof_incr` and `it_virt_incr` hold the values required to reinitialize the timers after they run out. `real_timer` is used for the implementation of the real-time interval timer. More information about this is given in the description of the timer interrupt in Section 3.2.5.

Interprocess communication The LINUX kernel implements a system of interprocess communication which is compatible with System V. Among other things, this provides semaphores. A process can occupy a semaphore, which blocks it. If other processes also wish to occupy this semaphore, they are halted until the semaphore is released. This uses the component

```
struct sem_queue *semsleeping;
```

When the process is terminated, the operating system must release all semaphores occupied by the process. The component

```
struct sem_undo *semundo;
```

contains the information required for this.

Miscellaneous The following components do not fit any of the above groups.

```
wait_queue_head_t wait_chldexit;
```

A process executing the system call *wait4* must be halted until a child process terminates. It joins the `wait_chldexit` wait queue in its own task structure, sets the status flag to the value `TASK_INTERRUPTIBLE`, and passes control to the scheduler. When a process terminates, it signals this to its parent process via this queue. There is more on this in the section on wait queues (Section 3.1.5), the section on the system *_exit* and *wait* (Section 3.3.3) and the source texts for the kernel function `sys_wait4()` (kernel/exit.c).

```
struct semaphore *vfork_sem;
```

The semantics of the system call *vfork* requires that the parent process, to continue working, waits until the child process either terminates or has loaded another program via *exec*. This waiting is carried out via the semaphore `vfork_sem`. More details about this are given in Section 3.3.3.

```
struct rlimit rlim[RLIM_NLIMITS];
```

Every process can check limits for the use of resources by means of the system calls *setrlimit* and *getrlimit* (see Section A.1). These are restored in the `rlim` structure.

```
int exit_code, exit_signal;
```

These contain the return code for the program and the signal by which the program has been terminated. This information can be polled by a parent process after completion of the child process.

```
char comm[16];
```

The name of the program executed by the process is stored in the component `comm`. This is used in debugging.

```
unsigned long personality;
```

As mentioned earlier, LINUX supports, via the iBCS interface, the execution of programs from other UNIX systems. Together with the `exec_domain` component described above, `personality` is used to give a precise description of the characteristics of this version of UNIX. For standard LINUX programs, `personality` takes the value `PER_LINUX` (defined as 0 in <linux/personality.h>).

```
int dumpable:1;
int did_exec:1;
```

The `dumpable` flag indicates whether a memory dump is to be executed by the current process if certain signals occur.

A rather obscure semantic in the POSIX standard needs, when calling `setpgid`, to distinguish whether a process is still running the original program or whether it has loaded a new program with the system *execve*. This information is monitored using the flag `did_exec`.

Another important component in the task structure is `binfmt`. This describes the functions responsible for the loading of the program.

```
struct linux_binfmt *binfmt;
struct thread_struct thread;
```

The `thread_struct` structure includes any kind of information about the current process status up to the point of the last transition from the user mode to the system mode.

All of the processor registers are saved here so that they can be restored via the return to user mode.

3.1.2 The process table

Every process occupies exactly one entry in the process table. Up to version 2.2, LINUX was statically organized and restricted in size to NR_TASKS (512). In the up-to-date version the process table is still just an abstraction. The individual tasks can be accessed via the `next_task` and `prev_task` concatenations available in the `task_struct` structure.

The `init_task` macro points at the first task in the system. It is initialized by starting the system (described in Section 3.2.4) using the **INIT_TASK** macro. After the system has been booted, this is only responsible for the use of unclaimed system time (idle process). For this reason it is out of place and should be regarded as a normal task rather than as a class of its own.

Even if the table process has a dynamic structure, the number of tasks is restricted to `max_threads` in the system.

```
int max_threads;
```

This value, however, can be altered at runtime using the *sysctl* interface.

Many algorithms in the kernel must take into account each individual task. To make this easier, the `for_each_task()` macro was defined as follows:

```
#define for_each_task(p) \
  for  (p = &init_task ; ( p = p->next_task) != &init_task ; )
```

As we can see, the `init_task` has changed. In version 1, the entry for the currently running task could be reached via the global variable `struct task_struct *current`.

Since version 2.0 multiprocessing (SMP) has been supported, so this had to be extended – now there is a task for every processor.

```
#define current get_current()
inline struct task_struct * get_current(void)
{
        struct task_struct *current;
        __asm__("andl %%esp,%0; ":"=r" (current) : "0" (~8191UL));
        return current;
}
```

The `get_current()` function is a bit magical; the task structure is placed in the stack segment of the actual task for the sake of efficiency.

3.1.3 Files and inodes

UNIX systems traditionally make a distinction between the file structure and the inode structure. The inode structure describes a file. The concept *inode* is used more than once in different contexts.

Both the data structure in the kernel and the data structure on the hard disk describe files (each from their own viewpoint) and are therefore inodes. In the following, we will always refer to the data structure in memory. Inodes contain information such as the file's owner and access rights. There is exactly one inode entry in the kernel for each file used in the system.

File structures (that is, data structures of the `struct file` type), on the other hand, contain the view of a process on these files (represented by inodes). This view on the file includes attributes, such as the mode in which the file can be used (read, write, read + write), or the current position of the next I/O operation.

File structure The structure file is defined in `include/linux/fs.h`.

```
struct file
{
        mode_t f_mode;
        loff_t f_pos;

        atomic_t f_count;
        unsigned int f_flags;

        struct dentry *fs_dentry;
        struct file_operations * f_op;
        ...
};
```

f_mode describes the access mode in which the file was opened (read-only, read + write, or write-only); f_pos holds the position of the read/write pointer at which the next I/O operation will be carried out. This value is updated by every I/O operation and by the system calls *lseek* and *llseek*. Note that the offset is stored in the kernel as a 64-bit value of the type loff_t. This enables LINUX to correctly handle files larger than 2 gigabytes (2^{31} bytes).

f_flags includes additional flags that control access to this file. These can be set by opening a file by means of the system call *open* and can be read and modified later on via the system call *fcntl*. f_count is a simple reference counter. A number of file descriptors can refer to the same file structure. As these are inherited through the system call *fork*, the same file structure may also be referenced from different processes. When a file is opened, f_count is initialized to 1. Every time the file descriptor is copied (by the system calls *dup*, *dup2*, or *fork*) the reference counter is incremented by 1, and every time a file is closed (using the system calls *close*, *exit*, or *exec*) it is decreased by 1. The file structure is only released once there is no longer any process referring to it.

f_dentry is a reference to an entry in the directory cache that includes all the files opened. Via this entry it is also possible to access the inode (the real description of the file). f_op refers to a structure of data pointers referencing all file operations. By comparison with other UNIX systems, LINUX supports a very large number of file system types. Each of these file systems implements accesses in a different way. For this reason, a "virtual file system" (VFS) has been implemented in LINUX. The idea is that the functions operating on the file system are not called directly, but via a function specific to the file (system). The file-system-specific operations are part of the file or inode structure, which corresponds to the principle of virtual functions in object-oriented languages. Comprehensive information on the VFS is given in Section 6.2.

Inodes The inode structure

```
struct inode
{
```

also is defined in include/linux/fs.h. Many components of this structure can be polled via the system call *stat*.

```
        kdev_t i_dev;
        unsigned long i_ino;
```

i_dev is a a description of the device (the disk partition) on which the file is located. i_ino[3] identifies the file within the device. The (i_dev, i_ino) pair thus provides an identification of the file which is unique throughout the system.

```
        umode_t i_mode;
        uid_t i_uid;
        gid_t i_gid;
```

```
    off_t i_size;
    time_t i_mtime;
    time_t i_atime;
    time_t i_ctime;
```

These components describe the access rights to the file, its owner (user and group), the size i_size in bytes, and the times of the last modification i_mtime, the last access i_atime, and the last modification to the inode i_ctime.

```
    struct inode_operations * i_op;
    ...
```

Like the file structure, the inode also has a reference to a structure containing pointers to functions which can be used on inodes (see Section 6.2.7). Further information on inodes is given in Section 6.2.

3.1.4 Dynamic memory management

Under LINUX, memory is managed on a page basis. One page contains 2^{12} bytes. The basic operations to request a free page are the functions

```
struct page * __alloc_pages(int gfp_mask, unsigned long order);
unsigned long __get_free_pages(int gfp_mask
                unsigned long order);
```

which are defined in the file mm/page_alloc.c. gfp_mask gives information to those who need to control the pages and the behavior of the functions, in case there are not enough pages free in the main memory. A process, for instance, can wait until memory is available again, but this is not possible for an interrupt routine. The values GFP_BUFFER, GFP_ATOMIC, GFP_USER, GFP_KERNEL, GFP_KSWAPD, and GFP_NFS are valid for gfp_mask.

order describes the number of the pages to be reserved. 2^{order} pages are reserved.

The pages requested can be freed by means of the functions

```
        void __free_pages(struct page *page, unsigned long order);
        void free_pages(unsigned long addr, unsigned long order);
```

In this way, the pages are entered in the uncommitted memory list.

Even though this represents the basic operation of getting and freeing a page, it should not be used in this form. The function

```
unsigned long get_zeroed_page(int gfp_mask);
```

is more suitable. It also initializes the memory requested with 0. This is important for two reasons. Firstly, some parts of the kernel expect the new memory to be initialized with 0

---

3 Here, too, i_ino stands for the inode, referring in this case to the block number of the data structure on the hard disk, describing the file on the external memory device.

(for instance, the system call *exec*). Secondly, this is a security procedure. If the page has already been used, it may contain the data of another user (e.g., passwords), which should not be made accessible to the process requesting a new page.

The C programmer is normally used to working with `malloc()` and `free()` for the management of memory. There is also something similar in the LINUX kernel: the function

```
void *kmalloc (size_t size, int flags);
```

works in a similar way to `malloc()`. The argument `flags` indicates, as in `get_zeroed_page()`, how `kmalloc()` should request new memory pages. The counterpart of `kmalloc()` is the function

```
void kfree (const void * objp);
```

which frees a memory area that was allocated with `kmalloc()`.

The reader can find further information on the operation of memory management under LINUX in Chapter 4.

3.1.5   Queues and semaphores

Often a process will be dependent on the occurrence of certain conditions. For example, the system call *read* has to wait until the data has been loaded into the process's area of memory from the hard disk, or a parent process may be using *wait* to wait for the end of a child process. In each of these cases it is not known how long the process will have to wait.

This "wait until condition met" is implemented in LINUX by means of wait queues. A wait queue is nothing more than a cyclical list containing pointers to the process table as its elements.

```
struct list_head {
        struct list_head *next, *prev;
};

typedef struct __wait_queue {
        struct task_struct * task;
        struct list_head task_list;
} wait_queue_t;

typedef struct __wait_queue_head {
        struct list_head task_list;
} wait_queue_head_t;
```

Cyclical lists are a fundamental data structure, therefore a uniform implementation was established for it using the structure `list_head` and the associated functions.

The data type `wait_queue_t` describes the element of a wait queue and `wait_queue_head_t` the wait queue itself. Wait queues should be modified with the help of the following two functions only. By means of the corresponding locking they make sure that access to the wait queues is synchronized.

```
void add_wait_queue(wait_queue_head_t *q,
            wait_queue_t *wait);
void remove_wait_queue(wait_queue_head_t *q,
            wait_queue_t *wait);
```

q contains the wait queue to be modified and `wait` the entry to be added or removed.

A process wishing to wait for a specific event enters itself into a wait queue of this type and relinquishes control. There is a wait queue for every possible event. When the relevant event occurs, all the processes in its wait queue are reactivated and can resume operation. This semantic is implemented by the functions

```
void sleep_on(wait_queue_head_t *q);
void sleep_on_timeout(wait_queue_head_t *q, long timeout);
void interruptible_sleep_on(wait_queue_head_t *q);
void interruptible_sleep_on_timeout(wait_queue_head_t *q,long timeout);
```

These set the status of the process (`current->state`) to the value `TASK_UNINTERRUPTIBLE` or `TASK_INTERRUPTIBLE`, enter the current process (`current`) in the wait queue and call the scheduler. The process then voluntarily relinquishes control.

It is only reactivated when the status of the process is set to `TASK_RUNNING`. This is generally done by another process calling one of the macros

```
void wake_up(struct wait_queue **p);
void wake_up_interruptible(struct wait_queue **p);
```

to wake up all the processes entered in its wait queue.

With the aid of wait queues, LINUX also provides semaphores. These are used to synchronize access by various kernel routines to shared data structures. These semaphores should not be confused with semaphores provided for user programs in UNIX System V.

```
struct semaphore {
        atomic_t count;
        wait_queue_head_t wait;
        . . .
};
```

A semaphore is taken to be occupied if `count` has a value less than or equal to 0. All the processes wishing to occupy the semaphore enter themselves in the wait queue. They are then notified when it is released by another process. There are two auxiliary functions to occupy or release semaphores:

```
void down( struct semaphore * sem )
```

```
{
  while( sem -> count <= 0 )
        sleep_on( & sem->wait );
  sem -> count -= 1;
}
void up( struct semaphore * sem )
{
  sem -> count += 1;
  wake_up( & sem -> wait );
}
```

For the sake of efficiency, the actual implementation is written in assembler and is substantially more complex.

3.1.6 System time and timers

In the LINUX system, there is just one internal time base. It is measured in ticks elapsed since the system was booted, with one tick equal to 10 milliseconds. These ticks are generated by a timer chip in the hardware and counted by the timer interrupt (see Section 3.2.5) in the global variable jiffies. All the system timings mentioned below always refer to this time base.

Why do we need timers? Many device drivers like to receive a message if the device is not ready. To support this, LINUX provides a facility to initiate functions at a defined future time. To achieve this, there is the interface in the form of:

```
struct timer_list {
        struct list_head list;
        unsigned long expires;
        unsigned long data;
        void (*function)(unsigned long);
};
```

The list entry in this structure helps the internal management of the timer using a double interlinked list. The component expires indicates the time when the function has to be called with the argument data. The functions

```
extern void add_timer(struct timer_list * timer);
extern int del_timer(struct timer_list * timer);
extern int mod_timer(struct timer_list * timer,
                     unsigned long expires);
```

help with the management of a global timer list. add_timer() activates a timer by entering it to the global timer list, del_timer() removes it, and mod_timer() modifies the expires time of an activated timer.

The timer interrupt (see Section 3.2.5) regularly calls the function

```
static inline void run_timer_list(void);
```

which searches for timers that have expired and calls the affiliated functions.

3.2 MAIN ALGORITHMS

This section describes the main algorithms for process management.

3.2.1 Signals

One of the oldest facilities for interprocess communication under UNIX consists of signals. The kernel uses signals to inform processes about certain events.

The user typically uses signals to abort processes or to switch interactive programs to a defined state. Processes use signals to synchronize themselves with other processes. Signals are usually sent via the function

```
int send_sig_info(int sig,
                struct siginfo *info,
                struct task_struct *t);
```

In addition to the signal number `sig` and a pointer to the task that is to receive the signal, it also contains a parameter `info` that identifies the sender as an argument. The kernel can send a signal to every process; a normal process can only do so in particular cases. It can have either superuser rights or the same IUD and GID as the receiver process. The `SIGCONT` signal is an exception. This can also be sent by an arbitrary process to the same session.

If there is authority to send the signal and the process is not inclined to ignore this signal, it is sent to the process. This is done by sending the signal in the `pending` component of the task structure for the receiving process. In this case, one has just to check if any signal is available for a process; the component `sigpending` of the task structure is also set. The signal has been sent. There is no immediate treatment of the signal by the receiving process: this happens only after the scheduler has returned the process to the `TASK_RUNNING` state (see Section 3.2.6).

When the process is reactivated by the scheduler, but before it is switched to user mode, routine `ret_from_sys_call` (Section 3.3.1) is run. It checks if any signal is available for the process. This happens when the flag `sigpending` is set in the task structure of the process. In this case, the function `do_signal()` is called, which takes over the actual signal handling. If, on meeting a signal, a user-defined function has to be called, `do_signal` calls the function `handle_signal()`.

It still remains to be explained how this function can call the signal management routine defined by the process. This is tricky. The function `handle_signal()` manipulates the stack and the register of the process. The instruction pointer is set to the first instruction of the signal handling routine and the parameter of the signal handling routine is added to the stack. If the process now carries on its work, it seems to it as if the signal handling routine had been called as a normal function.

This is the usual approach; however, in the actual implementation it is extended in two ways.

Firstly, LINUX claims to be POSIX compatible. The process can specify which signals are to be blocked while a signal handling routine is running. This is implemented by the kernel adding further signals to the signal mask `current->blocked` before calling the user-defined signal handling routine. There is a problem, however: the signal mask must be restored to its original state after the signal handling routine has terminated. To deal with this, an instruction which activates the system call *sigreturn* is entered on the stack as the return address of the signal handling routine. This then takes care of the cleaning-up operations at the end of the user-defined signal routine. The second addition is an optimization. If a number of signal handling routines need to be called, a number of stack frames are set up. As a result, the signal handling routines are executed one after the other.

3.2.2 | Hardware interrupts

Interrupts are used to allow the hardware to communicate with the operating system. Programming interrupt routines will be examined in more detail in Section 7.3.2. Here we are more interested in the principles governing the execution of an interrupt.

When creating an interrupt routine, the programmer faces a problem. On the one hand, the actual interrupt routine has to serve the hardware as quickly as possible and release the processor for other tasks, for instance to process further interrupts. On the other hand, this kind of interrupt can also carry out the processing of a large amount of data.

To solve this problem, interrupt handling under LINUX is carried out in two phases. First, the time-critical communication with the hardware is carried out, and in doing so other interrupts can be blocked. The actual processing of data is carried out asynchronously with the actual interrupt. "Software interrupts" are used for this, "tasklets" or "bottom halves". These are functions which will be called later on. They can be interrupted by other interrupts.

The main handling routine for hardware interrupts is simplified, as in the following:

```
unsigned int do_IRQ(struct pt_regs regs) {
  int irq;
  struct irqaction * action;

  /* take irq number from the register */
  irq = regs.orig_eax & 0xff;
```

```
/* find the respective handler */
action = irq_desc[irq].action;

/* and execute the actions */
while ( action )
{
      action->handler(irq, regs)
      action = action->next;
}
/* the actual hardware interrupt is exited here  */

if( softirq_active & softirq_mask)
      do_softirq();
}
```

3.2.3 Software interrupts

LINUX 2.4 introduces the concept of software interrupts. A software interrupt is like a hardware interrupt, an event that can be activated which leads to the processing of the interrupt handling routine. But these are not started immediately like hardware interrupts are, but only at certain times. In practice, this happens after every hardware interrupt and system call.

As with the number of hardware interrupts, the number of software interrupts is also limited.

```
enum { HI_SOFTIRQ=0,
       NET_TX_SOFTIRQ, NET_RX_SOFTIRQ,
       TASKLET_SOFTIRQ
};
static struct softirq_action softirq_vec[32];
```

HI_SOFTIRQ is the software interrupt with the superior priority, NET_TX_SOFTIRQ and NET_RX_SOFTIRQ are used by the network code, and TASKLET_SOFTIRQ is the software interrupt with whose aid tasklets are processed.

The registration of an interrupt handler is carried out via the function open_softirq(). Calling of raise_softirq() makes sure that the registered handling routine is executed as soon as do_softirq() is called again.

```
void open_softirq(int nr,
            void (*action)(struct softirq_action*),
            void *data);
raise_softirq(int nr);
void do_softirq();
```

Notice that in a multiprocessor system the same interrupt handler can be processed on several processors at the same time, therefore the functions have to be reentered or implement a serial access to general resources.

It is easier to work with tasklets than with software interrupts. The system guarantees that a particular tasklet is only executed once at a certain time; however, different tasklets can be processed in parallel.

The registration of a tasklet is carried out via the function `tasklet_init()`. Using `tasklet_schedule()` a tasklet is marked for processing and the software interrupt `TASKLET_SOFTIRQ` is activated. Its interrupt line executes the tasklets.

```
struct tasklet_struct;
void tasklet_init(struct tasklet_struct *t,
                void (*func)(unsigned long),
                unsigned long data);
void tasklet_schedule(struct tasklet_struct *t);
```

Software interrupts and tasklets are new in LINUX 2.4, whereas bottom halves have been available for a very long time. Previously these were implemented like software interrupts, but now they behave like tasklets. Bottom-half functionality should not be used in new development, therefore it is not described in detail here. The substantial difference from tasklets is that in a multiprocessor system only one bottom-half handler can be processed at one time.

3.2.4 Booting the system

There is something magical about booting a UNIX system (or, for that matter, any operating system). The aim of this section is to make the process a little more transparent.

Appendix D explains how LILO (the *LI*nux *LO*ader) finds the LINUX kernel and loads it into memory. It then begins at the entry point `start:` which is held in the `arch/i386/boot/setup.S` file. As the name suggests, this is assembler code responsible for initializing the hardware. Once the essential hardware parameters have been established, the process is switched into protected mode by setting the *protected mode* bit in the *machine status word*.

The assembler instruction

```
jmpi 0x100000 , __KERNEL_CS
```

then initiates a jump to the start address of the 32-bit code of the actual operating system kernel and continues from `startup_32:` in the file `arch/i386/kernel/head.S`. More sections of the hardware are initialized here (in particular the MMU (page table), the co-processor, and the environment (stack, environment, and so on) required for the execution of the kernel's C functions). Once the initialization is complete, the first C function, `start_kernel()` from `init/main.c` is called.

The function `setup_arch` saves all the data the assembler code has found about the hardware up to that point as well as the initialization of more architecture-dependent components. Finally, the hardware-independent parts of the kernel are initialized.

```
asmlinkage void __init start_kernel(void)
{
  char * command_line;
  printk(linux_banner);
  setup_arch(&command_line);
  parse_options(command_line);
  trap_init();
  init_IRQ();
  sched_init();
  time_init();
  softirq_init();
  console_init();
  init_modules();
...
```

The process now running is process 0. It now generates a kernel thread which executes the `init()` function.

```
  kernel_thread (init,NULL,...)
```

Subsequently, process 0 is only concerned with using up unused computing time.

```
  cpu_idle (NULL);
```

The `init()` function carries out the remaining initialization. Among other things, the `do_basic_setup()` function initializes all drivers for the hardware here.

```
static int init()
{
  do_basic_setup();
```

Now an attempt can be made to establish a connection with the console and to open the file descriptors 0, 1, and 2.

```
  if (open("/dev/console", O_RDWR, 0) < 0)
          printk("Warning: unable to open an initial console.\n");
  (void) dup(0);
  (void) dup(0);
```

Then an attempt is made to execute a boot program specified by the user or one of the programs /sbin/init, /etc/init, or /bin/init. These usually start the background process running under LINUX and make sure that the `getty` program runs on each connected terminal – thus a user can log on to the system.

```
if (execute_command)
        execve(execute_command,argv_init,envp_init);

execve("/sbin/init",argv_init,envp_init);
execve("/etc/init",argv_init,envp_init);
execve("/bin/init",argv_init,envp_init);
```

If none of the programs mentioned above exists, an attempt is made to start a shell, so that the superuser can repair the system. If this is not possible, the system is stopped.

```
execve("/bin/sh",argv_init,envp_init);
panic("No init found...");
```

The approach described here is intended just to provide a general overview of what happens when the system is started. The reality is more complex, depending on the hardware initialization (MMU, SMP) and the exceptions, such as the use of an Initial RAM disk (INITRD).

3.2.5   Timer interrupts

All operating systems need a way of measuring time and keeping a system time. The system time is usually implemented by arranging the hardware to trigger an interrupt at specific intervals. These interrupt routines take over the time "counting." Under LINUX, system time is measured in "ticks" since the system was started up. One tick represents 10 milliseconds, so the timer interrupt is triggered 100 times per second. The timer is stored in the variable

```
unsigned long volatile jiffies;
```

which should be modified by the timer interrupt. However, this method only provides an internal time base.

Applications, on the other hand, are more interested in the "actual time." This is held in the variable

```
volatile struct timeval xtime;
```

which is also updated by the timer interrupt.

The timer interrupt is called relatively often and is therefore somewhat time-critical. Therefore the implementation is bipartite.

The actual interrupt routine do_timer() only updates the variable jiffies and indicates the *bottom-half* routine (see Sections 3.2.2 and 7.3.5) of the timer interrupt as active. It is called by the system later on and handles the rest of the work.

```
void do_timer(struct pt_regs * regs)
{
    (*(unsigned long *)&jiffies)++;
```

```
    update_process_times(user_mode(regs));

  mark_bh(TIMER_BH);
  if (TQ_ACTIVE(tq_timer))
        mark_bh(TQUEUE_BH);
}
```

update_process_times() will be described later. To begin with, we want to have a look at the bottom-half routine of the timer interrupt.

```
void timer_bh(void)
{
  update_times();
  run_timer_list();
}
```

run_timer_list() takes care of the processing of the functions, described in Section 3.1.6, to update the system-wide timer. This also includes the real-time timers of the actual task. update_times() is responsible for updating the times.

```
static inline void update_times(void)
{
  unsigned long ticks;

  ticks = jiffies - wall_jiffies;

  if (ticks) {
  wall_jiffies += ticks;
  update_wall_time(ticks);
  }
  calc_load(ticks);
}
```

update_wall_time() deals with the update of the *real-time* xtime and is called when some time has passed since the last call of the function.

The function update_process_time collects data for the scheduler and decides whether it has to be called.

```
static void update_process_times(int user_ticks);
{
  struct task_struct * p = current;
  int cpu = smp_processort_id();

  unsigned long user = ticks - system;
```

First of all, the `counter` component of the task structure is updated. When `counter` is zero, the time slice of the current process has expired and the scheduler is activated at the next opportunity.

```
update_one_process(p, ticks, user, system, 0);
if(p->pid)
{
        p->counter -= 1;
        if (p->counter <= 0) {
            p->counter = 0;
            p->need_resched = 1;
}
```

After this, the `per_cpu_user` task structure components are also updated for statistical purposes.

```
        p->per_cpu_user[cpu] += user_ticks;
}
```

Under LINUX it is possible to limit a process's "**CPU** consumption" resource. This is done by means of the system call *setrlimit*, which also can be used to limit other resources of a process. Exceeding the time limit is checked in the timer interrupt, and the process is either informed via the `SIGXCPU` signal or aborted by means of the `SIGKILL` signal. Subsequently, the interval timers of the current task must be updated. When these have expired, the task is informed by a corresponding signal.

```
void update_one_process(p,user,system,cpu)
{
  p->per_cpu_utime[cpu] += user;
  p->per_cpu_stime[cpu] += system;
  do_process_times(p, user, system);

  do_it_virt(p, user);
  do_it_prof(p);
}

void do_process_times(p,user,system)
{
  psecs = (p->times.tms_utime += user);
  psecs += (p->times.tms_stime += system);
  if (psecs / HZ > p->rlim[RLIMIT_CPU].rlim_cur) {
        /* Send SIGXCPU every second.. */
        if (!(psecs % HZ))
                send_sig(SIGXCPU, p, 1);
```

```
                /* and SIGKILL when we go over max.. */
                if (psecs / HZ > p->rlim[RLIMIT_CPU].rlim_max)
                        send_sig(SIGKILL, p, 1);
        }
}
void do_it_virt(p, user) {
    unsigned long it_virt = p->it_virt_value;

    if (it_virt)
    {
            it_virt -= user;
            if (it_virt <= 0)
            {
                    it_virt = p->it_virt_incr;
                    send_sig(SIGVTALRM, p, 1);
            }
            p->it_virt_value = it_virt - user;
    }
}
```

3.2.6 | The scheduler

The scheduler is responsible for allocating the "processor" (that is, computing time) to the individual processes. The criteria by which this is done vary from operating system to operating system. UNIX systems prefer traditional interactive processes to enable short response times to be achieved and so make the system appear subjectively faster to the user. In compliance with POSIX standard 1003.4, LINUX supports various scheduling classes which can be selected via the *sched setscheduler()* system call. There are real-time processes in the scheduler classes SCHED_RR and SCHED_FIFO. Real-time does not mean "hard real time" with guaranteed process switching and reaction times, but "soft real-time." When a process with higher real-time priority (described in the rt_priority component of the task structure) wishes to run, all other processes with lower real-time priorities are cast aside.

The difference between SCHED_FIFO and SCHED_RR is that a process of the SCHED_FIFO class can run until it relinquishes control or until a process with higher real-time priority wishes to run. A process of the PROG_RR class, in contrast, is also interrupted when its time slice has expired or there are processes of the same real-time priority. Thus, a classic *round robin* procedure is created among processes of the same priority.

On the other hand, there is the scheduling class SCHED_OTHER which implements a classic UNIX scheduling algorithm. According to POSIX 1003.4, every real-time process has a higher priority than any process of the scheduling class SCHED_OTHER.

The LINUX scheduling algorithm is implemented in `schedule()` (`kernel/sched.c`). It is called at two different places. Firstly, there are system calls which call the `schedule()` function, usually indirectly by calling `sleep_on()` (see Section 3.1.5). Secondly, after every system call and after every slow interrupt, the flag `need_resched` is checked by the `ret_from_sys_call()` routine. If it is set, the scheduler is also called from here. Because the timer interrupt is called regularly and sets the `need_resched` flag, the scheduler is activated regularly.

The `schedule()` function consists of three parts. Firstly, all upcoming software interrupts are processed. Secondly, the process with the highest priority is determined. Here, *real-time* processes always take precedence over "normal" ones. Thirdly, the new process becomes the current process, and the scheduler has accomplished its task.

Unfortunately, the real source code of the scheduler has become relatively unclear in kernel version 2.0. The reason for this lies partly in the restructuring carried out for efficiency reasons, but more so because of the new multiprocessor support.

Therefore, we will present a highly simplified version of the `schedule()` function. Among other things, the details needed for SMP support have been omitted.

```
asmlinkage void schedule(void)
{
  struct task_struct * prev, * next, *p;
  prev = current;
  prev->need_resched = 0
```

First, the software interrupts are called. They are time-uncritical routines that have been taken out of the interrupt handlers for efficiency reasons. However, as these routines may well manipulate information capable of influencing the scheduling (for example, changing a task back into the `TASK_RUNNING` state), they must be processed here at the latest.

```
  if (softirq_active(this_cpu) & softirq_mask(this_cpu))
        do_softirq();
```

If `schedule()` was called because the current process has to wait for an event, it is removed from the run queue. If the current task belongs to the SCHED_RR scheduling class, and the task's time slice has expired, it is placed at the end of the run queue and thus after all other ready-to-run tasks belonging to the SCHED_RR scheduling class.

The run queue is a list of all processes applying for the processor, and is doubly linked by the component `run_list` of the task structure.

```
  if (!prev->counter && prev->policy == SCHED_RR)
  {


        prev->counter = prev->priority;
        move_last_runqueue(prev);
  }
```

```
if( prev->state != TASK_RUNNING )
{
        del_from_runqueue(prev);
}
```

Next, the scheduling algorithm itself is carried out, that is, the process in the run queue that has the highest priority is searched for. The function goodness() calculates the priority for every process; real-time processes are given preference.

```
next = idle_task;              /* next process */
next_p = -1000;                /* and the priority */

list_for_each(p,&runqueue_head)
{
        if( ! can_schedule(p) )
                continue;
        weight = goodness(p,prev,this_cpu);
        if( weight > next_p)
        {
                next_p = weight; next = p;
        }
}
```

If next_p is greater than zero, we have found a suitable candidate. If next_p is less than 0, there is no ready-to-run process and we must activate the idle task. In both cases, next points to the task to be activated next. If next_p is equal to zero, there are ready-to-run processes, but we must recalculate their dynamic priorities (the value of counter). The counter values of all processes are also recalculated. Then we restart the scheduler, but this time with more success.

```
if( next_p == 0 )
{
        for_each_task(p)
        {
                p->counter = (p->counter / 2) + p->priority;
        }
}
```

The task indicated by next is the next to be activated.

```
if( prev != next )
        switch_to(prev,next);
} /* schedule() */
```

This concludes the description of the scheduler. We stress again that the above source text is a highly simplified version of the scheduler, but is, in our opinion, sufficient to understand its functioning.

3.3   IMPLEMENTATION OF SYSTEM CALLS

The range of functions in the operating system is made available to the processes by means of system calls. In this section we will look at implementing system calls under LINUX.

3.3.1   How do system calls actually work?

A system call works on the basis of a defined transition from user mode to system mode. In LINUX, this is only possible using interrupts. The interrupt 0x80 is therefore reserved for system calls.[4]

Normally, the user will always call a library function (such as *fork()*) to carry out a certain task. This library function (as a rule generated from the _syscall macros in `<asm/unistd.h>`) writes its arguments and the number of the system call to the defined transfer register and then triggers the 0x80 interrupt. When the relevant interrupt service routine returns, the return value is read from the appropriate transfer register and the library function terminates.

The actual work of the system call is taken care of by the interrupt routine. This starts at the entry address `system_call()`, held in the `arch/i386/kernel/entry.S` file.

Unfortunately, this routine is written entirely in assembler. For better readability, it will be illustrated here by a C equivalent. Wherever symbolic labels occur in the assembler text, we have shown them as labels in the C text.

The parameters `sys_call_num` and `sys_call_args` represent the number of the system call (see `<asm/unistd.h>`) and its arguments.

```
PSEUDO_CODE system_call( int sys_call_num , sys_call_args )
{
system_call:
```

First, all the registers for the process are saved.

```
SAVE_ALL; /* Macro from entry.S */
```

If `sys_call_num` represents a legal value, the handling routine assigned to the system call number is called. This is entered in the `sys_call_table[  ]` (defined in the file `arch/i386/kernel/entry.S`). If the process flag **PF_TRACESYS** is set, it is monitored by its parent process. The work entailed in this is taken care of by the `syscall_trace()` function (`arch/i386/kernel/ptrace.c`). It amends the state of the current process to

---

4 This applies to LINUX system calls on the PC. The iBCS emulation uses a different procedure – the so-called `lcall7` gate.

TASK_STOPPED, sends a SIGTRAP signal to the parent process and calls the scheduler. The current process is interrupted until the parent process reactivates it. As this is done before and after every system call, the parent process has total control over the method of the child process.

```
  if (sys_call_num >= NR_syscalls)
  {
badsys:
        errno = -ENOSYS;
  }
  else
  {
        if (current->ptrace)
                syscall_trace();
        errno=(*sys_call_table[sys_call_num])(sys_call_args);
        if (current->ptrace)
                syscall_trace();
  }
```

The actual work of the system call is now complete. Before the process can continue, however, there may still be some administrative tasks to deal with.

```
ret_from_sys_call:
  if (softirq_active & softirq_mask)
handle_softirq:
        do_softirq()
```

If scheduling has been requested (need_resched != 0), the scheduler is called.

This causes another process to become active. schedule() will only return once the process has been reactivated.

```
ret_with_reschedule:
  if (current->need_resched) {
reschedule:
        schedule();
        goto ret_from_sys_call;
  }
```

If signals have been sent for the current process, and the process has not blocked receipt of them, they are now processed. The function do_signal() is described in Section 3.2.1.

```
  if (current->sigpending)
signal_return:
        do_signal();
```

This completes the necessary work, and the system call returns. All the registers are now restored and the interrupt routine is then terminated by the assembler instruction iret.

```
restore_all:
  RESTORE_ALL;
} /* PSEUDO_CODE system_call */
```

3.3.2 Examples of simple system calls

In the following we take a closer look at the implementation of some system calls. This will also demonstrate the use of the algorithms and data structures introduced above.

The system call *getuid*

This is a very simple system call – it merely reads a value from the task structure and returns it:

```
asmlinkage int sys_getuid(void)
{
  return current->uid;
}
```

The system call *nice*

The system call *nice* is a little more complicated. *nice* expects a number by which the static priority of the current process is to be modified as its argument.

All system calls which process arguments must test the arguments for plausibility.

```
asmlinkage int sys_nice (int increment)
{
  int newpriority;
```

Note that a larger argument for sys_nice() indicates a lower priority. This makes the name increment for the argument of *nice* a bit confusing.

```
  if (increment < 0 && !capable (CAP_SYS_NICE))
        return -EPERM;
```

capable() checks whether the current process has the right to increase its priority. This is the case with the classical UNIX systems when the process has privileges. LINUX provides a concept of subdividing these privileges in a finer way.

The new priority for the process can now be calculated. Among other things, a check is made at this point to ensure that the new priority for the process is within a reasonable range.

```
    newpriority = ...
    if (newpriority < -20)
          newpriority = -20;
    if (newpriority > 19)
          newpriority = 19;

    current->nice = newpriority;
    return 0;
} /* sys_nice */
```

The system call *pause*

The system call *pause* interrupts the execution of the program until the process is reactivated by a signal. This merely amounts to setting the status of the current process to TASK_INTERRUPTIBLE and then calling the scheduler. This results in another task becoming active.

The process can only be reactivated if the status of the process is returned to TASK_RUNNING. This occurs when a signal is received (see Section 3.2.6). The system call pause then returns with the fault ERESTARTNOHAND and carries out the necessary actions for the handling of the signal (as described in Section 3.2.1).

```
asmlinkage int sys_pause(void)
{
  current->state = TASK_INTERRUPTIBLE;
  schedule();
  return -ERESTARTNOHAND;
}
```

3.3.3 | Examples of more complex system calls

We will now turn to rather more complex system calls. This section examines the system calls for process management (*fork*, *execve*, *_exit*, and *wait*).

The system call *fork*

The system call *fork* is the only way of starting a new process. This is done by creating a (nearly) identical copy of the process that has called *fork*.

As a matter of fact, *fork* is a very demanding system call. All the data of the process has to be copied, and this can easily run to a few megabytes. In the course of developing UNIX, a number of methods were adopted to keep the demands of *fork* as low as possible. Frequently, *fork* is followed directly by a call to *exec*. It is not necessary to copy the data, as it is not needed. In the UNIX systems from the BSD family, therefore, the system call *vfork* has been introduced. Like *fork*, it creates a new process, but it shares the data segment between the two processes. This is a rather dubious approach, as one process can affect the data of the other process. To keep this interference as limited as possible, further execution of the parent process is halted until the child process has either been terminated by *_exit* or has started a new program with *exec*.

Newer UNIX systems such as LINUX, for example, take a different approach, using the *copy-on-write* technique. The thought behind this is that a number of processes may access the same memory at the same time – provided they do not modify the data.

Thus, under LINUX, the relevant pages of memory are not copied with a call to *fork*, but are used at the same time by the old and new processes. However, the pages used by both processes are marked as write-protected – which means that they cannot be modified by either process. If one of the processes needs to carry out a write operation on these pages of memory, a page fault is triggered by the memory management hardware (MMU), the process is interrupted and the kernel is informed. At this point, the kernel copies the pages of memory concerned and assigns the writing process a copy of its own. This procedure is completely transparent – that is, the processes themselves are unaware of it. The great advantage of this copy-on-write method is that uneconomical copying of memory pages is only carried out when it is actually needed.

The newer operating system concepts embody, in addition to the idea of process, the idea of threads, an independent sequence of events within a process. A number of different threads may be processed in parallel and independently of each other during the execution of a process. The main way this differs from the concept of a process is that the different threads within a process operate in the same area of memory and can therefore affect each other. There are a variety of approaches to implementing threads. Simple variants, such as the widely used Pthread library, manage without any support from the kernel of the operating system. The disadvantage of these methods is that the scheduling of the individual threads has to be carried out by the user program: the kernel sees it as an ordinary process. As a result, a blocking system call (for example, a read originating at the terminal) blocks the entire process and thus all the threads. The ideal situation would be one in which only the thread which has used the system call were to block. Later versions of UNIX (for example, Solaris 2.x) provide this support.

LINUX supports threads by making the (LINUX specific) system call *clone* available, which provides the necessary kernel support to implement threads.

clone works in a similar way to *fork*, that is, it creates a new task. The main difference is that with *clone* both tasks can work with common memory. As *fork* and *clone* essentially do the same thing, they are implemented by a common function, which is simply called in a different way depending on the system call used.

```
asmlinkage int sys_fork(struct pt_regs regs)
{
  return do_fork (SIGCHLD, regs.esp, &regs,0);
```

```
}

asmlinkage int sys_clone (struct pt_regs regs)
{
  unsigned long clone_flags;
  unsigned long newsp;

  clone_flags = regs.ebx;
  newsp = regs.ecx;
  if (!newsp)
        newsp = regs.esp;
  return do_fork (clone_flags, newsp, &regs,0);
}
```

The function do_fork() carries out the actual work:

```
int do_fork (unsigned long clone_flags,
        unsigned long start_stack,
        struct pt_regs *regs,
        unsigned long stack_size)
{
  int error = -ENOMEM;
  unsigned long new_stack;
  struct task_struct *p;
```

First the memory space required for the new task structure and the kernel stack is allocated.

```
  p = alloc_task_struct();
  if (!p)
        goto fork_out;
```

If the user has exceeded its limit of processes, the function is interrupted. The same happens if there are already too many tasks in the system.

```
  if (current->user->count >=
                current->rlim[RLIMIT_NPROC].rlim_cur)
        goto bad_fork_free;
  if (nr_threads >= max_threads)
        goto bad_fork_cleanup_count;
```

The child process p inherits all the parent process's entries.

```
  *p = *current;
```

However, some of the entries need to be initialized for a new process.

```
p->state = TASK_UNINTERUPTIBLE;
p->did_exec = 0;
p->swappable = 0;
p->pid = get_pid(clone_flags);
...
p->run_list.next = NULL;
p->run_list.prev = NULL;
...
p->start_time = jiffies;
...
```

Now the substructures in the task structure are copied. Depending on the value of clone_flags, data structures will be either copied or shared. This is where the differences between the system calls *fork* and *clone* are put into effect.

```
if (copy_files(clone_flags, p))
        goto bad_fork_cleanup;
if (copy_fs(clone_flags, p))
        goto bad_fork_cleanup_files;
if (copy_sighand(clone_flags, p))
        goto bad_fork_cleanup_fs;
if (copy_mm(clone_flags, p))
        goto bad_fork_cleanup_sighand;
copy_thread(0, clone_flags, start_stack, stack_size, p, regs);
```

Finally, the state of the new task is set to **TASK_RUNNING** so that it can be activated by the scheduler. The old task (the parent process) returns from the system call with the process identification number (PID) of the new process.

```
++nr_threads;
wake_up_process(p);
return p->pid;
```

If something has gone wrong, data structures requested up to that moment must be released.

```
bad_fork:
    ...
    return error;
}
```

The copy_thread() function which is called in the above coding is also responsible for initializing the registers for the new process. Among other things, the instruction pointer p->tss.eip is set to the start of the ret_from_sys_call() assembler routine, so that the new process begins processing as if it were the one which had issued the *fork* call. At the same time, the return value is set to zero to enable the program to tell the parent process and child process apart by reference to the different return values.

The system call *execve*

The system call *execve* enables a process to change its executing program. LINUX permits a number of formats for executable files. As in UNIX, they are recognized by the so-called "magic numbers" – the initial bytes of the file. By tradition, every UNIX system uses its own format for executable files. In the past few years a standard has developed, the ELF format.[5]

This has become predominant, as the treatment of dynamic libraries has been simplified drastically. Interested readers can find more information on the ELF format in [ELF]. In addition, LINUX supports the script files used in the BSD world. If a file begins with the pair of characters "#!", it is not loaded directly, but passed for processing to an interpreter program specified in the first line of the file. The familiar version of this is a line in the form

```
#!/bin/sh
```

at the start of the shell script. Executing this file (that is, issuing an *execve*) is equivalent to executing the file /bin/sh with the original file as its argument. The following gives (heavily abriged) the annotated source text of do_execve().

```
static int do_execve(char *filename, char **argv, char **envp,
struct pt_regs * regs)
{
```

First, an attempt is made to find the file relevant to the executing program (its inode) by reference to the name of the program. The structure bprm is used to store all the data about the file.

```
struct linux_binprm bprm;
struct file *file;

file = open_exec(filename);

if ( IS_ERR(file))
        return PTR_ERR(file);
brpm.file = file;
bprm.filename = filename;
bprm.argc = count(argv);
bprm.envc = count(envp);
...
```

5 ELF stands for Executable and Linkable Format.

The function `prepare_binrpm` checks the access rights and reads the first 128 bytes of the file.

```
retval = prepare_binrpm(&brpm);
if (retval <= 0)
        goto error;
```

Now, on the basis of the first bytes of the file, an attempt can be made to load the executable file. LINUX uses a separate loading function for each file format it is familiar with. They are each called in turn and "asked" whether they can load the file. If the file can be loaded, `execve()` terminates successfully; if not, it returns ENOEXEC.

```
return seach_binary_handler(&bprm.regs);
} /* do_execve() */

int search_binary_handler(struct linux_binprm *bprm,
                       struct pt_regs *regs)
{
  for( fmt = formats; fmt ; fmt = fmt->next )
  {
        if (!fmt->load_binary)
                continue;
        retval = (fmt->load_binary)(bprm, regs);
        if (retval >= 0) {
                current->did_exec = 1;
                return retval;
        }
        if( retval != -ENOEXEC )
                break;
  }
  return(retval);
}
```

The actual work is done by the function `fmt->load_binary()`. Let us take a closer look at a function of this type:

```
int load_aout_binary(struct linux_binprm *bprm,
                struct pt_regs *regs)
{
```

`bprm->buf` contains the first 128 bytes of the file to be loaded. First, this section of the file is inspected to confirm that it is in the correct file format. If not, the function returns the fault ENOEXEC. After this, `search_binary_handler()` can test for the formats. These tests also extract various pieces of information from the header which will be needed later.

```
struct exec ex;

ex = *((struct exec *) bprm->buf);
if ((N_MAGIC(ex) != ZMAGIC && N_MAGIC(ex) != OMAGIC &&
        N_MAGIC(ex) != QMAGIC && N_MAGIC(ex) != NMAGIC) ||
        N_TRSIZE(ex) || N_DRSIZE(ex) ||
        bprm->dentry->inode->i_size < ex.a_text+ ...)
{
        return -ENOEXEC;
}
...
fd_offset = N_TXTOFF(ex);
...
```

If these tests have been concluded successfully, the new program is loaded. The first action at this stage is to release the process's memory, which still contains the old program. If a fault occurs while the file is being loaded, the current process will have to be aborted.

```
flush_old_exec(bprm);
```

Now the task structure can be updated. At this point, a note that the program is in a LINUX-specific format is entered in the `personality` component.

```
set_personality(PER_LINUX);
current->mm->end_code = ex.a_text +
        current->mm->start_code = N_TXTADDR(ex));
        ...
```

The text and data segments are then inserted into memory using do_mmap(). Note that do_mmap() is not loading the file at this point, but only updating the page tables and thus telling the paging algorithm where to find the pages of memory to be loaded when it needs them. The paging is described in Section 4.4.

```
do_mmap(bprm->file, N_TXTADDR(ex), ex.a_text,
        PROT_READ | PROT_EXEC,
        MAP_FIXED | MAP_PRIVATE | ..., fd_offset);
...
```

Now the BSS segment is loaded. Under UNIX it contains the non-initialized data for a process. This is done by the function `set_brk()`. Initialization of the registers, and in particular, the instruction pointer for the new program is then carried out; this is the job of the function `start_thread()`. When the system call *execve* completes its work, program execution for the process continues from the new address.

```
set_brk(current->mm->start_brk, current->mm->brk);
current->mm->start_stack = ...;
```

```
    start_thread(regs, ex.a_entry, current->mm->start_stack);
    return 0;
} /* load_aout_binary */
```

In the kernel the functions do_execve() and load_aout_binary() are considerably more complicated than this, partly because of the necessary fault and exception handling.[6] Also, we have left a number of "unimportant" details out of this illustration; "unimportant" in the sense that they are unnecessary for an understanding of the basic principles of do_execve(). Those who wish to explore these functions seriously and perhaps implement a new file format will find they cannot avoid a study of the original.

The system call *exit*

A process is always terminated by calling the kernel function do_exit(). This is done either directly by the system call _exit or indirectly on the occurrence of a signal which cannot be intercepted.

As a matter of fact, do_exit() does not have much to do. It merely has to release the resources claimed by the process and, if necessary, inform other processes. However, this gives rise to a good deal of detail; so, once again, the following illustration of the do_exit() function is heavily abridged. For example, we shall not take account of actions necessary for clean management of the process groups.

```
NORET_TYPE void do_exit(long code)
{
```

First, the process releases all the structures it occupies.

```
    del_timer(&current->real_timer);
    sem_exit();
    __exit_mm(current);
    __exit_files(current);
    __exit_fs(current);
    __exit_sighand(current);
    exit_thread();
```

The parent process is informed of the termination of a child process. In some cases, it will already be waiting for this event via the system call *wait*. When a process completes its work, all the child processes are inherited by process 1. If it no longer exists, they are bequeathed to process 0. All this is done by the exit_notify() function. It also sets the status of the current process from TASK_RUNNING to TASK_ZOMBIE

```
    exit_notify();
```

---

6 It can also happen, for example, that the older LINUX binaries cannot be loaded using do_mmap(). This means that load_aout_binary() has to load the program code and data in full and cannot fall back on "demand loading."

All cleaning-up operations have now been completed. No memory space is needed for the process any longer (except for the task structure). It becomes a zombie process. It will remain a zombie process until the parent process issues the system call *wait*.

```
current->exit_code = code;
```

Finally, do_exit() calls the scheduler and allows the other processes to continue. As the status of the actual process is TASK_ZOMBIE, the function schedule() no longer returns.

```
schedule();
/* NOTREACHED */
} /* do_exit */
```

The system call *wait*

The system call *wait4* enables a process to wait for the end of a child process and interrogate the exit code supplied. Depending on the argument given, *wait4* will wait for a specified child process, a child process in a specified process group, or any child process. In this way, it is possible to control if *wait4* really has to wait for the end of a child process or if it has to take into account child processes that were already finished. As all these distinctions are rather boring, the following illustration shows a modified version of *wait4* with semantics more or less corresponding to those of *wait*. (Normally, *wait* is a library function which calls *wait4* with appropriate arguments.)

```
int sys_wait( … )
{
repeat:
```

sys_wait() consists of two parts. First, it tests whether there is already a child process in the TASK_ZOMBIE state. If there is, we have found the process we are looking for and sys_wait() can return successfully. Before it does so, however, it picks up statistical data (system time used, exit code, and so on) from the child process's process table and then releases its task structure. This is the only time a process entry can be removed from the process table.

```
nr_of_childs = 0;
for (p = current->p_cptr ; p ; p = p->p_osptr)
{
       ++nr_of_childs;

       if(p->state == TASK_ZOMBIE)
       {
               current->times.tms_cutime += p->times.tms_utime +
                                       p->times.tms_cutime;
```

```
                    current->times.tms_cstime += p->times.tms_stime +
                                                p->times.tms_cstime;
                    if (stat_addr)
                            put_user(p->exit_code, stat_addr);
                    release(p);
                    return p;

            }

    }
```

If there is no child process, `sys_wait()` returns immediately.

```
if (nr_of_childs == 0)
        return 0;
```

However, if there are child processes, it waits for one of the child processes to end. To do this, the parent process enters itself in the relevant wait queue in its own task structure. As we have already seen, on the _exit system call every process wakes up all the processes waiting in this wait queue via the `wake_up()` function. This guarantees that the parent process is informed of the end of a child process.

```
interruptible_sleep_on(&current->wait_chldexit);
```

The signal SIGCHLD sent by `do_exit()` on terminating the child process is ignored. If a signal is received in the meantime (`interruptible_sleep_on()` can, after all, be interrupted by another signal) the system call is terminated with an error message. In all other cases, we know that there is now a child process in the TASK_ZOMBIE state, and we can start looking for it again from the top.

```
current->signal &= ~(1<<(SIGCHLD-1));
if (current->signal & ~current->blocked)
        return -EINTR;
goto repeat;
} /* sys_wait */
```

4 MEMORY MANAGEMENT

A multitasking system like LINUX makes particular demands on memory management. The memory belonging to a process and used by the kernel needs to be protected against access by other processes. This protection is vital for the stability of a multitasking operating system. It prevents a process from writing at random into other processes' areas of memory, causing them to crash. This can happen in a C program, for example, simply by exceeding the limits of a field variable.

Memory protection prevents any system from crashing due to errors in the application programs as well as manipulations due to malicious programs, such as viruses and trojans.

Moreover, memory protection forces communication between application programs and operating system to take place over defined interfaces, rather than manipulating the memory of the operating system directly.

Primary memory (RAM) has been a scarce resource for a long time. Also, the demands for memory by applications and the primary memory that is usually available seem to be the same. Now, new database systems, desktop shells such as GNOME and KDE as well as Java, already known to be memory eaters, join the existing software for LINUX, such as the GNU C compiler or the X Window system. Java is an example of working at higher levels of abstraction in programming, with higher demands on memory.

As a multitasking system like LINUX can run a number of processes in quasi-parallel, it is possible that the memory requirement of all the processes to be carried out exceeds the size of the primary memory. Operating systems solve this problem by moving areas from primary memory to secondary memory (e.g., to areas on hard disks). It is also possible that a process's memory requirement exceeds the amount of primary memory available. The operating system should then be able to move individual parts of the memory out of a process.

If two process instances of a program are run in quasi-parallel, at least the data for the two processes must be stored in different physical areas of memory. This means that the data for the corresponding variables in each process will be stored at different physical addresses. By far the most elegant method of dealing with this problem is to introduce a virtual address space for each process. The programmer can then design his or her program without regard to the actual locations of the code and data in the physical address space.

Mapping the virtual addresses onto the physical addresses is the responsibility of the operating system's memory management system.

Memory protection prevents two processes exchanging data by changing the areas of memory used by both. In this case, interprocess communication must be carried out using system calls. But the use of a system call is bound up with a large and complex set of operations such as multiple saving of registers to the stack, copying areas of memory, and so on. If processes were able to share certain areas of memory, interprocess communication would be more efficient.

This concept of *shared memory* is not restricted to communication with processes. For example, areas of files could also be mapped into a process's memory: this could often save many repeated system calls to read and write the file.

The program code of a process can be executed in different threads at the same time. In principle, these threads share a common virtual address space.

The efficient implementation of a state-of-the-art system for memory management would be impossible without hardware support. As LINUX is also intended to run on systems not based on Intel architecture in the future, an *architecture-independent* memory model has to be defined. This memory model must be so universal that it can be used in conjunction with the memory architectures of a wide range of different processor types. This chapter starts by introducing this architecture-independent memory model. The implementation of the model for the i386 processor family is then presented. In the following, CPUs in this family will be referred to as x86 processors. Introducing the 64-bit architecture, Intel has described the underlying architecture as IA 32. We still refer to the old description, as it also includes the processors of other manufacturers.

To demonstrate the flexibility of the memory model, the mappings for other processor architectures also are shown.

In the past few years the kernel developers have continually optimized the memory management system. In particular, the optimization of multiprocessor systems has been the center of attention. A detailed representation of this optimization is not possible here. Version 2.4 also supports the concept of *non-uniform memory access* (NUMA) for the *Intel Architecture* 64 (IA 64) and MIPS64. The NUMA concept comes into play when any CPU of a multiprocessing system gets its own memory area that the processor can access faster than the memory of any other processor. The operating system should therefore minimize the number of accesses of the processor to the wrong memory.

The second part of this chapter will explain how the architecture-independent memory model is used to implement memory management. The algorithms used by LINUX for memory management are introduced. Notice that other systems have used and are using different algorithms and concepts for memory management. Interested readers can read [Bac86].

A typical computer today has a number of levels of memory with different access times. The first level mostly consists of cache memory within the processor. In the newest processors a second cache level is integrated in order to minimize access times even more. The actual working memory usually consists of inexpensive DRAM chips with access times up to 70 ns. These higher access times are today's bottleneck in increasing computer power. Technologies such as RAMBUS or DDR (*double data rate*) try to remove these limitations.

For a number of systems, the cache levels are transparent after their initialization when the computer is started. This happens, for instance, with the PowerPC platform, Alpha, or x86 systems. In other systems, the operating system has to take on a number of tasks for controlling the cache, for instance in the Sparc architecture.

4.1.1   Pages of memory

The physical memory is divided into *pages* (pages of memory). The size of a memory page is defined by the `PAGE_SIZE` macro of the `asm/page.h` file. For the 32-bit architecture, such as x86, this size is usually 4 Kbytes, normally 8 Kbytes for the 64-bit architectures, and up to 64 Kbytes in the IA 64 processor. Table 4.1 indicates the size of the memory pages of all the processor architectures supported by LINUX 2.4.

At the same time, the *memory management units* (MMU) of various architectures also support memory pages of up to 4 Mbytes. Such huge pages are particularly meaningful when one wishes to display the following physical memory in the virtual address space.

4.1.2   Virtual address space

A process is run in a *virtual address space*. Data and the code of the process are scattered in the virtual address space. The size of the complete virtual address space depends on the number of bits used in a memory address. The usual sizes now are 32 or 64 bits. With 32 bits a virtual address space of 4 Gbytes is available, and with 64 bits, 2^{24} terabytes, 2^{14} petabytes, or 16 exabytes are available.

This memory model simplifies the programming. The programmer can apply huge structures to consecutive addresses and does not have to take into account any segment or memory page limit; all pointers are the same size. The WIN16 programming with near-pointers and far-pointers shows how circumstantial it can be.

Under LINUX, a process can be either in user mode or in system mode. Each program started in a UNIX system is initially in a low-privileged user mode. When the program wants to access the system sources, it has to change into system mode. At this point the process executes the code in the kernel. The processes that have been started in the kernel display an unusual feature. These are permanently in kernel mode. In the x86 world, system mode is defined as ring 0 and user mode as ring 3. The standard procedure to change from user mode to system mode is to call the software interrupt 0x80. As hardware interrupts are also processed in system mode, the same procedure can be used.

In user mode it is forbidden for a process to access the memory of the kernel. This prevents the protective mechanisms of the process architecture. Access to a memory page can be granted to system and/or user mode.

LINUX usually maps the physical memory after an offset (PAGE_OFFSET) in the virtual memory area. However, access to this memory is only permitted in system mode. In the kernel, addresses always point to this area. But there is no rule without exception: the implementation for the Sparc64 architecture uses a separate virtual address space for the memory of system mode.

Therefore the address space available in the user mode is smaller than the theoretical maximum and is defined via the TASK_SIZE macro. The values for the different architectures are indicated in Table 4.1. Kernel programmers define the area of the virtual memory, accessible only in system mode, as kernel segments and the area available in user mode as user segments. The segment concept is derived from the x86 architecture.

Segments in the x86 architecture fix additional access limits to some areas of the virtual address space. Under version 2.0 there were respectively a data and a code segment for system and user mode, which limited access to the corresponding areas in the virtual address space. This meant that in system mode, various segment selectors had to be used in order to access the corresponding data. The management of the corresponding segment selectors leads to greater effort. Since version 2.2, segments have still been defined, but they are now defined for the whole virtual address space.

Even after this simplification the kernel cannot access the user area without being tested again. It has to be checked if the pointers actually refer to the user area. If this check is not carried out, a program could overwrite data in the kernel. Just think about a read call in which the contents of a previously created file are in an arbitrary place in the kernel.

In the older Intel processors, write protection bits were not taken into account for memory pages in system mode, but at the same time they were used in the user area for more efficient paging. In these processors, this bit has to be explicitly checked by the software. As the Sparc64 architecture supports two different kinds of address space for system and user mode, access to data in the user segment is not directly possible, but can only take place via macros or functions.

The asm/uaccess.h include file defines the macros and the functions to access user memory from the kernel.

The most important macro in this file is access_ok(). It checks whether it is possible to access a user address range by reading (VERIFY_READ) or writing (VERIFY_WRITE). The problem of write protection in the older processors is solved with this macro. If any fault occurs, 0 is returned. For compatibility with code for LINUX 2.0 there is the inline function verify_area(). If any fault occurs, this function returns EFAULT.

The following list provides an overview of all functions or macros that can be used to read and write data from a user segment.

```
/* Read a scalar value in the user segment */
get_user(val, ptr);
/* Write a scalar value in the user segment */
put_user(val, ptr);
/* Copy data from the user segment */
copy_from_user(to, from, n);
/* Copy data to the user segment */
copy_to_user(to, from, n);
/* Copy a character string from the user segment */
strncpy_from_user(to, from, n);
/* Determine the length of a character string in the user segment*/
strnlen_user(str, n);
strlen_user(str); /* should not be used any more */
/* clear the memory in the user segment */
clear_user(mem, len);
```

In the *get* and *put* functions, the type of the pointer indicates how large the data to be read or written is. For all functions apart from `strnlen_user()` and `strlen_user()` there is a counterpart that begins with two underscores (e.g., `__get_user()`), where the macro `access_ok()` is not called. A corresponding call of `access_ok()` for the accessed data has to precede the call of these functions. Macros and functions cannot be called in the interrupt context as it could be necessary to read the memory page from an external block device first.

4.1.3 | Converting the linear address

The linear addresses need to be converted into a physical address by either the processor or a separate MMU. In the architecture-independent memory model, this page conversion is a three-level process in which the address for the linear address space is split into four parts. The first part is used as an index in the page directory. The entry in the page directory refers to what is called a page middle directory in LINUX. The second part of the address serves as an index to a page middle directory. Referenced in this way, the entry refers to a page table. The third part is used as an index to this page table. The referenced entry should, if possible, point to a page in the physical memory. The fourth part of the address gives the offset within the selected page of memory. Figure 4.1 shows these relationships in graphical form.

The x86 processor only supports a two-level conversion of the linear address. Here, the conversion for the architecture-independent memory model can be assisted by means of a useful trick. An entry in the page directory is considered as a middle page directory. Obviously, the operations for accessing page conversion tables have to take this into account. If the x86 processor supports the *page size extension* (PSE), the physical memory is displayed as 4 Mbyte memory pages in the kernel segment. This saves memory and is quicker than access via 4 Kbyte memory pages. In this case, the address conversion is still one-level, since the reference to the 4 Mbyte page is written in the page directory.

x86 computers with more than 896 Mbytes become a problem for LINUX 2.2. The virtual address space of the kernel, the kernel segment, is one gigabyte in size. For vmalloc() and for the *advanced programmable interrupt controllers* (APICs) of multiprocessor systems, 128 Mbytes of address space is reserved. LINUX cannot display the whole physical memory in the kernel segment any more. LINUX creates a page table so it can display the remaining physical memory temporarily in the kernel segment. The reserved virtual address range begins with PKMAP_BASE (0xfe000000) and has a length of 4 Mbytes. Kernel programmers have called this feature "Highmem" in reference to the x86 *Real Mode*.

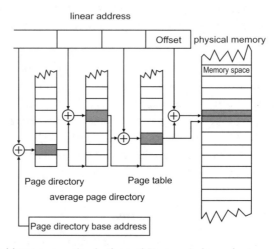

Figure 4.1: Linear address conversion in the architecture-independent memory model.

This Highmem support helps up to a physical memory size of 4 Gbytes; the address space is this large with 32-bit addresses. But with great foresight Intel added four additional address pins to the Pentium-Pro and created the *physical address extension* (PAE). This was necessary, since the previous two-level address conversion only supported 32-bit physical addresses. The PAE has control of a three-level address conversion, as in the LINUX abstract model. The size of the virtual address space remains unchanged at 4 Gbytes. The additional physical memory can be displayed via the Highmem feature in the kernel segment.

64-bit architectures such as the Alpha processor, like the PAE of the x86 processors, use a three-level address conversion. A two-level address conversion would lead to huge page directories and page tables, if the linear address were not reduced to 32 bits. On an Alpha processor, a memory page for LINUX has a length of 8 Kbytes. As the memory page directories and tables cover one memory page respectively and an entry has a length of 64 bits, only 1,024 entries per level can be managed. As the base address is also managed in the page directory, the size of the virtual address space is limited to 1,023 * 1,024 * 1,024 * 8.192 bytes = 8,184 Gbytes, which is only just 8 Tbytes. For a user segment, 4 Tbytes = 2^{42} bytes are available. Table 4.1 gives an overview of the conversion levels and user segment sizes for all architectures supported by LINUX 2.4. The number of levels refers to the memory in the user segment.

Table 4.1: Parameters of memory page management for the architectures supported by LINUX

Processor	Size of a memory page PAGE_SIZE	Level of page conversion	Size of the user address space TASK_SIZE
Alpha	8 Kbytes	3	4 Tbytes
ARM 26 bit	16 or 32 Kbytes	2	up to 26 Mbytes
ARM 32 bit	4 Kbytes	2	3 Gbytes
IA 64	4, 8, 16, or 64 Kbytes	3	10 Exabytes
M68000	4 Kbytes	3	224 Mbytes
Alpha	8 Kbytes	3	4 Tbytes
M68000 SUN3	8 Kbytes	2	3.75 Mbytes
MIPS	4 Kbytes	2	2 Gbytes
MIPS64	4 Kbytes	3	1 Petabyte
PARISC	4 Kbytes	2 or 3	3 Gbytes
PowerPC	4 Kbytes	2	2 Gbytes
S390	4 Kbytes	2	2 Gbytes
SH	4 Kbytes	2	1.984 Mbytes
Sparc	4 Kbytes	3	3.75 Gbytes
Sparc SUN4	8 Kbytes	2	3.75 Gbytes
Sparc64	8 Kbytes	3	16 Exabytes – 16 Gbytes
x86	4 Kbytes	2 or 3	3 Gbytes

4.1.4 Page directories

The kernel manages the page directories and tables for the kernel segment and the user segments of the processes. The necessary data types, macros, and functions are defined in the `asm/page.h`, `asm/pgtable.h`, and `asm/pgalloc.h` files.

The short identifiers for the page directories are `pgd` for the first level and `pmd` for the second level. The directory entry has the data type `pgd_t` or `pmd_t`. Both data types are defined as structures in order to avoid inadvertent conversions to integer data types. The kernel references the page directories by pointers to the first entry in the respective directory: `pgd_t*` and `pmd_t*`.

`pgd_val()`, `pmd_val()` These macros allow access to the real value of the directory entry. Depending on the processor architecture, this can be a 64-bit or a 32-bit value.

`pgd_alloc()`, `pmd_alloc()` These functions provide a memory page for the respective directory. All entries are initialized so that they do not reference an intermediate page directory or page table. In the kernel 2.4, the macros can use a so-called quick list in which only corresponding initialized memory pages are entered. The kernel defines variants of this macro which contain directories especially for the kernel (`pgd_alloc_kernel()` and `pmd_alloc_kernel()`). However, in most processor architectures these macros are identical to `pgd_alloc()` and `pmd_alloc()`.

`pgd_free()`, `pmd_free()` The page directories are freed. In kernel 2.4 they can be entered in the quick list mentioned above.

`pgd_clear()`, `pmd_clear()` This macro deletes the entry in the page directory. It no longer refers to an intermediate page directory or page table.

`pgd_none()`, `pmd_none()` Both macros test whether the directory entry refers neither to an intermediate page directory nor to a page table.

`pgd_present()`, `pmd_present()` When a directory entry contains a reference to a middle page directory or to a page table, these macros return a positive result. The result is the negation of `pgd_none()` or `pmd_none()`.

`pgd_bad()`, `pmd_bad()` These entries check the correctness of the entries in the directories which reference a middle page directory or a page table.

`pgd_page()`, `pmd_page()` These macros return the pointer to the referenced intermediate page directory or page table.

`__pgd_offset()`, `__pmd_offset()` This function returns the index to a linear address in the respective page directory. For the uppermost page directory, the macro is `pgd_index()`, identical to `__pgd_offset()`.

`pgd_offset()`, `pgd_offset_k()` The macro `pgd_offset()` determines from the memory management (`struct mm_struct`) and the linear address the pointer of the affiliated entry in the uppermost page directory. `pgd_offset_k()` uses the memory management structure of the kernel to retrieve the pointer into the page directory entry.

`pmd_offset()` To fix a pointer to an entry in the middle page directory from a linear address, the kernel programmers use this macro. However, for this purpose the affiliated superior page directory must be known.

`set_pgd()`, `set_pmd()` The kernel sometimes has to fill the page directories with entries. To achieve this, kernel programmers call this macro.

4.1.5 | The page table

An entry in the page table is defined by the data type `pte_t`. The kernel references a page table by a pointer to the first entry of the table. The fundamental task of the page table entry is to address a page in the physical memory.

`pte_val()` This macro returns the value of a page table entry.

`pte_alloc()`, `pte_alloc_kernel()` Using an entry of the middle page directory and of the linear address the page table entry for the linear address submitted is returned. If the affiliated page table does not exist yet, it is allocated. For addresses in the kernel, `pte_alloc_kernel()` has to be used. A quick list can be used so as not to initialize the page tables again.

`pte_free()`, `pte_free_kernel()` These functions free a page table. The table should no longer contain an initialized value, as the table can be entered in the quick list again.

`pte_page()` This function, using a page table entry finds a pointer into the `mem_map`, which contains all the physical memory pages of this computer.

`pte_offset()` This macro calculates by using an immediate page table entry and the linear address the affiliated page table entry.

`set_pte()` The values of the page table entry are set, but the entry must either not be present or cannot be updated by the hardware. Otherwise, `ptep_get_and_clear()` should be used.

`ptep_get_and_clear()` This function returns the page table entry and deletes it.

`pte_same()` This function compares two page table entries.

Flags in the page table entry describe the legal access modes to the memory page and their status. LINUX maps the architecture-dependent flags to attributes that are valid for any architecture. The "presence" attribute tells the MMU whether it is possible to access the memory page. The possiblity to read, write and execute a page is shown by three associated attributes.

One attribute indicates whether the memory page has been accessed – in other words, this attribute describes the "age" of the page. The "dirty" attribute is set when the contents of the memory page have been modified.

The kernel defines a series of attribute combinations as macros of the `pgprot_t` type. Further special attribute combinations are defined for single architectures:

`PAGE_NONE` No physical memory page is referenced by the page table entry.

`PAGE_SHARED` All types of access are permitted.

`PAGE_READONLY` Only read and execute access is allowed to this page of memory.

With write access, an exception is generated which allows this error to be handled. The memory page can be copied, and the page table entry can be set to the physical address of the new page and its attributes to `PAGE_SHARED`. This is exactly what is meant by "copy-on-write."

`PAGE_COPY` This macro corresponds to `PAGE_READONLY`.

`PAGE_KERNEL` Access to this page of memory is only allowed in the kernel segment.

`PAGE_KERNEL_RO` Access to this page of memory is only allowed when reading in the kernel segment.

asm/pgtable.h also defines the macros __P000 to __P111 and __S000 to __S111 which, together with the _PAGE_NORMAL() macro, enable any combination of protection attributes to be defined. The bit positions in the macro names are interpreted as "xwr." For the macros beginning with __P, the position of the "write" attribute is interpreted as the "copy-on-write" attribute. The macros beginning with __S describe pages that are marked as PAGE_SHARED; they are opened for write access.

The x86 architecture does not support all attribute combinations of the "read" and "execute" attributes. Table 4.2 shows the semantics of all the possible attribute combinations, using the classical UNIX "rwx" notation.

Table 4.2: Semantics for the combinations of protection attributes for x86 processors

Attribute combination	x86 semantics
---	---
--x	r-x
---	---
-w-	rwx
-wx	rwx
r--	r-x
r-x	r-x
rw-	rwx
rwx	rwx

The kernel manages the page table entries with a series of macros.

mk_pte(), mk_pte_phys() The mk_pte() macro creates a page table entry from the pointer in the directory of the physical memory pages mem_map and the protection attributes (pgprot_t). The mk_pte_phys() function does the same but uses the physical memory page address as input.

pte_modify() This function changes the attribute of a memory page entry.

pte_none(), pte_clear() The macro pte_none() checks if the page table entry is empty. The entry is deleted via pte_clear().

pte_present() This function checks whether the "presence" attribute of the page table entry is set.

pte_dirty(), pte_mkdirty(), pte_mkclean() These functions manage the "dirty" attribute of a page table entry. The function pte_mkdirty() sets the "dirty" attribute, and pte_mkclean() deletes it.

ptep_test_and_clear_dirty() This function checks the dirty flag of a page table entry and deletes it.

`pte_exec()`, `pte_mkexec()`, `pte_exprotect()` These functions manage the execution attribute. The function `pte_exec()` tests it, `pte_mkexec()` sets it, and `pte_exprotect()` deletes it.

`pte_young()`, `pte_mkyoung()`, `pte_mkold()` These functions manage an attribute that gives evidence for access to the memory page. The memory management unit of the processor sets the attribute to *young* in a memory access. Using this attribute, the kernel can determine whether the memory page has been accessed after the attribute was set to *old*.

`ptep_test_and_clear_young()` This inline function is used when the kernel has to check the "age" attribute and delete the attribute.

`pte_read()`, `pte_mkread()`, `pte_exprotect()` As happens with the attribute for execution rights, these functions are used to manipulate the read attribute.

4.2   THE VIRTUAL ADDRESS SPACE OF A PROCESS

As we have already mentioned in the last section, the virtual address space of a LINUX process is segmented. A distinction is made between the kernel segment and the user segment.

4.2.1   The user segment

In user mode, privilege level 3 in x86 processors, a process can only access the user segment. As the user segment contains the data and code for the process, this segment needs to be different from those belonging to other processes. This can be done via other page directories or a different page table. In the system call *fork*, the parent process's page directories and page tables are copied for the child process. An exception to this is the kernel segment, whose page tables are shared by all of the processes.

The system call *fork* has an alternative: *clone*. Both system calls generate a new thread, but *clone* can share its memory with the calling thread. Thus, LINUX regards threads as tasks which share their address space with other tasks. The handling of additional task-specific resources, such as the stack, can be controlled via parameters of the system call *clone*. The POSIX thread library available under LINUX uses this system call to create threads. Threads are always used when it is difficult to divide program functions between several processes, to make them parallel. This performance advantage also means that there is the risk of *race conditions* which are otherwise dealt with largely by the kernel.

The structure of the user segment during execution in ELF format is shown in Figure 4.2. The user segment for any process, other than the idle process (process number 0), is initialized by the loading or mapping of a binary file carried out by the system call *execve*. A process generated by *fork* inherits the structure of its parent process.

The shared libraries shown in the user segment need some explanation. Originally, under LINUX, the entire code of a program was statically linked into the binary. This led to the effect that, with the growth of libraries, binaries became ever larger. In order to prevent this, libraries were stored in separate library files and loaded at the program start. However, owing to restrictions in the a.out format, the shared libraries were linked to static addresses. With the ELF object file format, a file structure and some methods were defined which made this superfluous, and allowed shared libraries to be loaded during program execution. With a flexible design, shared libraries unknown at the time of compilation could now be linked into a program. The automatic modules of the script language Perl are a good example. The shared libraries are mapped at dynamically determined addresses. However, the libraries must have been generated as position-independent code (PIC), that is, there must be no absolute address references in the compiled code, and a register (x86: EBX) is always filled for references to global addresses.

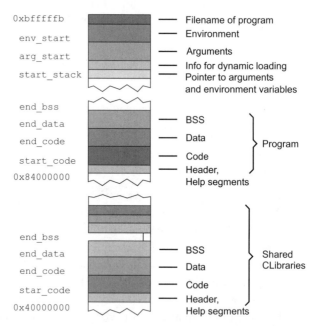

Figure 4.2: Structure of the user segment for a process with a binary file in ELF format.

LINUX still supports the classic a.out format. Here, however, the user segment is structured in a different way. The program text starts at the virtual address 0, and the dynamic libraries are mapped at static addresses between the heap and the stack. Because of the fixed address allocation and the much more laborious way of generating shared libraries in the a.out format, this binary format has been superseded.

In addition, LINUX can handle scripts as true binaries. When a script is called, the interpreter specified in the first line after the character combination #! is started with the script as its argument. For binary formats that cannot support #!, since LINUX 2.2 there has been the binfmt_misc feature which allows, along with the file extension or specific byte sequences, other specific programs to be called which act as interpreters for this file. In LINUX 2.0 there was only this kind of feature for Java files, even though emulators such as DOSEMU can profit from it.

At the end of the user segment above there is the file name of the program, the environment variables, and the arguments of the process saved as a sequence of zero-terminated character strings. Below it there are pointer tables for the arguments and the environment variables, which are referred to in a C program with `argv` or `environ`.

4.2.2 | Virtual memory areas

As a shared library can be very large, it would not be a good idea if all its code were constantly being loaded into physical memory. We can be sure that the processes running at any one time will not be using all the functions in a library at the same time. Loading the code for unused functions squanders memory resources and is unnecessary. Even in larger programs there will certainly be sections of code which will never be touched by a process because, for example, certain program features are not used. Loading these parts of the program is just as wasteful as loading the unused sections of a library.

Virtual memory areas are frequently used by the hardware devices that map their memory in the address space. The communication between an application and the hardware is carried out a lot faster via virtual memory areas than via system calls. Frame buffer devices are an example of this; using these the memory of the graphics board can be mapped in a memory area.

If two processes are being run by the same executable file, the program code does not need to be loaded into memory twice. Both processes can execute the same code in primary memory. It is also possible that large parts of the data segments of these processes will match. These also can be shared between the processes, provided neither process modifies this data. Only when a process modifies a page of memory does a copy-on-write need to be performed.

If a process reserves very large amounts of memory, the allocation of pages of physical memory would be extravagant. The process will only use these pages fully at a later stage, and possibly not even then. The way to get round this problem is to use copy-on-write, by which an empty page of memory is referenced more than once in the page tables for the process. It is only after a modification has been made at a specific address in the user segment that this page needs to be copied and mapped to the appropriate point in the linear address space.

It is clear from this that the separate areas of the user segment must have different attributes for the page table entries for the memory page, different handling routines for access errors, and different strategies to save to secondary memory. It was for this reason that the abstract process of virtual memory area was introduced during the development of LINUX. A virtual memory area is defined by the data structure `vm_area_struct` in the `linux/mm.h` file:

```
struct vm_area_struct {
        /* Parameter for virtual memory area */
        struct mm_struct * vm_mm;
```

```
        unsigned long vm_start;
        unsigned long vm_end;
        /* linked VM areas of a task, sorted by
        * addresses */
        struct vm_area_struct *vm_next;
        pgprot_t vm_page_prot;
        unsigned long vm_flags;
        /* AVL tree of the VM area of a task, sorted by
        * addresses */
        short vm_avl_height;
        struct vm_area_struct * vm_avl_left;
        struct vm_area_struct * vm_avl_right;
        /* For areas with an address space and background memory
        * one of the address_space->i_mmap{,shared}-Lists,
        * for SHM areas the lists of attachments; otherwise
        * unused.
        */
        struct vm_area_struct *vm_next_share;
        struct vm_area_struct **vm_pprev_share;
        struct vm_operations_struct * vm_ops;
        /* Offset in PAGE_SIZE units */
        unsigned long vm_pgoff;
        struct file * vm_file;
        unsigned long vm_raend;
        void * vm_private_data;
};
```

The components vm_start and vm_end determine the start and end addresses of the virtual memory area managed by the structure. vm_mm is a pointer to a part of an entry in a process table. The protection attributes for pages of memory in this area are fixed by vm_page_prot. Information on the memory area type is held in vm_flags. This includes the current access permissions for the memory area and rules as to which protection attributes can be set.

The virtual memory areas for a process are managed in two places: an AVL tree, sorted by address, and a singly linked list, also sorted by address. For special purposes, such as the mapping of a file or the use of System V shared memory, fields for a doubly linked circular list are also defined.

The inode pointer vm_file refers to the file or hardware device whose contents have been mapped to the virtual memory area starting at the offset vm_pgoff. If this pointer is set to NULL, the process is referred to as "anonymous mapping." The integer value vm_raend is used in the read-ahead of mapped files. The field vm_private_data is used in the implementation of the shared memory of System V.

As the virtual areas of memory are merely reserved, any attempt to access memory in one of these areas will produce a page error, because either no entry in the page directory exists as yet for the page, or else the referenced page of memory does not allow write access. The processor generates a page error exception interrupt and activates the appropriate handling routine. This routine then calls up an operation to provide the required pages in memory. There are pointers to these operations in vm_ops. As well as these, vm_ops also contains pointers for additional operations which organize the initializing and release of a virtual memory area. The structure vm_operations_struct defines the possible function pointers enabling different operations to be assigned to different areas. vm_ops is not used for anonymous mappings; these are treated via global functions.

```
struct vm_operations_struct {
  void (*open)(struct vm_area_struct * area);
  void (*close)(struct vm_area_struct * area);
  struct page * (*nopage)(struct vm_area_struct * area,
      unsigned long address,
      int write_access);
};
```

The open() function is called if a new virtual memory area is mapped to the user segment. To remove the mapped area of memory, close() is called. nopage() is used to treat errors if there is access to a page that is not available in the physical memory and has not been vacated. The function just has to read and map the memory page at the address submitted. The parameter write_access determines whether the file will be mapped privately or as a shared page.

The function do_mmap_pgoff() adds virtual memory areas to the process.

```
int do_mmap_pgoff(struct file * file, unsigned long addr,
        unsigned long len, unsigned long prot,
        unsigned long flags, unsigned long pgoff)
```

It maps the file referenced with file in the virtual address space. The offset in the file (pgoff) is indicated in the memory pages. The parameter prot establishes the address protection for the virtual memory area; Table 4.3 provides an overview of this.

If do_mmap_pgoff() is NULL and thus no file is referenced, the function creates an anonymous memory area. According to the process, the anonymous virtual memory areas are filled with zero bytes. When the process accesses a memory page in the virtual address space for the first time, the kernel always refers to the same global empty memory page in the corresponding page table. The global empty memory page is referenced via the ZERO_PAGE() macro. When the process writes to a memory page for the first time, the kernel writes the address of a newly allocated, empty memory page in the affiliated page table entry.

Attributes for the virtual memory area are given in flags. MAP_FIXED can be used to specify that the kernel maps the memory area exactly to the given address. Care should be taken to ensure that no other virtual memory area is mapped to this address. The flags

Table 4.3: Values for `prot` of the do_mmap() function

Value	Meaning
PROT_READ	Area can be read
PROT_WRITE	Area can be written to
PROT_EXEC	Area can be executed
PROT_NONE	Area cannot be accessed (not supported at present)

MAP_SHARED and MAP_PRIVATE control the handling of memory operations in the virtual memory area. MAP_SHARED specifies that all write operations will be carried out on the same pages of memory. With MAP_PRIVATE the memory pages are duplicated with a write access. By setting MAP_PRIVATE, the copy-on-write of the respective memory area is carried out. Because of the limitations of the x86 architecture – the rights to read and execute are held in a flag – a complete implementation of do_mmap_pgoff() on x86 processors is not possible.

4.2.3   The system call *brk*

At the start of a process, the value of the brk field in the process table entry (see also Section 3.1.1) points to the end of the BSS segment for non-statically initialized data. By modifying this pointer, the process can allocate and release dynamic memory. The standard C function malloc() modifies the brk pointer to increase the heap if necessary. The allocation of memory must of course be linked to the necessary changes to the page directory for the process. Of course, only the kernel can modify the page directory. To achieve this, the kernel provides the system call *brk* to read and modify the brk pointer. The system call checks the validity of a new value set. A test checks whether enough memory is available in the primary and secondary memories. LINUX 2.4 allows the switching on or turning off of this test via the sysctl entry VM_OVERCOMMIT_MEMORY. But the system call also verifies the current limitations predefined by the user memory expenditure of the process. The system call also excludes any overlap with any previously mapped memory area. If the brk pointer is increased, memory is allocated in the virtual address space of the process.

The system call *brk* maps an anonymous memory area or extends an already available anonymous memory area. The kernel also reserves memory when it is accessed by writing. When reading is carried out before writing, the kernel writes the global empty memory page (ZERO_PAGE()) in the page directory of the process.

4.2.4 | Mapping functions

In the header file `sys/mman.h` the C library also provides, among other things, the following three functions:

```
#include <sys/mman.h>
extern __ptr_t mmap(__ptr_t addr, size_t len,
                int prot, int flags, int fd, __off_t off);
extern int munmap(__ptr_t addr, size_t len);
extern int mprotect(__ptr_t addr, size_t len, int prot);
```

From the offset `off`, `mmap()` maps the file or the device to which the file descriptor `fd` refers as virtual memory area. The flag `MAP_ANONYMOUS` has to be used for anonymous mapping.

The `munmap()` function makes use of the system call *munmap* to remove memory areas previously mapped to the user segment.

The library function `mprotect()` implements the protection attributes for a memory area in the user segment using the macros `PROT_NONE`, `PROT_READ`, `PROT_WRITE`, and `PROT_EXEC` mentioned above. The implementation of this function is based on the system call *mprotect*. This system call will of course check whether an area of memory has been mapped at this point and whether the new protection attributes are legal for the area.

In x86 architecture, the semantics of setting the attributes `PROT_WRITE` and `PROT_EXEC` will cause `PROT_READ` to be set for all of these operations. The `PROT_EXEC` attribute is implicitly set when `PROT_READ` is set.

Furthermore, additional functions for synchronizing the working memory with the disk contents (`msync()`), blocking the evacuation of mapped memory areas to the secondary memory (`mlock()`), and moving the memory areas (`mremap()`) are supported. Since version 2.0 it has been possible to use `mmap()` without restrictions under LINUX.

4.2.5 | The kernel segment

When a system function is initiated, the process switches to system mode. LINUX usually triggers the software interrupt 128 (0x80). The processor then reads the gate descriptor stored in the interrupt descriptor table. This is a trap gate descriptor pointing to the assembler routine system call in `arch/i386/` that shows `kernel/entry.S`. The processor jumps to this address with the segment descriptor in the CS register pointing to the kernel segment. The assembler routine then sets the segment selectors in the DS and ES registers in such a way that memory accesses will read or write to data in the kernel segment.

As the page tables for the kernel segment are identical for all processes, this ensures that any process in system mode will encounter the same kernel segment. The physical memory is mapped to the virtual kernel address space after the standard address set via `PAGE_OFFSET`. In addition to this, virtual address areas can be mapped via `vmalloc()` or `ioremap()` in the kernel address space.

4.2.6 | Memory allocation in the kernel segment during booting

Before a kernel generates its first process when it is run, it calls initialization routines for a range of kernel components. These may have to allocate memory if the normal memory management of the kernel has not yet been initialized. This uses almost of all the console driver, which is useful for the debugging of memory management initialization. The kernel programmer defines the memory so allocated as boot memory; the routines to reserve and release boot memory can be found in `linux/bootmem.h`. After memory management has been successfully started, the kernel releases the boot memory again. The memory is occupied page by page, and by doing so the space previously not used by another memory page is used by a limited allocation.

4.2.7 | Dynamic memory management in the kernel segment

In the system kernel, it is often necessary to allocate dynamic memory, for example, for temporary buffers. Since LINUX 2.2 a new allocation procedure has been adopted. Therefore, the units used by this procedure are defined as *slab allocation*.

In principle, memory can be dynamically allocated and released using both `kmalloc()` and `kfree()+`.

```
void * kmalloc (size_t size, int priority);
void kfree (const void *obj);
```

The `kmalloc()` function attempts to reserve the extent of memory specified by `size`.

The `kfree()` function releases the reserved memory. Version 1.0 of LINUX only allowed memory to be reserved up to a size of 4,072 bytes. After repeated implementation, it is now possible to reserve memory of up to 128 Kbytes. The kernel reserves memory from the physical memory area. `kmalloc()` does not clear the allocated memory content. `kmalloc()` may interrupt the process when no empty memory pages are available in the kernel segment and the kernel only has to release or evacuate memory pages.

The slab allocation implements `kmalloc()` and `kfree()`. It uses kernel memory caches which provide memory sections of a particular size. Therefore, there is a special cache for directory entries. The `/proc/slabinfo` file indicates the active caches as well as the number of allocated and free objects in the cache.

```
kmem_cache_t* kmem_cache_create(const char *name,
  size_t size, size_t offset, unsigned long flags,
  void (*ctor)(void *, kmem_cache_t *, unsigned long),
  void (*dtor)(void *, kmem_cache_t *, unsigned long));
int kmem_cache_destroy(kmem_cache_t *cachep);
int kmem_cache_shrink(kmem_cache_t *cachep);
void* kmem_cache_alloc(kmem_cache_t * cachep, int flags);
void kmem_cache_free(kmem_cache_t * cachep, void *);
```

kmem_cache_create() creates a new cache for objects of the size size. If the function requires a special alignment for the objects, the caller has to set the offset parameter to something other than zero. The parameter cannot exceed the size of the object. The kernel calls the functions ctor() and dtor() when creating or deleting objects. It is important that the objects can be allocated and released in an arbitrary way. Different flags can be submitted to the constructor. Therefore the SLAB_CTOR_CONSTRUCTOR flag has to be set when the constructor is called. When calling the SLAB_CTOR_ATOMIC flag the constructor is not allowed to block, and with SLAB_CTOR_VERIFY the constructor has to check the object submitted.

With the SLAB_HWCACHE_ALIGN flag kmem_cache_create() is informed that all objects have to be aligned with the size of the level 1 cache lines of the processor. This helps with performance, particularly with small objects. Further flags act in conjunction with debugging, so the constructor can be used when the objects are released to check the object. Red zones between the single objects help to recognize any transgression of the borders of an allocated area. When looking for non-initialized memory, a kernel programmer can use SLAB_POISON which initializes slab memory with the value 0xA5. The kmem_cache_destroy() function closes the cache and releases the whole memory reserved by the cache. This function allows the use of caches in modules; this has been possible since LINUX 2.4. To reduce the cache, the kernel calls kmem_cache_shrink(). kmem_cache_alloc() and kmem_cache_free() reserve or release an object.

A cache manages several slabs in which the objects are contained. The size of a slab is a multiple of a memory page. The multiple is always a power of two and normally no more than 32. Therefore, the largest slab object can have a size of 128 Kbytes. Depending on the memory space, the slab allocator manages the slab management structures within or outside the slab. If the SLAB_NO_GROW flag is also set when an object is allocated, no new slabs should be created if none of the other slabs of the cache contain any free objects.

The kmalloc() function uses two tables of caches. One of these tables is used for ISA DMA memory, the other for the remaining memory. In both tables there is respectively a cache for each power of two from 64 bytes, 32 for 4 Kbyte memory pages, up to 128 Kbytes. If kmalloc() requires memory space, the kernel searches the cache with the smallest size in which the memory space fits. In the case of objects that do not correspond to the length of a power of two, kmalloc() reduces the memory. If many objects of the same size have to be created, a special slab cache should be used.

The flags parameter can control the allocation of the memory. Thus, using GFP_DMA it is possible to request ISA DMA memory or, using GFP_ATOMIC, to prevent the process from sleeping.

In very old kernel versions (0.x), kmalloc() was the only option for allocating memory in the kernel dynamically. Moreover, the size of the memory space to be reserved was limited to the size of a memory page.

The vmalloc() function and the affiliated vfree() solved this problem. Using these two functions it is possible to reserve memory in multiples of a memory page. Both functions are defined in mm/vmalloc.c.

```
void * vmalloc(unsigned long size);
void * vfree(void * addr);
```

A size that is not divisible by 4,096 can also be given; in this case it is rounded up. If areas smaller than 4,072 bytes have to be reserved, kmalloc() should be given preference. The largest value for size is restricted by the available free physical memory. As memory reserved by vmalloc() cannot be paged out, kernel programmers should not be too generous with it. Since vmalloc() calls the __get_free_page() function, the process could be blocked in order to free memory pages. The memory reserved is not initialized.

After rounding size up, vmalloc() carefully searches the help function __vmalloc() for a free address in which the area to be allocated in the kernel segment can be mapped. As already explained, the whole physical memory is mapped to the kernel segment at the beginning so that the virtual addresses correspond to the physical addresses plus an architecture-dependent offset.

__vmalloc() must map the memory to be allocated at the end of the physical memory. The search for a free address begins, in the x86 architecture, with the next address located in an 8 Mbyte limit (VMALLOC_OFFSET) behind the physical memory. The addresses located there could have been verified previously via vmalloc calls. A memory page is released between the single areas reserved to query accesses that go beyond the allocated memory area. __vmalloc() modifies the page directory accordingly. See Figure 4.3.

LINUX manages the virtual kernel address area easily by means of a linear list. The affiliated data structure vm_struct includes the virtual address of the area and its size, which also contains the page which is not registered in the page table.

The flags component distinguishes between the structures used by vmalloc() and by ioremap().

The advantage of the vmalloc() function certainly consists in the fact that the size of the required memory area can adapt to the requirements better than kmalloc(). To reserve more than 64 Kbytes of memory, kmalloc() needs 128 Kbytes of consecutive physical memory. Moreover, vmalloc() is only restricted to the size of the free physical memory and not to the segmentation size of kmalloc(). As vmalloc() does not return any physical address, and the memory areas reserved can be scattered among non-consecutive memory pages, this function is unfit to reserve memory for DMA. LINUX 2.4 has the vmalloc_dma() function which reserves memory in ISA-DMA-capable areas. However, it is never called in the kernel.

PCI devices are mapped to addresses at the top end of the physical address space. As these addresses are not mapped in the virtual address space of the process, at first it is not possible to access this memory. Using the ioremap() function, these kinds of physical addresses should be entered in the page directory of the kernel segment. The virtual address area used is scheduled by vmalloc(). iounmap() releases the virtual address space. ioremap_nocache() prevents the corresponding memory area in the processor cache from being stored intermediately.

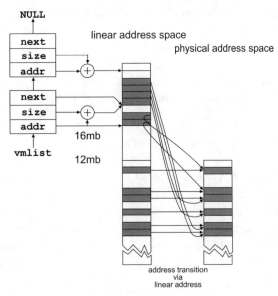

Figure 4.3: Mode of operation for `vmalloc()`.

4.3 BLOCK DEVICE CACHING

When judging the performance of a computer system, the speed of access in block devices plays a decisive role. LINUX makes use of a dynamic cache system which employs primary memory that is left unused by the processes as a buffer for block devices. If the requirement for primary memory increases, the space allowed for buffering is reduced.

Since version 2.0, block device caching has been complemented by the file-oriented memory page caching described further below.

4.3.1 Block buffering

Files are held on block devices which can process requests to read or write blocks of data. The size of the block for a device can correspond to a multiple of 512 up to the size of a memory page (`PAGE_SIZE`). These blocks must be held in the memory via a buffering system.

The device itself should only be accessed in two circumstances: a block may be loaded if it is not yet held in the buffer; and a block may be written if the buffer contents for the block no longer match what is held in the external medium. To handle the latter case, the respective block in the buffer is marked as "dirty" after a modification. There may be a delay in performing a delay operation, however, as the valid contents of the block are held in the buffer cache. A special case applies for blocks taken from files opened with the flag `O_SYNC`. These are transferred to disk every time their contents are modified.

The implementation of the buffer cache in LINUX was originally based (with slight modifications) on the concept described by Maurice J. Bach [Bac86] in *The Design of the*

Unix (R) Operating System. The changes that have been made in the meantime, however, justify our referring to a separate LINUX buffer cache system.

As mentioned earlier, the buffer cache manages individual block buffers of varying size. For this, every block is given a buffer_head data structure. For simplicity, it will be referred to below as the *buffer head*.

The definition of the buffer head is in linux/fs.h:

```
struct buffer_head {
  /* First cache line: */
  struct buffer_head * b_next;      /* hash list */
  unsigned long b_blocknr;          /* block number */
  unsigned short b_size;            /* block size */
  unsigned short b_list;            /* buffer list */
  kdev_t b_dev;                     /* device (B_FREE = free) */
  atomic_t b_count;                 /* number of the userfor
                                     * this block */
  kdev_t b_rdev;                    /* real device */
  unsigned long b_state;            /* buffer status bitmap*/
  unsigned long b_flush time;       /* time, when the buffer
                                     * should be written */
  struct buffer_head *b_next_free;  /* LRU or free list */
  struct buffer_head *b_prev_free;
  struct buffer_head *b_this_page;  /* list of the buffers of a
                                     * memory page */
  struct buffer_head *b_reqnext;    /* list of IO requirements*/
  struct buffer_head **b_pprev;     /* hash lists */
  char * b_data;                    /* pointer to the data block */
  struct page *b_page;              /* page in which the block
                                     * is embedded */
  void (*b_end_io)(struct buffer_head *bh, int up-to-date);
                                    /* called after the end
                                     * of the input/output */
  void *b_private;                  /* reserved for b_end_io */
  unsigned long b_rsector;          /* real place on the
                                     * hard disk */
  wait_queue_head_t b_wait;
  struct inode * b_inode;
  struct list_head b_inode_buffers;
                                    /* list of the modified
                                     * buffers of an inode */
};
```

The data structure is organized in such a way that frequently requested data lies very close together and may be kept in the processor cache.

The pointer b_data points to the block data in a specially reserved area of physical memory. The size of this area matches the block size b_size exactly. This area and the buffer head together form the block buffer. The value of b_dev specifies the device on which the relevant block is stored, and b_blocknr the number of this block on the storage medium used by the device. As it is possible that the referenced device is a pseudo-device which combines general block devices (such as several partitions on a hard disk) or a logic volume, there are additional pointers b_rdev and b_rsector which reference a real sector on a real device.

The number of processes currently using the block buffer is held in b_count. The bitmap variable b_state combines a series of status flags. The block buffer matches the disk contents if the BH_Uptodate flag is set. The block buffer must be written back to the medium if BH_Dirty is set. If BH_Lock is set, access to the block buffer is locked: in this case, processes must wait in the wait queue b_wait. The flag BH_Req indicates whether the block belonging to the buffer has been requested by a device. The buffers marked with BH_Protected can no longer be released. This feature is used for RAM disks. The memory area for RAM disks should be allocated statically in advance. BH_New indicates that the buffer content is new and has not been written to the hard disk yet. If the buffer is BH_Mapped, a block is assigned to the buffer on the device.

b_flushtime specifies the time in jiffies, for a block buffer marked as "dirty," from which the block buffer should be written back. When the block is marked as "dirty," the b_flushtime is set to the current time plus a delay parameter. The buffer is then only written back to the disk if no write access has been carried out over a lengthy period.

The handler b_end_io() is called when the IO operation for this buffer has been carried out successfully.

4.3.2 Bdflush and kupdate

Bdflush and kupdate are kernel threads that write the buffer back to the hard disk. Kupdate writes the old modified buffers back to the hard disk, including the superblock and the inode information.

kupdate writes all modified buffer blocks that have not been used since a certain time period back to the hard disk, including any superblock and inode information. The kupdate interval used under LINUX is five seconds by default. The time that kupdate waits to write a modified buffer to the disk is 30 seconds by default.

Bdflush writes the number of blocks (standard 64) provided by means of the bdflush parameter to the hard disk in an endless loop. If the total number of modified blocks is higher than a percentage (standard 30) the buffers are written back to the disk.

The system call *bdflush* sets the parameters for both kernel threads during the ongoing operation. Table 4.4 illustrates the single parameters.

The advantage of the combination of bdflush and kupdate is obvious: the number of block buffers contained in the modified buffer cache is minimized.

Table 4.4: Parameters for the `bdflush` process

Parameter	Default value	Description
nfract	30	Percentage for modified buffer blocks; if they are exceeded the `bdflush` process is activated
ndirty	64	Maximum number of buffer blocks that are written every time `bdflush` is activated
interval	500	Ticks, after which `kupdate` is started again (five seconds)
age_buffer	3,000	Ticks, after which the call of a modified buffer block is delayed (30 seconds)
nfract_sync	60	Percentage at which modified buffer blocks are issued, without waiting for the `bdflush` kernel thread to be activated

4.3.3 List structures for the buffer cache

LINUX manages its block buffers via a number of different lists. Free block buffers are managed in circular doubly linked lists. The table `free_list[]` contains this kind of list for the block sizes supported in LINUX. The available block sizes are 1, 2, 4, 8, 16, and 32 Kbytes and 512 bytes. The blocks contained in the `free_list[]` are marked in such a way that B_FREE (0xffff) is typed in the b_dev field of their buffer head. Block buffers in use are managed in a set of special LRU lists. The individual LRU lists are summarized in the table `lru_list[]`.

The indices in this table determine the type of the block buffers written in the individual LRU lists. Table 4.5 illustrates the possible indices and also the different types of LR lists. Like the lists of free blocks, the LRU lists are doubly linked circular lists, linked by means of the pointers `prev_free_list` and `next_free_list`. A block buffer is sorted into the correct LRU list by the function `refile_buffer()`.

Table 4.5: The various LRU lists

LRU list(index)	Explanation
BUF_CLEAN	Block buffers not managed in other lists – the content matches relevant blocks on the hard disk
BUF_LOCKED	Locked block buffers (b_lock != 0)
BUF_DIRTY	Block buffers with contents which do not match the relevant block on the hard disk
BUF_PROTECTED	Block buffers in a RAMDISK

The different blocks used are referenced in the table `hash_table[]`. It is used to trace block buffers by referring to their device and block numbers. The procedure used for this is open hashing. The hash lists are implemented as doubly linked linear lists. The pointers `b_next` and `b_prev` of the buffer head are used for this.

4.3.4 | Using the buffer cache

To read a block, the system routine calls the function `bread()`. This is defined in the file `fs/buffer.c file`:

```
struct buffer_head * bread(kdev_t dev, int block, int size)
```

First a check is made as to whether there is already a buffer for the device `dev` that contains the block, by accessing the block buffer hash table. If the buffer is found and the `BH_Uptodate` flag is set, `bread()` terminates by returning the block buffer. If the flag is not set, the buffer must be updated by reading the external medium, after which the routine can return.

The block is read using the function `ll_rw_block()`, which generates the appropriate request for the device driver. It is implemented in `ll_rw_blk.c` in the `drivers/block/` directory. However, after issuing the device driver request, the current process has to wait for the request to be processed. The memory block returned by `bread()` should be released once it is no longer required, using `brelse()`.

For reading and writing memory pages from and into the working memory, the `brw_page()` function is available:

```
int brw_page(int rw, struct page *page,
kdev_t dev, int b[], int size)
```

This function writes or reads (according to the parameter `rw`) the blocks whose numbers are given in vector `b[]` from the memory page `page`.

LINUX provides the classical system calls *sync* and *fsync*. *sync* writes back all modified buffer blocks in the cache, including the inodes and superblocks, without waiting for the end of the write requests. The function is based on `sync_buffers()`.

```
static int sync_buffers (kdev_t dev, int wait);
```

The `dev` parameter can be set to 0, so as to update all the block devices. `wait` determines whether the routines will wait for the write request to be performed by the device drivers. If not, the entire buffer cache is inspected for modified block buffers. If any are found by `sync_buffers()` it will generate the necessary write requests to the device drivers by calling `ll_rw_block()`.

A more complicated situation arises if the routine has to wait for successful execution of the write operation. This involves going through the entire buffer cache three times in all. In the first case, the appropriate requests are generated for all the modified blocks which are not locked. The second waits for the completion of all the locked operations. It could happen, however, that during the first pass a buffer locked by a read operation is modified by another process while the routine is waiting, so that write requests are also generated for modified buffers during this second pass. The third pass just involves waiting for all the operations which have locked buffers to be completed. This demonstrates a particular advantage of asynchronous control of the device drivers: while the block buffers are being written to the block device during the first pass, LINUX can already be searching for the next modified block buffer.

4.4   PAGING UNDER LINUX

The RAM memory in a computer has always been limited and, compared to fixed disks, relatively expensive. Particularly in multitasking operating systems, the limit of working memory is quickly reached. Thus it was not long before someone hit on the idea of offloading temporarily unused areas of primary storage (RAM) to secondary memory (for example, a hard disk).

The traditional procedure for this used to be the so-called "swapping" which involves saving entire processes from memory to a secondary medium and then reading them again. This approach does not solve the problem of running processes with large memory requirements in the available primary memory. In addition, saving and reading in all processes is very inefficient.

New hardware architectures (VAX) introduced the concept of *demand paging*. This concept divides the memory into memory pages. Under the control of a *memory management unit* the entire memory is divided into pages, with only complete pages of memory being saved as required. As all modern processor architectures, including the x86 architecture, support the management of paged memory, demand paging is employed by LINUX. Pages of memory which have been mapped directly to the virtual address area of a process using do_mmap() without write authorization are not saved, but simply discarded. Their contents can be read in again from the files which were mapped. Modified memory pages, in contrast, must be written into swap space.

Pages of memory in the kernel segment cannot be saved, for the simple reason that routine and data structures which read memory pages back from secondary memory must always be present in primary memory. The most straightforward way of making sure that this is the case is to lock all of the kernel segment pages so they cannot be saved.

LINUX can save pages to external media in two ways. In the first, a complete block device is used as the external medium. This will typically be a partition on a hard disk. The second uses fixed-length files in a file system for its external storage. The rather loose approach to terminology characteristic of LINUX has resulted in these areas being referred to, confusingly, as swap devices or paging files. Correctly, they should be called paging devices and paging files. However, as the two not quite correct terms have now become standard, they will be used here: the term swap space below may refer to either a swap device or a swap file. Two different formats are defined for a swap device and swap file.

The newest version 2 has been supported since LINUX 2.2. In the old format, a bitmap is contained in the first 4,096 bytes. Bits that have been set indicate that the page of memory for which the number in the swap space matches the offset of the bit at the start of the space is available. From byte 4,086 the character string "SWAP-SPACE" is also stored as an identifier. This means that the old format can only support 4,086 * 8 - 1 = 32,687 memory pages (130,784 Kbytes in 4-Kbytes pages) in a swap device or swap file. Given the size of hard disks usual today, this is not a lot. Therefore, a new format with the label "SWAPSPACE2" was introduced. This format supports sub-versions, of which only sub-version 1 is known at the moment. It does not support a bitmap. With this format, at the moment it is possible to use up to 2 Gigabytes for the swap space. This limit is associated with the maximum file offset previously available. LINUX 2.4 now supports 64- bit offsets, but the treatment of the swap space has not yet been adapted.

In addition, it is also possible to manage a number of swap files and devices in parallel. LINUX specifies this number as 8 in MAX_SWAPFILES. This value can be increased, but there should be hardly any applications that require a 2 * 63 = 126 Gigabyte swap space.

Using a swap device is more efficient than using a swap file. In a swap device, a page is always saved to consecutive blocks whereas in a swap file the individual blocks may be given various block numbers depending on how the particular file system fragmented the file when it was set up. These blocks then need to be found via the swap file's inode. On a swap device, the first block is given directly by the offset of the page of memory to be saved or read in. The rest then follows this first block. When a swap device is used, only one read or write request is needed for each page, whereas a swap file requires several, depending on the proportion of page size to block size. In a typical case (when a block size of 1,024 bytes is used) this amounts to four separate requests to read areas on the external medium which may not necessarily follow one after the other. On a hard disk, this causes movement of the read/write head, which in turn affects the access speed. The system call *swapon* logs on a swap device or file to the kernel:

```
int sys_swapon(const char * specialfile, int swap_flags);
```

The parameter specialfile is the name of the device or file. The priority of the swap space can be specified by swap_flags. The flag SWAP_FLAG_PREFER must be set, while the bits in the SWAP_FLAG_PRIO_MASK specify the positive priority of the swap space. If no priority is specified, the swap spaces are automatically assigned a negative priority, with the priority decreasing with each call to swapon. The system routine completes an entry for the swap space in the swap_info table.

This entry is of the swap_info_struct type:

```
struct swap_info_struct {
unsigned int flags;
kdev_t swap_device;
spinlock_t sdev_lock;
struct dentry * swap_file;
struct vfsmount *swap_vfsmnt;
unsigned short * swap_map;
unsigned int lowest_bit;
```

```
    unsigned int highest_bit;
    unsigned int cluster_next;
    unsigned int cluster_nr;
    int prio;
    int pages;
    unsigned long max;
    int next;
};
```

If the SWP_USED bit in flags is set, the entry in the swap_info table is already being used by the kernel of another swap space. The kernel sets flags to SWP_WRITEOK, once all the initialization stages for the swap space have been completed. If a structure refers to a swap file, the inode pointer swap_file will be set; otherwise the device number of the swap device will be entered in swap_device. The mount point of the file system is referenced with swap_vfsmnt. sdev_lock synchronizes access to the swap space and its data structures. The swap_map pointer shows a table allocated with vmalloc(), in which each memory page of the swap space is assigned. In this, the number of processes referring to this memory page is calculated. If the memory page cannot be used, the value in swap_map is set to SWAP_MAP_BAD (0x8000). The integer component pages holds the number of pages in the swap space that can be written to. The values of lowest_bit and highest_bit define the maximum offset of a page in the swap space. The integer max contains the value highest_bit plus one, as this value is frequently required. prio holds the priority assigned to the swap space.

New pages to be swapped are stored sequentially in groups (clusters) in the swap space. This serves to prevent excessive head movement of the hard disk during the consecutive swapping of memory pages. The variable cluster_nr specifies how many more free memory pages have to be included in the up-to-date cluster, and cluster_next saves the offset of the last memory page that has been allocated.

The index next of the structure swap_info_struct builds a list of the swap spaces according to their priority.

The system call swapoff may be used to attempt to log swap files or devices from the kernel. However, this requires enough space to be available in memory or in the other swap spaces to accommodate the pages in the swap space:

```
int sys_swapoff(const char * specialfile);
```

4.4.1 Memory management and the memory cache

For each memory page, a data structure struct page or mem_map_t is managed in the kernel in a table shown by the pointer mem_map. Data is organized in such a way that data that belongs together is stored in a cache line (16 bytes).

```
typedef struct page
{
  struct list_head list;
  struct address_space *mapping;
  unsigned long index;
  struct page *next_hash;
  atomic_t count;
  unsigned long flags;
  struct list_head lru;
  unsigned long age;
  wait_queue_head_t wait;
  struct page **pprev_hash;
  struct buffer_head * buffers;
  void *virtual; /* not ZERO if mapped with kmap */
  struct zone_struct *zone;
} mem_map_t;
```

The structure `list` is used for the management of memory pages in doubly linked circular lists. The `mapping` pointer refers to a structure that holds information about all memory pages within a file or block device, including the inode. The field `index` indicates the offset in the file or block device that displays the memory page. When the memory page is loaded in the working memory, it also references the kernel in `page_hash_table` using `next_hash` and `pprev_hash`. When a read request is made for a page from a file, the hash table is checked for the existence of that page first. If it is found there, it doesn't have to be read with the aid of a file system. Thus, file-oriented caching which supports arbitrary file systems (in particular NFS) is implemented. Also, normal file system read operations, such as `read()`, access data via the page cache.

Back to the page structure: the number of users of a page is held in `count`. The `buffers` pointer references the block buffer when the page is part of a block buffer. The wait queue contains entries for the tasks which are waiting for the page to be unlocked. Table 4.6 explains the meaning of the individual flags stored in `flags`.

The field `zone` refers to the memory area that contains the memory page. The kernel 2.4 has three zones: `ZONE_DMA`, `ZONE_NORMAL`, and `ZONE_HIGHMEM`. The DMA zone contains memory pages that are suitable for *direct memory access* (DMA) of the hardware. The normal zone contains memory pages that are directly addressable in the kernel. The `HIGHMEM` zone is filled with memory pages that can be mapped in the kernel temporarily. This happens when the hardware has more physical memory than addressable memory in the kernel segment, and `HIGHMEM` support is switched on. For `HIGHMEM` memory pages, the virtual pointer is initialized when the memory page is mapped in the kernel segment with `kmap()`.

Table 4.6: Memory page flags

Flag	Description
PG_locked	The page is locked. The flag is set when the page is read or issued
PG_error	This flag indicates an error condition in the input or output
PG_locked	The page is locked. The flag is set when the page is read or issued
PG_error	This flag indicates an error condition in the input or output
PG_referenced	The page is referenced through a buffer head
PG_uptodate	The loading of the page was successful
PG_dirty	The page was modified and no longer corresponds to the hard disk
PG_decr_after	After reading or writing the page, the nr_async_pages counter for pages that have to be temporarily stored or evacuated asynchronously decreases.
PG_active	The page is in use, which means that that it has been accessed, or more than two users are sharing it
PG_inactive_dirty	The page has been written to or locked, but for a long time there has been no access
PG_slab	The page is used for slab allocation
PG_swap_cache	The page is written in the swap cache
PG_skip	The page marks gaps in the physical memory (e.g. between the individual memory banks in the Sparc architecture) – not used in 2.4.2
PG_inactive_clean	The page corresponds to the hard disk and has not been accessed for a long time
PG_highmem	The page is contained in high memory, a memory that is not directly addressable in the kernel
PG_arch_1	This flag is an architecture-specific page flag. It is used for the Sparc64 architecture and by the A 64 to handle data caches
PG_reserved	The page should not be accessed, as either no memory is available or the hardware is mapped

4.4.2 | Reserving a page of memory

When physical pages of memory are reserved, the kernel function __get_free_pages() is called. This is defined in the file mm/page_alloc.c:

Table 4.7: Priorities for the function `__get_free_pages()`

Priority	Description
GFP_ATOMIC	When such a memory page is allocated, the kernel thread cannot be interrupted
GFP_BUFFER	When such a memory page is allocated, the ongoing process can be interrupted, although not for the evacuation of memory pages
GFP_KERNEL	To allocate memory pages, they can be freed and the process can be interrupted
GFP_NFS	Has the same priority as GFP_KERNEL
GFP_RPC	The same priority as GFP_KERNEL is also used here
GFP_USER	At present, practically corresponds to GFP_KERNEL, but it should be used so that the allocation has an inferior priority
GFP_HIGHUSER	Same priority as GFP_USER. However, the memory page can come from high memory. This means that it is not directly addressable in the kernel segment
GFP_KSWAPD	This priority is used by the GFP_KSWAPD kernel thread. However, it is not used to allocate memory pages but to free them if there is a memory shortage
GFP_DMA	Flag that requests a memory page from the architecture-dependent DMA area. The ISA DMA controller can, for example, use a smaller address area
GFP_HIGHMEM	Flag that requests a memory page in high memory. These memory pages are not mapped in the kernel segment permanently

```
unsigned long __get_free_pages(int gfp_mask, unsigned long order)
```

The parameter `gfp_mask` controls the processing of the function. The values are listed in Table 4.7. These also have to be used for `kmalloc()` and `kmem_cache_alloc()` explained above, in which a series of priorities with the prefix SLAB_ in place of GFP_ are defined for the last function.

GFP_ATOMIC is used for calls to `__get_free_pages` from interrupt routines. It does not interrupt the task when waiting for the provision or even the freeing of memory pages. A GFP_BUFFER call can be interrupted, but not for the freeing of memory pages. For all of the remaining priorities, the kernel can interrupt the current task and wait for the memory pages to be freed.

The `order` parameter establishes the order of the memory block of consecutive pages that have to be reserved. A block with order x has a length of 2x memory pages. In the LINUX kernel, only orders that are less than the MAX_ORDER macro (standard value 10) are accepted. In the x86 architecture with a size of 4 Kilobytes per page, it is possible to reserve at least $2^0 = 4$ and at most $2^9 = 2.048$ Kilobytes.

If __get_free_pages() is able to reserve a suitable block, it returns the address of this block. The current implementation ensures that the block will begin at an address which is divisible by its size in bytes.

The kernel has three memory zones. The first, ZONE_DMA, contains memory pages intended for direct memory access of peripheral equipment. The memory pages that cannot be mapped in a kernel segment are managed in the ZONE_HIGHMEM zone. All the other memory pages are assigned to the "normal" zone ZONE_NORMAL.

Every possible priority for __get_free_pages() is assigned a list of zones. __get_free_pages() tries to satisfy the memory area according to the order of the zones in the list. Thus it is guaranteed that the DMA memory is only used for normal memory requests. If there are not enough memory zones available, kernel threads are activated to provide free memory pages. The evacuation of memory pages may also be carried out. If no memory page can be found, the function returns 0.

The zones and zone lists are managed in the pglist_data structure. The kernel accesses this structure via the global variable contig_page_data, if NUMA is not supported.

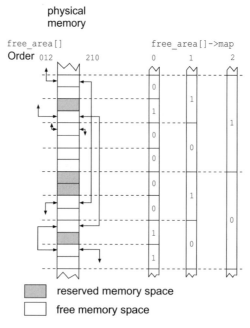

Figure 4.4: Example of the contents of maps in free_area.

For every zone, the kernel manages the `free_area[]` table in order to support the different large memory areas. A doubly linked circular list of memory pages of the corresponding size is entered into a table. The map pointer of the entry refers to a bitmap. In this bitmap, a bit for two consecutive memory blocks of the respective order is reserved. The bit is set when one of the two memory blocks is free and the other is only partly reserved. This method is described by Donald E. Knuth in [Knu98] as a buddy system. Figure 4.4 shows a possible occupation of maps for the first three orders.

The LINUX implementation ensures that there are never two consecutive memory blocks free which could be combined into a larger block. This can sometimes mean that no blocks are free for the smaller orders of size. If a request for one of these is made, the higher-order block will have to be split. The `expand()` function in `mm/page_alloc.c` updates the `free_area` data structures accordingly.

The LINUX user can specify the number of memory blocks for the individual zones and memory sizes by pressing a specific key combination on the console. For Suse LINUX, the shift and scroll keys have to be pressed simultaneously. Here is an extract from the output that combines the free memory lists for the DMA and the normal zone:

```
1*4kB 1*8kB 1*16kB 0*32kB 0*64kB 0*128kB 0*256kB 1*512kB
0*1024kB 0*2048kB = 540kB)
23*4kB 6*8kB 1*16kB 2*32kB 1*64kB 0*128kB 1*256kB 1*512kB
0*1024kB 0*2048kB = 1052kB)
```

If `kreclaimd` is not active, it is activated. The function `get_free_pages()` calls the inline function `alloc_pages()`. It activates the kernel thread `kswapd` if there are too many free and inactive memory pages available. The kernel thread looks for inactive memory pages and inserts them in the corresponding list. If enough inactive memory pages are available, the `bdflush` kernel thread is activated, which evacuates memory pages. After this, a free memory area is searched for in the individual zones. If only a few free memory pages are still active for the last function and the `kreclaimd` kernel thread is not active, the thread writes inactive, clean memory pages into the `free_area` maps again.

4.4.3 Optimization of memory page management via kernel threads

The kernel can only begin the search and evacuation of memory pages if it cannot find any free ones during the allocation of memory pages. This was also done in previous LINUX versions. However, this approach is problematic, as the CPU load increases if a lot of memory is required.

LINUX 2.4 optimizes memory page management. Global lists for the active memory pages and "dirty" memory pages are managed for this purpose. Every memory zone has its own list of inactive clean memory pages.

If inactive memory pages have not been accessed for a long time, and clean inactive memory pages match the content on the disk, dirty inactive memory pages must be written either in the swap area or to the disk. If free memory pages are required, inactive pages are candidates for memory pages that are rejected and used again.

Kernel threads act so that the `free_area` maps and the lists are filled with the inactive memory pages. The `kswapd` kernel is activated once every second, as long as memory is not particularly scarce. Via the function `do_try_to_free_pages()`, `kswapd` fills the list of inactive clean pages. Otherwise, the `kswapd` kernel thread is always reserved when too few inactive memory pages are available in the system.

The `kreclaimd` kernel thread writes inactive clean pages in the `free_area` maps. It is only activated when, during allocation, it is established that there are too few free pages in a memory zone.

If, when allocating memory pages, enough memory pages are active, but there are too few free ones, the kernel `bdflush` thread is activated. The kernel thread writes blocks to the hard disk so that memory pages can be entered in the lists of inactive clean memory pages when `do_try_to_free_pages()` is called again.

4.4.4 Page errors and reloading a page

If the MMU processor is not able to access a page, it will generate a page fault interrupt. In an x86 processor an error code is written to the stack and the linear address at which the interrupt was triggered is stored in register `CR2`. In other architectures there are similar mechanisms.

In this case, LINUX calls the architecture-specific function `do_page_fault()`:

```
void do_page_fault(struct pt_regs *regs,unsigned long error_code);
```

This routine will submit the values of the registers and the error number at the time of the interrupt. The routine searches for the virtual memory area of the currently active process in which the address in the user segment which caused the fault is to be found.

If the address is not in a virtual memory area, `do_page_fault()` checks whether the flag `VM_GROWSDOWN` is set for the next virtual memory area. An area of this sort provides memory for the stack and may grow downwards.

If the function cannot find a virtual memory area, the function `handle_mm_fault()` is called. If `handle_mm_fault()` cannot assign a memory page, the signal `SIGBUS` is generated. When not enough memory is available, the current process is concluded with `SIGKILL`. If `handle_mm_fault()` was successful, it returns `do_page_fault()`.

If no virtual memory area could be assigned, and this is an address in the user segment, the `SIGSEGV` signal is generated. This segmentation violation signal will be familiar to any serious UNIX programmer.

If the error occurs in system mode, a check is made to see whether this is the F00F bug in Pentium processors. It is treated as an invalid machine code error.

If a kernel error occurs, an exception table is searched and the instruction pointer of the register record is manipulated accordingly.

If none of these checks is successful, there is certainly an error in the kernel, and corresponding information is issued on the console.

The function `handle_mm_fault()` mentioned above is architecture-independent. It determines the page table entry that belongs to the memory page. If the memory page is not present and the corresponding bit is not set, `do_swap_page()` is called if a swap index can be found in the page table entry. Otherwise, `do_no_page()` is called. If the page is available but write-protected, `do_wp_page()` is called.

```
static int do_no_page(struct mm_struct * mm,
        struct vm_area_struct * vma,
        unsigned long address, int write_access,
        pte_t *page_table);
static int do_swap_page(struct mm_struct * mm,
        struct vm_area_struct * vma,
        unsigned long address, pte_t * page_table,
        swp_entry_t entry, int write_access);
static int do_wp_page(struct mm_struct *mm,
        struct vm_area_struct * vma,
        unsigned long address, pte_t *page_table,
        pte_t pte);
```

The function `do_no_page()` checks whether this is an anonymous mapped memory page. If so, `do_anonymous_page()` is called and executes the corresponding copy-on-write operations. This means that during read access, the ZERO_PAGE is mapped, and with write access a completely new memory page is displayed. Otherwise, the corresponding management routine is called from the virtual memory area and the page table entry is set according to the write or read access.

`do_swap_page()` checks whether the memory page is already available in the swap cache. If not, the memory page is read via `swapin_readahead()`. This function can also asynchronously read the current page as well as the pages following it that are available in the swap area.

The function `do_wp_page()` checks whether a write-protected memory page can be found under the address indicated. If it is only referenced once, the write protection is simply removed. If it is referenced repeatedly, a copy of the memory page is created and this is not entered as write-protected in the appropriate page table of the process that has solved the error.

5 INTERPROCESS COMMUNICATION

There are many applications in which processes need to cooperate with each other. This is always the case, for example, if processes have to share a resource (such as a printer). It is important to make sure that no more than one process is accessing the resource – that is, sending data to the printer at any given time. This situation is known as a race condition. Communication between the processes must prevent these kinds of situations. However, eliminating race conditions is only one possible use of interprocess communication, which we will take to mean the simple exchange of information between the processes of one or more computers. There are many different types of interprocess communication. They differ in a number of ways, including their efficiency. The transfer of a small natural number between two processes could be effected, for example, by one of these generating a matching number of child processes and the other counting them.

This example, which is not meant entirely seriously, is of course very unwieldy and slow and would not be considered. Shared memory can provide a faster and more efficient answer to the problem.

Recently, threads have become more popular. Threads allow the execution of codes in the same address space. Switching between threads is less expensive than between processes, as the page directories do not have to be exchanged. In multiprocessor environments, threads allow, for example, the execution of two methods of the same object instance at the same time. This is particularly interesting for CORBA applications. However, the advantages offered come with many race conditions, because the threads of a program can access the whole address space. Single threads also have to communicate with each other, in order to avoid these race conditions.

This communication is made possible by the use of programming interfaces that are known as POSIX threads. We will not deal with these programming interfaces here because they are not created in the kernel, yet. In his implementation of threads, Linus Torvalds supported the opinion that threads are only processes that share the address space with other processes. Further support of threads cannot be found in the kernel yet. This leads to some incompatibilities with the POSIX standard, in particular regarding signal treatment. After years of debate, Linus Torvalds agreed to a design for the POSIX-compatible support of threads. The kernel designers will incorporate this into the 2.5 design kernels.

A variety of forms of interprocess communication can be used under LINUX. These support resource sharing, synchronization, connectionless and connection-oriented data exchange, or combinations of all of these. Synchronization mechanisms are used to eliminate the race conditions mentioned above.

Connectionless and connection-oriented data exchange differ from the first two variants in their different semantic models. In these models, a process sends messages to a process or a specific group of processes.

In connection-oriented data exchange, the two parties must set up a connection before communication can start. In connectionless data exchange, a process simply sends data packets, which may be given a destination address or a message type, and leaves it to the infrastructure to deliver them. The reader will already be familiar with these models from everyday life: when we make a telephone call we are using a connection-oriented data exchange model, and when we send a letter we rely on a connectionless model.

It is possible to implement one concept (for example, semaphores) based on another (for example, connectionless data exchange). LINUX implements all the forms of interprocess communication possible between processes in the same system by using shared resources, kernel data structures, and the "mutual exclusion" synchronization system, Mutex. The kernel programmers make use of the spin lock concept which describes the procedure more and the effect of the synchronization mechanism less.

LINUX processes can share memory by means of the System V shared memory facility. The file system has been implemented from the start to allow files and devices to be used by several processes at the same time. To avoid race conditions when files are accessed, various file locking mechanisms can be used.

System V semaphores can be used as a synchronization mechanism between processes in a computer.

There is also a POSIX specification of these IPC mechanisms mentioned above. LINUX 2.4 implements these mechanisms by means of the shared memory file system. The GNU-C Library version 2.2 supports POSIX semaphores and shared memory. As the POSIX message queues can be created on the basis of semaphores and shared memory, the kernel will no longer hinder POSIX compatibility.

Interested readers can read the book by W. Richard Stevens [Ste98] about interprocess communication, which discusses the new POSIX functions in detail. The book [Gal95] by Bill O. Gallmeister contains another representation.

Signals are the simplest variant of connectionless data exchange. They can be understood as very short messages sent to a specific process or process group (see Chapter 3). In this category, LINUX still provides System V message queues and the datagram sockets in the INET address family. The datagram sockets are based on the UDP section of the TCP/IP code and can also be used in the network (see Chapter 8).

The available methods for connection-oriented data exchange are *pipes*, *named pipes* (also known as FIFOs[1]), UNIX domain sockets, and Stream sockets of the INET address family. The stream sockets are the interfaces of the TCP part of the network and are used to implement services such as FTP and TELNET, amongst others. These are also looked at in Chapter 8. The use of the socket program interface does not always amount to interprocess communication, as the opposite number on the network need not be a process. It could, for example, be a program in an operating system, with no process concept.

[Bac86] introduces the system call *ptrace* as a variant of interprocess communication. This can be used by a process to control the operation of another process right down to single-step processing and modify both the memory and the registers for this process. It is used particularly in debugging work. Its implementation will be discussed in this chapter.

Table 5.1 gives a summary chart of the types of interprocess communication supported by LINUX. As NFS is based on datagram sockets, the facility to send files over the NFS file system is not included. In version 2.0 of the kernel, the system call *mmap* is fully implemented, which means that shared memory can be effected via anonymous mapping, as in BSD systems. Kernel 2.4 also allows the mapping of the /dev/zero device as simultaneously used memory without any problem. The System V Transport Library Interface is not supported.

5.1   SYNCHRONIZATION IN THE KERNEL

Because the kernel manages the system resources, access by processes to these resources must be synchronized. Normally, a process will not be interrupted by the scheduler as long as it is executing a system call. This only happens if it locks or it calls `schedule()`, to explicity allow the execution of other processes. In kernel programming it should be remembered that functions like `__get_free_pages()` and `down()` can lock processes. Processes in the kernel, however, can be interrupted by interrupt handling routines: this can result in race conditions even if the process is not executing any functions that can lock files.

In a multiprocessor system the situation is even more difficult, as several processes can be executed on different processors at the same time. Race conditions also occur between ongoing processes.

Race conditions between the current process and the interrupt routines are excluded by the processor's interrupt flag being cleared when the critical section is entered and reset on exit. While the interrupt flag is being cleared, the processor will not allow any hardware interrupts except for the non-maskable interrupt (NMI), used in PC architecture by default to indicate RAM errors. In normal operation, the NMI should not occur. This method has the advantage of being very simple but has the drawback that, if used too freely, it slows the system down.

---

1   FIFO stands for "First In/First Out," which describes the action of a pipe very well.

Table 5.1: Types of interprocess communication supported by LINUX

	In the kernel	Between processes	In the network
Resource division	Data structures, buffer	System V shared memory, files, anonymous mmap, /dev/zero mmap	
Synchronization method	Wait queues, semaphores	System V semaphores, file locking, lock file	
Connectionless	Signals	Signals, System V message queues, UNIX domain sockets in the datagram mode	Datagram sockets (UDP)
Connection-oriented data exchange		Pipes, named pipes, UNIX domain sockets in the stream mode	Stream sockets (TCP)

Because there can be race conditions between the processes of the various processors, this method is no longer useful. Data that is ignored by the interrupt handling routines does not have to be protected by blocking the interrupts. The base synchronization mechanism in multiprocessor systems, also used by other operating systems, is called a spin lock. These locks carry out the mutual exclusion of processes in the kernel. The critical section can only be executed by the process that is in possession of the spin lock. This concept is also known as mutex. The implementation depends on the specific computer architecture. A spin lock for an x86 multiprocessor system is defined via the C data type spinlock_t:

```
typedef struct { volatile unsigned int lock; } spinlock_t;
```

In the default status, the variable lock has a value of 1. The process that wants to block the spin lock tries to set the lock to 0, if it has not yet been set to 0. This is possible with an x86 machine command in which the bus access of the other processors are blocked during the processing of this command. Thus the process of testing and setting up the lock variable is atomic. If the spin lock cannot be set, the processor waits in a loop until the lock variable is released again. However, during this process, the other processors are not blocked. When the lock variable is free again, it tries once more to block the spin lock. The process of unlocking and resetting the lock variable is atomic.

The wait for the release of the lock variable is known as busy waiting. No modification of the process is possible, since this has to be locked again in order to access the global process table. Spin locks are also the atomic synchronization mechanisms in the LINUX kernel. Moreover, the decisive advantage of spin locks is that they can be used in the interrupt handling routines. Therefore, spin locks can be used in cases where the locking only lasts a short time and the effort of locking the process is not worthwhile, or if locks for the process change itself are necessary. Spin locks do not prevent interruption due to interrupts. Single processor systems do not need a spin lock, therefore the corresponding operations are defined empty by default. The read-write locks are an alternative to the spin locks. It is established whether a process wants to read from or write to a resource. Processes that only read the resources do not exclude each other. However, a write process excludes all other processes. In the LINUX kernel, a read-write lock for x86 multiprocessor systems is represented via the `rwlock_t` data structure as in the following:

```
typedef struct {
  volatile unsigned int lock;
} rwlock_t;
```

In x86 processors the lock variable has the value `RW_LOCK_BIAS` (0x01000000) in the default status. A write lock tries to set this value to 0 by means of subtraction from `RW_LOCK_BIAS`, and waits in a loop until it is successful. A read lock tries to subtract 1 without the result being negative. Also in this case, the waiting is carried out in a busy loop. It is more time consuming to set and lock read-write locks than spin locks. Therefore, they should be used when read accesses are much more frequent than write accesses.

Ingo Molnar and David S. Miller have also implemented *big reader locks* for LINUX 2.4. They have the same semantics as read-write locks, but only set read locks per processor. This does not force the processor caches to be updated for one read lock. These spin locks need more memory than read-write locks but can accelerate read-write locks with a high quota of read locks. These big locks are currently used for global interrupt handling and for some network related code.

Spin and read-write locks also are created via hand-optimized assembler routines that minimize the number of operations when the lock is set successfully.

The initialization of spin locks is possible via the `SPIN_LOCK_UNLOCKED` macro, while `RW_LOCK_UNLOCKED` has to be used for read-write locks. It is possible to set and unlock spin locks easily using `spin_lock()` or `spin_unlock()`. The macros `spin_lock_irq()` and `spin_unlock_irq()` lock and also allow interrupts for the current processor. These macros are problematic when the interrupts have been disabled before these functions have to be called, because the interrupts are enabled again via `spin_unlock_irq()`. Here `spin_lock_irqsave()` and `spin_unlock_irqrestore()` have to be used. They save the interrupt status of the local processor against the locking of the interrupts and restore it by unlocking it.

It is necessary to lock the interrupts in the interrupt handling routines for the respective CPU. If the interrupts are not locked, the same interrupt handling routine may be called using another interrupt. This routine would lock on the same spin lock that has been locked in the previous handling of the interrupt. Because the locking runs in a loop, the spin lock is no longer unlocked. Software interrupts can also interrupt themselves, as they are called after the handling of the hardware interrupts. To avoid this, the execution of further software interrupts on the current CPU should be avoided for the spin lock. To make this possible, the kernel defines `spin_lock_bh()` and `spin_unlock_bh()`.

The `read_lock()` and `write_lock()` macros set a read or write lock. The unlocking is carried out via `read_unlock()` or `write_unlock()`. The variants for interrupt handling are provided in the same way as the spin lock macros in include/linux/spinlock.h. The variants for the big reader locks have the prefix br_ and the locks are selected using an index and have to be declared in include/linux/brlock.h as the values of enumeration during compilation.

It can often happen that processes in the kernel need to wait for particular events, such as a block being written to the hard disk. The current process should block to allow other processes to be executed. The alternative is busy waiting, where the process runs through the loop until it encounters the event. However, the corresponding computing time could be used by other processes.

In the LINUX kernel, processes are locked and particular events are waited for via waiting queues. A process can sit on a waiting queue and will not be interrupted until the processes in the waiting queue are reactivated by an interrupt handling routine or another process.

The data types wait_queue_head_t and wait_queue_t are available for the waiting queues.

```
struct __wait_queue_head {
  wq_lock_t lock;
  struct list_head task_list;
};
typedef struct __wait_queue_head wait_queue_head_t;
struct __wait_queue {
  unsigned int flags;
  struct task_struct * task;
  struct list_head task_list;
};
typedef struct __wait_queue wait_queue_t;
```

The wait queue is a doubly linked circular list of pointers into the process table and an associated spin lock. LINUX 2.4 provides generic doubly linked circular lists in the include/linux/list.h header. This extremely elegant solution enables the management of a data structure in many circular lists, in which a field with the type struct list_head is included per circular list. The type wq_lock_t can be defined either as a spin lock or as a read-write lock. It is currently set to spin lock. In LINUX 2.2 there was a global lock for all waiting lists; this is now refined.

If the kernel programmer wants to use wait queues, he or she has to include a field with the type wait_queue_head_t in the data structure and initialize it with the function init_waitqueue_head(). After initialization the wait queue is empty. The kernel adds a process (which the kernel programmers also call a task) to the wait queue in two steps. In the first step, the DECLARE_WAITQUEUE() macro declares and initializes a wait_queue_t data structure using the pointer to the task structure. In the second step, the data structure is written into the data structure by means of add_wait_queue(). It is possible to determine whether any entry is already contained in the list, by means of waitqueue_active(). Using remove_wait_queue() the task can be removed from the task list. While the wait queue is modified, the interrupts are locked so that the interrupt routines can access the wait queues.

However, by using these functions processes cannot be locked, and sleep_on() moves the process into the TASK_UNINTERRUPTIBLE status. In this status the process cannot be interrupted by the use of signals. The function interruptible_sleep_on() keeps the process in the TASK_INTERRUPTIBLE status so that signals can activate the process. It is possible to lock the process for a certain time by means of sleep_on_timeout() and interruptible_sleep_on_timeout().

The implementation of sleep_on() is represented in pseudo code here as an example:

```
__pseudo__ sleep_on(struct wait_queue **p)
{
  struct wait_queue wait;

  current->state = TASK_UNINTERRUPTIBLE;
  wait.task = current;

  add_wait_queue(p, &wait);
  schedule();
  remove_wait_queue(p, &wait);
}
```

A process is responsible for entering itself into the wait queue and for deleting itself from it. The real sleep_on() functions use macros to accelerate these frequently used routines in the kernel. It is possible to write both interruptible and non-interruptible processes into the same wait queue. Sleeping processes that cannot yet be interrupted by signals, are condemned to eternal sleep, as in the *Sleeping Beauty* fairytale. However, there are certain macros that are able to wake up processes.

The wake_up() macro wakes up a process in the wait queue, wake_up_nr() wakes up a certain number of processes, and wake_up_all() wakes up all processes in the wait queue. Using wake_up_interruptible(), wake_up_interruptible_nr(), and wake_up_interruptible_all() it is also possible to limit the waking up to processes that had slept as interruptible in the wait queue. Moreover, there are so-called synchronous variants, such as wake_up_sync(), which are only different because they do not lead to the next possible time for rescheduling, but wait until the scheduler is activated for another reason. Wait queues are used to implement the kernel semaphores. Semaphores are counters that can be incremented at any time, but can only be decremented when their value is greater than zero. If this is not the case, the decrementing process is blocked, and is entered in a wait queue for a semaphore. Semaphores can be used as mutexes for mutual exclusion, when situations with a counter of 0 are interpreted as locked. The incrementing of a counter is equal to the leaving of a mutex while its decrement equals the entering of a mutex. However, it has to be taken into account that decrements and increments are carried out in pairs. The implementation chosen by LINUX 2.4 is a bit more complex than this:

```
struct semaphore {
  atomic_t count;
```

```
  int sleepers;
  wait_queue_head_t * wait;
};
```

The variable `count` is of type `atomic_t`. It is only possible to access it via atomic operations. From the kernel programmer's point of view, atomic operations are such that they do not lead to any race condition. The multiprocessor hardware provides these operations, in which it uses more complex cache-consistent protocols.

The `up()` function increments `count` and wakes up all sleeping processes when the value of `count` is less than or equal to 0. If `count` were to represent the correct value of the semaphore, `up()` should wake a sleeping process if `count` is equal to 1. However, there is no atomic operation for the increment and test for equality to 1. Therefore `count` is corrected so that it is less than 0 if processes are waiting for semaphores.

This allows the function `down()` to simply decrement `count` and sleep in the wait queue if the value is less than 0. In doing so, `down()` modifies `sleepers` so that when all the processes in the semaphore wait queue are sleeping or working out of the semaphore routine, the sum of `sleepers` and `count` is equal to the correct value of the semaphore. This is implemented so that sleepers is 1 if possible and count is -1 if possible. In the case of several consecutive `up()` calls, only the first call has to wake up a process in the waiting queue. The first process that is woken up, wakes up the next process which tries to set `count` to less than 0 again and then sleep. If the second `up()` call is quicker, this is not successful and the next blocked process is woken up, until there is no longer a sleeping process or `count` is less than 0 again. There are two more variants for `down()`: `down_interruptible()` and `down_trylock()`. In the first, the process is put to sleep and can be interrupted, and in the second the process is not blocked if the semaphore cannot be decremented.

5.2   COMMUNICATION VIA FILES

Communication via files is in fact the oldest way of exchanging data between programs. Program A writes data to a file and program B reads it. In a system in which only one program can be run at any given time, this does not present any problems.

In a multitasking system, however, both programs could be run as processes at least quasi-parallel to each other. Race conditions then usually produce inconsistencies in the file data which result from one program reading a data area before the other has finished modifying it, or both processes modifying the same area of memory at the same time.

The situation therefore calls for locking mechanisms. The simplest method, of course, would be to lock the whole file. For this, LINUX, like other UNIX derivatives, offers a range of facilities. More common and more efficient, however, is the practice of locking file areas. This locking of file access can be either *mandatory* or *advisory*. Advisory locking allows reading and writing to the file to continue even after the lock has been set.

However, locks are mutually exclusive, depending on the semantics determined by their respective types. Mandatory locking blocks read and write operations throughout the entire area.

With advisory locking, all processes accessing the file for read or write operations have to set the appropriate lock and release it again. If a process does not obey this rule, inconsistencies are possible. However, mandatory locking provides no better protection against malfunctions within processes: if processes have write authorization to a file, they can produce inconsistencies by writing to unlocked areas. The problems produced by faulty programs when mandatory locking is employed are extremely critical, because the locked files cannot be modified as long as the process in question is still running. Since version 2.0, LINUX has supported mandatory locking, but the corresponding kernel configuration parameter is disabled by default. For the reasons given above and as POSIX 1003.1 does not require mandatory locking, this is perfectly acceptable.

If mandatory locking is supported by a generated LINUX kernel, for each file that is to support mandatory locking the SGID bit is set. Mandatory locking does not function with files mapped with mmap() and with the MAP_SHARED flag.

5.2.1 Locking entire files

There are two methods of locking entire files:

1

In addition to the file to be locked there is an auxiliary file known as a lock file which refuses access to the former when it is present. In his book *Programming Unix Networks* [Ste92b] and in the reprint [Ste98], W. Richard Stevens lists the following procedures:

■ It makes use of the fact that the system call *link* fails if the reference to the file it is instructed to set up already exists. A file with the process number as its file name is set up and then attempts to set up a link to the name of the lock file, which will only be successful if this link does not yet exist. The reference with the process number as its name can then be deleted. After a failure, the process can call the library function sleep() to pause it (but only for a short time) and then reattempt the link.

■ Next the characteristic of the system call *create*: it aborts with an error code if the process which is being called does not possess the appropriate access rights. When the lock file is set up, all of the write access bits are canceled. This variant, however, also involves active waiting and cannot be used for processes running with the superuser's access rights.

■ The variant recommended for LINUX programming is based on the use of a combination of the O_CREAT and O_EXCL flags with the system call *open*. The lock file can then only be opened if it does not already exist; otherwise an error message will appear.

■ It is also possible to create the lock file via open() with O_CREAT | O_WRONLY | O_TRUNC and a mode 0 without any rights. However, this trick does not work as a superuser.

The drawback to all four of these variants, however, is that after a failure the process must repeat its attempts to set up a lock file. Usually, the process will call `sleep()` to wait for one second and then try again. However, the process which has set up the lock file may be terminated by a `SIGKILL` signal, so that the lock file can no longer be deleted. It must now be explicitly deleted. For this reason many programs, such as the mail reader `elm`, place a restriction on the number of attempts to set up a lock file and abort with an error message once this number is exceeded to draw the user's attention to this sort of situation.

2 The second method is to lock the entire file by means of the system call *fcntl*. This is also suitable for locking file areas, which is covered in the next section. This is the variant recommended to lock the entire file. Since version 2.0, the library function `flock()` to lock the entire file, derived from BSD 4.3, has been implemented as a separate system call. `flock()` only supports advisory locking and is based on the same data structures in the kernel as locking with `fcntl()`. As `flock()` is not defined by the POSIX standard, programmers are advised against using it.

5.2.2 | Locking file areas

Locking file areas is usually referred to as *record locking*. This should be defined as data record locking. However, this terminology does not help users of UNIX systems a great deal, because the UNIX file concept does not support records.

Under LINUX, advisory locking of file areas can be achieved with the system call *fcntl*. Nowadays the kernel supports the 64-bit variant for larger offsets as well.

```
int sys_fcntl (unsigned int fd, unsigned int cmd,
               unsigned long arg);
int sys_fcntl64 (unsigned int fd, unsigned int cmd,
                 unsigned long arg);
```

The parameter `fd` is used to pass a file descriptor. For locking purposes, only the commands F_GETLK, F_SETLK, and F_SETLKW are of interest; and if one of these commands is used, `arg` must be an indication of a `flock` structure. The F_GETLK command tests whether the lock specified in `flock` would be possible; if not, the attempted lock is returned. F_SETLK sets the lock. If it cannot do so, the function returns. F_SETLKW locks if the lock cannot be set. The last two commands can release a lock if the lock type `l_type` is set to F_UNLCK. The 64-bit variants of the macros are indicated by 64.

```
struct flock {
  short l_type; /* F_RDLCK, F_WRLCK, F_UNLCK */
  short l_whence; /* SEEK_SET, SEEK_CUR, SEEK_END */
  off_t l_start; /* Offset relative to l_whence */
  off_t l_len; /* length of the area to be locked */
  pid_t l_pid; /* is returned with F_GETLK */
};
```

The type **F_RDLCK** is used to set up a read lock for the file area, and **F_WRLCK** a write lock. Table 5.2 shows the mutually exclusive nature of the locks. The access mode of the files which are being partially locked must allow the process read or write access as appropriate. The 64-bit variant uses the type **loff_t** in place of the type **off_t**.

A peculiarity of LINUX is that for **l_type**, **F_SHLCK** and **F_EXLCK** are also possible. These were used by an older implementation of the library function **flock()**. Under LINUX, the lock types mentioned above are mapped to **F_RDLCK** or **F_WRLCK**, with the difference that the file to be locked must be opened for reading and writing. This means that if a shared lock is interpreted as a read lock and an exclusive lock as a write lock, the semantics are the same as for **F_RDLCK** and **F_WRLCK** (see Table 5.2). However, the semantics of **fcntl** and **flock** locks differ in that **flock** locks are not associated with processes. For this reason, this ad hoc implementation is faulty.

Table 5.2: Semantics of **fcntl** locks

Existing locks	Setting a read lock	Setting a write lock
None	Possible	Possible
More than one	Possible	Not allowed
A write lock	Not allowed	Not allowed

The new **flock** locks are managed in the kernel using the same data structures as **fcntl()** locks, but they are marked accordingly to prevent locks of different types being mixed up. When an attempt is made to set a lock on a file in which locks of the other type have already been set, an **EBUSY** error is returned. The two lock types have different handling routines.

Locks can be moved using **F_UNLCK**, with the starting position given in **l_whence** and **l_start**. For the **l_whence** parameter, the "seek" parameters familiar to **lseek()** can be used: **SEEK_SET** for the start of the file, **SEEK_CUR** for the current position in the file, and **SEEK_END** for the end of the file. These values are then incremented by **l_start**. LINUX converts **SEEK_END** to the current end of the file, so that the lock is not set relative to the end of the file. For example, it is not possible to use the same lock independently of write operations to inhibit access to the last two bytes at the end of the file.

By doing this, LINUX behaves in the same way as SVR4 but differs from BSD.

The parameter **l_len** defines the length of the area to be locked; and a **l_len** of 0 indicates that the area stretches to the current end, and any future end, of the file. This is the method accepted by the POSIX specification.

If the **F_GETLK** call finds an existing lock which would exclude locking the area specified, the process number of the process which set up the lock is returned in **l_pid**. The implementation of these functions centers on the doubly linked list **file_lock_table** (with entries consisting of **flock**-like **file_lock** data structures).

```
struct file_lock {
  struct file_lock *fl_next;
  struct list_head fl_link;
  struct list_head fl_block;
  fl_owner_t fl_owner;
  unsigned int fl_pid;
  wait_queue_head_t fl_wait;
  struct file *fl_file;
  unsigned char fl_flags;
  unsigned char fl_type;
  loff_t fl_start;
  loff_t fl_end;

  void (*fl_notify)(struct file_lock *);
  void (*fl_insert)(struct file_lock *);
  void (*fl_remove)(struct file_lock *);
  struct fasync_struct * fl_fasync;
  union {
  struct nfs_lock_info nfs_fl;
} fl_u;
};
extern struct list_head file_lock_list;
```

The pointer fl_next is used to contruct a linear list linking all locks for one file (inode->i_flock).

The component fl_owner saves the file descriptors of the process, which have set the lock, fl_pid, to the corresponding process identifier. Both details are used for the command F_GETLK. The locked file is identified via fl_file.

This parameter is used to distinguish between the fcntl locks (FL_POSIX), the new flock locks (FL_FLOCK), the old flock locks (FL_BROKEN), absolute locks (FL_ACCESS), locked locks (FL_LOCKD) for NFS, and FL_LEASE for the lease concept.

By means of the lease concept, the network client can guarantee the consistency of the data in its file cache and on the server. SAMBA and the experimental SODA file system use this feature. fl_type indicates the type of lock. The parameters fl_start and fl_end indicate the locked area in the file. They are given in absolute offsets.

From this comes the POSIX-conforming handling of SEEK_END.

The remaining parameters support callbacks for locking operations and are used for the NFS locked daemon and the lease concept.

These structures determine the implementation of the commands GET_LK, SET_LK, and SET_LKW. GET_LK is executed by the function fcntl_getlk() in fs/locks.c and tests whether the file descriptors are open and whether the values of the flock structure are valid. The flock structure is then copied into a file_lock structure and the lock function of the file is called when it is defined. This is not valid, for example, for the ext2 file system. In this case fcntl_getlk() tracks down possible conflicts with posix_test_lock(). The function posix_test_lock() calls the function posix_locks_conflict() in a loop for all POSIX file locks. In this case, the blocking lock is written into flock and the function returns.

The commands SET_LK and SET_LKW are executed by fcntl_setlk().

After the validity of the parameters has been checked, this function checks whether the file is opened in the correct mode. The lock is set using the function posix_lock_file(). All locks will search for conflicts via posix_locks_conflict().

If a conflict is found, the function returns EAGAIN if called using SET_LK, or blocks if SET_LKW is used. In the latter case, the current process is entered in the wait queue for the lock. When locked, the actual process is entered into the wait queue of the lock. When this lock is removed, all the processes in the wait queue are woken up and retest the existing locks for conflicts. If no conflict can be found, the lock is entered in the list of file locks.

In Figure 5.1, process 1 has locked the first byte in the file for read access and process 2 has locked the second byte. Process 1 then attempts to place a write lock on the second byte, but is blocked by process 2. Process 2 in turn attempts to lock the first byte and is likewise blocked.

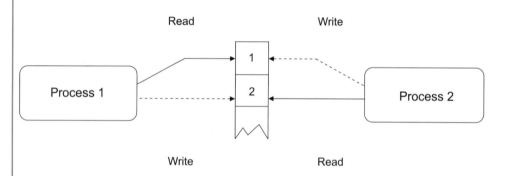

Figure 5.1: A deadlock scenario arising when locking files.

Both processes would now wait for the other to release its lock, producing a deadlock situation. The scenarios for deadlocks are generally more complex, as a number of processes may be involved. LINUX tracks down situations of this type via posix_locks_deadlock(), and the system call *fcntl* returns the error EDEADLK.

Fcntl locks are not transferred to the child process by *fork*, but are retained by *execve*. This method conforms to POSIX but is very simple to implement.

The flock locks are not assigned to individual processes so that locks remain set as long as the file is open. This is not hard to implement either.

5.3   PIPES

Pipes are the classical method of interprocess communication under UNIX. Users of UNIX should not be unfamiliar with a command line such as

```
% ls -l | more
```

Here, the shell runs the processes *ls* and *more*, which are linked via a pipe. ls writes the data to the pipe and more reads it.

Another variant of pipes consists of named pipes, also known as FIFOs (pipes also operate on the "First in – First out" principle).

In the following pages, the terms pipe and FIFO will be used interchangeably. Unlike pipes, FIFOs are not temporary objects that only exist as long as a file descriptor is still open for them. They can be set up in a file system using the command

```
mkfifo pathname
```

or

```
mknod pathname p
```

See the following example:

```
% mkfifo fifo
% ls -l fifo
prw-r--r--   1 kunitz users    0   Feb    27    22:47    fifo|
```

Linking the standard inputs and outputs of two processes is a little more complicated with FIFOs.

```
% ls -l >fifo & more <fifo
```

There are obviously many similarities between pipes and FIFOs, and these are exploited by the LINUX implementation. The inodes have the same specific components for pipes and FIFOs.

```
struct pipe_inode_info {
  wait_queue_head_t wait;           /* wait queue              */
  char *base;                       /* address of FIFO buffer */
  unsigned int start;               /* offset for current area */
  unsigned int readers;             /* number of processes
                                     * reading at this moment  */
  unsigned int writers;             /* number of processes
                                     * writing at this moment  */
  unsigned int waiting_readers;     /* number of blocked processes
                                     * reading at this moment  */
  unsigned int waiting_writers;     /* number of blocked processes
                                     * writing at this moment  */
```

```
    unsigned int r_counter;    /* number of read processes
                               * that have opened              */
    unsigned int w_counter;    /* number of write processes
                               * that have opened              */
};
```

The length of the area of the pipe is managed in the i_size field. The system call *pipe* creates a pipe which involves setting up a temporary inode and allocating a page of memory to base.

The architecture-dependent size of the memory page then defines the size of a pipe. The system call returns one file descriptor for reading and one for writing.

Table 5.3: Opening a FIFO

		Blocking	Non-blocking
For reading	No writing processes	Block	Open FIFO
	Writing processes	Open FIFO	Open FIFO
For writing	No reading processes	Block	Error ENXIO
	Reading processes	Open FIFO	Open FIFO
For reading and writing		Open FIFO	Open FIFO

Table 5.4: Semantics of the pipe/FIFO read operation

	Blocking	Non-blocking
Empty pipe	Block the calling process if write processes are available, otherwise return 0	Error EAGAIN if there are write processes, otherwise 0
Otherwise	Maximum number of characters up to the required length, wait for blocked write processes	As with the blocking operation, but no wait for write processes

For FIFOs there is an open function, which allocates a memory page and returns a file descriptor that has been assigned an operation vector with read and write operations. Its process is summarized in Table 5.3.

FIFOs and pipes use the same read and write operations. The memory belonging to FIFO or the pipe is interpreted as a circular buffer. Data which has not yet been read is saved from start with a length of i_size bytes. The O_NONBLOCK flag checks whether the write or read operations block, if there is nothing to do. If the number of bytes to be written does not exceed the internal buffer size for the pipe, the write operation must be carried out atomically – that is, if a number of processes are writing to the pipe/FIFO, byte sequences for the individual write operations are not interrupted. The semantics implemented in LINUX are shown in Tables 5.4 and 5.5.

As processes very often block when accessing pipes or FIFOs, it follows that the read and write operations often have to wake up processes in the inode's wait queue. All the processes are managed in a single wait queue, although they may be waiting for different events.

Table 5.5: Semantics of pipe/FIFO write operation

	Blocking	Non-blocking
Not a reading process	Signal SIGPIPE is sent to the writing process and returned with EPIPE error	–
Atomic writing	Block the calling process if not enough space	EAGAIN error if not enough space
Otherwise	Always continue to block until the required number of bytes is written	Write maximum possible number to bytes

5.4 DEBUGGING USING *ptrace*

No programmer is capable of writing a bug-free program first time. Tools that are able to track down errors are also required. UNIX provides the system call *ptrace*, which gives one process control over another process. The process under its control can be run step by step and its memory can be read and modified. Data can also be read from the process table. Debuggers such as gdb are based on the ptrace() system call. Because it is dependent on the process architecture, this call is defined in the file arch/i386/kernel/ptrace.c.

```
int sys_ptrace(long request, long pid, long addr, long data);
```

The function processes various requests defined in the parameter request. The parameter pid specifies the process number of the process to be controlled.

Using the request PTRACE_TRACEME, a process can specify that its parent process controls it via ptrace() – in other words, the trace flag (PT_PTRACED) for the process is traced via sys_ptrace().

The calling process can use PTRACE_ATTACH to make any process its child process and set its PT_PTRACED flag. However, the user and group numbers for the calling process must match the effective user and group numbers of the process to be controlled. The new child process is sent a SIGSTOP signal, which will usually cause it to stop running. After this request it will be under the control of its parent process.

With the exception of PTRACE_KILL, the following requests are only processed by ptrace once the child process has been stopped. The requests PTRACE_PEEKTEXT and PTRACE_PEEKDATA can be used to read 32-bit values from the controlled process's user memory area. LINUX does not make any distinction between the two requests. PTRACE_PEEKTEXT will read the code, while PTRACE_PEEKDATA can be used to read data. The request PTRACE_PEEKUSR will cause a long value to be read from the user structure for the processes.

This is where debugging information, such as the process's debug register, is saved. It is updated by the processor after a debugging trap and written to the process table using the appropriate handling routine.

The user structure is virtual. The sys_ptrace() function uses the address to decide what information should be returned and outputs it. Therefore, the registers on the child process's stack and the debug registers saved in the process table will be read by the function.

The requests PTRACE_POKEDATA and PTRACE_POKETEXT allow the user area for the process under control to be modified. If the area to be modified is write protected, the relevant page is copied by copy-on-write. However, the page of memory retains its access attribute. This is used, for example, to write a special instruction to a particular location in the machine code so that a debugging trap is triggered. In this way, breakpoints can be set by debuggers. The code will be executed until the instruction triggering the trap (in int3 in the case of x86 processor) is processed, at which point the debugging trap handling routine will interrupt the process and inform the parent process.

It is also possible to use PTRACE_POKEUSR to modify the virtual user structure. The main use for this is to modify the process's register.

After being interrupted by a signal (in most cases SIGSTOP), the child process can be continued using the request PTRACE_CONT. The argument data can be used to decide what signal the process will handle when it resumes execution. On receipt of the signal, the child process informs the parent process and stops. The parent process can now continue the child process and decide whether it should process the signal. If the data argument is zero, the child process will not process a signal.

The request PTRACE_SYSCALL causes the child process to resume in the same way as PTRACE_CONT, but only until the next system call. The sys_ptrace() function will also set the PT_TRACESYS flag. When the child process arrives at the next system call, it halts and receives the SIGTRAP signal. The parent process could at this point, for example, inspect the arguments for the system call. If the process is continued with a further PTRACE_SYSCALL request, the process will halt on completion of the system call, and the result and (eventually) the error variable can then be read by the parent process.

The request PTRACE_SINGLESTEP differs from PTRACE_CONT in setting the processor's trap flag. The processor thus executes only one machine code instruction and generates a debug interrupt (No. 1). This sets the SIGTRAP signal for the process, which is then interrupted again. In other words, the PTRACE_SINGLESTEP request allows the machine code to be processed instruction by instruction. The request PTRACE_KILL continues the child process with the signal SIGKILL set. The process is then aborted.

Using PTRACE_DETACH, the process controlled by PTRACE_ATTACH is detached from the controlling process. The former process is given back its old parent process and the flags PT_PTRACED and PT_TRACESYS are canceled along with processor's trap flag.

In version 2.2 of LINUX there are also requests to select and set all general and floating point registers. The process of selecting and modifying via the user structure using single 32-bit values in modern processors is too slow. The requests for general registers are PTRACE_GETREGS and PTRACE_SETREGS. For floating point registers, the requests PTRACE_GETFPREGS and PTRACE_SETFPREGS can be used. LINUX 2.4 introduced the new commands PTRACE_GETFPXREGS and PTRACE_SETFPXREGS to support the additional MMX registers of the new x86 CPU for debugging.

Another new request is PTRACE_SETOPTIONS. It sets or deletes the flag PT_TRACESYSGOOD. It allows the parent process to recognize whether a SIGTRAP signal is from an interrupt after a system call or a normal SIGTRAP signal.

A debugger uses *ptrace* in the following way: it executes the system call *fork* and calls the function in the child process with PTRACE_TRACEME. The program to be inspected is then started by *execve*. Since the PT_PTRACED flag is set, the *execve* call sends a SIGTRAP signal to itself. The system call will not allow *ptrace* to process programs for which a S bit is set. It is not difficult to imagine the options that would otherwise be open to hackers. On return from *execve* the SIGTRAP signal is processed, the process is stopped, and the parent process is informed by being sent a SIGCHLD signal. The debugger will wait for this via the system call *wait*. It can then inspect the child process's memory, modify it and set breakpoints. The simplest way of doing this with x86 processors is to write an int3 instruction at the appropriate address in the machine code. This instruction is only one byte long.

If the debugger calls ptrace() with the request PTRACE_CONT, the child process will continue running until it processes the int3 instruction, at which point the relevant interrupt handling routine sends a SIGTRAP signal to the child process, the child process is interrupted, and the debugger is again informed. It could then, for example, simply abort the program to be inspected.

There are, of course, other ways of using this system call. The program provides a report (trace) on all the system calls that have been carried out. This is illustrated below by the output listing of strace cat motd. Naturally, strace uses PTRACE_SYSCALL.

```
%strace cat motd
uselib("/lib/ld.so")                                    = 0
getuid()                                                = 15211
geteuid()                                               = 15211
getgid()                                                = 15200
getegid()                                               = 15200
stat("/etc/ld.so.cache", {st_mode=S_IFREG|0644, st_size=3653,
...})                                                   = 0
open("/etc/ld.so.cache", O_RDONLY)                      = 3
```

```
mmap(0, 3653, PROT_READ, MAP_SHARED, 3, 0)              = 0x40000000
close(3)                                                = 0
uselib("/lib/libc.so.4.6.27")                           = 0
munmap(0x40000000, 3653)                                = 0
munmap(0x62f00000, 24576)                               = 0
brk(0)                                                  = 0x3000
brk(0x6000)                                             = 0x6000
brk(0x7000)                                             = 0x7000
stat("/etc/locale/C/libc.cat", 0xbffff1b0)              = -1 ENOENT
                             (No such file or directory)
stat("/usr/lib/locale/C/libc.cat", 0xbffff1b0)          = -1 ENOENT
                             (No such file or directory)
stat("/usr/lib/locale/libc/C/usr/share/locale/C/libc.cat", 0
bffff1b0)                                               = -1 ENOENT
                             (No such file or directory)
stat("/usr/local/share/locale/C/libc.cat", 0xbffff1b0)
                                                        = -1 ENOENT
                             (No such file or directory)
fstat(1, {st_mode=S_IFCHR|0622, st_rdev=makedev(4, 195), …}
)                                                       = 0
open("motd", O_RDONLY)                                  = -1 ENOENT
                             (No such file or directory)
write(2, "cat: ", 5cat: )                               = 5
write(2, "motd", 4motd)                                 = 4
write(2, ": No such file or directory", 27: No such file or
directory)                                              = 27
write(2, "\n", 1)                                       = 1
close(1)                                                = 0
_exit(1)                                                = ?
```

The range of functions offered by ptrace() is wide enough to debug programs in multitasking environments. On the negative side, it should be mentioned that it is very inefficient to use a single system call to read or write a 32-bit value in the address area.

5.5   SYSTEM V IPC

As long ago as 1970, the classical forms of interprocess communication – semaphores, message queues, and shared memory – were implemented in a special variant of UNIX.

These were later integrated into System V and are now known as System V IPC. LINUX supports these variants, although they are not included in POSIX. The original LINUX implementation was produced by Krishna Balasubramanian but it has been continually modified by several developers.

For interprocess communication there are also POSIX specifications that are completely different from the interfaces of the V-IPC system. Using `mmap()`, the kernel allows the creation of these interfaces in the user segment. The GNU C library in version 2.2 includes the interfaces for shared memory and semaphores according to POSIX. It is also possible to create POSIX message queues on this basis.

5.5.1 Access rights, numbers, and keys

In System V IPC, objects are created in the kernel. These must be assigned unique identifiers to ensure that operations activated by the user process are carried out on the right objects. The simplest form of identifier is a number: these numbers are dynamically generated and returned to the process generating the object. A process entirely separate from the creator process cannot access the object, as it does not know the number.

In this kind of case, the two processes will have to agree on a static key by which they can reference the IPC object. The C library has the `ftok` function, which generates a unique key from a filename and a character. A special key is `IPC_PRIVATE`, which guarantees that no existing IPC object is referenced. Access to objects generated using `IPC_PRIVATE` is only possible via their object numbers.

As with UNIX System V, access permissions are managed by the kernel in the structure `kern_ipc_perm`.

```
struct kern_ipc_perm
{
        key_t key;
        uid_t uid;                      /* owner              */
        gid_t gid;                      /* owner              */
        uid_t cuid;                     /* creator            */
        gid_t cgid;                     /* creator            */
        mode_t mode;                    /* access modes       */
        unsigned long seq;              /* counter, used
                                         * to calculate the
                                         * identifier         */
};
```

As LINUX 2.4 now supports the user and group numbers with 32 bits, the system call interface must support two versions of the interface: `IPC_OLD` and `IPC_64`. In the kernel, the data structures are treated independently of the interface that is used by the system call. The interfaces for the System V IPC system calls for the `IPC_64` version are described in the following.

If a process accesses an object, the routine `ipcperms()` is called, once again using the standard UNIX access flags for the user, the group, and others. If the effective user number of the attempting process matches that of the owner or the creator, the user access rights are checked. The same applies to checks on group access rights.

5.5.2 | Semaphores

The use of semaphores expands the classical semaphore model. An array of semaphores can be set up using a system call. It is possible to modify a number of semaphores in an array in a single operation. A process can set semaphores to any chosen value, and they can be incremented or decremented in steps greater than 1. The programmer can specify that certain operations are reversed at the end of the process.

LINUX provides the following data structure for every reserved semaphore array:

```
struct sem_array {
  struct kern_ipc_perm sem_perm;    /* access permissions      */
  time_t sem_otime;                 /* time of the last semaphore
                                     * operation               */
  time_t sem_ctime;                 /* time of the last
                                     * change                  */
  struct sem *sem_base;             /* pointer to first
                                     * semaphore               */
  struct sem_queue *sem_pending;    /* operations
                                     * to be reversed          */
  struct sem_queue **sem_pending_last;
                                    /* last operation
                                     * to be carried out       */
  struct sem_undo *undo;            /* Undo operations, to be
                                     * carried out when semaphores
                                     * are deleted             */
  unsigned long sem_nsems;          /* number of the semaphores in
                                     * this array              */
};
```

It is possible to access individual semaphores via an offset from sem_base. In the structure sem_queue there is, among other things, a wait queue in which processes whose operations cannot be executed are blocked. The structure sem manages a single semaphore:

```
struct sem {
  int semval;        /* current value    */
  int sempid;        /* process number of the last
                      * operation        */
};
```

A more complex situation is presented by the task of undoing individual semaphore operations at the end of a process. The process can require any call to a semaphore operation to be undone when it terminates: for these calls, sem_undo structures are generated dynamically.

```
struct sem_undo {
  struct sem_undo *proc_next;        /* list of all Undo structures
```

```
                                         *  in  a  process              */
  struct sem_undo *id_next;              /* list of all Undo structures
                                         *  in  a  semaphore  array     */
int semid;                               /* number of semaphore array */
short * semadj;                          /* values to which semaphores
                                         *  are  reset                  */
};
```

A `sem_undo` structure stores all the semaphore operations of a process that are to be undone. The kernel sets up a maximum of one `sem_undo` structure per process. When the process terminates, the system call *exit* attempts to reset the semaphores to the `semadj` values. The process will not block on *exit*, if this would produce a value less than zero: the value of the semaphore is simply set to 0. This feature is often referred to as "adjust on exit." The semaphore operations are implemented with the structures explained below.

```
asmlinkage long sys_semget(key_t key, int nsems, int semflg);
asmlinkage long sys_semop(int semid, struct sembuf *sops,
                          unsigned nsops);
asmlinkage long sys_semctl(int semid, int semnum, int cmd,
                          union semun arg);
```

Together with other operations in System V IPC, they are called using the system call *ipc*. This in turn calls the appropriate functions by referring to its first argument. The C library must convert all the relevant library calls into system calls. This might be called system call multiplexing.

sys_semget() is used to find the number of a semaphore array with nsems semaphores.

The values which can be used for `semflg` are listed in Table 5.6.

The `semop()` call executes the number of operations defined by means of nsops from the table `sops`. An operation is described by the structure `sembuf`:

```
struct sembuf {
  unsigned short sem_num; /* index to semaphores in the array */
  short sem_op; /* operation */
  short sem_flg; /* flags */
};
```

The value in `sem_op` is added to the semaphore. The operation blocks if the sum would yield a negative value. It must then wait for the semaphore to be incremented. If `sem_op` is 0, the process waits for the semaphore to become 0. It never blocks if `sem_op` is greater than 0. If the value increases, all the processes waiting for this event for this semaphore array are woken up. Similarly, all the processes waiting for a semaphore in the array to reach 0 are woken up if this event occurs.

Two values are possible for `sem_flg`: IPC_NOWAIT and SEM_UNDO. If IPC_NOWAIT is set, the process will never block. The effect of SEM_UNDO is to cause a `sem_undo` structure to be set up or updated for all operations in this function call. The negative operation value is entered in the `sem_undo` structure or added to the old adjust value on updating.

Table 5.6: Flags for `segmet()`

Flag	
0400	Read permission for creator
0200	Write permission for creator
0040	Read permission for creator group
0020	Write permission for creator group
0004	Read permission for all
0002	Write permission for all
IPC_CREAT	A new object will be created is it is not available
IPC_EXCL	If IPC_CREAT is set and there is such an object, the function is returned with EEXIST error

Table 5.7: Components of the `seminfo` structure

Component	Value	Description
semmni	128	Maximum number of arrays
semmns	32,000	Maximum number of semaphores in the system
semmsl	250	Maximum number of semaphores per array
semopm	32	Maximum number of operations per semop call
semvmx	32,767	Maximum value of a semaphore
semmap	32,000	Is ignored by LINUX – number of entries in a "semaphore map"
semmnu	32,000	Is ignored by LINUX – maximum number of sem_undo structures in the system
semume	32	Is ignored by LINUX – maximum number of sem_undo entries for a process
semusz	20	Is ignored by LINUX – size of sem_undo structure (value is too high)
semaem	16,383	Is ignored by LINUX – maximum value for a sem_undo structure

The `sys_semctl()` call can be used to perform a wide range of commands, and has to be entered as a parameter. Another parameter of this function is the `union semun`.

```
union semun {
  int val;                    /* value for SETVAL           */
  struct semid_ds *buf;       /* buffer for IPC_STAT & IPC_SET */
  unsigned short *array;      /* field for GETALL & SETALL  */
struct seminfo *__buf;        /* buffer for IPC_INFO        */
  void *__pad;
};
```

`IPC_INFO` enters values in the `seminfo` structure (see Table 5.7). All values are specified as fixed values by separate macro definitions.

The `ipcs` program, which displays information about IPC objects, uses the `SEM_INFO` variant of this command. This gives the number of semaphores that have been set up in `semusz` and the total number of semaphores in the system in `semaem`. `IPC_STAT` returns the `semid64_ds` structure for the semaphore array. For `ipcs` there is again the `SEM_STAT` variant, which requires the index in the table of arrays to be specified rather than the number of semaphore arrays. The `ipcs` program can provide information about all of the arrays by counting from 0 to `seminfo.semmni` in a loop and calling `semctl()` with `SEM_STAT` and the counter as arguments.

`IPC_SET` allows the owner and mode of the semaphore array to be set to new values. `IPC_SET` requires the `sem_setbuf` structure as a parameter. `IPC_RMID` deletes a semaphore array if the caller is the owner or creator of the array or if the superuser has called `semctl()`. The remaining commands for `sys_semctl()` are listed in Table 5.8.

Table 5.8: Commands for `sys_semctl()`

Command	Value returned and function
GETVAL	Value of semaphore
GETPID	Process number of last process to modify the semaphore
GETNCNT	Number of processes waiting for semaphore to be incremented
GETZCNT	Number of processes waiting for a value of 0
GETALL	Values of all semaphores of the array in the parameter field `semun.array`
SETVAL	Sets value of semaphore
SETALL	Sets values of semaphores

5.5.3 | Message queues

Messages consist of a sequence of bytes. In addition to this, IPC messages in System V include a type code. Processes send messages to the message queues and can receive messages, restricting reception to messages of a specified type if required. Messages are received in the same order in which they are entered in the message queue. The basis of the implementation in LINUX is the structure msg_queue.

```
struct msg_queue {
  struct kern_ipc_perm q_perm;      /* access permissions     */
  time_t q_stime;                   /* time of last send      */
  time_t q_rtime;                   /* time of last receipt   */
  time_t q_ctime;                   /* time of last change    */
  unsigned long q_cbytes;           /* current number of bytes in
                                     * queue                  */
  unsigned long q_qnum;             /* number of messages in
                                     * queue                  */
  unsigned long q_qbytes;           /* capacity of the
                                     * wait queue in bytes    */
  pid_t q_lspid;                    /* process number of last
                                     * sender                 */
  pid_t q_lrpid;                    /* process number of last
                                     * receiver               */
  struct list_head q_messages;      /* list of messages       */
  struct list_head q_receivers;     /* list of blocked
                                     * receivers              */
  struct list_head q_senders;       /* list of blocked
                                     * senders                */
};
```

As well as management information, the structure contains two wait queues of its own: q_senders and q_receivers. A process enters itself in q_senders if the message queue is full – that is, when it is no longer possible to send the message without exceeding the maximum number of bytes allowed in the message queue.

The message queue q_receivers includes messages that wait for messages to enter the wait queue.

The doubly linked ring list q_messages includes the messages of the message queue.

Single messages are stored in the kernel in the structure msg_msg.

```
struct msg_msgseg {
  struct msg_msgseg *next;
  /* the message segment follows here */
};
struct msg_msg {
```

```
  struct list_head m_list;          /* list of messages in
                                     * message queue              */
  long m_type;                       /* message type              */
  int m_ts;                          /* length of message         */
  struct msg_msgseg* next;           /* next segment of
                                     * message                    */
/* message or first message segment
 * follows here */
}
```

LINUX stores the message immediately after this structure. If structure and message are longer than a page of memory, the message is segmented, where the following segments only include the structure msg_msgseg. In this way the available memory can be used very efficiently.

As with semaphores, functions are now required for initialization, for sending and receiving messages, for returning information, and for releasing message queues.

Although the operations to be performed are relatively simple, access protection and the updating of statistical data make things more complicated.

The relevant library functions call the system call *ipc*, which passes on the call to appropriate kernel functions. The function sys_msgget() creates a message queue using the standard parameters for the IPC get functions.

```
int sys_msgget (key_t key, int msgflg);
```

The parameter key is a mandatory key and msgflg is the same as for the flags in semget() (see Table 5.6). Messages are sent using the function sys_msgsnd().

```
struct msgbuf {
  long mtype;            /* message type           */
  char mtext[1];         /* text of message        */
};
int sys_msgsnd (int msqid, struct msgbuf *msgp, size_t msgsz,
int msgflg);
```

The parameter msgsz is the length of the text in mtext and must be no greater than MSGMAX. The process blocks if the new number of bytes in the message queue exceeds the value in the component msg_qbytes, the permitted maximum. It only resumes processing once other processes have read messages from the queue or when non-blocked signals are sent to the process. Blocking can be prevented by setting the flag IPC_NOWAIT.

A message can be read back from the queue by means of sys_msgrcv().

```
int sys_msgrcv (int msqid, struct msgbuf *msgp, size_t msgsz,
                long msgtyp, int msgflg);
```

The messages to be received are specified in msgtyp. If the value is 0, the first message in the queue is selected. For a value greater than zero, the first message of the given type in the message queue is read. However, if the flag MSG_EXCEPT is set, the first message not matching the message type is received. If msgtyp is less than zero, the function selects the first message of the type with the smallest integer value that is smaller than or equal to the absolute value of msgtyp. The length of the message must be smaller than msgsz. However, if MSG_NOERROR is set, only the first msgsz bytes of the message will be read. If no message matching the specification is found, the process blocks. This can be prevented by setting the IPC_NOWAIT flag.

Another function that can be used to manipulate the message queue is sys_msgctl(). This function is very similar to sys_semctl().

```
int sys_msgctl (int msqid, int cmd, struct msqid_ds *buf);
```

The command IPC_INFO outputs the maxima for the values relevant to message queues in the structure msginfo. These maxima are listed in Table 5.9. LINUX uses only a small number of these values.

Table 5.9: Components of the msginfo structure

Component	Value	Explanation
msgmni	16	Maximum number of message queues
msgmax	8,192	Maximum size of a message in bytes
msgmnb	16,384	Standard value for the maximum size of a message queue in bytes
msgmap	16,384	Not used – number of entries in a "message map"
msgpool	256	Not used – size of "message pool"
msgtql	16,384	Not used – number of "system message headers"
msgssz	16	Not used – size of message segment
msgseg	0x4000	Not used – maximum number of segments

The macro for each of the components is defined in msg.h. The command MSG_INFO is the variant of IPC_INFO designed for the ipcs program. This gives the number of wait queues used in msgpool, the number of messages in msgmap, and the total number of bytes of messages saved in the system in msgtql.

IPC_STAT copies the msqid_ds structure of the referenced message queue to the user memory area. Like SEM_STAT, the MSG_STAT variant allows an index to the system-internal table of the message queue as a parameter. This LINUX feature is also used by the ipcs command.

IPC_SET enables the owner, mode, and maximum possible number of bytes for the message queue to be modified. Processes without superuser rights must not set this value higher than MSGMNB (16,384). Without this restriction, a normal process would be in a position, by sending messages to the queue after setting this value high, to allocate kernel memory which cannot be moved to the secondary memory.

The owner or creator of the message queue as well as the superuser can delete the queue by means of IPC_RMID.

Under LINUX 2.0, message queues have the task of communicating with the kerneld daemon. This daemon was responsible for loading kernel modules via modprobe, when the kernel required it. Now the LINUX 2.2 kernel thread kmod fulfills this task by calling this program directly. Thus a whole series of specific modifications would be superfluous to the message queue and could be deleted.

5.5.4 | Shared memory

Shared memory is the fastest form of interprocess communication. Processes using a shared section of memory can exchange data using the usual machine code commands for reading and writing data. In all other methods this is only possible by recourse to system calls to copy the data from the memory area of one process to that of the other. The drawback of shared memory is that the processes need to use additional synchronization mechanisms to ensure that race conditions do not arise. Faster communication is only achieved by increased programming effort. Performing the synchronization via other system calls makes for a portable implementation, but reduces the speed advantage. Another option would be to exploit the machine code instructions for conditional setting of a bit in the processors for different architectures: these instructions set a bit depending on its value. As this occurs within a machine code instruction, the operation cannot be halted by an interrupt. These instructions provide a very simple and quick way of implementing a system of mutual exclusion. In Section 4.2.2, it was explained how complex the shared use of memory areas is. Since version 2.0 it has become possible, with mmap(), to map memory areas that can be written to by several processes. This mechanism can also be used to implement shared memory applications.

As in the other IPC variants of System V, a shared segment of memory is identified with a number, which refers to a shmid_kernel data structure containing public information, only used in the kernel. This segment can be mapped to the user segment in the virtual address space by a process with the aid of an attach operation, and the procedure can be reversed with a detach operation. For simplicity, we will refer to the memory managed by the shmid_kernel structure as a segment, although this term is already used for the segments of the virtual address space in x86 processors.

```
struct shmid_kernel
{
  struct kern_ipc_perm shm_perm;    /* access permissions     */
  struct file * shm_file;           /* file in the SHM file
                                     * system                  */
  int id;                           /* Id                      */
```

```
unsigned long shm_nattch;        /* number of attachments  */
unsigned long shm_segsz;         /* size of segment         */
time_t shm_atim;                 /* time of last attach     */
time_t shm_dtim;                 /* time of last detach     */
time_t shm_ctim;                 /* time of creation        */
pid_t shm_cprid;                 /* creator PID             */
pid_t shm_lprid;                 /* PID of last
                                  * operation               */
};
```

The modal components in the `kern_ipc_perm` structure are used to store two flags. The flag `SHM_LOCKED` prevents pages in the shared memory segment from being swapped out to secondary devices, while `SHM_DEST` specifies that the segment is released on the last detach operation.

The field `shm_file` refers to a file in the SHM file system, created with the segment. The SHM file system is not assigned to any device and only uses the memory page cache. This file can then be mapped in the memory area of a process via `do_mmap()`; this means that the memory management treats the LINUX System V shared memory as the memory mapped via `mmap()`.

This is new for LINUX 2.4 and has saved a number of codes for the special treatment of System V shared memory. The kernel automatically mounts the SHM file system at an internal mount point that is not visible outside the kernel. It is possible to mount a further shared memory file system, for example under /dev/shm. Logically, the shared memory segments of the System V IPCs are not visible there. However, the file system mounted under /dev/shmem can be used to convert the POSIX shared memory.

There are also kernel patches that allow the reading of the files created in the shared memory file system via `read()` and `write()`. It is possible to use this file system as a file system for temporary files, for instance. Solaris uses such a file system for the /tmp directory.

By calling `sys_shmget()` a process can create a reference to a segment.

```
asmlinkage long sys_shmget(key_t key, size_t size, int shmflg);
```

The parameter `size` specifies the size of the segment. If the segment has already been set up, the parameter may be smaller than the actual size. The flags listed in Table 5.6 may again be set in the parameter `shmflg`.

This function only initializes the `shmid_kernel` data structure. The entry in the kernel-internal SHM file system is created, although no memory page is reserved for the file.

By far the most important function when using shared memory is `sys_shmat()`. This maps the segment to the process's user segment.

```
int sys_shmat (int shmid, char *shmaddr, int shmflg,
        unsigned long *addr);
```

The parameter shmaddr can be used by the process to specify the address at which the segment is to be mapped. If this is zero, the function will find a free area of memory for itself and the address will then be returned under addr. This rather complicated procedure using the parameter is unavoidable, since otherwise addresses over 2 gigabytes would be interpreted as errors on return to the user process.

The flags allowed in shmflg are SHM_RND and SHM_RDONLY. If SHM_RND is set, the address that is passed will be rounded down to a page boundary, as LINUX only allows segments to be mapped to a page boundary. SHM_RDONLY indicates whether the mapped segment is to be read-only.

To map the memory area, do_mmap() has to be called. Again, the shared memory area cannot yet be allocated. This only happens when access to a memory page in the shared memory segment displayed is not successful. shmem_nopage() then acts so that a corresponding memory page is mapped. It checks whether the memory page has been entered into the swap space. If it has, the memory page is mapped, otherwise a new memory page is allocated.

The function sys_shmdt() removes a common segment from the user segment of a process.

```
int sys_shmdt (char *shmaddr);
```

The sys_shmctl() function is the counterpart of the functions sys_semctl() and sys_msgctl() that were mentioned earlier.

```
int sys_shmctl (int shmid, int cmd, struct shmid_ds *buf);
```

A call to this function using the IPC_INFO command will return the maximum values that apply when using LINUX's implementation of shared memory. The shminfo structure used for this is summarized in Table 5.10.

Table 5.10: Components of the shminfo structure for the IPC_INFO command

Component	Value for x86	Explanation
shmmni	4,096	Maximum number of shared memory segments
shmmax	33,554,432	Maximum size of a segment in bytes
shmmin	1	Minimum size of a segment
shmall	2,097,152	Minimum number of shared pages of memory in entire system
shmseg	4,096	Permitted number of segments per process

Even though the value 1 is accepted for the size of the segment, LINUX always allocates at least one memory page (4,096 bytes) for general use.

The SHM_INFO command fills the shm_info structure, which is shown in Table 5.11. The IPC_STAT command can be called to read the segment data structure shmid_ds. The SHM_STAT variant of this command performs the same task, but needs an index to the table of segment data structures as a parameter in place of the segment number.

Table 5.11: Components of the shm_info structure for the SHM_INFO command

Components	Explanation
used_ids	Number of segments used
shm_tot	Total number of shared pages
shm_rss	Number of shared pages allocated in main memory
shm_swp	Number of currently swapped pages
swap_attempts	Attempts to swap shared pages
swap_successes	Number of shared pages swapped since the start-up of the system

If sys_shmctl() is called with the command IPC_SET, the owner and the access mode for a segment can be modified by the old owner or the process that initialized the shared memory segment.

Unlike the functions sys_semctl() and sys_msgctl(), the IPC_RMID command does not enable the IPC data structure to be released in all cases. There may still be processes with the segment mapped. To mark the segment structure as deleted, the SHM_DEST flag in the mode field of the ipc_perm component is set.

The commands SHM_LOCK and SHM_UNLOCK allow the superuser to disable and re-enable the swapping of pages in a segment.

5.5.5 The ipcs and ipcrm commands

One drawback to the System V IPC is that testing and developing programs that use it can easily give rise to the problem whereby IPC resources remain present after the test programs have been completed, when this was not intended. The ipcs command allows the user to investigate the situation and to delete these resources using ipcrm.

For example, a program may have set up three semaphore arrays. Information can be obtained via ipcs on the shared memory segments, semaphore arrays, and message queues to which the user has access.

```
% ipcs
-- shared memory segments ----
shmid   owner  perms bytes nattch status
```

```
-- Semaphore Arrays ----
semid    owner  perms  nsems  status
kunitz   666    1
1153     kunitz 666    1
1154     kunitz 666    1

-- Message Queues ----
msqid    owner  perms  used-bytes    messages
```

ipcrm can delete one of these semaphore arrays. The command can be used similarly for message queues and shared memory segments.

```
%         ipcrm sem    1153

resource deleted
%        ipcs

-- shared memory segments ----
shmid    owner  perms  bytes  nattch status

-- Semaphore Arrays ----
semid    owner  perms  nsems  status
1152     kunitz        666    1
1154     kunitz        666    1

-- Message Queues ----
msqid    owner  perms  used-bytes    messages
```

In LINUX 2.4, information about the System V IPC resources is available under /proc/sysvipc. In /proc/sys/kernel PC parameters can be modified without requiring new compilation of the kernel.

5.6   IPC WITH SOCKETS

So far, we have only looked at forms of interprocess communication supporting communication between processes in one computer. The socket programming interface provides for communication via a network as well as locally on a single computer. The advantage of this interface is that it allows network applications to be programmed using the long-established UNIX concept of file descriptors. A particularly good example of this is the INET daemon.

The daemon waits for incoming network service requests and then calls the appropriate service program using the socket file descriptor as standard input and output. For very simple services, the program called need not contain a single line of network-relevant code.

In this chapter we limit ourselves to the use and implementation of UNIX domain sockets. Sockets for the INET domain will be explained in Chapter 8.

5.6.1 A simple example

Similarly to FIFOs, UNIX domain sockets enable programs to exchange data in a connection-oriented way. The following example illustrates how this works. The same include files are used both for client and server programs.

```
/* sc.h */
#include <sys/types.h>
#include <sys/socket.h>
#include <sys/un.h>
#include <stdio.h>
#include <stdlib.h>
#include <unistd.h>
#define SERVER "/tmp/server"
```

The job of the client is to send a message to the server along with its process number and to write the server's response to the standard output.

```
/* cli.c - client connection-oriented model */
#include "sc.h"
int main(void)
{
        int sock_fd;
        struct sockaddr_un unix_addr;
        char buf[2048];
        int n;
        if ((sock_fd = socket(AF_UNIX, SOCK_STREAM, 0)) < 0)
        {
                perror("cli: socket()");
                exit(1);
        }
        unix_addr.sun_family = AF_UNIX;
        strcpy(unix_addr.sun_path, SERVER);
        if (connect(sock_fd, (struct sockaddr*) &unix_addr,
                sizeof(unix_addr.sun_family) +
                strlen(unix_addr.sun_path)) < 0)
        {
```

```
                perror("cli: connect()");
                exit(1);
        }
        sprintf(buf, "Hello Server, this is %d.\n", getpid());
        n = strlen(buf) + 1;
        if (write(sock_fd, buf, n) != n)
        {
                perror("cli: write()");
                exit(1);
        }
        printf("Client sent: %s", buf);
        if ((n = read(sock_fd, buf, 2047)) < 0)
        {
                perror("cli: read()");
                exit(1);
        }
        buf[n] = 0;
        while (buf[n] == 0) { n--; }
        if (buf[n] == '\n')
        buf[n] = '\0';
        printf("Client received: %s\n", buf);
        exit(0);
}
```

First a socket file descriptor is created with socket(). Then the address of the server is generated. For UNIX domain sockets this consists of a filename – in our example this is /tmp/server. The client then attempts to set up a connection to the server using connect(). If this is successful, it is possible to send data to the server using standard read and write functions. To be precise, the client does this by sending the message

Hello Server! This is *Process number of client*.

To enable the server to reply, we need a few more lines of C programming.

```
/* srv.c - server, connection-oriented model */
#include <signal.h>
#include "sc.h"
static void stop(int n)
{
  unlink(SERVER);
  exit(0);
}
static void server(void)
```

```
{
  int sock_fd, cli_sock_fd;
  struct sockaddr_un unix_addr;
  char buf[2048];
  int n, addr_len;
  pid_t pid;
  char *pc;

  signal(SIGINT, stop);
  signal(SIGQUIT, stop);
  signal(SIGTERM, stop);
if ((sock_fd = socket(AF_UNIX, SOCK_STREAM, 0)) < 0)
{
  perror("srv: socket()");
  exit(1);
}
unix_addr.sun_family = AF_UNIX;
strcpy(unix_addr.sun_path, SERVER);
addr_len = sizeof(unix_addr.sun_family) +
        strlen(unix_addr.sun_path);
unlink(SERVER);
if (bind(sock_fd, (struct sockaddr *) &unix_addr,
        addr_len) < 0)
{
  perror("srv: bind()");
  exit(1);
}
if (listen(sock_fd, 5) < 0)
{
  perror("srv: client()");
  unlink(SERVER); exit(1);
}
while ((cli_sock_fd =
        accept(sock_fd, (struct sockaddr*) &unix_addr,
                &addr_len)) >= 0)
{
  if ((n = read(cli_sock_fd, buf, 2047)) < 0)
  {
        perror("srv: read()");
        close(cli_sock_fd);
        continue;
  }
```

```
        buf[n] = '\0';
        for (pc = buf; *pc != '\0' &&
        (*pc < '0' || *pc > '9'); pc++);
        pid = atol(pc);
        if (pid != 0)
        {
        sprintf(buf, "Hello client %d, this is the server.\n",
        pid);
        n = strlen(buf) + 1;
        if (write(cli_sock_fd, buf, n) != n)
        perror("srv: write()");
        }
        close(cli_sock_fd);
        }
        perror("srv: accept()");
        unlink(SERVER); exit(1);
  }
  int main(void)
  {
        int r;
        if ((r = fork()) == 0) server();
        if (r < 0)
        {
        perror("srv: fork()");
        exit(1);
        }
        exit(0);
}
```

The server calls fork() and terminates its running. The child process continues running in the background and installs the handling routine for interrupt signals.

Once a socket file descriptor has been opened, the server's own address is bound to this socket and a file is created under the path name given in the address. By limiting the access rights to this file, the server can reduce the number of users able to communicate with it. A client's connect call is only successful if this file exists and the client possesses the necessary access rights. The call listen() is necessary to inform the kernel that the process is now ready to accept connections to this socket. It then calls accept() to wait.

If a connection is set up by a client using connect(), accept() will return a new socket file descriptor. This will then be used to receive messages from the client and reply to them. The server simply writes back:

Hello Client *process number of client*, this is the Server.

The server then closes the file descriptor for this connection and again calls `accept()` to offer its services to the next client.

The read and write operations usually block the socket descriptor if either no data is present or there is no more space in the buffer. If the `O_NONBLOCK` flag has been set with `fcntl()`, these functions do not block.

Since version 2.0 it has been possible to use UNIX domain sockets under LINUX in the connectionless mode by means of the functions `sendto()` and `recvfrom()`.

5.6.2 The implementation of UNIX domain sockets

A socket is represented in the kernel by the data structure socket. Data contained in the sockets is stored in `sk_buff` structures. These are described in Chapter 8.

There is a range of socket-specific functions, such as `socket()` and `setsockopt()`. These are all implemented via a system call, `socketcall`, which calls all necessary functions by reference to the first parameter. The file operations `read()`, `write()`, `poll()`, `ioctl()`, `lseek()`, `close()`, and `fasync()` are called directly via file operations in the file descriptors.

The socket functions in the user area have affiliated functions in the kernel that are provided with the `prefix sys_`. These functions support different protocols and address families. The function `sys_socket()` determines which function has to be initialized by the socket by using an address family table. All other socket operations use protocol-specific functions included in the operation vector `proto_ops`, which is contained in the socket structure. The semantics of operations for UNIX domain sockets are briefly described below.

```
long sys_socket(int family, int type, int protocol);
```

This sets up a socket file descriptor. This function calls the protocol operation `unix_create()`. This function may block. The status of the sockets on completion of this operation is `SS_UNCONNECTED`.

```
long sys_bind(int fd, struct sockaddr *umyaddr, int addrlen);
```

The address `umyaddr` is bound to the socket. The protocol operation naturally tests whether the address belongs to the UNIX address family, and attempts to set up the socket address. `sys_bind()` is only successful if the socket address file has not yet been bound by another program.

```
long sys_connect(int fd, struct sockaddr *uservaddr,
                int addrlen);
```

This operation attempts to bind the socket to the address `uservaddr`. This address must of course be a UNIX domain address. An attempt is made to open the server's socket address file which, for datagram sockets, is sufficient.

With stream sockets, the protocol operation `unix_connect()` checks whether any connections are being accepted at the server address. If the operation has been successful, the socket status is `SS_CONNECTED`.

```
long sys_listen(int fd, int backlog);
```

With this operation the server informs the kernel that connections are being accepted, from now on. The status in the `sock` structure is set to `TCP_LISTEN` and `max_ack_backlog` is given the value of the parameter `backlog`.

```
long sys_accept(int fd, struct sockaddr *upeer_sockaddr,
                int *upeer_addrlen);
```

A process can only call this operation if `listen()` has been called for this socket previously. The process blocks if there are no processes that have called `connect()` for the address of the socket.

```
long sys_getsockname(int fd, struct sockaddr *usockaddr,
                int *usockaddr_len);
```

The protocol operation `unix_getname()` is the basis of this function. The address bound to the socket is returned.

```
int sys_getpeername(int fd, struct sockaddr *usockaddr, int *usockaddr_len);
```

This operation is also based on the `unix_getname()` protocol operation for the socket. However, a parameter for this function specifies that the address of the bound socket (the peer) should be returned.

```
long sys_socketpair(int family, int type, int protocol,
                int usockvec[2]);
```

Two sockets descriptors are generated and bound to each other

```
long sys_send(int fd, void * buff, int len, unsigned flags);
long sys_sendto(int fd, void * buff, int len, unsigned flags,
                struct sockaddr *addr, int addr_len);
long sys_sendmsg(int fd, struct msghdr *msg, unsigned int flags);
```

These are the different socket operations for sending messages. Depending on whether the socket is a datagram or a stream socket, `unix_dgram_sendmsg()` or `unix_stream_sendmsg()` is called. The messages are divided across several `sk_buff` structures and written into the receive list of the peer socket.

```
long sys_recv(int fd, void * buff, int len, unsigned flags);
long sys_recvfrom(int fd, void * ubuf, int size, unsigned flags,
                struct sockaddr *addr, int *addr_len);
long sys_recvmsg(int fd, struct msghdr *msg, unsigned int flags);
```

These functions call `unix_dgram_recvmsg()` or `unix_stream_recvmsg()` depending on whether it is a datagram or a stream socket. This operation blocks if the peer has not written any data.

```
long sys_shutdown(int fd, int how)
```

This socket operation is activated via `unix_shutdown()`. The socket status is marked as to whether sending and receiving is still allowed.

```
long sys_getsockopt(int fd, int level, int optname, char *optval,
                int *optlen)
long sys_setsockopt(int fd, int level, int optname, char *optval,
                int optlen)
```

As there are no specific options for UNIX sockets, only the public socket options are supported on the `SOL_SOCKET` layer.

Since some processes should be able to use sockets as normal file descriptors, the functionality of almost all operations must be supported. Only the operations `readdir()` and `fsync()` are not supported. Sockets have a special treatment `sock_no_open()` for the open calls, UNIX sockets have established for `mmap()` `sock_no_mmap()`. The `lseek()` treatment routine only returns `ESPIPE`.

Most of the operations are treated generally for all sockets on the socket layer. UNIX sockets treat `poll()` and `ioctl()` in a special way, and the `close()` call is treated via `unix_release()`. The function `unix_ioctl()` enables the user process to query the number of the bytes via `SIOCOUTQ`. The IOCTL command `SIOCINQ` questions the number of bytes in the send queue. It should also be mentioned that the process can be prevented from blocking while performing this operation by setting the descriptor's `O_NONBLOCK` flag. The file set up using `bind()` can only be opened and closed.

The flag `S_IFSOCK` in the file's inode structure is set by marking the file as a special socket address file. An `ls -lF` for the socket address file in the example will produce the message:

```
% ls -lF server
srwxr-xr-x   1   kunitz   mi89   0   Mar   7   00:09   server=
```

6 THE LINUX FILE SYSTEM

In the PC field, variety in a file system is common: practically every operating system has its own file system. And each of these of course claims to be "faster, better and more secure" than its predecessors.

The large number of file systems supported by LINUX is undoubtedly one of the main reasons why LINUX has gained acceptance so quickly in its short life. Not every user is in a position to put in the time and effort to convert his or her old data to a new file system.

The range of file systems supported is made possible by the unified interface of the LINUX kernel. This is the *Virtual File System Switch* (VFS), which will be referred to below simply as the "virtual file system." Note that it is not a file system on its own but an interface providing a clearly defined link between the operating system kernel and the different file systems (illustrated in Figure 6.1).

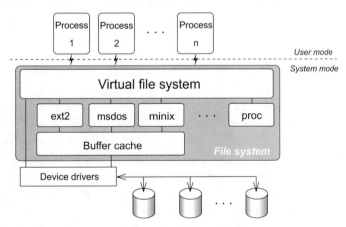

Figure 6.1: The layers of the file system.

The virtual file system supplies the applications with the system calls for file management (see Section A.2), maintains internal structures, and passes tasks on to the appropriate actual file system. Another important task of the VFS is the performance of default actions. As a rule, for instance, no file system implementation will actually provide an `lseek()` function, as the functions of `lseek()` are provided by a default action of VFS. We are therefore justified in calling VFS a file system.

In this chapter, we take a closer look at how VFS works and how it interacts with specific file system implementations. The implementation of the *Proc* file system will be looked at as an example. In addition to this, we will examine the design and structure of the *Ext2* file system serving as the standard LINUX file system.

6.1 BASIC PRINCIPLES

The importance of a good file management system is often underestimated. Where human beings can use their memory or a notebook, a computer has to resort to other means.

A central demand made of a file system is the *purposeful structuring* of data. When selecting a purposeful structure, however, two factors that should not be neglected are the *speed of access* to data and a facility for *random access*.

Random access is made possible by block-oriented devices, which are divided into a specific number of equal-sized blocks. When using these, LINUX also has the buffer cache described in Section 4.3 at its disposal. Using the functions of the buffer cache, it is possible to access any of the sequentially numbered blocks in a given device. The file system itself must be capable of ensuring unique allocation of the data to the hardware blocks.

In UNIX, the data is stored in a hierarchical file system containing files of different types. These consist not only of normal files and directories but also of device files, FIFOs (*named pipes*), symbolic links, and sockets. These enable all resources of the system to be accessed via files.

From a programming point of view, files are simply data flows of unspecified content containing no other structuring. The file system takes on the task of managing these "data flows" efficiently and allowing the *representation of different file types* (including pseudo files).

In UNIX, the information required for management is kept strictly apart from the data and collected in separate inode structures for each file. Figure 6.2 shows the arrangement of a typical UNIX inode. The information contained includes access times, access rights, and the allocation of data to blocks using the physical media. As is shown in the figure, the inode already contains a few block numbers to ensure efficient access to small files (which are often encountered under UNIX). Access to larger files is provided via indirect blocks, which also contain block numbers. Every file is represented by just one inode, which means that, within a file system, each inode has a unique number and the file itself can also be accessed using this number.

Directories allow the file system to be given a hierarchical structure. These are also implemented as files, but the kernel assumes them to contain pairs consisting of a filename and its inode number. There is no reason why a file cannot be accessed via a number of names, which can even be held in different directories (in the form of a hard link). In older versions of UNIX it was possible to modify directory files using a simple editor, but to ensure consistency this is no longer permitted in more recent versions. LINUX file systems will not even allow these to be read using a normal systems call.

The basic structure is the same for all the different UNIX file systems (see Figure 6.3). Each file system starts with a boot block. This block is reserved for the code required to boot the operating system (see Appendix D). As file systems should usually be able to exist on any block-oriented device, and on each device, in principle, they will always have the same structure (to ensure uniformity), the boot block will be present whether or not the computer is booted from the device in question.

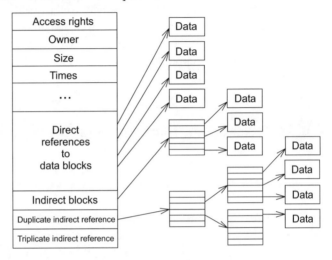

Figure 6.2: The structure of a UNIX inode.

All information which is essential for managing the file system is held in the superblock. This is followed by a number of inode blocks containing the inode structures for the file system. The remaining blocks for the device provide the space for the data.

These *data blocks* thus contain ordinary files along with the directory entries and the indirect blocks.

As file systems must be able to be implemented on different devices, the implementation on the file system must also adapt to different device-level characteristics, such as block devices, and so on. At the same time, all operating systems strive for *device independence*, which will make it immaterial as to what media the data has been stored on. In LINUX, this task is carried out using file system implementation, enabling the virtual file system to work with device-independent structures.

In UNIX, the separate file systems are not accessed via device identifiers (such as drive numbers), as is the case for other operating systems, but are combined in a hierarchical directory tree.

The arrangement is built up by the action of mounting the file system, which adds another file system (of whatever type) to an existing directory tree. A new file system can be mounted onto any directory. This original directory is then known as the mount point and is occupied by the root directory of the new file system along with its subdirectories and files. Unmounting the file system releases the hidden directory structure again.

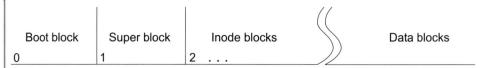

| Boot block | Super block | Inode blocks | | Data blocks |
| 0 | 1 | 2 . . . | | |

Figure 6.3:   Schematic structure of a UNIX file system.

A further aspect of major importance to the quality of a file system is data security. On the one hand, this comprises facilities to maintain consistency and a mechanism to ensure data protection. On the other hand, the file system should behave robustly in the event of system errors, corruption of data, or program crashes. The prime example for this is the new XFS from SGI.

6.2   THE REPRESENTATION OF FILE SYSTEMS IN THE KERNEL

The representation of data on a floppy disk or hard disk may differ considerably from case to case. In the end, however, the actual representation of data in LINUX's memory works in the same way.

Here, once again, LINUX sticks closely to its "model" UNIX, because the management structures for the file systems are very similar to the logical structure of a UNIX file system.

These are the responsibility of the VFS, which calls the file-system-specific functions for the various implementations to fill the structures. These functions are provided by every current implementation and are made known to the VFS via the function `register_filesystem()`, by the fact that they are appended to the list of known file systems.

```
int register_filesystem(struct file_system_type * fs)
{
        int res = 0;
        struct file_system_type ** p;
        ...
        write_lock(&file_systems_lock);
        p = find_filesystem(fs->name);
        if (*p)
                res = -EBUSY;
        else
                *p = fs;
        write_unlock (&file_systems_lock);
        return res;
}
```

In the example with the *Ext2* file systems this happens with `init_ext2_fs()`, which in turn calls the `register` function[1]:

```
static DECLARE_FSTYPE_DEV (ext2_fs_type, "ext2", ext2_read_super);
static int __init init_ext2_fs (void)
{
        return register_filesystem (&ext2_fs_type);
}
```

The VFS therefore contains the name of the file systems (`"ext2"`), a function to mount, as well as (via the macro expansion) a flag, which shows whether it is absolutely necessary to mount a device. The `read_super()` function submitted forms the mounting interface. Other functions of the file system implementation are given to the virtual file systems first.

The function sets up the structure `file_system_type`, which was submitted to it in a simply linked list. `file_systems` shows the beginning of this list.

```
struct file_system_type {
  const char *name;
  int fs_flags;
  struct super_block *(*read_super) (struct super_block *,
  void *, int);
  struct module *owner;
  struct vfsmount *kern_mnt;
  struct file_system_type *next;
}
static struct file_system_type *file_systems;
```

In older LINUX kernels (before version 1.1.8) the structures were still managed in a static table, as all the file system implementations were known when the kernel was compiled. With the introduction of modules it became desirable to load new file systems after the LINUX system had started running.

Different flags can be used when registering a file system. These control the behavior of the kernels, if a file system is later mounted using this type. In version 2.4 the LINUX kernel defines the following registration flags:

FS_REQUIRES_DEV This file system uses a device for mounting.
FS_NO_DCACHE Instruction to the VFS, not to use the directory cache (see Section.2.4) for this file system. Presently not implemented.
FS_NO_PRELIM Presently not implemented.
FS_SINGLE The file system has only one superblock.
FS_NOMOUNT No mount operations can be executed later on this file system.
FS_LITTER If a file system is unmounted with this flag, all `Dcache` entries for this file system will be deleted.

1 The conversion is carried out in the file `super.c` of the respective file system.

After a file system implementation by VFS is registered, it becomes possible to mount file systems of this type.

6.2.1 Mounting

Before a file can be accessed, the file system containing the file must be mounted. This can be done using either the system call *mount* or the function `mount_root()`.

The `mount_root()` function takes care of mounting the first file system (the root file system). It is called at the start of the system after registration of the device and file system implementation of the `do_basic_setup()` function.

Every mounted file system is represented by a `super_block` structure. These structures are placed in a dynamic table `super_blocks` held by the `struct list_head` type. The maximum length of this list is limited by the `max_super_blocks` variable, initialized by `NR_SUPER`. It can, however, be changed at runtime with the `Systlc` interface (see Section A.1).

The function `read_super()` of the virtual file system is used to initialize the superblock. It creates an empty superblock, puts it in the superblock list, and calls the function provided by every file system implementation to create the superblock. This file-system-specific function will have been made known on registering the implementation with the VFS. When called, it will contain the superblock structure filled with general information (the device and the flags, the latter filled according to Table 6.1), a character string (`void *`) containing further mount options for the file system, and a flag `silent` which shows whether the mounting failed using messages. This flag is only used by the `mount_root()` kernel function, because this calls all available `read_super()` functions in the various system implementations when mounting the root file system, and constant error messages during start-up would be disruptive.

Table 6.1: The file-system-independent mount flags in the superblock

Macro	Value	Remark
MS_RDONLY	1	File system is read only
MS_NOSUID	2	Ignores S-bits
MS_NODEV	4	Inhibits access to device files
MS_NOEXEC	8	Inhibits execution of program
MS_SYNCHRONOUS	16	Immediately writes to disk
MS_REMOUNT	32	Flags have been changed
MS_MANDLOCK	64	Allows absolute file access locking
MS_NOATIME	1,024	Time of the last access is not updated
MS_NODIRATIME	2,048	Time of the last access to the directory is not updated

6.2.2 The superblock

The file-system-specific function `read_super()` reads information from the corresponding block device if necessary, using the functions of the LINUX cache introduced in Section 4.3. This is also the reason why a process is necessary for mounting file systems.[2] This can be stopped by the device driver since the access to the corresponding device takes time. The sleep wake-up mechanism (see Section 3.1.5) is used for this, which works with processes. The LINUX superblock looks like the following:

```
struct super_block {
  struct list_head s_list;         /* serve for chaining
                                    * in the list of superblocks */
  kdev_t s_dev;                    /* device for the file system */
  unsigned long s_blocksize;       /* block size                */
  unsigned char s_blocksize_bits;  /* ld (block size)           */
  unsigned char s_lock;            /* superblock lock           */
  unsigned char s_rd_only;         /* not used (= 0)            */
  unsigned char s_dirt;            /* superblock changed        */
  struct file_system_type *s_type; /* file system type          */
  struct super_operations *s_op;   /* superblock operations     */
  struct dquot_operations *dq_op;  /* quota operations          */
  unsigned long s_flags;           /* flags                     */
  unsigned long s_magic;           /* file system identifier    */
  struct dentry *s_root;           /* DEntry from '/'           */
  wait_queue_head_t s_wait;        /* s_lock waiting queue      */
  struct list_head s_dirty;        /* list of all dirty inodes  */
  struct list_head s_files;
  struct block_device *s_bdev;     /* block device structure    */
  struct list_head s_mounts;       /* list of mountings         */

  union {
        struct minix_sb_info minix_sb;
        ...
        void *generic_sdp;
  } u;                                    /* file-system-specific
                                          * information */
  struct semaphore s_vfs_rename_sem;      /* semaphore for renaming
                                          * directories      */
  struct semaphore s_nfsd_free_path_sem;  /* semaphore for access
                                          * to sub-directories */
};
```

2 When the root file system is mounted, no user process yet exists; however, the Kernel-Thread `init()` which calls `do_basic_setup()` is available.

The superblock contains information about the complete file system, such as block size, access rights, and type of file system. Furthermore, the union at the end of the structure contains special information about the corresponding file system. Therefore the character string `generic_sdp` is available for special file system modules.

The `s_lock` and `s_wait` components ensure synchronization of accesses to the superblock. The functions `lock_super()` and `unlock_super()`, defined in the file `<linux/locks.h>`, are used for this.

```
extern inline void lock_super(struct super_block * sb)
{
  if (sb->s_lock)
        __wait_on_super(sb);
  sb->s_lock = 1;
}
extern inline void unlock_super(struct super_block * sb)
{
  sb->s_lock = 0;
  wake_up(&sb->s_wait);
}
```

In addition to this, a reference to the `dentry` (directory entry) of the filesystem `s_root` is in the superblock. A further task of the function `read_super()` of the concrete file system implementation is therefore to provide the root inode of the file system so that it can be changed into a `dentry` and written in the superblock. This can be done by the functions of the VFS, as well as by the `iget()` function which is described later, provided that the components `s_dev` and `s_op` are set correctly.

6.2.3 Superblock operations

In the vector `s_op`, the superblock structure provides functions for accessing the file system, and these form the basis for further processing of the file system.

```
struct super_operations {
  void (*read_inode) (struct inode *);
  void (*write_inode) (struct inode *);
  void (*put_inode) (struct inode *);
  void (*delete_inode) (struct inode *);
  int (*notify_change) (struct dentry * dentry,
                        struct iattr * attr);
  void (*put_super) (struct super_block *);
  void (*write_super) (struct super_block *);
  void (*statfs) (struct super_block *, struct statfs *, int);
  int (*remount_fs) (struct super_block *, int *, char *);
```

```
  void (*clear_inode) (struct inode *);
  void (*umount_begin) (struct super_block *);
};
```

The functions in the `super_operations` structure are used to read and write an individual inode, to write the superblock, and to read file system information. This means that the superblock operations therefore contain functions to transform the specific representation of the superblock and inode on the data media into their general form in the memory and vice versa. As a result, this layer completely hides the actual representation. Strictly speaking, the inodes and the superblock do not even have to exist.

An example of this is the MS-DOS system, in which the FAT and the information in the boot block are transferred to the UNIX-internal view consisting of the superblock and inodes. If a superblock operation is not implemented, that is, if the pointer is `NULL`, no further action will take place.

`read_inode(inode)` This function must be implemented and is responsible for filling the submitted inode structure. It is called by the `get_new_inode()` function already mentioned, which covers the following entries:

```
  inode->i_sb = sb;
  inode->i_dev = sb->s_dev;
  inode->i_ino = ino;
  inode->i_flags = 0;
  inode->i_count = 1;
  inode->i_state = I_LOCK;
```

`read_inode()` is responsible for the distinction between the different file types, mainly because it enters the inode operations into the inode, depending on the file system and file type. Almost every `read_inode` function, such as the *Ext2* file system, contains the following lines:

```
if (S_ISREG(inode->i_mode))
  inode->i_op = &ext2_file_inode_operations;
else if (S_ISDIR(inode->i_mode))
  inode->i_op = &ext2_dir_inode_operations;
else if (S_ISLNK(inode->i_mode))
  inode->i_op = &ext2_symlink_inode_operations;
```

`write_inode(inode)` The `write_inode()` function is used to save information about the inode structure. It is the counterpart of `read_inode()`, and makes sure that all information of the VFS inode is written back to the file system setup. This operation is optional, but must be implemented on all file systems that permit write access.

put_inode(inode) is called by iput() if the inode is no longer required, for example if the files belonging to the file system are closed. Its main task is to release all blocks that are occupied by inodes and release other resources. This operation is optional.

delete_inode(inode) This function is also called by iput(), if the i_nlink component is zero, therefore it will no longer be referenced on the file system. You have to delete this inode. This operation is optional, but must, however, be implemented by all file systems that permit write access.

notify_change(inode, attr) The modification made to the inode by the system call is acknowledged by calling the operation notify_change(). This is done using the iattr structure:

```
struct iattr {
  unsigned int ia_valid;      /* flags for changed components  */
  umode_t ia_mode;            /* new access rights             */
  uid_t  ia_uid;              /* new user                      */
  gid_t  ia_gid;              /* new group                     */
  off_t ia_size;              /* new size                      */
  time_t ia_atime;            /* time of last access           */
  time_t ia_mtime;            /* time of last modification     */
  time_t ia_ctime;            /* time of creation              */
  unsigned int ia_attr_flags; /* inode flags                   */
};
```

The file-system-specific flags are in ia_attr_flags. The VFS provides a standard implementation for this operation, which all other file system implementations fall back upon.

put_super(sb) The virtual file system calls this function when unmounting file systems. During the process, it should also release the superblock and other information buffers (e.g., inode bitmap, free block lists, etc.) (see brelse() in Section 4.3) and restore the consistency of the file system. This operation is optional.

write_super(sb) The write_super() function is used to save the information of the superblock. This does not necessarily have to guarantee the consistency of the file system.[3] If the current file system supports a flag indicating inconsistency, the flag should be set. Normally, the function will cause the buffer of the superblock to be written back to the cache: this simply makes sure that the buffer's s_dirt flag is set. The function is used to synchronize the device and is ignored by read-only file systems such as Isofs.

---

3 The date and inode blocks as well as the free block list or bitmaps must not be written back; therefore perhaps the file system is not solid.

statfs(sb, statfsbuf, int) The two system calls *statfs* and *fstatfs* (see Section A.2) call the superblock operation which in fact does no more than fill in the statfs structure. This structure provides information on the file system, for example the number of free blocks and the preferred block size. Note that the structure is located in the user address space. If the operation fails, the VFS returns ENODEV.

remount_fs (sb, flags, options) The remount_fs() function changes the status of a file system (see Table 6.1). This generally involves entering the new attributes for the file system in the superblock and restoring the consistency of the file system.

clear_inode (inode) This function is called by iput() and deletes the information from an inode. The implementation of VFS also releases the quotas and sets the status of the inode to 0.

umount_begin(sb) This function will be called when unmounting a device, if the MNT_FORCE option is set. It is optional, and is currently only implemented by NFS. Therefore, all calls which access the file system are broken off and the error message -EIO is displayed.

6.2.4 | The directory cache

The directory cache comes originally from the *Ext2* file system. Since LINUX version 1.1.37 it has belonged to VFS and can be used by all file system implementations. In order to accelerate access via the reading of directories, directory entries are kept in this cache because they are needed to open files. It should provide a solution to the old problem that the user works with file names but the kernel works with inodes. The kernel must determine a name for the inode and then again during the next access. In contrast to the inodes that exist permanently on the hard drive, the entries in the directory cache are purely RAM based. The entries in this cache have the following structure:

```
struct dentry {
  int d_count;                        /* user counter           */
  unsignedint d_flags;                /* flags                  */
  struct inode * d_inode;             /* inodes                 */
  struct dentry * d_parent;           /* parent directory       */
  struct list_head d_vfsmnt;          /* mount information      */
  struct list_head d_hash;            /* entry in the hash list */
  struct list_head d_lru;             /* unused entries         */
  struct list_head d_child;           /* list of the children   */
  struct list_head d_subdirs;         /* subdirectories         */
  struct list_head d_alias;           /* inode alias list       */
  struct qstr d_name;                 /* file name              */
```

```
  unsigned long d_time;              /* time stamp (Network FS) */
  struct dentry_operations *d_op;    /* operations              */
  struct super_block * d_sb;         /* accompanying superblock */
  unsigned long d_reftime;           /* last access             */
  void * d_fsdata;                   /* FS-specific data        */
  unsigned char d_iname[DNAME_INLINE_LEN]; /* short name        */
};
```

The file name is saved in an extra structure, along with its length and hash value:

```
struct qstr {
  const unsigned char * name;    /* name        */
  unsigned int len;              /* length      */
  unsigned int hash;             /* hash value  */
};
```

The directory cache is a global (hash) list in which doubly linked lists are entered. The position of the sublist in the global hash list determines the hash value of the name and the address of the DEntry entry of the parent directory.

```
static struct list_head *dentry_hashtable;
```

A new DEntry is produced using d-alloc(). The function

```
struct dentry * d_alloc(struct dentry * parent,
                const struct qstr *name);
```

receives the DEntry of the parent directory and submits the name of the current file. The kernel allocates memory for the new DEntry, enters the submitted DEntry as parent, and writes the child list in the subdirs list of its parent. The name is entered and the DEntry is returned. At this point the DEntry is still "negative," and does not yet carry any inode information.

The remainder is done by d_add(), which, by calling

```
void d_instantiate(struct dentry *entry,
                struct inode * inode);
```

validates the DEntry, because of the inode in the DEntry and in the i_dentry entry of the inodes in the alias list entry. It then puts the DEntry in its hash list by using d_rehash().

The most important function is d_lookup(). It is used to look up names. It gets the start directory DEntry and the name in qstr form as a parameter. However, it only searches the existing cache. The creation of a DEntry takes place (see Section 6.2.10) elsewhere.

```
struct dentry * d_lookup(struct dentry * parent,
                struct qstr * name);
```

The function searches for the list in the global hash table; it runs through it first and compares the hash value and the parent entry of the found DEntry with the current DEntry. If the parent is to define a `d_compare` operation, the name will be compared with it, otherwise a simple `memcmp()` is used. A reason for defining a comparison operation is that a file system may not distinguish between small and capital letters. If the right entry is found, the statistics will be updated and the entry is returned, otherwise zero is returned.

6.2.5 | DEntry operations

Like (more or less) every essential structure of a file system, the DEntry also has its own operations. New DEntries can be created, managed, and deleted.

```
struct dentry_operations {
  int (*d_revalidate)(struct dentry *, int);
  int (*d_hash) (struct dentry *, struct qstr *);
  int (*d_compare) (struct dentry *, struct qstr *,
             struct qstr *);
  void (*d_delete)(struct dentry *);
  void (*d_release)(struct dentry *);
  void (*d_iput)(struct dentry *, struct inode *);
};
```

`d_revalidate (dentry, int)` is used in network file systems to update the information of the local DEntry copy. `dentry` is the current DEntry, and `int` contains flags with which, for example, timeout behaviors can be controlled.

`d_hash (dentry, qstr)` calculates the position of the list in the hash table from the address in `dentry`, and the hash value from `qstr`. Here, DEntry is the parent directory, as this function is also called from positions where the current DEntry is negative.

`d_compare (dentry, qstr, qstr)` compares the two `qstr` entries with each other. Since things like capital/small letters must be taken into account, this function is a matter for the special file system. DEntry is also the parent directory here, as this function is also called from positions where the current DEntry is negative.

`d_delete (dentry, qstr)` first of all tests the usage counter of the DEntry. It tests whether `d_count` equal to 1, whether the process is the only user of the DEntry, and whether it is able to clear it. This encloses the release of the inode structure using `d_iput()` (if defined, otherwise `iput` is used) and the entries from the alias list is done here. Thus the DEntry is negatively marked. Then the DEntry is dropped from the hash list by means of `d_drop()`, so that it will no longer be found by `d_lookup()`.

d_release (dentry, qstr) releases the memory of a DEntry. This function is only implemented by file systems that save data in **d_fsdata**.

d_iput (dentry, qstr) opens the information of an inode. This function is only implemented by file systems where the inode is still managed in special lists (HFS). If this function is not implemented, iput() is called. The directory cache is also used to accelerate the file-system-specific lookup function. Finally, we have to mention that the directory cache accelerates file access for systems with little memory. In systems with a lot of memory, this is used for the caching of the block device and therefore also keeps directories in the memory.

6.2.6 | The inode

The structure inode has the following appearance:

```
struct inode {
    struct list_head i_hash;    /* inode chainings             */
    struct list_head i_list;
    struct list_head i_dentry;
    unsigned long i_ino;        /*  inode number               */
    unsigned int i_count;       /* reference counter           */
    kdev_t i_dev;               /* device number of the file   */
    umode_t i_mode;             /* file type and access rights */
    nlink_t i_nlink;            /* number of hard links        */
    uid_t i_uid;                /* owner                       */
    gid_t i_gid;                /* owner                       */
    kdev_t i_rdev;              /* device at device files      */
    off_t i_size;               /* size                        */
    time_t i_atime;             /* time of last access         */
    time_t i_mtime;             /* time of last modification   */
    time_t i_ctime;             /* time of creation            */
    unsigned long i_blksize;    /* block size                  */
    unsigned long i_blocks;     /* number of blocks            */
    unsigned long i_version;    /* DCache version management   */
    struct semaphore i_sem;     /* access control              */
    struct semaphore i_zombie;  /* access control              */
    struct inode_operations *i_op;   /* inode operations       */
    struct file_operations *i_fop;   /* file operations        */
    struct super_block *i_sb;        /* superblock             */
    struct wait_queue *i_wait;       /* wait queue             */
    struct file_lock *i_flock;       /* file locks             */
    struct address_space *i_mapping; /* memory areas           */
```

```
     struct address_space i_data;
     struct dquot *i_dquot[MAXQUOTAS];
     struct pipe_inode_info *i_pipe;
     struct block_device *i_bdev;      /* block device              */
     unsigned long i_state;            /* status (DIRTY, …)        */
     unsigned int i_flags;             /* flags                     */
     unsigned char i_sock;             /* inode represents socket */
     atomic_t i_writecount;            /* flag for write access     */
     unsigned int i_attr_flags;
     __u32 i_generation;
     union {
             struct minix_inode_info minix_i;

                 …

             void *generic_ip;
     } u;                              /* file system specific information */
};
```

This structure contains essential information about the file. In this structure, you will find management information as well as the file-system-dependent union u.

In the kernel, there are three storage areas where inodes are saved. First, there are two (doubly chained) lists – one saves all the used inodes, the other all the unused inodes. In addition, there is a hash table (inode_hashtable) containing all the used inodes. With a hash value built from the superblock address and the inode number the inode can be found in this list.

Of course, the kernel permanently needs the number of all used and free inodes for statistical purposes. For this purpose there is the structure inodes_stat:

```
struct {
        int nr_inodes;
        int nr_free_inodes;
        int dummy[5];
} inodes_stat = {0, 0,};
```

The functions iget() and iput() are used when working with inodes. They are used to create or release the inode structures.

```
static inline struct inode *iget(struct super_block *sb,
                              unsigned long ino)
{
        return iget4(sb, ino, NULL, NULL);
}
```

The iget() function provides the inode via the superblock sb and the inode number ino of the inode. However, it is only a capsule for the iget4() function. This function can additionally take a function and a parameter that controls the search for inodes at the same time. This is used by NFS, so it can handle 64-bit inodes.

The `iget4()` function calls `find_inode()`, which finds the inode with the correct number from the submitted list (`head`). If the inode searched for is contained in the list, the reference counter `i_count` will increase. If it is not found, a free inode will be selected using `get_new_inode()`. They are inserted in both lists (all and used), and the implementation of the corresponding file system is arranged by the superblock operation `read_inode()`, to fill the inode with information.

An inode that was retrieved with `iget()` must be "opened" again using the function `iput()`. It calls the `put_inode` function of the file system and reduces the reference counter by 1. If this is then zero and there are no references to the inode, it will be deleted. If there still are references, it will be moved into the list of unused inodes.

The linking of a file name with its inode is carried out via the DEntry. Section 6.2.4 describes the DEntry and the directory cache in which it is stored

6.2.7 | Inode operations

The inode structure also has its own operations which are held in the `inode_operations` structure and are mainly used for file management. These functions are usually called directly from the implementations of the appropriate system calls. If one of the inode operations is omitted, the calling function carries out default actions; however, often only an error is returned.

Since not all of the operations for each file type are meaningful, most file system implementations have defined various operations; e.g., there are some special ones for simple files or for directories.

Functions that have previously been used for mapping files to memory are now an extra sub-structure of the address spaces (memory areas) that are managed by the inode.

```
struct inode_operations {
  int (*create) (struct inode *,struct dentry *,int);
  struct dentry * (*lookup) (struct inode *,struct dentry *);
  int (*link) (struct dentry *,struct inode *,struct dentry *);
  int (*unlink) (struct inode *,struct dentry *);
  int (*symlink) (struct inode *,struct dentry *,const char *);
  int (*mkdir) (struct inode *,struct dentry *,int);
  int (*rmdir) (struct inode *,struct dentry *);
  int (*mknod) (struct inode *,struct dentry *,int,int);
  int (*rename) (struct inode *, struct dentry *,
  struct inode *, struct dentry *);
  int (*readlink) (struct dentry *, char *,int);
  struct dentry * (*follow_link) (struct dentry *,
  struct nameidata *);
```

```
  void (*truncate) (struct inode *);
  int (*permission) (struct inode *, int);
  int (*revalidate) (struct dentry *);
  int (*setattr) (struct dentry *, struct iattr *);
  int (*getattr) (struct dentry *, struct iattr *);
};
```

create(inode, dentry, int) is called by the open_namei() function of the VFS. This function serves several purposes. Firstly, it takes, with help from the get_empty_inode() function, a free inode from the list of all inodes. The inode structure must now be filled file system specifically. Therefore, for example, a free inode from the medium will be searched for. In addition to this, create() enters the file names from dentry into the directory and fills the mode attribute. If create() is missing in a file system implementation, the error EACCES will be returned by the VFS.

lookup (inode, dentry) searches the directory inode for the inode of the file whose name is in dentry. If the inode is found, by using the d_add(), it will be bound on the DEntry and zero will be returned.

link ((dentry, inode, dentry) is used to create a hard link. The old file is set in the first DEntry, and the name of the new file in the second one. In inode is the inode of the parent directories of the second DEntry. If this function is absent, the calling function returns the error EPERM.

unlink (inode, dentry) deletes the file indicated by dentry in the directory given by the inode. In the calling function it is first ensured that this operation has the relevant rights. The VFS returns the error EPERM, if unlink() is not implemented.

symlink (inode, dentry, char) establishes the symbolic link char in the inode directory. Before this function is called from VFS, the access rights will already have been checked by a call to permission(). If the symlink() is missing in a concrete implementation, VFS will return the error EPERM.

mkdir (inode, dentry, int) corresponds to the system call *mkdir()*, in which dentry contains the directory name, inode contains the inode of the parent directory and int, the access rights. First of all, the function must check whether further subdirectories can be created in the directory, and then allocate a free inode to the data carrier as well as a free block, in which the directory with its default entry "." and ".." will be written. The access rights will already have been checked in the calling VFS function. If the mkdir() function is not implemented, the error EPERM is returned.

rmdir (inode, dentry) deletes the subdirectory dentry from the directory. The function must check whether the directory to be deleted is empty and whether it is being used by a process, as well as whether the process is the owner of the subdirectory if the *sticky bit* is set in the directory dir. As with the functions already described, the access rights are checked beforehand by a VFS function. If rmdir() is not available, the VFS returns the error EPERM.

mknod (inode, dentry, int, int) sets up a new inode with the mode of the first int parameter. This inode gets the name from dentry. The parent directory (as usual) is in inode. If the inode is a device file (in which case either S_ISBLK(mode) or S_ISCHR(mode)), the second int parameter will contain the number of the device. If this function is not implemented, the error EPERM will be returned.

rename (inode, dentry, inode, dentry) moves a file or changes its name. The first two parameters define the source, the next two the target. The call function of the VFS checks the respective access rights in the directories beforehand. If this function is missing, the error EPERM will be returned by the VFS.

readlink (dentry, buf, size) reads the symbolic link dentry and copies the path of the file that this link points to into the buffer. When implementing this yourself, make sure that buf is placed in user address space! If the buffer is too small, the pathname should simply be truncated. If the inode is not a symbolic link, EINVAL should be returned. This function is called from sys_readlink() once the write access permission to the buffer buf has been checked and the DEntry been determined with lnamei(). If the implementation is missing, the system call will return the error EINVAL.

follow_link (dentry, nameidata) resolves a symbolic link, by the function filling nameidata with the values of the file, which show the first link in the DEntry. To avoid endless loops,[4] the maximum number of links is set to eight by executing the lookup_dentry() function in LINUX.

    This number is in the do_follow_link() function, which will be called in path_walk(), "hard wired." If follow_link() is missing, the calling function of the same name in the VFS simply returns inode, as if the link were pointing to itself. This behavior means that the VFS function can always be called without testing whether the current inode describes a file or a symbolic link.

truncate (inode) is mainly used to shorten a file, but can also lengthen a file if this is supported by the specific implementation. The only parameter required by truncate() is that the inode of the file is amended, with the i_size field set to the new length before the function is called. The truncate function is used in a number of places in the kernel, both by the system call *sys_truncate()* and when a file is opened. It will also release the blocks that are no longer required by a file.

---

4 Finally a symbolic link can be displayed on another symbolic link.

`permission (inode, int)` checks the inode to confirm access rights to the file given by the mask. If the function is not available, the calling function in the virtual file system checks the standard UNIX rights, which means that the implementation is actually unnecessary, unless additional access mechanisms are to be implemented.

`revalidate (dentry)` refreshes the information on an inode. This function is used by distributed file systems (e.g., NFS), because it is necessary (e.g., using `notify_change`) to make the inode information more consistent.

`setattr (dentry, iattr)` checks the values from `iattr` in the inode belonging to DEntry. Each file system can use its own attributes by implementing this function. The VFS has a default implementation.

`getattr (dentry, iattr)` checks the values from the inode belonging to DEntry in `iattr`.

6.2.8 | The file structure

In a multitasking system, there is often the problem that a number of processes want to access a file at the same time, both to read and to write. A single process may even be reading and writing at different points in the file. To avoid synchronization problems and allow shared access to files by different processes, UNIX has introduced an extra structure.

This relatively simple structure `file` contains information on a specific file's access rights `f_mode`, the current position `f_pos`, the type of access `f_flags`, and the number of accesses `f_count`.

```
struct file {
  struct list_head      f_list;       /* chaining              */
  struct dentry         *f_dentry;     /* DEntry entry          */
  struct vfsmount       *f_vfsmnt;     /* mount data            */
  struct file_operations *f_op;        /* file operations       */
  atomic_t              f_count;       /* reference counter     */
  unsigned short        f_flags;       /* open() flags          */
  mode_t                f_mode;        /* access type           */
  loff_t                f_pos;         /* file position         */
  unsigned long         f_reada, f_ramax, f_raend, f_ralen, f_rawin;
                                       /* control information
                                        * for cache access      */
  struct fown_struct    f_owner;       /* data about the owner*/
  unsigned int          f_uid, f_gid;  /* owner                 */
  int f_error;
  unsigned long         f_version;     /* Dcache version management*/
```

```
        void *private_data;                        /* data for a.o. terminal
                                                    * driver          */
        };
```

6.2.9 | File operations

The file_operations structure is the general interface for working on files, and contains the functions to open, close, read, and write files. The reason why these functions are not held in inode_operations but in a separate structure is that they need to make changes to the file structure. The inode's inode_operations structure also includes the default_file_ops, in which the standard file operations are already specified.

```
struct file_operations {
  struct module *owner;
  loff_t (*llseek) (struct file *, loff_t, int);
  ssize_t (*read) (struct file *, char *, size_t, loff_t *);
  ssize_t (*write) (struct file *, const char *, size_t, loff_t*);
  int (*readdir) (struct file *, void *, filldir_t);
  unsigned int (*poll) (struct file *,
  struct poll_table_struct *);
  int (*ioctl) (struct inode *, struct file *, unsigned int,
  unsigned long);
  int (*mmap) (struct file *, struct vm_area_struct *);
  int (*open) (struct inode *, struct file *);
  int (*flush) (struct file *);
  int (*release) (struct inode *, struct file *);
  int (*fsync) (struct file *, struct dentry *);
  int (*fasync) (int, struct file *, int);
  int (*lock) (struct file *, int, struct file_lock *);
  ssize_t (*readv) (struct file *, const struct iovec *,
  unsigned long, loff_t *);
  ssize_t (*writev) (struct file *, const struct iovec *,
  unsigned long, loff_t *);
};
```

These functions are also useful for sockets and device drivers, as they contain the actual functionality for sockets and devices. The anode operations, on the other hand, only use the representation of the socket or device in the related file system or its copy in the memory.

The old functions responsible for media changes have been moved to the operations for block devices.

llseek(file, offset, origin) The job of the llseek function is to deal with positioning within the file. If this function is not implemented, the default implementation (default_llseek()) simply converts the file position f_pos of the file structure.

read(file, buf, count, ppos) This function reads count bytes from the file and copies them into the buffer buf in the user address space. Before calling the function, the virtual file system first confirms that the entire buffer is located in the user address space and can be written to, and also that the file pointer is valid and the file has been opened for reading. ppos therefore shows the current file position using this. The read function should match the file position if work with file positions is supported. A device driver usually ignores these, so that it says zero in the file position. If no read function is implemented, the error EINVAL is returned.

write(file, buf, count, ppos) The write function operates in an similar way to read() and copies data from the user address space to the file.

readdir(file, buf, callback) This function returns the next directory entry in the dirent structure or an ENOTDIR or EBADF error. If this function is not implemented, the virtual file system returns ENOTDIR. The implementation is only necessary for directory entries. The callback is necessary as the function is used by system calls *readdir* and *getdents*, which have various output formats.

```
struct old_linux_dirent {
  unsigned long       d_ino;
  unsigned longd_offset;
  unsigned short      d_namlen;
  char d_name[1];
};
struct readdir_callback {
        struct old_linux_dirent * dirent;
        int count;
};
/* __buf is interpreted as readdir_callback */
int fillonedir(void * __buf, const char * name, int namlen,
        off_t offset, ino_t ino);
int old_readdir(…)
{
  struct readdir_callback buf;
…
  error = file->f_op->readdir(file, &buf, fillonedir);
…
}
```

The second variant looks like this:

```
struct linux_dirent {
  unsigned long d_ino;
  unsigned long d_off;
  unsigned short d_reclen;
char      d_name[1];
};
struct getdents_callback {
  struct linux_dirent * current_dir;
  struct linux_dirent * previous;
  int count;
  int error;
};
/* __buf is interpreted as getdents_callback */
int filldir(void * __buf, const char * name, int namlen,
off_t offset, ino_t ino);
  int sys_getdents(…)
{
  struct getdents_callback buf;
…
  error = file->f_op->readdir(file, &buf, filldir);
…
}
```

In both cases, the read_dir function does not show any interest in the buf parameter; it is merely passed on to the callback function callback. readdir() must make sure that the name, the length of the name, the file position of the current directory entries, and the inode number of the entries on the callback function are passed on.

poll (file, poll_tbl) This function checks whether data from a file can be read or written to a file. You also can test whether exceptional conditions are present. This function is only meaningful for device drivers and sockets. You will find an in-depth analysis of the poll() function in Section 7.4.8.

ioctl (inode, file, cmd, arg) Strictly speaking, the ioctl() function sets device-specific parameters. However, before the virtual file system calls the ioctl operation, it tests the following default arguments:

FIONCLEX clears the Close-on-exec bit.
FIOCLEX sets the Close-on-exec bit.
FIONBIO If the additional argument arg refers to a value not equal to zero, the
    O_NONBLOCK flag is set; otherwise it is cleared.

FIOASYNC sets or clears the O_SYNC flag as for FIONBIO. The `fasync()` function is also called.

If `cmd` is not among these values, a test is carried out to see whether `file` refers to a normal file. If so, the function `file_ioctl()` is called and the system call is terminated. For other functions the VFS tests for the presence of an `ioctl` function. If there is not one present, the ENOTTY error is returned, otherwise the file-specific `ioctl` function is called.

The following commands are available to the `file_ioctl()` function:

In the argument `arg`, FIBMAP expects a pointer to a block number and returns the logical number of this block in the file on the device if the inode relating to the file has a `get_block` function. This logical number is written back to the address `arg`. The absence of the inode operations or `get_block()` generates an EBADF or EINVAL respectively.

FIGETBSZ returns the block size of the file system in which the file is located. It is written to the address `arg` if a superblock is assigned to the file. Otherwise, an EBADF error is generated.

FIONREAD writes the number of bytes within the file which have not been read in the address `arg`.

As all of these commands write to the user address, permission for this is always obtained via the function `verify_area()` and an access error may be returned. If the command `cmd` is not among the values described, `file_ioctl()` also calls an existing file-specific `ioctl` function; otherwise the ENOTTY error is returned.

`mmap(file, vm_area)` This function maps part of a file to the user address space of the current process. The structure `vm_area` specifies all the characteristics of the memory area that is to be mapped: the components `vm_start` and `vm_end` give the start and end address of the memory area to which the file is to be mapped and the position in the file from which the mapping is to be carried out. For a more comprehensive description of `mmap` see Section 4.2.2.

`open(inode, file)` This function is only useful in two cases, since the default function in the virtual file system will already have taken care of all the necessary actions for files, such as allocating the file structure. The first case concerns the device driver and the second the opening of files from 32-bit systems.

`flush(file)` The `flush` function is called from VFS if a file is closed by using the system call *close*. In doing so, you ensure that the possible buffered data will be written. If this function is absent, the VFS takes no further action; however, `flush` can return an error code which is then returned as the error code of the *close* system call.

release(inode, file) This function is called when the file structure is released, that is, when its reference counter f_count is zero. This function is primarily used for device drivers, and its absence will be ignored by the virtual file system. Updating of the inode is also taken care of automatically by the virtual file system.

fsync(file, dentry) The fsync() function ensures that all buffers for the file have been updated and written back to the device, which means that the function is only relevant for file systems. If a file system has not implemented an fsync function, EINVAL is returned.

fasync(fd, file, on) This function is not implemented in file systems, but is used by device drivers (see Section 7.4.11) and sockets. With this function, a process can keep itself informed about asynchronous data.

lock(file, op, file_lock) lock is called if file locks are set or read by means of the system call *fnctl*. If lock is not implemented, the VFS default actions posix_test_lock() and posix_lock_file() are executed (see Section 5.2.1).

readv(file, iovec, count, offset) This function reads data from a file. In contrast to the normal read function, the data is not put in a buffer, but in a number of I/O vectors. During the filling of the vectors, the data is read from the file.

```
struct iovec
{
  void *iov_base;            /* address        */
  __kernel_size_t iov_len;   /* size           */
};
```

writev(file, iovec, count, offset) This function writes the contents of the submitted vectors to the file file one at a time.

6.2.10 Opening a file

One of the most important operations when accessing data is opening a file with the system call *open*. For this, the system not only has to make the appropriate preparations to ensure there are no problems with access to data, but also has to check the authorizations for the process. This is also where the actual switching function of the virtual file system is implemented, passing data between the specific file system implementations and the various devices.

If the function sys_open() is called, it gets a free file descriptor using get_unused_fd() and then calls filp_open() with the parameters submitted. Using the get_empty_filp() function, this function creates a new file structure and inserts this in the file descriptor table of the process. In this structure, the fields f_flags and f_mode are occupied and the open_namei() function is called in order to obtain the inode for the file to be opened.

Before this function is called, the open() flags are modified, leaving the two lowest bits holding the access permissions – bit 0 for read and bit 1 for write operations. The advantage of representing access to the file in this way is clear: it is possible to query the authorization rights using a simple command. The function open_namei() overlaps the submitted rights using the process-specific Umask, and carries out the resolution of the name. The nameidata structure as well as the path_init() function and path_walk() are used for this purpose. The structure has the following appearance:

```
struct nameidata {
  struct dentry *dentry;     /* DEntry of file              */
  struct vfsmount *mnt;      /* mount data                  */
  struct qstr last;          /* qstr structure of the names */
  unsigned int flags;        /* flags                       */
  int last_type;             /* type of the last parent     */
};
```

Table 6.2: Conversion of the open () flags

open () flag	Value	Bit 1 & 0	of the open_namei () flag
		00	No permission required (symbolic links)
RD_ONLY	0	01	Read permission required
O_WRONLY	1	10	Write permission required
O_RDWR	2	11	Write and read permission required
O_CREAT	1,000	1*	Write permission required
O_TRUNC	2,000	1*	Write permission required

The function path_init() has the following definition:

```
int path_init(const char *name,unsigned int flags,
       struct nameidata *nd);
```

You enter the submitted flags in nd.

Possible flags are:

LOOKUP_FOLLOW – Links are resolved.
LOOKUP_CONTINUE – Flag for internal use. Used by NFS in order to ignore small page variations.

LOOKUP_POSITIVE – If no inode is found for the DEntry, and this flag is set, an error (instead of 0) will be returned.

LOOKUP_DIRECTORY – The current path component is a directory.

LOOKUP_PARENT – The type of the parent directory is registered in the nd structure. There are five possible types; only the first three are used by path evaluation.

> LAST_DOT – . is the parent directory.
>
> LAST_DOTDOT – .. is the parent directory.
>
> LAST_NORM – . is the parent directory.
>
> LAST_ROOT – will be registered by path_init() by default.
>
> LAST_BIND – is registered by *Proc* file systems and influences the correct resolution of the links there.
>
> LOOKUP_NOALT – If the flag is set fs->altroot (if not NULL) will be used, and not fs->root, by path_init().

The path_init() function also uses the values mnt and dentry. If the submitted name is an absolute path name, the root values of the current process will be used (current->fs->rootmnt and current->fs->root), otherwise one of the other directories (current->fs->pwdmnt and current->fs->pwd) are used. We now have a starting point for decomposing the name.

The path_walk() function takes on the actual decomposing of the name. It replaces the old dir_namei(), _namei(), d follow_link(), and lookup_dentry() functions. The DEntry for name will be built up in it if it does not yet exist or return. It has the following calling convention:

```
int path_walk(const char * name, struct nameidata *nd);
```

In the process, name is the name of the file and nd the initialized structure from path_init().

An endless loop now starts, which tries to break down the name part by part. The name is decomposed directory wise, separated by "/". A qstr structure is built up for the next part of the name.

When we have arrived at the last part of the name, another branch appears, where the same instructions as in the loop are executed, but only once. If the name ends with "/", the do_follow_link() will still be called, and the error ENOTDIR will be returned if the DEntry found is a file.

Now the actual search starts. If the current part of the name is "..", then the parent directory is determined and the search continues with the next part of the name. If a DEntry operation d_hash is implemented for dentry, a new hash value will be calculated with this.

Now the directory cache is searched using cached_lookup(). If this function does not deliver a valid result, real_lookup() is called, and the work must be finished by the implementation of the respective file system. The current directory is locked, it will only be shown in the cache again. Using d_alloc(), a new DEntry will be created and is filled with the lookup() inode operation (this also calls d_add()).

Now we have a valid DEntry, but there are still two things that have to be done: We will have to be careful with mount points and links. Mount points are decomposed recursively, as long as the DEntry is a mount point and the __follow_down() function delivers a value that is unequal to 1. Links are followed, by either (if the LOOKUP_FOLLOW flag is set and there is an inode operation follow_link()) the inode operation being called by the do_follow_link() function and the result returned or (otherwise) the current DEntry being returned. Regardless of which of the two cases applies, the result will in any case be assigned to base, and with this we are one (directory) step further. Now the loop is run again.

Now we are on the open_namei() layer, and a number of tests are carried out. Finally, the following actions are executed:

- Has the DEntry now got an inode? If not, the call returns the error ENOENT. Is the inode a symbolic link? If so, we have a link loop and return ELOOP.

- Does the inode belong to a directory? And have we set write access in the flag? If so, the error EISDIR is returned.

- Check the submitted mode.

- Is the file a FIFO, a socket? If so, then allow write access (delete the O_TRUNC flag), even if it is a read-only file system, otherwise EROFS is returned.

- Is O_TRUNC (still) set? If so, truncate the file; it could be because there is no write access (get_write_access()) or because there are locks (locks_verify_locked()) on the file.

If all of this has been done, the DEntry will have been returned, and we will again be in filp_open(). Now the file structure is filled in dentry_open(): The DEntry is entered, f_pos is initialized with 0, and the standard file operations of the inode are typed in as *File Operation*. If an open() function has been defined, this is also called.

If the open file is a file of a character-oriented device, the chrdev_open() function will be called, which in turn changes the file operations depending on the major and minor number of the device:

```
int chrdev_open(struct inode * inode, struct file * filp)
{
  int ret = -ENODEV;
  filp->f_op = get_chrfops(MAJOR(inode->i_rdev),
                    MINOR(inode->i_rdev));
  if (filp->f_op != NULL){
        ret = 0;
        if (filp->f_op->open != NULL)
             ret = filp->f_op->open(inode,filp);
```

```
    }
    return ret;
}
```

The file operations of the device driver are in the `chrdevs[]` table and were entered during the initialization of the driver using the `register_chrdev()` function (see Chapter 7) . The minor number is required in order for the module to be reloaded when serial devices are demanded, provided, of course, that the kernel module loader was configured during the conversion of the kernel.

The `open()` function of the device driver will enter further file operations depending on the minor numbers of the device. They are described in the next chapter.

The file pointer is returned, and we are still in `sys_open()`. Now the file pointer is connected to the descriptor using `fd_install()`. If this is successful, the call is ended and delivered to the descriptor.

6.3   THE *EXT2* FILE SYSTEM

As LINUX was initially developed under Minix, it is hardly surprising that the first LINUX file system was the Minix.

However, this file system restricts partitions to a maximum of 64 Mbytes and filenames to no more than 14 characters, so it was not long before the search for a better file system was started. The result, in April 1992, was the *Ext* file system – the first to be designed especially for LINUX. Although this allowed partition of up to 2 Gbytes and filenames up to 255 characters, it left the LINUX community far from satisfied as it was slower than its Minix counterpart and the simple implementation of the free file block administration led to extensive fragmentation of the system. A system which is now little used was presented by Frank Xia in January 1993: the Xia file system. This is also based on the Minix file system and permits partitions of up to 2 Gbytes in size along with filenames of up to 248 characters, but its administration of free blocks in bitmaps and optimizing block allocation functions makes it faster and more robust that the *Ext* file system.

At about the same time, Rémy Card, Wayne Davidson, and others presented the *Ext2* file system as a further development of the *Ext* file systems. It now can be considered to be the LINUX file system, as it is used in most LINUX systems and distributions.

6.3.1   The structure of the *Ext2* file system

The design of the *Ext2* file system was very much influenced by BSD's *Fast File System* (BSD FFS). Thus, a partition is divided into a number of *block groups*, corresponding to the cylinder groups in FFS, with each block group holding a copy of the superblock and inode and data blocks, as shown Figure 6.4. The block groups are employed with the aim of keeping

■ data blocks close to their inodes, and

■ file inodes close to their directory inodes,

and thus reducing positioning time to a minimum, thereby speeding up access to data. As well as this, every group contains the superblock, along with information on all block groups, allowing the file system to be restored in an emergency.

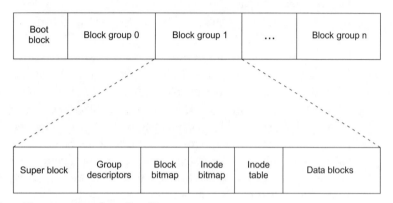

Figure 6.4: The structure of the *Ext2* file system.

The physical superblock – defined as the structure `ext2_super_block` – is shown in Figure 6.5. It contains the control information on the file system, such as the number of inodes and blocks. The block size used is not held directly, but as the dual logarithm of the block size minus the minimum block size supported by *Ext2* file system – normally 0. To use this, all that needs to be done is to "shift" the minimum block size `EXT2_MIN_BLOCK_SIZE` by the value given. In addition, the superblock includes

0	1	2	3	4	5	6	7
0	Number of inodes			Number of blocks			
8	Number of reserved blocks			Number of free blocks			
16	Number of free inodes			First data block			
24	Block size			Fragment size			
32	Blocks per group			Fragment per group			
40	Inodes per group			Mounting time			
48	Time of last writing			Mount counters		Max mount counters	
56	Ext2 signature		Status		Error handling		Minor revision
64	Time of last test			Max test time interval			
72	Operating system			File system revision			
80	RESUID		RESGID					

Figure 6.5: The superblock of the *Ext2* file system. Because of filler bytes it has grown to the size of 1,024 bytes.

information on the number of inodes and blocks per block group, along with the times of the last mount operation, the last write to the superblock, and the last file system check. It also holds information about the behavior of the file system in the event of errors, the maximum time interval to the next file system check, a mount counter, and the maximum number of mount operations which indicates when a mandatory file system test should be carried out. The resuid and resgid specify which users or groups are allowed to use the reserved blocks in addition to the superuser.

The superblock is made up to a size of 1,024 bytes – the minimum block size EXT2_MIN_BLOCK_SIZE – by inserting filler bytes. This makes it simple to use the space for expansions and to also read the superblock using bread().

The superblock is followed in each block group by the *block group descriptors*, which provide information about the block groups. Each block group is described by a 32-byte descriptor (see Figure 6.6). This contains the block numbers in the inode bitmap, block bitmap and inode table, the number of free inodes and blocks, and the number of directories in the block group. The number of directories is used by the inode allocation algorithm for the directories, which attempts to spread directories as evenly as possible over the block groups – in other words, a new directory will be mounted in the block group with the smallest number of directories.

The bitmaps are each the size of one block. This restricts the size of a block group to 8,192 blocks for blocks of 1,024 bytes.

The inode table for a block group lists consecutive blocks, starting with the one specified, and consists of inodes 128 bytes in size (see Figure 6.7). In addition to the data already mentioned, these contain the time when the file was deleted (for use in restoring deleted files), entries for ACLs (access control lists to enable access permissions to be differentiated more precisely), and information specific to the operating system in use. At present, ACLs are not implemented, which means that the function ext2_permission() tests only the UNIX permissions and the S_IMMUTABLE flag.

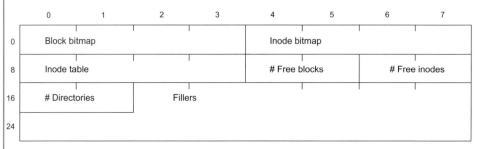

Figure 6.6:   The block group descriptors in the *Ext2* file system.

If the inode refers to a device file (that is, if S_IFCHR or S_IFBLK in i_mode is set), the first block number (i_block[0]) will give the device number. For a short symbolic link (S_IFLNK) the block numbers include the path, so that no additional data block is

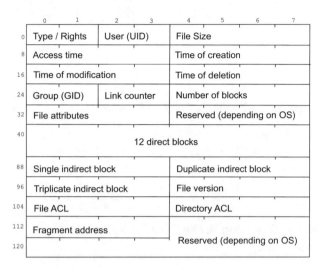

Figure 6.7: The inode of the *Ext2* file system.

required and the, "number of blocks" field, i_blocks, will contain a value of zero. If the symbolic link is longer than

```
EXT2_N_BLOCKS * sizeof (long)
```

it will be stored in the first block. This limits the maximum length of a reference to the size of a block.

6.3.2 | Directories in the *Ext2* file system

In the *Ext2* file system, directories are administered using a singly linked list. Each entry in the list has the following structure:

```
struct ext2_dir_entry_2 {
    __u32 inode;                  /* inode number               */
    __u16 rec_len;                /* length of directory entry  */
    __u8 name_len;                /* length of filename         */
    __u8 file_type;               /* type of file               */
    char name [EXT2_NAME_LEN];    /* filename                   */
};
```

The field rec_len contains the length of the current entry, and is always rounded up to a multiple of 4. This enables the start of the next entry to be calculated. The name_len field holds the length of the filename. It is perfectly possible for a directory entry to be longer than is required to store the filename. A possible structure is shown in Figure 6.8.

An entry is deleted by setting the inode number to zero and removing the directory entry from the linked list: that is, the previous entry is simply extended. This eliminates the need

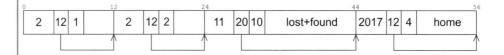

Figure 6.8:   A directory of the *Ext2* file system.

for shift operations in the directory, which might otherwise exceed the limits of the buffers. However, the "lost space" is not wasted, but is reused when a name is entered, either by overwriting an entry with a value of 0 or by using the additional space provided by removal of the link.

6.3.3 | Block allocation in the *Ext2* file system

A problem commonly encountered in all file systems is the fragmentation of files – that is, the "scattering" of files into small pieces as a result of the constant deleting and creating of new files. The problem is usually solved by the use of "defragmentation programs," such as defrag for LINUX. Some file systems attempt to prevent fragmentation as far as possible by sophisticated systems of block allocation. The *Ext2* file system similarly uses two algorithms to limit the fragmentation of files.

Target-oriented allocation

New data blocks are always searched for near a "target block." If this block is free, it is allocated. Otherwise, a free block is sought within 32 blocks of the target block, and if found, is allocated. If this fails, the block allocation routine tries to find a free block which is at least in the same block group as the target block. Only after these avenues have been exhausted are other block groups investigated.

Pre-allocation

If a free block is found, a number of the following blocks are reserved (if they are free). The number can be inserted in the *Ext2* superblock, otherwise EXT2_ DEFAULT_PREALLOC_BLOCKS (8) blocks are reserved. If the file is closed, the rest of the reserved blocks will be released. This also guarantees that as many data blocks as possible are collected into one cluster. Pre-allocation of blocks can be deselected by removing the definition of EXT2_PREALLOCATE from the file <linux/ext2_fs.h>.

How is the target block itself determined? Let n be the relative number in the file of the block to be allocated. The block allocation algorithm then applies the following heuristics in the order given:

■ In u.ext2_i.i_next_alloc_goal a target block number is written in the inode of the file.

- All existing blocks of the file, starting at block number n−1, are scanned to confirm that they have been assigned logical blocks (that is, the block is not a "hole"). The target block is given the number of the first logical block found.

- The target block is in the first block in the block group in which the inode for the file is located.

6.3.4 Extensions of the *Ext2* file system

The *Ext2* file system has additional file attributes beyond those which exist in standard UNIX file systems (see Table 6.3). In version 0.5a, which is current at the time of writing, these are:

EXT2_SECRM_FL If a file has this attribute, data blocks are first overwritten with random bytes before they are released via the truncate function. This ensures that the contents of the file cannot possibly be restored after it has been deleted. This property causes problems with linked files and is therefore deactivated.

EXT2_UNRM_FL In the future, this attribute should be used in the restoration of deleted files. However, this function is not yet implemented.

EXT2_COMPR_FL This attribute will be used later on to indicate that the file has been compressed. At present, online compression has not yet been implemented.

EXT2_SYNC_FL If a file has this attribute, all write requests are performed synchronously, i.e., not delayed by the buffer cache.

EXT2_IMMUTABLE_FL Files with this attribute cannot be deleted or amended. The renaming and setting up of further hard links is also prohibited. Even the superuser cannot modify the file so long as it possesses this attribute. Directories with this attribute cannot be changed – that is, no new files can be created or deleted. Existing files or subdirectories, however, can be modified as desired.

Table 6.3: The file attribute of the *Ext2* file system (n.i. = not yet implemented)

Macro	Value	Remark
EXT2_SECRM_FL	1	Secure deletion (n.i.)
EXT2_UNRM_FL	2	Undelete (n.i.)
EXT2_COMPR_FL	4	Compressed file (n.i.)
EXT2_SYNC_FL	8	Synchronous file
EXT2_IMMUTABLE_FL	16	"Append-only" file
EXT2_APPEND_FL	64	Do not archive file
EXT2_NOATIME_FL	128	Do not update access time

EXT2_APPEND_FL As for the previous attribute, files with this attribute cannot be deleted, renamed, or relinked. However, this attribute does allow a write to the end of the file to add fresh data. Directories with this attribute will only allow new files to be created. These will inherit the EXT2_APPEND_FL attribute when they are created.

EXT2_NODUMP_FL This attribute is not used by the kernel. It is intended to be used to mark files which are not required in a backup. This flag is currently not implemented.

EXT2_NOATIME_FL If this is flag set, the access rights will not be updated during access to a file.

These attributes can, however, be modified with the aid of the chattr program. The program lsattr displays them.

The development of the *Ext2* file system is not yet complete. The list of planned expansions includes:

- restoration of deleted files
- ACLs
- automatic file compression
- fragments.

6.4   THE *PROC* FILE SYSTEM

As an example of how the virtual file system interacts with a file system implementation, we now take a closer look at the *Proc* file system. The *Proc* file system in this form is peculiar to LINUX. It provides, in a portable way, information on the current status of the LINUX kernel and running process. It also allows modifications of kernel parameters in simple ways during runtime.

Each process in the system that is currently running is assigned a directory /proc/*pid*, where *pid* is the process identification number of the relevant process. A detailed breakdown of these files and their contents is given in Appendix C. There are also files and directories for process-independent information such as loaded modules, used bus systems, etc.

However, there are some disadvantages. There is no interface for the individual files; every user has to find out where and how the information that is required is hidden in the file. Another disadvantage is that all information is output as strings, therefore conversion is always necessary for further processing.

As far as its ideas are concerned, the process file system of the SystemV Release 4 is similar to the experimental system Plan 9.[5]

5 Plan 9 has been developed by such notable names as Rob Pike and Ken Thompson at AT&T's Bell Labs, and provides a perspective on what the developers of UNIX are currently doing. A good survey of Plan 9 is given in [PT+91].

Now, let us look at how this file system is used. The complete implementation is in the fs/proc directory.

6.4.1 | Structures of the *Proc* file system

Because the file system cannot fall back upon inodes in the conventional meaning and the structure can be changed at runtime, there is a *Proc Dir* entry:

```
struct proc_dir_entry {
    unsigned short low_ino;           /* (sub) inode nummer    */
    unsigned short namelen;           /* length of the name    */
    const char *name;                 /* name of the entry     */
    mode_t mode;                      /* mode                  */
    nlink_t nlink;                    /* link counter          */
    uid_t uid;                        /* UID                   */
    gid_t gid;                        /* GID                   */
    unsigned long size;               /* size of the file      */
    struct inode_operations * proc_iops;    /* inode-op        */
    struct file_operations * proc_fops;     /* file-op         */
    get_info_t *get_info;
    struct module *owner;
    struct proc_dir_entry *next, *parent, *subdir;
                                      /* connection            */
    void *data;
    read_proc_t *read_proc;           /* read function         */
    write_proc_t *write_proc;         /* write function        */
    unsigned int count;               /* user counter          */
    int deleted;                      /* delete flag           */
    kdev_t rdev;
};
```

We will refer to this structure as a PD entry below. Many entries correspond to the inode. The pointers next, parent, and subdir are used for linking: next shows the next entry in the current directory, parent shows the parent directory (at the root directory as itself), and subdir shows a subdirectory (if available). One can go through all PD entries in a directory, starting at the Parent PD entry, using the following loop:

```
for (de = de->subdir; de ; de = de->next) {
    ...
}
```

There are a number of constant PD entries that are initialized at the start of the system, and most of them only define the values up to the file operations. These entries are the files and directories lying directly under /proc/. Because there are almost 30 of them, and because they are dependent on the configuration of the kernels, the author saves him or herself from writing a list at this point, and refers to the function proc_root_init() in the file fs/proc/root.c. It is important that by creating this entry the proc_register() will be called at the end, in which the PD entries are linked together and entered using the correct inode and file operations for the file type.

The inodes are then created from the PD entries. A component of the inode has a special meaning in *Proc* file systems: In the inode number is stored the PID of the process that has created it (shifted by 16 bits) and the file type. The type also reveals whether it is a file in the /proc directory, a process directory, etc. There are a number of fixed enumeration types defined, which can be found under pid_directory_inos.

6.4.2 Implementation of the *Proc* file system

Now that the structures of the *Proc* file system have been explained, we will describe the mounting of the *Proc* system: As has just been described in Section 6.2.1, the function read_super() of VFS is called by do_mount(). This is found in the file_systems list, in the entry belonging to *Proc* file system, and calls the proc_read_super() function. The superblock submitted at this point is still empty apart from the flags submitted during the mounting and the device number.

```
struct super_block *proc_read_super(struct super_block *s,
                                    void *data, int silent)
{
  struct inode * root_inode;
  lock_super(s);
  s->s_blocksize = 1024;
  s->s_blocksize_bits = 10;
  s->s_magic = PROC_SUPER_MAGIC;
  s->s_op = &proc_sops;
  root_inode = proc_get_inode(s, PROC_ROOT_INO, &proc_root);
  if (!root_inode)
        goto out_no_root;
  /*
  * processes as subdirectories …
  */
  read_lock(&tasklist_lock);
  for_each_task(p) if (p->pid) root_inode->i_nlink++;
  read_unlock(&tasklist_lock);
  s->s_root = d_alloc_root(root_inode, NULL);
  if (!s->s_root)
        goto out_no_root;
```

```
  parse_options(data, &root_inode->i_uid, &root_inode->i_gid);
  s->u.generic_sbp = (void*) proc_super_blocks;
  proc_super_blocks = s;
  unlock_super(s);
  return s;
out_no_root:
  printk("proc_read_super: get root inode failed\n");
  iput(root_inode);
  s->s_dev = 0;
  unlock_super(s);
  return NULL;
}
```

Amongst other things, the function initializes the superblock operation (s_ops) using the special structure proc_sops:

```
static struct super_operations proc_sops = {
  read_inode: proc_read_inode,
  put_inode: proc_put_inode,
  delete_inode: proc_delete_inode,
  put_super: proc_put_super,
  statfs: proc_statfs,
};
```

In addition, the inode structure for the superblock is created with the proc_get _inode() function. The proc_read_inode() function is then called via the iget() interface of the VFS. Its mode of operation is described below.

When producing the root inode, of course, the corresponding PD entry is returned. This is strictly defined:

```
struct proc_dir_entry proc_root = {
PROC_ROOT_INO, 5, "/proc",
S_IFDIR | S_IRUGO | S_IXUGO, 2, 0, 0,
0, &proc_root_inode_operations, &proc_root_operations,
NULL, NULL,
NULL,
&proc_root, NULL
};
```

The PD entry is entered into the inode (u.generic_ip), and the following information will also be submitted to the inode: Mode, UID, GID, size, and the operations.

After creating the inode, the number of references to the directory is calculated. This is normally 2 + the number of subdirectories, as every subdirectory with ".." has this kind of reference. There is a problem here. Because the proc_get_inode() function is only called once during the "lifetime" of the memory inode and the number of processes during the runtime of a LINUX system surely changes, this value has to be recalculated later on. This happens in the `proc_root_lookup()` function described below.

With the help of the inode, the `d_alloc_root()` function then creates the PD entry of the *proc* root directories, which are entered into the superblock.

The `parse_options()` function then searches the submitted mount options for `data` entries from UID and GID (e.g., "`uid=1701,gid=42`") and sets the owner of the root inode. If no values are given, those of the current process are entered. The completed superblock is then returned and the function is exited.

The operations for the inode and file management are very scantily implemented: the structure `proc_root_inode_operations` only implements the lookup component as the `proc_root_lookup()` function.

```
static struct dentry *proc_root_lookup(struct inode * dir,
                     struct dentry * dentry);
```

This function is used for decomposing the name for the PID directory (for the other directories `proc_dir_inode_operations` is inserted for inode operations). Firstly, the number of running processes (minus the number of idle tasks) in `nlinks` is updated. As this can take quite a long time (relatively), this code part will only be run if the value `total_forks` has changed since the last time. It then calls `proc_lookup()` in order to determine the PD entry. Finally it calls `proc_pid_lookup()`. This function checks whether the process whose PID forms the name of the desired directory still exists, and creates a special inode, not with PID, GID, UID taken from the PD entry, but from the process. This new inode is then entered in the PD entry and overwrites the old one created by `proc_lookup()`.

Now we look at what happens when accessing this file system. It is interesting to see that the corresponding file is always generated first, if it is required. Let us assume that we want to access a file using the system call *open*, and after a while we end up in the *proc*-specific `lookup()` function:

```
struct dentry *proc_lookup(struct inode * dir,
             struct dentry *dentry);
```

An absolute pathname is indicated when opening, and the root inode is found in `dir`. The function gets the PD entry from this, and runs through the next list. If the name of an entry matches the PD entry a new inode is created with `proc_get_inode()`. The value `low_ino` from the PD entry is used as the inode number.

In this, the function for the reading of inodes entered in the superblock operations, `proc_read_inode()`, is called via the `iget()` function of the VFS and `get_new_inode()`. The submitted inode is already allocated, but is empty. This function sets the times of the inode nicely.

```
inode->i_mtime = inode->i_atime =
         inode->i_ctime = CURRENT_TIME;
```

After the call from iget(), UID, GID, size, links, and the operations in the inode are taken from the PD entry of the mode. The PID saved within the inode number is then extracted from it and the process is searched. If we open a process directory and the dumpable flag of the process is set, EUID and EGID of the processes will be taken as the UID and GID of the inode. Now the inode is filled and the function exited.

As a third example, we shall explain what happens if a file is selected. The origin is the call of the read() function of the VFS. In the *Proc* file system, files are inserted during the registration of files (see Section 6.4.1) for the proc_file_read function.

```c
#define PROC_BLOCK_SIZE (3*1024)
static ssize_t proc_file_read(struct file * file, char * buf,
        size_t nbytes, loff_t *ppos)
{
  struct inode * inode = file->f_dentry->d_inode;
  int eof=0;
  ssize_t n, count;
  char *start;
  struct proc_dir_entry * dp;

  dp = (struct proc_dir_entry *) inode->u.generic_ip;
  if (!(page = (char*) __get_free_page(GFP_KERNEL)))
        return -ENOMEM;

  while ((nbytes > 0) && !eof)
  {
        count = MIN(PROC_BLOCK_SIZE, nbytes);

        if (dp->get_info) {
                /*
                 * compatibility with old network routines …
                 */
                n = dp->get_info(page, &start, *ppos, count);
                if (n < count)
                        eof = 1;
        } else if (dp->read_proc) {
                n = dp->read_proc(page, &start, *ppos,
                        count, &eof, dp->data);
        } else
                break;
        …
  }
  …
}
```

It is no longer possible to select more than 4 Kbytes due to memory limitations, and because of this, the `while` loop cannot be selected. As you can see, the selection is made using the function that is entered in the PD entry under `read_proc`. From this it follows that every file that is registered in *Proc* file systems will have to define this kind of function!

If a process, for example, wants to select the file `/proc/loadavg`, the `loadavg_read_proc()` function is also called, which was entered during the initialization of the file. The function generates the contents of the file by entering the necessary values in the memory page, and returns the size of the buffer (that is, the file). This has the following appearance in the source:

```
static int loadavg_read_proc(char *page, char **start, off_t off,
        int count, int *eof, void *data)
{
  int a, b, c;
  int len;
  a = avenrun[0] + (FIXED_1/200);
  b = avenrun[1] + (FIXED_1/200);
  c = avenrun[2] + (FIXED_1/200);
  len = sprintf(page,"%d.%2d %d.%2d %d.%2d %d/%d %d\n",
        LOAD_INT(a), LOAD_FRAC(a),
        LOAD_INT(b), LOAD_FRAC(b),
        LOAD_INT(c), LOAD_FRAC(c),
        nr_running, nr_threads, last_pid);
  ...
  return len;
}
```

The functions of the individual files are implemented in `fs/proc/proc_misc.c` or by special source code. Therefore, the `get_module_list()` function for the file `/proc/module` is found in the file `kernel/module.c` of the module implementation.

7 DEVICE DRIVERS UNDER LINUX

In the computer stone age, the hardware-specific part of a program was simply connected to the executable program as a library. At that time these were neither several users nor programs that had to share a CPU and the necessary software. If an operating system had these qualities, one had to think about how to implement hardware control without disturbing the various processes or the users. This is where the concept of device drivers came from.

Device drivers are a collection of routines, which write magical numbers to magical places in the hardware. So that these routines can be sensibly fitted into an operating system, an interface is implemented, which can be called by the operating system with definite actions to be carried out on the hardware. The operating system, in addition to hardware access, takes on the task of coordinating resource distribution. The device driver runs in the memory of the kernel, and therefore has the same rights as the kernel. Therefore special care and attention should be taken when implementing a device driver, as an entry in the wrong register can have devastating consequences. The device driver should always use the resources as economically as possible, especially if it is permanently inserted in the kernel.

In UNIX systems, the driver interface, as with many other driver interfaces, is implemented as part of the access to the file system. Special entry points to the driver are created in UNIX as special virtual files in file systems. The user can then access devices using quite normal file operations like, for example, open, read, write, and close.

The virtual files are assigned a specific identification in the file system, so that the operating system can distinguish the device driver. Access to a driver file is redirected to the correct routines in the kernel using the so-called *major number*.

Some of the major numbers that are currently allocated are listed in Table 7.1. The `Documentation/devices.txt` file contains a complete list.

Devices can frequently have several logical subunits (for example, hard disks or serial devices), and therefore there is another identification system, the *minor numbers*, that will be submitted to the driver by means of the file system. The numbers, which are between 0 and 255, also can be used to switch between several operating modes of a device.

Table 7.1: Excerpt from the LINUX major number list

Major	Signal devices	Block devices
0	*unnamed* for NFS, network, etc.	
1	Memory devices (mem)	RAM disk
2	Pseudo TTY master (pty*)	Disks (fd*)
3	Pseudo TTY slaves (ttyp*)	IDE hard disks (hd*)
4	Terminals	
5	Terminals & AUX	
6	Parallel interfaces	
7	Virtual consoles (vcs*)	Loopback devices
8		SCSI hard disks (sd*)
9	SCSI tapes (st*)	Metadisk devices (RAID)
10	Bus mice (bm, psaux)	
11	Keyboard raw device	SCSI CD-ROM (sr*)
12	QICo2 tape	MSCDEX CD-ROM callback support
13	PC speaker driver	XT 8-bit hard disks (xd*)
14	Sound cards	BIOS hard disk support
15	Joystick	Cdu31a/33a CD-ROM
16	Non-SCSI scanner	GoldStar CD-ROM
17	Chase serial card	Optics storage CD-ROM
18	Chase serial card – alternative	Sanyo CD-ROM
19	Cyclades drivers	Double – compressed driver
20	Cyclades drivers	Hitachi CD-ROM
21	SCSI generic	Acorn MFM hard drive interface
22	Digiboard serial card	2. IDE interface driver
23	Digiboard serial card – alternative	Mitsumi CD-ROM (mcd*)
24	Stallion serial card	Sony535 CD-ROM
25	Stallion serial card – alternative	Matsushita CD-ROM 1
26	QuantaWinVision frame grabber	Matsushita CD-ROM 2
27	QIC117 tape	Matsushita CD-ROM 3

(continues)

Table 7.1: Excerpt from the LINUX major number list *(contd)*

Major	Signal devices	Block devices
28	Stallion serial card – programming	Matsushita CD-ROM 4
29	Frame buffer drivers	Other CD-ROMs
30	iCBS2	Philips LMS-205 CD-ROM

7.1   CHARACTER AND BLOCK DEVICES

In LINUX systems, block-oriented devices and character-oriented devices are distinguished.

Character devices deliver and read data character by character or in sequential byte streams, or replace the data in sequential data streams. For example, data transfer occurs by serial or parallel interfaces or tape streamer by character. As this access mode is very simple, very many drivers are implemented as character-oriented device drivers.

These access modes would be very inefficient for hard disks as in order to read data bytes in an asynchronous operation it would always have to wait for a whole rotation of the disk before the next byte can be read. To avoid this, these kinds of devices will always be read in blocks, i.e., the system always requests a number of whole blocks of a definite size from the hardware and puts these blocks in an intermediate buffer. If a block limit is reached when writing or reading, the old block will be synchronized with the hardware and then a new block will be processed. Drivers for this kind of device usually only have the functions that are necessary for the transfer of blocks or the management of block sizes. Therefore they are called block device drivers.

In LINUX file systems, character and block devices are distinguished by means of a flag, which is submitted as a parameter when creating a virtual driver file through mknod.

```
# mknod /dev/name type major minor
```

Character-oriented drivers implement the necessary functions directly and register these in the system with the file_operations structure.

```
struct file_operations busmouse_fops=
{
  owner:                THIS_MODULE,
  read:                 busmouse_read,
  write:                busmouse_write,
  poll:                 busmouse_poll,
  open:                 busmouse_open,
  release:              busmouse_release,
  fasync:               busmouse_fasync,
};
```

By calling *read* and *write*, the corresponding routines are called directly in the driver.

In version 2.4, the `file_operations` structure is divided up. In a block-oriented driver, the necessary routines are only registered in the `block_device_Operations` structure – as in the floppy driver here:

```
static struct block_device_operations floppy_fops = {
  open:                     floppy_open,
  release:                  floppy_release,
  ioctl:                    fd_ioctl,
  check_media_change:       check_floppy_change,
  revalidate:               floppy_revalidate,
};
```

Like character-oriented devices, there is also a registration function `register_blkdev()` for block devices, with which the `block_device_operations` structure is registered with the system.

7.2   HARDWARE

There should be, in fact, no discussions about hardware in a kernel book. Nevertheless, knowledge of the hardware is the most important prerequisite when writing a device driver. Therefore, we will briefly go through the specialities of the current PC hardware.

7.2.1   Port I/O

The simplest access to the hardware is the port access, i.e., to addresses in the address room of the CPU – the I/O ports called `0x0000–0xffff`. With the aid of macros, the corresponding functions for these accesses are defined in `include/asm/io.h`. The `inb_p()` function is used for byte access. In the same way, the `outw()` and `inw()` functions are used for word access and `outl()` as well as `inl()` for double word access.

As expected, the `outX` function is used to write and `inX` is used to read the given ports. The functions with the ending `_p` wait for a small period of time after the I/O operations. This can be necessary in some cases, in particular on old ISA hardware. For ancient hardware and for problematic timing situations, the behavior of the `*_p()` functions can be changed with the help of the macro `REALLY_SLOW_IO`. This macro must be defined before the inclusion of the `include/asm/io.h` file, to give a little more time after an I/O access of the bus.

LINUX usually uses a read access to the port 0x80 for this delay on x86 systems. This port is used by the BIOS in order to output status messages during the boot; therefore the reading of this port should always be harmless. Previously, unconditional jumps were used in the deceleration of I/O access. These were adequate on processors of the 386 class for a long time. However, today's processors execute unconditional jumps so fast that this method is unsuitable.[1] Despite this, it is possible to execute the delay by adding two unconditional jumps on x86 systems with the help of the SLOW_IO_BY_JUMPING macro.

So that different parts of the kernel are not in an undefined state, and in particular so that several device drivers do not write to the same I/O port and bring the hardware to an undefined state, access to I/O ports can be prohibited in LINUX.

Therefore, at boot time a parameter can be submitted to the kernel, which contains all the locked areas. If the system does not start after the installation of a new card, you should try to remove the address space from this card. A fictitious example should clarify this:

A scanner card covers the addresses 0x300–0x30f (there could also be a network card). Using the boot parameter

reserve=0x300,0x10

the region will be locked.

Within a driver, the following macros are used for I/O port management:

```
check_region(from, num)
request_region(from, num, name)
release_region(from, num)
```

The check_region() macro asks the kernel whether the num I/O ports at the beginning of the I/O address from are free. If at least one I/O port in the region is already locked, the error EBUSY is returned, otherwise 0.

The macro request_region() locks num I/O ports from the beginning of the I/O address. The third parameter is the name of the driver that wants to lock the port. The name of the drivers from the *Proc* file system is now used, and from this it is possible to determine which I/O ports are occupied by which drivers. This macro also returns the error EBUSY if there are errors. The release_region() macro opens locked I/O ports. This is necessary, for example, when dealing with modules when they are removed from the kernel.

7.2.2 The PCI bus

The PCI[2] bus architecture is not only common among Intel PCs, it has also gained acceptance in other architectures. The unusual feature of the PCI bus is the complete separation between the bus subsystem and the CPU subsystem. A special controller, the so-called PCI bridge, is responsible for most of the transfer.

On a PCI bus, all bus lines are shared as both data and address lines, which is why address and data packages always have to be sent alternately over the bus. With 16-bit access you also could use the remaining lines at the same time as a data bus.

During the transmission of a complete data block, the bridge can optimize the transfer, by only sending the start address via the bus and then sending all the data packages in blocks. The addresses are automatically incremented in the bridge as well as in the adapter. This procedure is also called *PCI burst cycles*. With 64-bit data transfer, the speed could reach

---

1 The faster execution of unconditional jumps after the introduction of the first 486 computers led to serious problems since disk drives suddenly no longer worked stably.
2 Peripheral Components Interconnect.

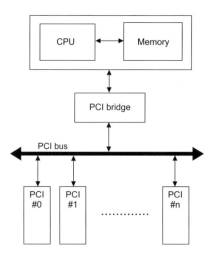

Figure 7.1:   Schematic construction of the PCI subsystem.

266 Mbytes/s.[3] Because the PCI bridge selects the fastest transfer mode itself, the driver programmer does not have to worry about this.

A PCI adapter can also send data without the involvement of the CPU into the memory area of the PC. For this purpose, the controller transfers itself to the busmaster mode, and can then take the data transfer to the bridge and thereby into the main memory of the PC or the memory area of another PCI adapter. Since this method is carried out similarly to the ISA-DMA, it is also frequently called *Busmaster DMA*.

A configuration address space of 256 bytes is provided for every device on the PCI bus, in which the parameters for this device are placed.

The first 64 bytes are provided in the PCI specification, and the rest is dependent on the manufacturer. During the boot, the PCI-BIOS determines the necessary resources of all devices and assigns all their parameters such as base address and IRQ by inserting them in this header. The driver gets the assigned parameters from reading from there.

Furthermore, every device on the PCI bus has a definite address. In contrast to the ISA bus, where the slots of the hardware cannot be distinguished, the position of every PCI device can be determined. The position depends on the bus number, and the device and function number. The bus number gives information on which bus the device is on, and there can definitely be several PCI buses on a computer (the AGP port also appears as an independent bus). The device number clearly determines the PCI slot where the PCI device is placed, while the function number permits several subunits, such as two SCSI controllers, to be put in a PCI device. If you put a PCI device in another slot, the address will change. This can lead to the PCI-BIOS assigning other resources.[4]

LINUX provides a number of useful functions and macros for handling the PCI configuration space. The functions which are necessary for the recognition of the card and

---

3 Only Serverboads fulfill this specification at present, however.
4 This is also the reason that other operating systems suddenly "discover" new hardware.

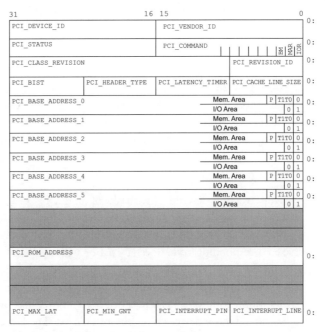

Figure 7.2: The PCI header and the macros from `pci.h`.

the determination of the base addresses or the interrupt number are mostly sufficient for the driver programmer; nevertheless, we will briefly go through the most essential configuration features here.

The accompanying macro definitions are found in `include/linux/pci.h`. For a clear identification of the card, a vendor code (`PCI_VENDOR_ID`), a device code (`PCI_DEVICE_ID`), a class, and a vendor-specific revision code are placed in the header, which cannot be overwritten. If a PCI frontend made by other vendors is used, the subvendor (`PCI_SUB_VID`) and the subdevice code (`PCI_SUB_ID`) give further information about the vendor of the subsystem.

Using class codes, you can determine which device class (e.g., mass memory controller or network card) you are dealing with. Every PCI device can cover up to six I/O areas, which are inserted over the PCI-BIOS in the configuration space (`PCI_BASE_ADDRESS_0-5`). The last bit of the value marks whether it is an address of an I/O address area or whether the area is displayed in the memory area. If the address is a memory address, it can be a 64-bit or a 32-bit memory address, or it can be marked that it must be mapped below 1 Mbyte.

The PCI driver model

With version 2.4, a new PCI driver model has made an appearance. The advantage of the new approach is that it can respond to *Hot Plug* devices (during the runtime of the added device). While Hot Plug PCI devices are still seldom talked about, this approach allows us to talk about PC card devices as PCI devices. When we mention PCI devices in the following, this includes PC card devices.

Next a table of all supporting devices must be created in the driver. The structure pci_device_id is used to do this:

```
struct pci_device_id {
  unsigned int vendor, device;       /* vendor and device code */
  unsigned int subvendor, subdevice; /* subsystem codes       */
  unsigned int class, class_mask;    /* class and subclass mask*/
  unsigned long driver_data;         /* desired driver data   */
};
```

This structure describes the masks of all devices in which the driver is interested. The vendor and device components take the vendor and device code of the PCI devices. subvendor and subdevice take on the subsystem codes. PCI_ANY_ID must be used in case a corresponding code doesn't exist or will not be taken into account by the selection. Therefore a driver, for example, can be registered for all devices of a vendor, by the vendor code being inserted while the device code of PCI_ANY_ID is being set. The class and class_mask components allow a driver to register itself for a device class. The value 0 has to be entered if the device class will not be used. The last component allows specific driver data to be entered into the structure.

A driver can now register a number of pci_device_id entries (ID table). The following example comes from the PCnet32 driver:

```
static struct pci_device_id pcnet32_pci_tbl[] __devinitdata = {
  { PCI_VENDOR_ID_AMD, PCI_DEVICE_ID_AMD_PCNETHOME,
  PCI_ANY_ID, PCI_ANY_ID, 0, 0, 0 },
  { PCI_VENDOR_ID_AMD, PCI_DEVICE_ID_AMD_LANCE,
  PCI_ANY_ID, PCI_ANY_ID, 0, 0, 0 },
  { PCI_VENDOR_ID_AMD, PCI_DEVICE_ID_AMD_LANCE,
        0x1014, 0x2000, 0, 0, 0 },
  { 0, }
};
```

The __devinitdata modifier should be used for the registration fields. It makes sure that the table can be automatically removed from the kernel if the Hot-Plugin is deactivated.

The pcnet32_pci_tbl field contains three entries. The first entry declares that the driver takes an interest in the AMD HomePNA network adapter. The second entry is to do with PCnet LANCE network cards. The third entry specifies a subsystem vendor and device code. The last entry signals the end of the field.

The second structure necessary for registration is pci_driver:

```
struct pci_driver {
  struct list_head node;
  char *name;
  /* pointer to the ID table*/
  const struct pci_device_id *id_table;
  /* new device was found*/
  int (*probe)(struct pci_dev *dev,
  const struct pci_device_id *id);
  /* device was removed */
  void (*remove)(struct pci_dev *dev);
  /* power management; device is suspended */
  void (*suspend)(struct pci_dev *dev);
  /* power management; device is woken up */
  void (*resume)(struct pci_dev *dev);
};
```

The node component is used to link together all entries in the PCI bus driver. name contains the name of the driver. The probe() function is called from PCI bus driver if a new device is found. Similarly, the PCI bus driver calls remove(), as the device was removed. The suspend() and resume() functions are used for power management. Now we look at the PCnet32 driver:

```
static struct pci_driver pcnet32_driver = {
name:    "pcnet32",
probe:   pcnet32_probe_pci,
remove: NULL,
id_table:        pcnet32_pci_tbl,
};
```

The PCnet32 driver registers a probe() function, as well as the ID table that has already been created. As long as the driver does not support a Hot-Plugin, the remove() function can be NULL. Our example does not support power management either.

```
static int __init pcnet32_init_module(void)
{
int err;
...
/* find the PCI devices */
if ((err = pci_module_init(&pcnet32_driver)) < 0 )
        return err;
  return 0;
}
```

pcnet32_init_module() now registers the driver with the PCI bus driver. This can happen using two functions:

```
int pci_register_driver(struct pci_driver *drv);
int pci_module_init(struct pci_driver *drv);
```

pci_register_driver() registers the driver with the bus driver and immediately tests whether there are already devices in the system for which the driver would like to register itself and for which no other driver has yet registered. If so, the probe() function of the driver will be called at this point. pci_register_driver() returns the number of devices on which the probe() function was called. The value 0 indicates that there are no devices in the system that the driver has registered for. Notice that in this case the driver is registered anyway. The pci_module_init() function forms a thin layer around pci_register_driver() and is used as an auxiliary function for modules.

```
static inline int pci_module_init(struct pci_driver *drv)
{
  int rc = pci_register_driver (drv);

  if (rc > 0)
  return 0;

  /* If the driver is statically entered in the kernel
   * and the CONFIG_HOTPLUG option is activated, the
   * driver should remain active, to be able to react to plug-ins
   * of hardware.
   * On the other hand, if the driver is compiled as a module,
   * a daemon should make sure that the driver
   * is reloaded, if hardware
   * is added to the system. */
#if defined(CONFIG_HOTPLUG) && !defined(MODULE)
  if (rc == 0)
        return 0;=
#endif
  /* If the flow of control reaches this point,
   * the driver must be removed as well as a suitable
   * error generated. */
  pci_unregister_driver (drv);
  return -ENODEV;
}
```

If there is no device in the system yet and the driver is compiled as a module, pci_module_init() removes the driver and returns an error. In this way it can prevent a module from being loaded before there is at least one device in the system.

The `pci_unregister_driver()` function removes a driver. If there are still devices in the system, the `remove()` function of the driver is called for every device. This function must at least be called in the exit function of a module.

The probe function

If there already is a suitable device in the system or if a device is added after registration, the `probe()` function of the PCI driver will be called.

```
int probe(struct pci_dev *dev, const struct pci_device_id *id);
```

The first argument of the function is a pointer to the `pci_dev` structure. The second argument points to the entry in the ID table that has matched the device code. If the ID table equals zero, then this argument equals NULL too. The `pci_dev` structure already contains all the resources of the PCI devices. In contrast to older LINUX versions, resources in version 2.4 should no longer be read directly from the PCI configuration space. In particular, the interrupt entry in the configuration space can be different.

```
struct pci_dev {
  struct list_head global_list;      /* chaining of the list of all
                                      * PCI devices             */
  struct list_head bus_list;         /* chaining in the list of
                                      * accompanying buses      */
  struct pci_bus      *bus;          /* bus where the device is
                                      * placed                  */
  struct pci_bus      *subordinate;  /* bus to where the device
                                      * builds a bridge         */
  void                *sysdata;      /* indicator for possible
                                      * additional data         */
  struct proc_dir_entry *procent;    /* device entry in
                                      * /proc/bus/pci           */
  unsigned int devfn;                /* device and function
                                      * index                   */
  unsigned short      vendor;        /* vendor code of the device */
  unsigned short      device;        /* device code of the device */
  unsigned short      subsystem_vendor;   /* vendor code of the
                                      * subsystem               */
  unsigned short      subsystem_device;   /* device code of the
                                      * subsystem               */
  unsigned int        class;         /* device class            */
  u8                  hdr_type;      /* PCI header type         */
  u8                  rom_base_reg;  /* base address of the ROM*/
  struct              pci_driver *driver  /* pointer to belonging
                                      * drivers    */
```

```
    void            *driver_data;           /* pointer to possible
                                             * addtional data of the
                                             * driver                 */
    dma_addr_t      dma_mask;               /* bit mask of the valid
                                             * address bits for the DMA
                                             * transfer, normally
                                             * 0xFFFFFFFF              */
    /* list of compatible devices    */
    unsigned short vendor_compatible[DEVICE_COUNT_COMPATIBLE];
    unsigned short device_compatible[DEVICE_COUNT_COMPATIBLE];
    unsignedint  irq;                       /* interrupt number       */
    /* I/O, memory and ROM resources         */
    struct resource resource[DEVICE_COUNT_RESOURCE];
    struct resource dma_resource[DEVICE_COUNT_DMA];
    struct resource irq_resource[DEVICE_COUNT_IRQ];
    char   name[80];           /* device name                 */
    char   slot_name[8];       /* slot name, where the
                               * device is placed            */
    int    active;            /* ISAPnP: device is active     */
    int    ro;                /* ISAPnP: resources are read-only*/
    unsigned short regs;       /* ISAPnP: supported register   */
    /* ISAPnP functions          */
    int (*prepare)(struct pci_dev *dev);
    int (*activate)(struct pci_dev *dev);
    int (*deactivate)(struct pci_dev *dev);
};
```

The contents of this returned structure should not be changed; the driver_data
component could merely be used by a driver to append specific data to a device. The
following auxillary functions are used for this:

```
void *pci_get_drvdata(struct pci_dev *pdev);
void pci_set_drvdata(struct pci_dev *pdev, void *data);
```

The resource information is saved in the resource structure:

```
struct resource {
  const char *name;          /* resource name                 */
  unsigned long start, end; /* start and end of theresource   */
  unsigned long flags;       /* flags, explaining the resource
                             * type                           */

  /* used to link together resources in the tree structure */
```

```
      struct resource *parent, *sibling, *child;
};
```

The following macros should be used to select the resource components:

```
pci_resource_start(dev,bar)
pci_resource_end(dev,bar)
pci_resource_flags(dev,bar)
pci_resource_len(dev,bar)
```

We turn to our example code again:

```
static int __init
pcnet32_probe_pci(struct pci_dev *pdev, const struct pci_device_id *ent)
{
  static int card_idx;
  long ioaddr;
  int err = 0;
  printk(KERN_INFO "pcnet32_probe_pci: found device %#08x.%#08x\n",
  ent->vendor, ent->device);
  ioaddr = pci_resource_start (pdev, 0);
  printk(KERN_INFO " ioaddr=%#08lx resource_flags=%#08lx\n",
          ioaddr, pci_resource_flags (pdev, 0));
  if (!ioaddr) {
          printk (KERN_ERR "no PCI IO resources, aborting\n");
          return -ENODEV;
  }
  if (!pci_dma_supported(pdev, PCNET32_DMA_MASK)) {
          printk(KERN_ERR "pcnet32.c: architecture does not support"
                        " 32bit PCI busmaster DMA\n");
          return -ENODEV;
  }
  if ((err = pci_enable_device(pdev)) < 0) {
          printk(KERN_ERR "pcnet32.c: failed to enable device"
                        " -- err=%d\n", err);
          return err;
  }
  pci_set_master(pdev);
  return pcnet32_probe1(ioaddr, pdev->irq, 1, card_idx, pdev);
}
```

First, the I/O addresses of the card are read. As the driver knows the PCnet32 network card, it knows that it is an I/O address.

Since the PCnet32 network board works by using busmaster DMA, it should first check whether this is possible with the current architecture. The following structure is used for this:

```
int pci_dma_supported(struct pci_dev *hwdev, dma_addr_t mask);
```

As the second parameter, the function must be submitted a mask of all possible address bits that the PCI device can generate. In the case of the PCnet32 network card, this is the PCNET32_DMA_MASK constant, which is defined as 0xFFFFFFFF, since this network card can generate every possible 32-bit address. There are even PCI cards that, for example, can only produce 24-bit addresses. The 0x00FFFFFF constant must be submitted for these devices. If the pci_dma_supported() function returns the value 0, the DMA access cannot be carried out on the current architecture.

If the DMA access is now supported, the driver activates the device. This occurs with the help of the following function:

```
int pci_enable_device(struct pci_dev *dev);
```

This function activates the resources of the card, if they aren't already activated. This function can fail if it runs into resource conflicts. However, this shouldn't happen if the PCI-BIOS is free from errors. With busmaster-capable cards, the PCI specification allows the busmaster bit mode to be turned off. If the device will be used in busmaster mode, the busmaster bit must be put in the PCI command register. The following function is used to do this:

```
void pci_set_master(struct pci_dev *dev);
```

This function sets the master bit and also increases the PCI latency counter to 64 if it was previously set to a value smaller than 16. Notice that the occupancy of the interrupt line isn't necessarily exclusive; the PCI specification even stipulates that a driver has to cope with shared interrupts from various devices (see also Section 7.3.3).

Compatibility mode

LINUX 2.4 also supports the old PCI access functions which are not Hot-Plugin capable. However, these should no longer be used for newer driver implementations. Therefore only a short summary follows:

```
struct pci_dev *pci_find_device(unsigned int vendor, unsigned int device,
  const struct pci_dev *from);
struct pci_dev *pci_find_subsys(unsigned int vendor, unsigned int device,
  unsigned int ss_vendor, unsigned int ss_device,
  const struct pci_dev *from);
struct pci_dev *pci_find_class(unsigned int class,
  const struct pci_dev *from);
```

pci_find_device() permits it to look for a device in the PCI address space. The vendor vendor code and device device code are required for this. If a device is found, this function returns a pointer to the pci_dev structure of the device. To search for further devices, pci_find_device can be called again. For this purpose, the last parameter must be the pointer to the pci_dev structure of the device found last. NULL starts the search all over again. pci_find_subsys allows the specification of a subsystem vendor and device code. Finally, pci_find_class looks for a device class in the PCI address space.

There is also the option of going through the list of all the PCI devices of the system. The following code is used to do this:

```
struct pci_dev *dev;
pci_for_each_dev(dev) {
        /* Loop, will be gone through for every device */
}
```

In addition to the pci_for_each_dev macro, there is also a version pci_for_each_dev_reverse, which goes through the list from the finish to the start. This was the order used in older LINUX versions.

Access to the configuration space

To be able to access the configuration space, LINUX has the following functions:

```
int pci_read_config_byte(struct pci_dev *dev, int where, u8 *val);
int pci_read_config_word(struct pci_dev *dev, int where, u16 *val);
int pci_read_config_dword(struct pci_dev *dev, int where, u32 *val);
int pci_write_config_byte(struct pci_dev *dev, int where, u8 val);
int pci_write_config_word(struct pci_dev *dev, int where, u16 val);
int pci_write_config_dword(struct pci_dev *dev, int where, u32 val);
```

These functions should not be used to query the resources of a PCI device, but only to read and write other configuration registers.

Access to the device address space

Before the I/O address space of a PCI device can be accessed, it should be allocated by using request_region(). Memory areas are allocated similarly to this by means of the macro

request_mem_region(from, num, name)

This makes sure that the driver only accesses the resources of the PCI device.

To be able to access the memory of a PCI device it must be mapped first into the virtual address space of the CPU. This is done using the ioremap() and iounmap() functions. ioremap() then returns a virtual address, which can be used to directly access the memory.

Furthermore, it can be necessary to "convert" the memory addresses into the respective view. The problem then is that there are at least three kinds of memory addresses on a PC these days:

Physical addresses These addresses exist on the memory bus as well as on the CPU.
Virtual addresses These addresses only exist within the CPU. The CPU undertakes a
  conversion to a physical address during access to a virtual address.
Bus addresses These addresses correspond to physical addresses "from the other side"
  of the PCI buses. The bus addresses are also the ones that a PCI device has to generate
  in order to be able to select a memory cell.

In the x86 architecture, the bus address is identical to the physical address. This is unfortunately not the case for all LINUX-supporting architectures. Therefore, special care must be taken during address conversion to make the driver compatible with all architectures. The following functions serve this purpose:

```
unsigned long virt_to_phys(volatile void * address);
unsigned long phys_to_virt(volatile void * address);
unsigned long virt_to_bus(volatile void * address);
unsigned long bus_to_virt(volatile void * address);
```

Virtual addresses are used in order to be able to access memory areas from the kernel. Bus addresses are used to access memory from a PCI device. Physical addresses are never used directly, only as parameters for functions of memory management.

7.2.3   The dinosaur – the ISA bus

Automatic hardware recognition

The ISA bus, which many still swear by, is still available on many PC boards because of its historical meaning. However, only a few cards for this bus are still in circulation today. With more recent boards, the ISA is created over a bridge on the PCI bus. This could remove many problems but unfortunately could also create new ones. Even though limits for the possible port addresses[5] are set by the design of ISA buses, it often leads to address overlaps.

The most common example was the grabbing of the I/O addresses of the COM4 interface by ISA cards with the S3 chip.

Moreover, the market trend led to different hardware using the same I/O address space. Usually it was possible to select different basic addresses by using *jumpers*. This was often necessary, but confused ordinary users as there was usually only a note in the documentation, that one should "keep the standard occupancy and in the case of a non-functioning jumper xx set to position YY."

---

5   Most PC hardware only decodes the first 10 bits of a port address. This means that all the possible port addresses in the area 0–0x3ff are shown.

During the development of a driver, there is the option of the "safe" way. All the parameters are set before compiling. This is very safe, but not very comfortable. Who wants to compile the kernel every time they change a jumper setting?

Algorithms which try to "recognize" the hardware are also searched for. In an ideal case it should be possible only by reading the I/O ports, but unfortunately this was often not the option during the development of the hardware. Therefore, one is forced to write in values in blue, select I/O ports, and make an independent decision from this. Normally, certain unusual features of single chips are used (bugs or "unused features"), which can lead to compatible hardware from another vendor not being recognized.

However, by far the most unpleasant problem is that the "test writing" of the functions can impede other hardware or bring the system down. The second case frequently occurs during the development of a driver, because usually one only notices that another device does not work much later on.

If a device driver wants to test I/O ports, permission should first be obtained using the macro `check_region()`. For this purpose, we want to look at a fragment of the skeleton for ISA network drivers.

```
#include <linux/ioport.h>
netcard_probe(struct device *dev)
{
  ...
  for (i = 0; netcard_portlist[i]; i++) {
        int ioaddr = netcard_portlist[i];
        if (check_region(ioaddr, NETCARD_IO_EXTENT))
                continue;
        if (netcard_probe1(dev, ioaddr) == 0)
                return 0;
  }
  return -ENODEV;
}
```

If the `check_region()` returns a value unequal to 0, at least one port in the area may not be accessed, and a test has to be carried out. If a driver has its hardware clearly identified, the accompanying I/O ports should be locked with the help of the `request_region()` macro.

Automatic interrupt recognition

On many ISA expansion cards the IRQ used must be set by using the jumper. First of all, extensions such as PCI or Plug and Play allow the setting and selection of the configuration of extension cards. They therefore pose the problem of determining the IRQs used during the initialization of the kernel. However, because an automatic interrupt identifier represents an element of uncertainty and can bring the system down, it should not be used when modules are being loaded.

The procedure for inquiring about IRQs used is actually always the same. All the possible IRQs are simply occupied, the device to be mentioned is forced to trigger an IRQ and – if only one IRQ from those previously allocated responds – we have probably found one. All other IRQs must now be released. LINUX already has functions which simplify this recognition. Next we will look at a fragment, as an example, from the WaveFront-Sound driver:

```c
unsigned long irq_mask;
short reported_irq;

irq_mask = probe_irq_on ();

outb (0x0, dev.control_port);
outb (0x80 | 0x40 | bits, dev.data_port);
wavefront_should_cause_interrupt(0x80|0x40|0x10|0x1,
                    dev.control_port,
                    (reset_time*HZ)/100);

reported_irq = probe_irq_off (irq_mask);

if (reported_irq != dev.irq) {
        if (reported_irq == 0) {
                printk(KERN_ERR LOGNAME
                        "No unassigned interrupts detected "
                        "after h/w reset\n");
        } else if (reported_irq < 0) {
                printk(KERN_ERR LOGNAME
                        "Multiple unassigned interrupts detected "
                        "after h/w reset\n");
        } else {
                printk(KERN_ERR LOGNAME "autodetected IRQ %d not the "
                        "value provided (%d)\n", reported_irq,
                        dev.irq);
        }
        dev.irq = -1;
        return 1;
} else {
        printk (KERN_INFO LOGNAME "autodetected IRQ at %d\n",
        reported_irq);
}
```

IRQ recognition begins with a call of the `probe_irq_on()` function. This returns a bitmap `irqs`, that contains all currently unassigned and available IRQs for automatic probing. After this, a function is called which triggers an IRQ through the sound card. This function should also wait a short period of time, in order to bridge the time up to the triggering of the interrupt through the hardware. After this, the call of `probe_irq_off()` ends the recognition. This function must have the bit mask delivered by `probe_irq_on()` as an argument, and delivers the number of displayed IRQs as the return value. If this number is smaller than 0, more than one IRQ had appeared. This can be an indication that a card is configured incorrectly or that another piece of hardware is in conflict. You can try the recognition once more, or give up as in the example. The value 0 shows that no IRQ has appeared, for example because no IRQ jumper was set at all. In this case the user must intervene. Only a positive return value indicates that the IRQ has been recognized.

The recognition of DMA channels is more difficult. Fortunately, most cards support only a few DMA channels, and these are selectable in the configuration register. If you do not have this option, the DMA channel will be created by a setup parameter. One can also try simply to allocate all possible channels and trigger a DMA transfer. This is only possible if the hardware has the option of establishing whether the transfer is successful.

DMA operation

If a particularly large amount of data is to be continuously transported from or to a device, the DMA operation can be used. In this operation mode, the DMA controller transfers data without assistance from the CPU to a device's memory. Usually, the device will then trigger an IRQ, so that the next DMA transfer can be prepared in the treated ISR. This way of working is ideal for multitasking, since the CPU can take on other tasks during the data transfer. Unfortunately there are also examples of DMA-capable devices that do not support an IRQ. Some hand scanners belong to this category. If you want to write a device driver for this class, you will have to poll the DMA controller in order to determine the end of a transfer.

In addition to this, one must also struggle with problems of a completely different manner with DMA operations from devices which come partly from compatibility with an ancient PC.

Since the DMA controller works independently of the processor, it only recognizes physical addresses.

The base address register of the DMA controller only has a width of 16 bits. No DMA transfer over the limit of 64 KB can be carried out using this. Since the first available controller in the AT carries out an 8-bit transfer, with the help of the four first DMA channels no more than 64 KB can be transferred at once. The second available DMA controller in the AT carries out a 16-bit transfer, i.e., two bytes are transferred in a cycle. Since the basic address register only has a width of 16 bits here as well, the second controller adds a 0 and the transfer must therefore always start with direct addresses (the contents of the register are therefore multiplied by 2). By doing this, the second controller can transfer a maximum of 128 KB, but not exceed a 128 KB limit.

In addition to the basic address register there is also a DMA page register, which takes on the address bits above A15. As this register in the AT only has a width of 8 bits, the DMA transfer can only be carried out within the first 16 MB. Although the EISA bus and many chipsets lifted this restriction (unfortunately not compatible there), LINUX doesn't support this.

In order to solve these problems, in earlier versions of LINUX the sound driver carried out the DMA transfer to the sound card using a special buffer.

Because in protected mode the DMA concept is disturbed by the necessary physical addresses, only the operating system or the device driver can use DMA. Therefore, the sound driver copies the data first with the help of the processors in the DMA buffer, and then transfers it to the sound card by using DMA. Although this procedure actually contradicts the idea of transmitting data without the help of the processor, it is still reasonable since one does not have to worry about the timing of the data transfer to the sound card or other devices. In the following we will look more closely at the concept of DMA.

An example of the DMA operation

To examine DMA in more detail, we need to start by considering how the DMA controller is programmed. However, the following is intended only as a brief introduction: for more detailed information the reader is referred to [Mes02].

As mentioned earlier, the DMA has a base register which holds the lower 16 bits of the address of the area of memory to be transferred. A second 16-bit register, the base count register, contains the number of data transfers to be carried out. This register is decremented on each data transfer, and the point at which a value of 0xFFFF is reached is called *Terminal Count* (TC). Every DMA controller possesses four channels, with a base register and a base count register assigned to each channel. An input signal DREQx and an output signal DACKx are also assigned to each channel. A device requests a DMA transfer by activating the DREQ signal. When the DMA controller has obtained control over the bus, it indicates this by means of the DACK signal. At any given time, however, a maximum of one DACK can be active, and the individual DREQ signals are therefore given different priorities. Usually it is DREQ0 which has the highest and DREQ3 the lowest priority. By modifying the request register, DMA transfer can also be activated "by hand," as if the relevant DREQ signal had been received. However, this facility is not normally used; it is provided in the PC/XT and other machines to allow a memory-to-memory transfer, but this is not possible on an AT, as the DMA channel 0 of the master controller, which is required for this mode, is used to cascade the slave controller.

In all, each DMA controller possesses 12 different registers governing its operation. However, the functions in the LINUX kernel fully encapsulate these registers, so a further explanation is required here.

The DMA controller also supports a number of different transfer modes, which must be set in the mode registers for each channel. These include the following operation modes:

Demand transfer In this mode, the DMA controller continues transferring data until the terminal count is reached or the device deactivates the DREQ. The transfer is then suspended until the device reactivates the DREQ.

Single transfer In this mode, the DMA controller transfers one value at a time and then returns the bus to the processor. Each further transfer must be requested by the DREQ signal or an access to the request register. This mode is used for slow devices, such as floppy disks and scanners.

Block transfer In this mode, the DMA controller carries out a block transfer without relinquishing the bus. The transfer is initiated by a DREQ.

Cascade Cascading of another DMA controller: in this mode the DMA controller passes on the DMA request it receives and thus enables more than one controller to be used. By default, DMA channel 0 of the second controller (or DMA channel 4 in consecutive numbering), which is the master in the AT, is in this mode.

These basic modes may be used in both read and write transfers. The DMA controller can both increment and decrement the memory addresses, enabling a transfer to start with the highest address. In addition, auto-initialization can be selected and deselected. If it is selected, the relevant DMA channel will automatically be reinitialized to the starting value when the terminal count is reached. This allows constant amounts of data to be transferred to or from a fixed buffer in memory.

Let us take as an example of DMA operation the implementation of a driver for a hand-held scanner. In the same way as the IRQs to be used, the DMA channel must first be allocated.

```
if ( (err = request_dma(AC4096_DMA, AC4096_SCANNER_NAME)) ) {
  printk("AC 4096: unable to get DMA%d\n", AC4096_DMA);
  return err;
}
```

The functions `request_dma()` and `free_dma()` work in a similar way to `request_irq()` and `free_irq()` described earlier. The `request_dma()` function expects to be given the number of the DMA channel and the driver wishing to use this channel. However, this name is only inspected by the *Proc* file system. As with IRQs, DMA channels should only be allocated if they are about to be used: as a rule, this will be done in a device driver's open function. If a driver is using both IRQ and DMA channels, the interrupt should be allocated first, followed by the DMA channel.

The allocation of buffers can also be carried out in the open function, but also as late as the `read()` or `write()` stages, memory is a far less critical resource. Since LINUX version 1.2 it has no longer been necessary to assign permanent buffers for DMA transfer when booting the kernel. This means that device drivers can now be implemented as modules using DMA transfers. The LINUX memory administration routines themselves ensure that memory allocated for DMA buffers is below the 16 MB limit and no 64 KB boundaries are crossed. To use this facility, memory must be allocated using the kmalloc() function and the additional GFP_DMA flag must be passed to it.

```
tmp = kmalloc(blksize + HEADERSIZE, GFP_DMA | GFP_KERNEL);
```

The DMA transfer can now be initiated. As mentioned above, the functions for this encapsulate the hardware to an extreme degree, so that the DMA transfer is easy to program. As a general rule, it will even confirm cases in the sequence shown in the following example.

```
static void start_dma_xfer(char *buf)
{
unsigned long flags;
flags = claim_dma_lock(void);
disable_dma(AC4096_DMA);
clear_dma_ff(AC4096_DMA);
set_dma_mode(AC4096_DMA, DMA_MODE_READ);
set_dma_addr(AC4096_DMA, (unsigned int) buf);
set_dma_count(AC4096_DMA, hw_modeinfo.bpl);
enable_dma(AC4096_DMA);
release_dma_lock(flags);
}
```

The function disable_dma() disables the DMA transfer on the channel given to the function as an argument. The programming of the DMA controller can now be carried out. The clear_dma_ff() function deletes the DMA pointer flip-flop. As the DMA controller only has 8-bit data ports, accesses to internal 16-bit registers have to be broken up. The DMA pointer flip-flop indicates whether the next value is to be interpreted as LSB (least significant bit) or MSB (most significant bit). Each time it is deleted, the DMA controller expects the LSB as the next value. As the calls to set set_dma_addr() and set_dma_count() rely on this, clear_dma_ff() should be called once before these functions are used. The function set_dma_mode() sets the mode of the DMA channel. The modes supported by LINUX via pre-defined macros are:

DMA_MODE_READ Single transfer from device to memory without auto-initialization, addresses incremented.

DMA_MODE_WRITE Single transfer from memory to device without auto-initialization, addresses incremented.

DMA_MODE_CASCADE Cascading of another controller.

However, these modes are adequate for most cases.

All that remains is to set the address of the buffer area by a call to set_dma_addr()
and the number of bytes to be transferred via set_dma_count(). Both functions take care
of the proper conversion of the values they are given for the DMA controller and therefore
expect even addresses and an even number of bytes if a DMA channel for the second
controller is used.

The functions claim_dma_lock() and release_dma_lock() make sure that the
programming of the DMA controllers is interrupted neither by an interrupt nor by a kernel
thread.

If the device generates an interrupt after the transfer is complete, an ISR should be
implemented matching the one pure interrupt operation. After testing, if necessary, to find
out whether the interrupt really has been triggered by the device concerned, the waiting
process must be woken up by a call wake_up_interruptible(), and if there is still data
to be transferred the next DMA transfer must be initiated.

If, as in our example, the device does not trigger an interrupt, the DMA controller must
be queried as to whether the end of the DMA transfer has been reached. This involves
querying the status register in the relevant DMA controller. The lower four bits of the
register indicate whether the corresponding channel has reached a terminal count. If the bit
is set, the TC has been reached and the transfer is complete. Every time the status register
is read, however, these bits are cleared. The following function can be used for the
interrogation procedure.

```
int dma_tc_reached(int channel)
{
  if (channel < 4)
        return ( inb(DMA1_STAT_REG) & (1 << channel) );
  else
        return ( inb(DMA2_STAT_REG) & (1 << (channel & 3)) );
}
```

This can be used in a polling routine, for example as follows:

```
  int dma_polled(void)
{
        unsigned long count = 0;

        do {
                count ++;
                if (current->need_resched)
                        schedule();
        } while (!dma_tc_reached(dma_channel) && count < TIMEOUT );
        …

}
```

However, depending on the device concerned, this may result in a loss of data as the time before the process is next activated (that is, when the process returns from schedule()) cannot be predicted. When using a scanner, this may mean the loss of scan lines if the device has no buffer or only a very small one. Our example therefore uses a different option: The DMA controller is queried in a timer routine which is called 50 times per second. This routine operates just like the corresponding ISR, but instead of testing whether the device had triggered the interrupt, it tests whether the DMA transfer has been completed.

```c
static inline void start_snooping(void)
{
  timer.expires = jiffies + 2;
  timer.function = test_dma_rdy;
  add_timer(&timer);
}

static void test_dma_rdy(unsigned long dummy)
{
  static int needed_bytes;
  char cmd;

  if (! xfer_going) return;
  start_snooping(); /* restart timer */

  if ( dma_tc_reached(AC4096_DMA) ) {
        ...

        stop_scanner(); /* Stop scanner */

        /* if a sufficiently large buffer is still free */
        if (WR_BUFSPC >= hw_modeinfo.bpl) {
              ...
              /* initiate next DMA transfer */
              start_dma_xfer(WR_ADDR);
        }
        else xfer_going = 0;
  }
}
```

7.2.4 ISA-PnP

The worst thing that was done to the ISA bus (and LINUX) was to introduce ISA plug and play (PnP).[6] The basic idea of PnP is to initialize the card during the first access and adjust the parameters such as basic addresses, and IRQ and DMA channels, during the boot. Therefore, particular addresses must be reserved with which the card can be detected and initialized. The problem here is: With ISA buses there are no opportunities to recognize and exclude hardware conflicts. Because of this, neither can be excluded, and the hard disk controller XY is now not at the address and the hard disk is formatted (this is very improbable... but ...).

LINUX 2.4 now supports ISA-PnP in the kernel. It is therefore possible to integrate drivers in the kernel for ISA-PnP cards. Before version 2.4 the `isapnptools` package from Peter Fox was used to initialize PnP cards; and a suitable driver then had to be loaded as a module, in which the initializing parameter was entered as parameter. The handling of ISA-PnP relied on the PCI bus handling, and the same structure `pci_dev` was even used to include the allocated resources.

Searching for ISA-PnP devices

In the world of PnP, the concepts device and function are used to recognize hardware units. The concept device then corresponds to a complete function unit, e.g., a PnP plug-in card. Every device has at least one or more functions. Functions are therefore the smallest hardware unit. This is why, for example, a sound card can contain the functions Audio DSP and Gameport. Before a device can be responded to, the driver must first determine whether such a device is actually available. The following function is used for this purpose:

```
struct pci_bus *isapnp_find_card(unsigned short vendor,
                                 unsigned short device,
                                 struct pci_bus *from);
```

The `isapnp_find_card` function searches through the ISA-PnP bus for a PnP card. The card is then recognized by a vendor and a device code. Both these codes are 16 bits wide. The vendor code is a string of 3 letters which are all coded with respectively 5 or 6 bits. The `ISAPNP_VENDOR` code produces this representation from the vendor code. The coding of the device code is produced from the `ISAPNP_DEVICE` macro. The third parameter gives the start point of the search; NULL begins the search with the first PnP card. If the `from` parameter is not NULL, the search begins after the device indicated in `from`.

If the device is found, it can be searched for functions. The following function is used:

```
struct pci_dev *isapnp_find_dev(struct pci_bus *card,
                                short vendor,
                                unsigned short function,
                                struct pci_dev *from);
```

---

6 Because of the frequent problems, also called "Plug and Pray."

The card parameter describes the device the function should search for. This is normally the return value of the isapnp_find_card function. If this parameter is equal to NULL the complete ISA-PnP bus is searched for the function. The function is then labeled by the two 16-bit codes vendor and function, in which the macro ISAPNP_FUNCTION is used for the production of the function code.

Alternatively, it is also possible to search for a device in a similar way to searching for the PCI bus driver with the callback function. The following structures and functions are used to do this:

```
struct isapnp_card_id {
  /* wanted driver data */
  unsigned long driver_data;
  /* vendor and device code */
  unsigned short card_vendor, card_device;
  struct {
        /* function code */
        unsigned short vendor, function;
  } devs[ISAPNP_CARD_DEVS];
};
  struct isapnp_device_id {
  /* vendor and device code */
  unsigned short card_vendor, card_device;
  /* function code */
  unsigned short vendor, function;
  /* wanted driver data */
  unsigned long driver_data;
};
int isapnp_probe_cards(const struct isapnp_card_id *ids,
  int (*probe)(struct pci_bus *_card,
                const struct isapnp_card_id *_id));
int isapnp_probe_devs(const struct isapnp_device_id *ids,
  int (*probe)(struct pci_dev *dev,
                const struct isapnp_device_id *id));
```

The isapnp_probe_cards function searches the entire list of the PnP devices for a particular device with one or more particular functions and calls of the probe() function for every matching combination that is submitted as a parameter. If a vendor or device code does not match, the value ISAPNP_ANY_ID is used. The list of the functions to be found is exited with the value of 0 for the components vendor and function. The probe() function should return a value larger or equal to NULL if the initialization of the device was positive.

isapnp_probe_cards returns the number of matched and positively "tried" devices as the return value.

The function `isapnp_probe_devs` works in a similar way; however, it only looks for a device with a function.

As no driver presently uses the functions that were named last, we have to make do with the example from the ISA-PnP documentation (`Documentation/isapnp.txt`):

```
static struct isapnp_card_id card_ids[] __devinitdata = {
  {
        ISAPNP_CARD_ID('A','D','V', 0x550a),
        devs: {
                ISAPNP_DEVICE_ID('A', 'D', 'V', 0x0010),
                ISAPNP_DEVICE_ID('A', 'D', 'V', 0x0011)
        },
        driver_data: 0x1234,
  },
  {
        ISAPNP_CARD_END,
  }
};
ISAPNP_CARD_TABLE(card_ids);
```

The `ISAPNP_CARD_ID` macro generates the vendor as well as the device code. Then, only devices which show at least two functions are searched for. The vendor and device code produce the macro `ISAPNP_DEVICE_ID`. The macro `ISAPNP_CARD_END` finally produces an entry with a zero vendor and device code and completes the search list. The `ISAPNP_CARD_TABLE` macro finally makes sure that the table is exported if the driver is compiled as a module. In this way, a daemon working in user mode could notice which modules have to be loaded.

The second example shows the usage of the `isapnp_probe_devs` function:

```
static struct isapnp_device_id device_ids[] __devinitdata = {
  { ISAPNP_DEVICE_SINGLE('E','S','S', 0x0968, 'E','S','S', 0x0968), },
  { ISAPNP_DEVICE_SINGLE_END, }
};
MODULE_DEVICE_TABLE(isapnp, device_ids);
```

The macro `ISAPNP_DEVICE_SINGLE` produces a complete function definition consisting of the vendor and device code as well as function code. The `ISAPNP_DEVICE_SINGLE_END` macro then in turn exits the table. With help of the macro `MODULE_DEVICE_TABLE` the table is then exported if the driver is compiled as a module.

Configuring ISA-PnP devices

If the function that should respond to the driver is now also found, the PnP card can be configured. In order to do this, it is necessary to call the returned `prepare` function of the `pci_dev` structure. This function initializes all the resource entries in the `pci_dev` structure. For this, no concrete values are assigned, but just the resource types and their qualities (I/O port, memory, IRQ). If the function has been configured already (e.g., through the BIOS or other mechanisms), it returns `EBUSY`, but does not change the configuration. All the resources which carry the `IORESOURCE_AUTO` attribute can now be explicitly assigned. The following function is used to do this:

```
void isapnp_resource_change (struct resource *resource,
                                    unsigned long start,
                                    unsigned long size);
```

It is worth noting that this function doesn't distinguish between the resource types; therefore it is possible to assign I/O ports as well as memory. The `flags` component in the `resource` structure gives the resources information in this way. The function `activate()` of the structure `pci_dev` now takes on the automatic assignment of all resources that have not yet been assigned and activates the function. If they have already been activated, `activate()` returns the current settings.

Let us have a look at PnP recognition in the example of the sound blaster driver:

```
static struct {
  char *name;
  unsigned short      card_vendor, card_device,
                      audio_vendor, audio_function,
                      mpu_vendor, mpu_function,
                      opl_vendor, opl_function;
                      short dma, dma2, mpu_io, mpu_irq;
} sb_isapnp_list[] = {
{"Sound Blaster 16",
ISAPNP_VENDOR('C','T','L'), ISAPNP_DEVICE(0x0024),
ISAPNP_VENDOR('C','T','L'), ISAPNP_FUNCTION(0x0031),
0,0,0,0,
0,1,1,-1},
  ...
  {0}
};
```

The field `sb_isapnp_list[]` contains the vendor and device codes of all the sound blaster cards as well as their cloning. In addition to this, it also contains the coding of all the possible functions on the cards, like Audio-DSP, MPU, and OPL. The recognition starts with the `sb_isapnp_probe` function:

```
int sb_isapnp_probe(struct address_info *hw_config,
  struct address_info *mpu_config, int card)
{
```

```
...
while ((bus = isapnp_find_card(
             sb_isapnp_list[i].card_vendor,
             sb_isapnp_list[i].card_device,
             bus))) {
  if(sb_isapnp_init(hw_config, mpu_config, bus, i, card)) {
        /* found */
        return 0;
        }
        ...
    }
...
}
```

This function calls isapnp_find_card() for all cards in the sb_isapnp_list[] field. If the device is found the sb_isapnp_init() function is called.

```
int sb_isapnp_init(struct address_info *hw_config,
  struct address_info *mpu_config, struct pci_bus *bus,
  int slot, int card)
{
  ...
  if(sb_init(bus, hw_config, mpu_config, slot, card)) {
             /* found */
             return 1;
        }
  ...
}
```

This function first calls sb_init() to activate all functions on the sound card:

```
struct pci_dev *sb_init(struct pci_bus *bus,
  struct address_info *hw_config,
  struct address_info *mpu_config,
  int slot, int card)
{
  /* configuring audio*/
  if((sb_dev[card] = isapnp_find_dev(bus,
             sb_isapnp_list[slot].audio_vendor,
             sb_isapnp_list[slot].audio_function,
             NULL))) {
        int ret;
        ret = sb_dev[card]->prepare(sb_dev[card]);
        /* if the audio function should already be configured
```

```
                * break off the configuration and then proceed
                * and use anyway. Some other way to check this? */
                if(ret && ret != -EBUSY) {
                printk(KERN_ERR "sb: ISAPnP found device that could not"
                                    " be autoconfigured.\n");
                    return(NULL);
            }
        if(ret == -EBUSY)
                audio_activated[card] = 1;
        if((sb_dev[card] = activate_dev(
                    sb_isapnp_list[slot].name,
                    "sb", sb_dev[card]))) {
            hw_config->io_base = sb_dev[card]->resource[0].start;
            hw_config->irq = sb_dev[card]->irq_resource[0].start;
            ...
        } else
                return(NULL);
    } else
            return(NULL);
    ...
    return(sb_dev[card]);
}
```

In this function, all ISA-PnP functions belonging to the card found now become activated. After this, the returned structure is then selected to initialize values such as I/O address, interrupt channel, etc. In the audio_activated[] field a note is made of whether the function was already activated or not.

If a driver is activated as a module and it has activated the PnP hardware, it should deactivate this before it is unloaded. To do this, the deactivate() function of the pci_dev structure is used. In our example, with help from the field audio_activated[] it was established whether the function has to be deactivated or not.

7.3   POLLING, INTERRUPTS, AND WAITING QUEUES

In comparison to the CPU, most of the hardware is very slow. It therefore is not desirable in multiprocessing operations to let the CPU wait for the time it takes a hardware operation to complete, i.e., one would like to use the spare time for other tasks. Because of these circumstances, no simple query loops can be used to query the hardware status, unless one gives control back to LINUX. There are several methods that can be used for these tasks.

7.3.1 | **Polling**

One of these methods is to call `schedule()`, which arranges for the LINUX scheduler to assign control to a new process via the CPU.

The "number randomizer" (/dev/random) works by default in the polling operation. It queries the "entropy pool" until sufficient random values have accumulated. The source of this procedure is as follows:

```
static ssize_t
random_read(struct file * file, char * buf, size_t nbytes,
loff_t *ppos)
{
  ...
  ssize_t                     n, retval = 0, count = 0;

  if (nbytes == 0)
        return 0;


  ...
  while (nbytes > 0) {
        set_current_state(TASK_INTERRUPTIBLE);

        n = nbytes;
        if (n > SEC_XFER_SIZE)
                n = SEC_XFER_SIZE;
        if (n > random_state->entropy_count / 8)
                n = random_state->entropy_count / 8;
        if (n == 0) {
                if (file->f_flags & O_NONBLOCK) {
                        retval = -EAGAIN;
                        break;
                }
                if (signal_pending(current)) {
                        retval = -ERESTARTSYS;
                        break;
                }
                schedule();
                continue;
        }
        n = extract_entropy(sec_random_state, buf, n,
                EXTRACT_ENTROPY_USER | EXTRACT_ENTROPY_SECONDARY);
        if (n < 0) {
```

```
                    retval = n;
                    break;
            }
     ...
}
```

If the entropy group is empty, it will first test whether the device was opened non-blocking. In this case, the error EAGAIN will be returned. Otherwise it must be checked whether there are signals for the process. The function signal_pending() tests this.

7.3.2 | Interrupt mode

In interrupt mode, the device informs the CPU via an interrupt channel (IRQ) if it has exited an operation. The prerequisite for this is that the hardware supports the triggering of interrupts.

This interrupts the running operation and executes an interrupt service routine (ISR). Further communication with the device is then carried out within the ISR.

A process that wants to write to the serial interface in interrupt mode is stopped by the device driver after writing a character with the interruptible_sleep_on(&lp->lp_wait_q) function. If the serial interface can accept additional characters, it triggers an IRQ. After that, the ISR wakes the process again and the event recurs. Another example is the serial mouse, which, with every movement, transfers data to the serial port that triggers an IRQ. The ISR then reads the data from the serial port first and provides the application program.

IRQs are installed with the help of the following function:

```
int request_irq(unsigned int irq,
        void (*handler)(int, struct pt_regs *),
        unsigned long irqflags, const char * devname,
        void *dev_id)
```

There are at least two possibilities of IRQ processing under LINUX. The irqflags argument gives information about which kind of interrupt is to be used. Older LINUX versions used to distinguish between slow and fast interrupts. Slow interrupts could be interrupted by other interrupts, fast ones couldn't. In addition to this, the bottom half handler was only started at the end of the slow interrupt.

LINUX 2.4 doesn't make this distinction any more, only the choice between interruptible and non-interruptible remains.

The installation of interruptible IRQs proceeds without the SA_INTERRUPT flag in the irqflags argument, the installation of non-interruptible IRQs with the SA_INTERRUPT flag. The name argument has no further meaning for the kernel; however, it is used by the *Proc* file system to show the owner of an IRQ. Therefore it should point to the name of the driver which uses the IRQ. The argument dev_id is given to the interrupt routine unchanged, and can therefore be used freely to submit additional data. If the IRQ was free and could be occupied, `request_irq()` returns 0.

The handler routine of an IRQ has the following appearance:

```
void do_irq(int irq, void *dev_id, struct pt_regs * regs);
```

Every ISR is given the called IRQ as an argument. Therefore, theoretically one can use the same ISR for several IRQs. The second argument is the pointer already described, `dev_id`, and the last argument is a pointer to the structure `pt_regs` and contains all the registers of the process which was interrupted by the IRQ. In this way, the timer interrupt can, for example, establish whether a process was interrupted in the kernel or in user mode and count the respective time up.

An example will show the installation of a non-interruptible interrupt:

```
if (request_irq(rtc_irq, rtc_interrupt, SA_INTERRUPT,
        "rtc", (void *)&rtc_port)) {
  printk(KERN_ERR "rtc: cannot register IRQ %d\n", rtc_irq);
  return -EIO;
}
```

Normally you would use non-interruptible interrupts for communication with the hardware.

7.3.3 Interrupt sharing

The number of free IRQs in a PC is restricted. Thus it can be sensible for various pieces of hardware to share interrupts. For PCI boards, this is mandatory.

The conditions required for this kind of interrupt sharing are the option of interrogating the hardware as to whether it generated the current interrupt or not, and the capability of the ISR to forward an interrupt not triggered by its hardware.

LINUX version 2.4 supports interrupt sharing by its ability to build chains of interrupt handling routines. When an interrupt occurs, each ISR in the chain is called by the function `handle_IRQ_event()`.

```
int handle_IRQ_event(unsigned int irq,
  struct pt_regs * regs, struct irqaction * action)
{
  int status;

  ...
  if (!(action->flags & SA_INTERRUPT))
        __sti();
  do {
        status |= action->flags;
        action->handler(irq, action->dev_id, regs);
```

```
        action = action->next;
    } while (action);
    if (status & SA_SAMPLE_RANDOM)
            add_interrupt_randomness(irq);
    __cli();
    ...
}
```

If an ISR capable of interrupt sharing is installed, this must be communicated to the `request_irq` function by setting the `SA_SHIRQ` flag. If another ISR also capable of interrupt sharing was already installed on this IRQ number, a chain is built. However, it is not possible to mix interruptible and non-interruptible interrupts, that is, an IRQ's handling routines must all be of the same type. As an example, we show a fragment of the DE4x5 Ethernet driver:

```
request_irq(dev->irq, (void *)de4x5_interrupt, SA_SHIRQ,
        lp->adapter_name, dev)
...
static void de4x5_interrupt(int irq, void *dev_id,
        struct pt_regs *regs)
{
    ...
    sts = inl(DE4X5_STS); /* read IRQ status register */
    outl(sts, DE4X5_STS); /* reset the interrupt board */
    if (!(sts & lp->irq_mask)) break; /* not from board, finished */
    ...
}
```

7.3.4 | Software interrupts

It is often the case that after the appearance of an interrupt, not all functions have to be executed immediately: "Important" actions must be carried out; others can be taken care of later or would take a relatively long time and it is better not to block the interrupt. The bottom halves were originally created for this purpose. This mechanism was replaced by the concept of software interrupts in LINUX 2.4 (see also Section 3.2.3). After every jump by `ret_from_syscall` and also after every interrupt, a set of a maximum of 32 software interrupts is called if no further hardware interrupts are running on the current processor at the same time.[7]

---

7 This can definitely happen, if e.g. an interruptible interrupt is interrupted.

7.3.5 Bottom halves – the lower interrupt halves

Bottom halves are the predecessors of software interrupts. If they are marked as active, they are each executed once and are then automatically marked as inactive. These bottom halves are atomic, that is, as long as one bottom half is active, none of the others can be executed, so that it is not necessary to protect them against interruptions.

The function used to install a bottom half is `init_bh()` which enters the bottom half into the function pointer table `bh_base`.

```
void init_bh(int nr, void (*routine)(void));
enum {
  TIMER_BH = 0,
  TQUEUE_BH,
  DIGI_BH,
  SERIAL_BH,
  RISCOM8_BH,
  SPECIALIX_BH,
  AURORA_BH,
  ESP_BH,
  SCSI_BH,
  IMMEDIATE_BH,
  CYCLADES_BH,
  CM206_BH,
  JS_BH,
  MACSERIAL_BH,
  ISICOM_BH
};
```

All bottom halves are authorized by default; however, they can be enabled and disabled using the functions:

```
void disable_bh(int nr);
void enable_bh(int nr);
```

The function

```
void mark_bh(int nr);
```

marks a bottom half, so that this bottom half is executed at the next available opportunity.

We will now examine how bottom halves are used, taking the timer interrupt as an example.

```
void do_timer(struct pt_regs *regs)
{
  (*(unsigned long *)&jiffies)++;
  ...
```

```
  mark_bh(TIMER_BH);
  ...
  }
  void timer_bh(void)
{
        update_times();
        run_timer_list();
  }
  void __init sched_init(void)
  {
        ...
        init_bh(TIMER_BH, timer_bh);
  ...
}
```

The init function of the scheduler installs timer_bh() as the bottom half. With every call to the timer interrupt, mark_bh(TIMER_BH) is called – that is, the bottom half is run at the first opportunity after completion of the keyboard interrupt, ideally immediately after it.

Bottom halves are implemented in version 2.4, assisted by software interrupts. The highest prioritized software interrupt HI_SOFTIRQ is used to execute the bottom half.

7.3.6 | Task queues

As the previous section shows, direct use of bottom halves is somewhat difficult because there are only 32, and some tasks are already assigned to fixed numbers. Since version 2.0, LINUX has therefore offered task queues as a dynamic extension of the concept of bottom halves.

Task queues allow an arbitrary number of functions to be entered in a queue and processed one after another at a later time. The linking together of the functions to be executed is carried out by means of the tq_struct structure.

```
struct tq_struct {
  struct list_head list ;    /* chaining with the next entry  */
  unsigned long sync;        /* synchronization flag          */
  void (*routine)(void *);   /* function to be called         */
  void *data;                /* arbitrary function argument    */
};
typedef struct list_head task_queue;
```

Before a function can be entered in a task queue, a tq_struct structure must be created and initialized. The routine component contains the address of the function to be called, while data holds an arbitrary argument to be passed to the function at call time.

The sync component must be initialized to 0. Insertion into a task queue is carried out by means of one of the following functions:

```
int queue_task(struct tq_struct *bh_pointer, task_queue *bh_list)
{
  int ret = 0;
  if (!test_and_set_bit(0,&bh_pointer->sync)) {
        unsigned long flags;
        spin_lock_irqsave(&tqueue_lock, flags);
        list_add_tail(&bh_pointer->list, bh_list);
        spin_unlock_irqrestore(&tqueue_lock, flags);
        ret = 1;
  }
  return ret;
}
```

The special versions queue_task_irq() and queue_task_irq_off() are no longer supported in version 2.4.

The function   run_task_queue()   processes a task queue.

```
run_task_queue(task_queue *list)
```

It takes a task queue as argument and processes all tq_struct structures inserted in the queue by calling their functions. Before the function is called, the sync flag is deleted so that within this function it would be possible to insert the tq_struct structure into an arbitrary task queue again.

In LINUX version 2.4, among other things the following task queues are defined:

tq_timer is called after each timer interrupt or processed on the next possible occasion.

tq_immediate is called at the next possible point in time after a call of the function mark_bh(IMMEDIATE_BH) and thus corresponds to the bottom half of version 1.x.

tq_disk is used by block devices and called at different points where the VFS must wait for incoming buffers or similar.

tq_disk shows that task queues need not necessarily be linked only to bottom halves. Task queues are implemented as pointers to a tq_struct structure and should be declared by means of the DECLARE_TASK_QUEUE() macro. They can be processed at any point by calling the function run_task_queue().

Processing of task queues inside interrupt service routines should, however, be avoided to prevent interrupts from being blocked for an unnecessarily long time.

7.3.7 | Timers

In many cases, the waiting process has to be woken up after a certain amount of time. For example, if the process waits for an interrupt which never happens because of a hardware fault or another problem.

In this case, LINUX offers the option of programming a timer, which wakes up the process again after a certain time (which can be adjusted). In the following example, after a while the timer calls for a timer interrupt routine, which registers the lost interrupts.

In the `init` routine of the driver the timer is initialized first, and then sets the timer interrupt routine.

```
...
static struct timer_list rtc_irq_timer;
...
static int __init rtc_init(void)
{
  ...
  init_timer(&rtc_irq_timer);
  rtc_irq_timer.function = rtc_dropped_irq;
  ...
}
```

After the hardware has been programmed for the triggering of the interrupts, a timer is programmed and started with `add_timer()` at a specific time (the number of timer ticks in jiffies):

```
  if (!(rtc_status & RTC_TIMER_ON)) {
        spin_lock_irq (&rtc_lock);
        rtc_irq_timer.expires = jiffies + HZ/rtc_freq + 2*HZ/100;
        add_timer(&rtc_irq_timer);
        rtc_status |= RTC_TIMER_ON;
        spin_unlock_irq (&rtc_lock);
  }
```

If the desired interrupt doesn't occur at the time that has been programmed, the timer expires and the `rtc_dropped_irq()` routine is called. This re-programs the corresponding module and starts the timer again. For this, the function `mod_timer()` is used.

```
void rtc_dropped_irq(unsigned long data)
{
  ...
  if (rtc_status & RTC_TIMER_ON)
        mod_timer(&rtc_irq_timer, jiffies + HZ/rtc_freq + 2*HZ/100);
  ...
```

```
}
static void rtc_interrupt(int irq, void *dev_id,
            struct pt_regs *regs)
{
  /*
   * Can be an alarm interrupt, update complete interrupt,
   * or a periodic interrupt. We store the status in the
   * low byte and the number of interrupts received since
   * the last read in the remainder of rtc_irq_data.
   */
  ...
  if (rtc_status & RTC_TIMER_ON)
        mod_timer(&rtc_irq_timer, jiffies + HZ/rtc_freq + 2*HZ/100);
  ...
}
```

The "real" interrupt routine must also restart the timer again, since a timer interrupt would otherwise follow. Finally, there is the del_timer() function, with which a timer can be deleted.

7.4 IMPLEMENTING A DRIVER

7.4.1 Example of a PC loudspeaker driver

If we are proposing to write a device driver for the internal loudspeaker, we cannot avoid taking a closer look at the hardware concerned and its control system. Although it has been part of the package since the earliest days of the PC, the internal speaker is not well suited to reproducing samples. As Figure 7.3 shows, the construction and programming of the speaker are both very simple.

The 8235 timer chip has three internal timers. Timer 2 is designed for use with the speaker, for which the output from timer 2 is connected via an AND gate to bit 1 of the system control latch at I/O address 0x61, with bit 0 used for starting or restarting timer 2.

Thus the speaker can only be fully turned on or switched off. The normal procedure is for timer 2 to be programmed as a frequency divider (meaning that both bits are set). This generates square waves, which account for the "typical" sound of internal speakers. The frequency is given by dividing the timer's basic frequency of 1.193MHz (= 4.77MHz / 4) by the timer constant that has been set.

To output an analog signal via the speaker, pulse-length modulation is employed. By rapid variation between on and off phases of different lengths, corresponding to the instantaneous analog value to be output, the mechanical inertia of the speaker can be

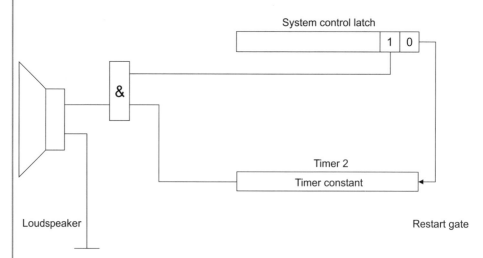

Figure 7.3:   Block diagram of PC speaker connections.

exploited to give a similar output. However, pulse-length modulation is very sensitive: even one missing sample will produce an annoying click from the speaker.[8]

The central problem in using pulse-length modules lies in determining and implementing the required time intervals. The first possibility is not to use timer 2 at all and control the output entirely with 1 bit of the system control latch. The time intervals can be generated by wait loops. This approach is the simplest to implement, but has two decisive drawbacks.

- The delay loops depend on the processor clock.
- Most of the time during output is spent on busy waiting; this is not acceptable in a multitasking operating system.

The second approach is to program timer 2 as a retriggerable oneshot. The timer is started by applying a 1 to the restart gate and produces 0 at the output. Once the timer constant has counted down, 1 is output. After a certain time, corresponding to the maximum sample value, a new constant is transferred to timer 2 and the timer is restarted. This constant time interval can then be generated again using a delay loop or timer 0, which generally runs in divider mode and generates an IRQ of 0 each time the timer constant reaches 0. This frequency generated by the timer 0 is also the sampling rate at which samples can be output. We shall refer to it below as the real sampling rate. Timer 2 must then be reinitialized in the interrupt handling routine. This procedure is shown in Figure 7.4.

The timer chip has four I/O ports. Port 0x43 is the mode control register. Data ports 0x40 to 0x42 are assigned to timers 0 to 2. This means that to program a timer, an instruction must be written to 0x43 and the timer constant in the appropriate data port. The structure of an instruction is very simple: bits 7 and 6 contain the number of the timer

---

8 This also accounts for the extraneous noise which sometimes accompanies floppy disk access or even mouse movements. If even a single interrupts fails to be handled, the dynamics of the speaker break down.

to be programmed, bits 5 and 4 contain one of the access modes shown in Table 7.2, and bits 3 to 1 the timer mode.

For example, to generate a 10,000 Hz tone the following steps are required:

```
outb_p (inb_p (0x61) | 3, 0x61);
          /* opens the AND gate and
           * sets the restart gate to active */
tc = 1193180 / 10000;
          /* calculates the timer required */
outb_p (0xb6, 0x43);
          /* corresponds to the instruction:
           * timer 2, Read/Write LSB then MSB, timer mode 3 */
outb_p (tc & 0xff, 0x42); outb ((tc >> 8) & 0xff, 0x42);
          /* writes the time constant to timer 2;
           * from now on the internal loudspeaker will emit a tone */
```

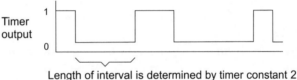

Length of interval is determined by timer constant 2

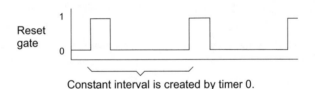

Constant interval is created by timer 0.

$$\text{Interval length} = \frac{\text{Timer constant}}{1{,}193{,}180} \text{ sec}$$

Figure 7.4: Pulse-length modulation using timers 0 and 2.

Table 7.2: Bits 4 and 5 in the timer instruction

Bits 54	Mode	Explanation
00	Latch	The counter is transferred to an internal register and can then be read out
01	LSB only	Only the bottom 8 bits of the counter are transferred
10	MSB only	Only the top 8 bits of the counter are transferred
11	LSB/MSB	First the bottom, and then the top 8 bits are transferred

The speaker can be silenced by: `outb(inb_p(0x61) & 0xfc, 0x61);`. This switches off the speaker as well as halting the timer.

Unfortunately, only timer 0 can generate an interrupt in a standard PC, which means that the second possibility described above is not entirely safe, since the timer interrupt IRQ0, which is so important under LINUX, is modified. The new interrupt routine must ensure that the original procedure is called again at exactly the same intervals. In addition, interrupt handling in protected mode needs considerably more time than in real mode, so the larger number of interrupts triggered consumes noticeably more computing time.

Let us now return to pulse-length modulation. As mentioned earlier, the choice of time interval is very important. Tests have shown that the best results are achieved with a real sampling rate between 16,000 and 18,000 Hz. The higher the sampling rate the better, as this specific frequency is audible as whistling.[9] When using timer 2, these frequencies give possible timer constants between 1 and 74 (0 would mean 65,536 and is therefore not admissible); so, as the constants are directly related to the samples, only six bits (1 to 65) can be output.

The maximum value possible for the real sampling rate is thus 18,357 Hz (or 1,193 MHz/65). However, this is not a very widely used figure; therefore other sampling rates are supported by generating and adding extra samples (*oversampling*). For the time, a simple algorithm arranges for the data to be "stretched" by repeating[10] each of the samples. For example, if the output is to be 10,000 Hz, each sample will need to be repeated on average about 1.8 times.

Compared with this, output via a digital–analog converter (DAC) is very straightforward. This simply connects to a parallel port and converts the incoming 8-bit sequence to an analog signal. As the parallel port buffers the incoming values, the structure of a DAC can be very simple, and in most basic versions it just consists of a resistor network. The parallel port can also output the data at virtually any speed, so timer 0 can be programmed with the true sampling rate.

This solution also avoids the need to transform the samples into a 6-bit representation; output via a DAC thus makes less demand on processor time than output via the internal speaker. And the final "plus" is that missing interrupts only make themselves heard as a slow-down in the output sound and in practice are as good as inaudible (within certain limits).

7.4.2 A simple driver

Now that the internal speaker's hardware has been discussed in detail, the question arises as to why a special device driver is required to take care of writing and reading at some I/O ports. To generate "noises" we could write a program `auplay`,[11] which would release the relevant ports by means of the system call `ioperm`:

---

9 The point at which this frequency becomes audible depends on the individual: I start hearing it from about 14,500 Hz onwards, others hear it from as far as 17,000 Hz.
10 Normally, the extra samples would be calculated by interpolation. However, this will not produce any improvement in quality when using the internal speaker for the output.
11 Rick Miller's `auplay` program provided the initial impetus for implementing a PC speaker driver.

```
if (ioperm(0x61,1,1) || ioperm(0x42,1,1) || ioperm(0x43,1,1)) {
    printf("can't get I/O permissions for internal speaker\n");
    exit(-1);
}
```

and then output the samples itself. However, this would have the following drawbacks:

■ The *ioperm* system call only works successfully with privileged authorizations. The program thus requires the set UID rights assigned to root. As a rule, no programs with the root set UID rights should exist in UNIX systems, as they would present a major security problem. This can normally be guaranteed by setting up special users and groups (for example, the group kmem to use the device /dev/kmem), but it is difficult to avoid this in our example.

A device driver, on the other hand, operates with kernel authorizations and thus free access to all resources – a fact which should always be borne in mind when implementing a driver, as errors in a driver could have more serious consequences than errors in a program.[12]

■ Probably the main problem is precise time determination for a program in a multi-tasking system. The only way of doing this is to use wait loops of the type:

```
for ( j = 1; j < DELAY; j++);
```

The busy waiting is not acceptable, as no precise determination of the sampling rate is possible. Use of the timer interrupt is a distinctly more elegant variant, but can only be done in the kernel.

■ Another problem is control of the PC speaker. Who guarantees that no other process will access the I/O ports at the same time and corrupt the sample? Using system V-IPC here (in this case semaphores) is like using a sledgehammer to crack a nut, especially as there is no way of knowing whether other programs may be accessing the same ports.

Compared with this, access restriction for devices is relatively simple and will be described below.

Writing an "audio daemon" which will read the sampled data from a named pipe and be run via the file rc.local when the system is booted is only of limited help. The problem of coordinating the timing remains.

This makes the device driver the best option. The actual implementation of the PC speaker driver involves filling in the structure file_operations described in the previous chapter, although the programmer will not need to complete all the functions, depending on the type of device. A further procedure used to initialize the driver must also be provided.

The names of these C functions should all be formed on the same principle to avoid conflicts with existing functions. The safest approach is to place an abbreviation for the name of the driver in front of the function name. For the PC speaker, or "pcsp" for short,

---

12 This is only true up to a point, as incorrect use of the mode control register for I/O address 0x43 by the auplay program could confuse the timer interrupt and cause the computer to crash.

this gives the functions `pcsp_init()`, `pcsp_read()` and so on, which will be explained in detail below. The same principle should be applied for external and static C variables.

7.4.3   The setup function

Sometimes it is desirable to pass parameters to a device driver on to the LINUX kernel. This may be necessary where automatic detection of hardware is not possible or may result in conflicts with other hardware, and can be passed to the kernel during the boot process. As a rule, these parameters will come in the form of a command line from the LINUX loader LILO (see Section D.2.5).

This command line will be analyzed in its component parts by the function `parse_options()`, which is located in `init/main.c`. The `checksetup()` function is called for each of the parameters and compares the beginning of the parameter with the string stored in the `__setup_start` field, calling the corresponding `setup` function whenever these match. If this returns a value unequal to zero, the editing of this parameter will be ended, otherwise it searches for other matches. A parameter should therefore have the following structure in version 2.4:

If empty space characters occur in the parameter string, the complete string must be split up using commas.

> *name=parameter*

The parameter string simply is passed on to the `setup` function, which must have the following construction:

```
int setup_func(char *);
```

The `setup` function for the PC loudspeaker will be used as an example here.

```
static int __init pcsp_setup(char *str)
{
  if (!strcmp(str, "off")) {
        pcsp_enabled = 0;
        return 1;
  }
  pcsp.maxrate = simple_strtol(str, NULL, 0);
  pcsp_enabled = 1;
  return 1;
}
__setup("pcsp=", pcsp_setup);
```

As this shows, the function first tests for the presence of the word "off," and therefore the boot parameter "pscp=off" switches the PC driver off. It is otherwise assumed that the submitted string is a numeric parameter which is used for the initialization of one of the global variables of the PC loudspeaker driver.

This function now needs to be registered. In LINUX versions earlier than 2.4, the function then had to be entered in the global array `bootsetups[]`. The current version implements an elegant mechanism, however, which uses something like "link magic." For this, the following macro is used:

```
struct kernel_param {
  const char *str;
  int (*setup_func)(char *);
};
#define __setup(str, fn)                                     \
  static char __setup_str_##fn[] __initdata = str;           \
  static struct kernel_param __setup_##fn                    \
  __attribute__((unused)) __initsetup =                      \
          { __setup_str_##fn, fn }
```

This macro produces a static entry of the type `kernel_param`. The special attribute `unused` makes sure that the compiler doesn't produce any warnings because of unused variables. Finally, the `__initsetup` macro makes sure that this produced variable is entered in a special section of the LINUX kernel. A linker-script makes sure that the variables `__setup_start` and `__setup_end` are placed at the beginning and the end of the array of variables that were produced in this way.

When the `setup` function is used, it should always be called before the device driver is initialized using its `init` function. This means that the `setup` function should only set global variables, which can then be evaluated by the `init` function.

7.4.4 Init

`init()` is only called during kernel initialization, but is responsible for important tasks. This function tests for the presence of a device, generates internal device driver structures, and registers the device.

While in older versions the call of the `init` function still had to be entered in other functions, version 2.4 again uses the linker to create the list of all `init` functions dynamically.[13]

The `__initcall()` is used for this:

```
typedef int (*initcall_t)(void);
typedef void (*exitcall_t)(void);
#define __initcall(fn) \
  static initcall_t __initcall_##fn __init_call = fn
#define __exitcall(fn) \
  static exitcall_t __exitcall_##fn __exit_call = fn
```

---

13 This includes `chr_dev_init()` and `blk_dev_init()`.

As you can see, an __exitcall() macro is also defined, but is not used for static drivers. However, the macro __initcall() isn't normally used directly, but instead is used by statically linked drivers:

```
#define module_init(x)  __initcall(x);
#define module_exit(x)  __exitcall(x);
```

Therefore, the same code can be used for the initialization of both the static and the dynamic drivers (see Section 9.4). The following code makes sure that the init function of the PC speaker driver is called automatically by the function do_initcalls():

```
int __init pcsp_init(void)
{
  ...
}
module_init(pcsp_init);
```

So that LINUX can start something with the driver, this must be registered. The register_chrdrv() function, which contains the major number of the device driver, the symbolic name of the device driver, and the address of the file_operations structure (in this case, pcsp_fops), is used to do this.

If zero is returned, the new driver is registered. If the major number has already been taken by another device driver, register_chrdrv() returns the error EBUSY.

```
if (register_chrdev(PCSP_MAJOR, "pcsp", &pcsp_fops))
  printk ("unable to get major %d for pcsp devices\n",PCSP_MAJOR);
else {
  printk("PCSP-device 1.0 init:\n");
  ...
}
```

In this case, an attempt can be made to allocate a free major number by giving the register_chrdrv() function 0 as the major number. The function then scans the list of all major numbers, starting at MAX_CHRDEV-1, and registers the driver under the first free number, returning this number. If no free number can be found, register_chrdrv() returns the EBUSY error.

```
if (!register_chrdev(DEFAULT_MAJOR, "device", &device_ops))
  printk("Device registered.\n");
else {
  major = register_chrdev(0, "device", &device_ops));
  if (major > 0)
        printk("Device registered using major %d.\n", major);
else {
        printk("Cannot register device!\n");
```

```
      ...
  }
}
```

init() is also the right place to test whether a device supported by the driver is present at all. This applies especially to devices which cannot be connected or changed during runtime, such as hard disks. If no device can be found, this is the time for the driver to say so (failure to detect a device could also indicate a hardware fault) and make sure that the device is not accessed later.

For example, if a CD-ROM driver is unable to find a CD drive, there is no point in the driver taking up memory for a buffer, as the drive cannot be added during the running of the program. For devices which can be connected at a later stage, the situation is different: If the PC speaker driver fails to detect a Stereo-on-one,[14] it will still allow it to be connected afterwards.

If one or more devices are detected, these should be initialized within the init function if necessary.

7.4.5 | Open and release

The open function is responsible for administering all the devices and is called as soon as a process opens a device file. If only one process can work with a given device (as in the example we are following), -EBUSY should be returned. If a given device can be used by a number of processes at the same time, open() should set up the necessary wait queues where these cannot be set up in read() or write(). If no device exists (for example, if a driver supports a number of devices but only one is present), it should return ENODEV. The open() function is also the right place to initialize the default settings needed by the driver. If the file has been opened successfully, 0 should be returned.

```
static int pcsp_open(struct inode *inode, struct file *file)
{
  if (pcsp_active)
        return -EBUSY;
  switch (minor & 0x0f) {
        case 3: /* DSP device /dev/dsp* */
                if (pcsp_set_format(AFMT_S16_LE) != AFMT_S16_LE)
                    pcsp_set_format(AFMT_U8);
                break;
        case 4: /* Sun Audio device /dev/audio* */
                pcsp_set_format(AFMT_MU_LAW); /* ULAW-Format */
                break;
        ...
  }
```

---

14 A Stereo-on-one is a stereo digital–analog converter designed by Mark J. Cox, which only occupies one parallel port and can be detected by software.

```
if (! (pcsp.buf[0] = vmalloc(pcsp.ablk_size)))
        return -ENOMEM;
if (! (pcsp.buf[1] = vmalloc(pcsp.ablk_size))) {
        vfree(pcsp.buf[0]);
        return -ENOMEM;
}
pcsp.buffer = pcsp.end = pcsp.buf[0];
pcsp.in[0] = pcsp.in[1] = 0;
pcsp.timer_on = pcsp.frag_size = pcsp.frag_cnt = 0;
...
pcsp_active = 1;
return 0;
}
```

The release function is called when the file descriptor for the device is released (see Section 6.2.9). The tasks of this function consist of cleaning-up activities that are global in nature, such as clearing wait queues.

For some devices it also can be useful to pass all the data that is still in the buffers to the device. In the case of the PC speaker driver, this could mean that the device file can be closed before all the data in the output buffers has been played. The function pcsp_sync() therefore waits until both buffers have been emptied and then releases them.

```
static int pcsp_release(struct inode *inode,
                        struct file *file)
{
        pcsp_sync();
        pcsp_stop_timer();
        outb_p(0xb6,0x43); /* binary, mode 2, LSB/MSB, ch 2 */
        vfree(pcsp.buf[0]);
        vfree(pcsp.buf[1]);
        pcsp_active = 0;
        return 0;
}
```

The release function is optional; however, configurations where it might be omitted are difficult to imagine.

7.4.6 Read and write

In principle, the read() and write() functions are a symmetrical pair. As no data can be read from the internal loudspeaker, only write() is implemented in the PC speaker driver. Since the creation of a read function for drivers in the polling operation was looked at in

Section 7.3, we now will consider the simplified write function of the PC speaker driver as an example of the interrupt operation.

```
static int pcsp_write(struct inode *inode, struct file *file,
                char *buffer, int count)
{
  unsigned long copy_size;
  unsigned long max_copy_size;
  unsigned long total_bytes_written = 0;
  unsigned bytes_written;
  int i;
  ...
  max_copy_size = pcsp.frag_size \
  ? pcsp.frag_size : pcsp.ablk_size;
  do {
        bytes_written = 0;
        copy_size = (count <= max_copy_size) \
        ? count : max_copy_size;
        i = pcsp.in[0] ? 1 : 0;
        if (copy_size && !pcsp.in[i]) {
                copy_from_user(pcsp.buf[i], buffer, copy_size);
                pcsp.in[i] = copy_size;
                if (! pcsp.timer_on) pcsp_start_timer();
        bytes_written += copy_size;
        buffer += copy_size;
  }
  if (pcsp.in[0] && pcsp.in[1]) {
        interruptible_sleep_on(&pcsp_sleep);
        if (signal_pending(current)) {
                if (total_bytes_written + bytes_written)
                        return total_bytes_written + bytes_written;
        else return -EINTR;
        }
    }
    total_bytes_written += bytes_written;
    count -= bytes_written;
  } while (count > 0);
  return total_bytes_written;
}
```

Data from the user area is first transferred into the first free buffer by using copy_from_user().

This is always necessary, as the interrupt may occur independently of the current process, with the result that the data cannot be fetched from the user area during the interrupt since the pointer buffer would be pointing to the user address space for the current process. If the corresponding interrupt is not yet initialized, it is now switched on (`pcsp_start_timer()`). As the transfer of data to the device takes place in the ISR, `write()` can begin filling the next buffer.

If all buffers are full, the process must be halted until at least one buffer becomes free. This makes use of the `interruptible_sleep_on()` function (see Section 3.1.5). If the process has been woken up by a signal, `write()` terminates; otherwise the transfer of data to the newly released buffer continues.

Let us now take a look at the basic structure of the ISR.

```
static int pcsp_do_timer(void)
{
  if (pcsp.index < pcsp.in[pcsp.actual]) {
        /* output of bytes */
        ...
  }
  if (pcsp.index >= pcsp.in[pcsp.actual]) {
        pcsp.xfer = pcsp.index = 0;
        pcsp.in[pcsp.actual] = 0;
        pcsp.actual ^= 1;
        pcsp.buffer = pcsp.buf[pcsp.actual];
        if (pcsp_sleep)
                wake_up_interruptible(&pcsp_sleep);
        if (pcsp.in[pcsp.actual] == 0)
                pcsp_stop_timer();
  }
  ...
}
```

As long as there is still data in the current buffer, this is output. If the buffer is empty, the ISR switches to the second buffer and calls `wake_up_interruptible()` to wake up the process. If the second buffer is empty too, the interrupt is disabled. The `if` before the call to the function is not in fact necessary, as `wake_up_interruptible()` carries out this test itself.

As the example shows, this ISR does not fit into the framework of fast and slow interrupts explained earlier. This is because the timer interrupt in LINUX is a slow interrupt, but for reasons to do with speed the PC speaker driver requires a fast interrupt. The PC speaker driver therefore contains a "third" type, which consists of both fast and slow interrupts. The routine `pcsp_do_timer()` is called like a fast interrupt (but with the interrupt flag set, meaning that it is interruptible): If it returns 0, the interrupt is terminated. Otherwise, the original timer interrupt is started as a slow interrupt. As the original timer interrupt needs to be called far less often, this approach gives a major speed advantage.

7.4.7 │ IOCTL

Although a device driver aims to keep the operation of devices as transparent as possible, each device has its own characteristics, which may consist of different operation modes and certain basic settings. It may also be the case that device parameters such as IRQs, I/O addresses, and so on need to be set during runtime.

The parameters passed to the ioctl function are an instruction and an argument. Since, under LINUX, the following applies:

```
sizeof(unsigned long) == sizeof(void *)
```

a pointer to data in the user address space can also be submitted as the argument. For this reason, the ioctl function usually consists of a long switch instruction, with an appropriate type conversion occurring for the argument. Calls to ioctl usually only change variables global to the driver, or global device settings.

Let us consider a fragment of the PC speaker driver's ioctl function.

```
static int pcsp_ioctl(struct inode *inode, struct file *file,
        unsigned int cmd, unsigned long arg)
{
  unsigned long ret;
  unsigned long *ptr = (unsigned long *)arg;
  int i, error;
  switch (cmd) {
        case SNDCTL_DSP_SPEED:
                if (get_user(arg, ptr))
                return -EFAULT;
                arg = pcsp_set_speed(get_user(ptr));
                arg = pcsp_calc_srate(arg);
                return pcsp_ioctl_out(ptr, arg);

        ...
        case SNDCTL_DSP_SYNC:
                pcsp_sync();
                pcsp_stop_timer();
                return (0);

        ...

  }
}
```

The command SNDCTL_DSP_SPEED converts the argument arg into a pointer and uses it to read the new sampling rate. The function pcsp_calc_srate() then simply calculates a number of time constants depending on the new sampling rate. SNDCTL_DSP_SYNC, on the other hand, completely ignores the argument and calls the function pcsp_sync(), which suspends the process until all the data still in the buffer has been played. The synchronization procedure becomes necessary if, for example, the sampling rate or the play mode (mono or stereo) is changed during the playback of audio data or if the output of audio data needs to be synchronized with events in another process.

Thus, the ioctl function can also be used to execute other functions within the driver, which are not included in the virtual file system. Another example of this behavior is contained in the driver for the serial interface; the TIOCSERCONFIG command initiates automatic detection of the UART chip and of the IRQs used for the interface.

When developing a custom driver, the coding of the IOCTL commands should conform to a standard. The file ‹linux/ioctl.h› contains macros which should be used to code the individual commands. If these macros are used, the various IOCTL commands can easily be decoded.

As illustrated in Figure 7.3, bits 8–15 of the command contain a unique identifier for the device driver. This ensures that if the IOCTL command is used on the wrong device, an error will be returned instead of possibly incorrectly configuring this device driver. The unique identifier recommended for the device driver is its major number.

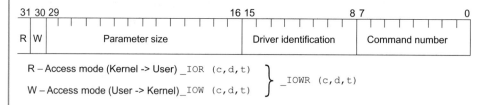

Figure 7.5:   Coding of IOCTL commands.

The macros to encode the IOCTL commands are given by the driver identifier as the first argument and the command number as the second:

_IO(c,d) for commands with no argument,

_IOW(c,d,t) for commands which write back to the user address space a value of the type t,

_IOR(c,d,t) for commands which read a value of the C type t from the user address space,

_IOWR(c,d,t) for commands which both read and write.

Finally, let us take the definitions for some IOCTLs for the sound driver.

```
#define SNDCTL_DSP_RESET  _IO ('P', 0)
#define SNDCTL_DSP_SYNC   _IO ('P', 1)
#define SNDCTL_DSP_SPEED  _IOWR('P', 2, int)
#define SNDCTL_DSP_STEREO _IOWR('P', 3, int)
```

Thus, while the `SNDCTL_DSP_RESET` command, for example, needs no arguments, `SNDCTL_DSP_SPEED` reads an argument of the int type from the user address space and writes one back. Of course, the file `<linux/ioctl.h>` also contains macros to simplify the decoding of the IOCTL commands:

`_IOC_DIR(cmd)` returns whether it is an input or output command,
`_IOC_TYPE(cmd)` returns the device identifier,
`_IOC_NR(cmd)` returns the command without type information,
`_IOC_SIZE(cmd)` returns the size of the argument received in bytes.

The file `documentation/ioctl-number.txt` holds information on device identifiers that are already in use.

7.4.8 | Poll

Since version 2.1.23 LINUX has supported the System V system call *poll* as well as the system call *select*. For this reason it was necessary to change the former `select` function of the file operation to support both system calls. It was then renamed as `poll`. Even though `poll()` is not implemented in our example, the operation is described here, since this function is particularly meaningful for character devices.

The task of the `poll` function is to check whether data can be read from the device or written to it, without blocking the reading or writing process. It also checks whether there is an exception condition.

As the virtual file system handles almost all of this, the task of the `poll` function is simple to describe:

```
static unsigned int aux_poll(struct file *file, poll_table * wait)
{
  poll_wait(file, &queue->proc_list, wait);
  if (!queue_empty())
        return POLLIN | POLLRDNORM;
  return 0;
}
```

The `poll` routine returns a bit vector, in which the corresponding vector is set depending on whether the device is ready to read (`POLLIN`) or to write (`POLLOUT`). Some devices provide special data such as error codes for the kernel interface, or arrange for the treatment of an exceptional situation.

For this differentiation, additional macros, which can be set by `poll()`, are defined in `<asm/poll.h>`:

POLLIN The device has returned data.
POLLOUT The device can now accept data.
POLLRDNORM It is normal readable data. This bit is usually put together with `POLLIN`.
POLLRDBAND It is "highly prioritized" data.

POLLWRNORM Normal data can be written. This bit is normally put together with POLLOUT.

POLLWRBAND It is "highly prioritized" data.

POLLHUP When reading, this bit signals that the driver has recognized the end of the data stream. This bit is, for example, set in the TTY driver if the distant terminal is disconnected (e.g., the modem signals a hang-up).

POLLERR This bit informs about an error. The FIFO implementation, for example, sets this bit if the reading process terminates (and POLLHUP if the writing process terminates).

POLLPRI With this bit, the process can be informed that highly prioritized data is ready for reading. A set bit arranges for the system call select(), passing an exceptional situation on to the process.

POLLNVAL The submitted file descriptor is disabled. This bit is automatically set by VFS and does not call poll.

POLLMSG At present, defined but not used.

If wait is not NULL, the process must be held up until the device becomes available. However, sleep_on() is not used; instead the task is taken care of by the function:

```
void poll_wait(struct file * filp,
wait_queue_head_t * wait_address, poll_table *p);
```

The function expects a wait queue and the last argument given to the poll function as arguments. As poll_wait() immediately returns if this latter argument is NULL, a query does not have to be made, and a function construction like that in the sample function shown above is produced.

If the device becomes available (usually indicated by an interrupt), the process is woken up by a wake_up_interruptible (wait_address). This is indicated by the driver's mouse interrupt.

```
static void keyboard_interrupt(int irq, void *dev_id,
            struct pt_regs *regs)
{
      spin_lock_irq(&kbd_controller_lock);
      handle_kbd_event();
      spin_unlock_irq(&kbd_controller_lock);
}
static unsigned char handle_kbd_event(void)
{
      ...
      if (status & KBD_STAT_MOUSE_OBF)
            handle_mouse_event(scancode);
      else
            handle_keyboard_event(scancode);
      ...
}
```

```
static inline void handle_mouse_event(unsigned char scancode)
{
        ...
        add_mouse_randomness(scancode);
        if (aux_count) {
                int head = queue->head;
        queue->buf[head] = scancode;
        head = (head + 1) & (AUX_BUF_SIZE-1);
        if (head != queue->tail) {
                queue->head = head;
                kill_fasync(&queue->fasync, SIGIO, POLL_IN);
                wake_up_interruptible(&queue->proc_list);
        }
    }
}
}
```

7.4.9 | Llseek

This function is not implemented in the PC speaker driver. It is also only of limited relevance to character devices as these cannot position. However, as the virtual file system's standard function llseek() does not return an error message, an llseek function must be explicitly defined if the driver is required to react to llseek() with an error message.

7.4.10 | Mmap

This function is not implemented in the PC speaker driver example, but nevertheless, memory mapping is very useful and for some driver implementations indispensable, therefore we will go briefly through it here.

The data must be copied to and from the data interchange between the kernel and process area with read() and write() every time. However, for some devices this is too slow. For example, you do not want a flickering picture with a video driver, as it is more efficient to write directly in the video card. LINUX and other UNIX-like operating systems therefore offer a technique called "memory mapping." A physical memory area is mapped for this into the address space of a process so the user process can have direct access, without having to copy the data.

An mmap() routine must be implemented for the driver, which carries out the actual mapping, and there is also a corresponding user-side counterpart. The X server, for example, uses the /dev/kmem device to obtain access to the memory area of the video map. The corresponding driver in the kernel implements an mmap() function which forms this memory range in the memory range of the process using remap_page_range(). The appropriate parameters will be submitted in the structure vm_area_str.

```
static int mmap_mem(struct file * file, struct vm_area_struct * vma)
{
  unsigned long offset = vma->vm_pgoff << PAGE_SHIFT;
  /*
  * the caching for these memory areas must be switched off
  * if the mapping addresses are above the
  * highest memory address or the O_SYNC
  * flag was set
  */
  if (noncached_address(offset) || (file->f_flags & O_SYNC))
  vma->vm_page_prot = pgprot_noncached(vma->vm_page_prot);
  /*
    * mapped memory areas cannot be swapped
  */
  vma->vm_flags |= VM_RESERVED;
  /*
  * only real memory areas can be in the core file
  */
  if (offset >= __pa(high_memory) || (file->f_flags & O_SYNC))
        vma->vm_flags |= VM_IO;
  if (remap_page_range(vma->vm_start, offset,
            vma->vm_end-vma->vm_start,
            vma->vm_page_prot))
        return -EAGAIN;
  return 0;
}
```

In the example, the offset is used for the physical address of the video card, which is mapped over the address in the process area `vma->vm_start`. Here separate values for separate drivers can be submitted, as they can be converted within the kernel into physical addresses.

After the call of `remap_page_range()` the inode used by the device becomes bound to the `vma` structure. In this way, it indicates that there are mappings for both the inode and for the corresponding memory. The example also shows an unusual feature which must be taken into account with Intel architectures. Since hardware addresses can be placed in the normal memory area of Intel architectures, it can happen that the processor stops access to this area because it is in its cache, which is not desirable with genuine hardware addresses we want to react immediately. The used memory page is therefore marked with the help of the function `pgprot_noncached()` and removed from the cache area.

Another unusual feature has to be taken into account if a memory area is to be mapped which is placed in the normal area of the kernel such as, for example, a memory page which has been allocated for a DMA buffer. This is because `remap_page_range()` only works on memory areas marked as reserved.

With `mem_map_reserve()`, this reservation can be carried out, and `mem_map_unreserve()` then removes it. In the example, `page_ptr` is an address that has already been allocated for the memory area.

```
for (i = MAP_NR (page_ptr);
        i <= MAP_NR (page_ptr+PAGE_SIZE-1); i++)
{
    mem_map_reserve (i);
}
```

7.4.11 | Fasync

The function `fasync()` offers the possibility of informing a process asynchronously about data arriving.[15] Unlike the `poll()` function, with which a process waits for an event, the signal `SIGIO` can be triggered with the assistance of `fasync()`, and the process then can react to this.

The LINUX kernel already provides complete functionality of this in the form of two functions.

The function `fasync_helper()` makes sure that the process interested in events arriving is set or removed from the special waiting list by the type `struct fasync_struct`.

```
int fasync_helper(int fd, struct file * filp, int on,
            struct fasync_struct **fapp)
{
  struct fasync_struct *fa, **fp;
  struct fasync_struct *new = NULL;
  int result = 0;
  /*
  * memory allocation can schedule, therefore
  * it is given priority over the locked area
  */
  if (on) {
        new = kmem_cache_alloc(fasync_cache, SLAB_KERNEL);
        if (!new)
            return -ENOMEM;
  }
  /* search first at the end of the list */
  for (fp = fapp; (fa = *fp) != NULL; fp = &fa->fa_next) {
        if (fa->fa_file == filp) {
                /* entry already exists*/
                if (on) {
```

---

15 This is normally data arriving; however, it says nothing about not informing about other events.

```
                              fa->fa_fd = fd;
                              kmem_cache_free(fasync_cache, new);
                    } else {
                              *fp = fa->fa_next;
                              kmem_cache_free(fasync_cache, fa);
                              result = 1;
                    }
          }
          goto out;
    }
}
  /*
  * put file description number on the list
  *and enter all data
  */
  if (on) {
          new->magic = FASYNC_MAGIC;
          new->fa_file = filp;
          new->fa_fd = fd;
          new->fa_next = *fapp;
          *fapp = new;
          result = 1;
  }
out:
  write_unlock_irq(&fasync_lock);
  return result;
}
```

Sending a signal to all processes uses the following function.

```
void kill_fasync(struct fasync_struct **fp, int sig, int band)
{
  read_lock(&fasync_lock);
  __kill_fasync(*fp, sig, band);
  read_unlock(&fasync_lock);
}
void __kill_fasync(struct fasync_struct *fa, int sig, int band)
{
  while (fa) {
          struct fown_struct * fown;
          if (fa->magic != FASYNC_MAGIC) {
                  printk(KERN_ERR "kill_fasync: bad magic number in "
                         "fasync_struct!\n");
                  return;
```

```
        }
        fown = &fa->fa_file->f_owner;
        /* Don't send SIGURG to processes which have not set a
                queued signum: SIGURG has its own default signaling
                mechanism. */
        if (fown->pid && !(sig == SIGURG && fown->signum == 0))
                send_sigio(fown, fa->fa_fd, band);
        fa = fa->fa_next;
    }
}
```

As you can see, a signal SIGIO is sent out using the function send_sigio() if a process has entered its name as an "owner" of a file descriptor. For this, the system call *fcntl* (see Section A.2) is used. The implementation of a fasync function in the driver is therefore simple, as the following example from the PS/2 mouse driver shows:

```
static int aux_fasync(int fd, struct file *filp, int on)
{
        int retval;
        retval = fasync_helper(fd, filp, on, &queue->fasync);
        if (retval < 0)
                return retval;
        return 0;
}
```

With this simple implementation, the question still remains: Why does the virtual file system need help to do this from a driver, and why does it not process all tasks itself? To do this it needs to know the fasync_struct of the driver.

If data has now arrived, all processes must be informed. The kill_fasync function does this, and in our example this occurs in the mouse interrupt after it has established that there is new mouse data.

```
static inline void handle_mouse_event(unsigned char scancode)
{
  ...
  kill_fasync(&queue->fasync, SIGIO, POLL_IN);
  ...
}
```

kill_fasync only uses the second parameter for a comparison in the current implementation (see above), and it is therefore not possible to create other signals like SIGIO.

It is also necessary to take a process from the fasync_struct list if it closes the file. Therefore, the release function of the driver normally just calls the fasync function.

```
static int aux_release(struct inode * inode, struct file * file)
{
  aux_fasync(-1, file, 0);
  ...
}
```

Since the file descriptor number isn't needed to remove a process, release_mouse() submits a -1 here. Every other value would have the same effect. As is usual in the LINUX kernel, this function can also be called if the current process was not on the list, so it doesn't have to be checked as to whether the process takes an interest in asynchronous events.

7.4.12 Readdir, Fsync

These functions are primarily intended for file systems and are not implemented in the PC speaker driver. As the file_operations structure is not only used for devices, it includes functions that are not used by device drivers. The readdir() and fasync() functions, for example, are meaningless for devices.

7.5 DYNAMIC AND STATIC DRIVERS

In earlier LINUX versions, device drivers were statically integrated into the kernel. Today, drivers can be reloaded dynamically during the runtime of the kernel.

Reloading drivers dynamically has many advantages. On the one hand, one can save considerably more memory if the module isn't needed, and on the other, one can indicate some parameters via the module-loading mechanism for the driver module directly when loading (e.g., the major number of the buffer size). However, the greatest advantage is the fundamentally shorter test period during driver development, as the whole kernel does not need to be compiled and rebooted each time.

The effort to develop a dynamically loading driver module is minimal; however, one must stick to some rules. The essential components of a dynamically loading driver are:

```
#include <linux/module.h>
...
  int driver_init(void) {
        ...
        if (register_chrdev(MY_MAJOR,"mydriver",&my_fops)) {
                printk("mydriver: unable to get major %d\n", MY_MAJOR);
                return -EIO;
  }
        ...
  }
  void driver_term(void)
```

```
{
        ...
        unregister_chrdev(MY_MAJOR,"mydriver");
        ...
  }
module_init(driver_init);
module_exit(driver_term);
```

If a driver is converted into a module, the meaning of the macros `module_init()` and `module_exit()` changes. The initialization routine, indicated by `module_init()`, is called by loading the modules with `insmod`. The driver must now register with the system by registering its `Fops` structure on the system. The registered functionality is now available until the driver is removed from the system using `rmmod`. Before the module is deleted from the memory, the routine indicated by `module_exit()` is called so that the driver can release resources requested by the system.

It should be noted that all processes should have the driver closed, or the removal of a module that is still needed could have devastating consequences.

8 NETWORK IMPLEMENTATION

Nowadays, support for network communication is one of the basic demands made on an operating system. For LINUX, this requirement has been there from the start. This kind of communication lays the foundations for a range of network services, including services which are familiar to most users such as http (WWW), ftp (file transfer), and rlogin (remote login). There are also options of using file systems on other computers (NFS), of receiving e-mail and NetNews, and much more. The type of network used (OSI, IPX, UUCP, and so on) is a secondary consideration as far as the user is concerned.

In UNIX, the dominating protocols are those that come under the name of TCP/IP. LINUX is modelled on UNIX and so, as might be expected, an implementation of TCP/IP is provided which concentrates mainly on communication via Ethernet. But LINUX can do more than this. Using SLIP (serial line interface protocol) or PLIP (parallel line interface protocol) or PPP (point to point protocol) it is possible to link computers together using their serial or parallel interfaces. The capabilities of the PPP protocol are particularly impressive, since it can use modems and telephone lines to set up network links to anywhere in the world.

In its AX.25 protocol, LINUX even provides a way of communicating between computers by radio. Communication via IPX, a protocol developed by Novell, has also been developed. The world of Apple data is accessible via an adaptation of AppleTalk. Both for AppleTalk and IPX, software packages have been developed that allow file access and printing.

In this chapter, we will deal with the characteristics of the LINUX implementation of TCP/IP.[1] It is not our intention to provide a description of how TCP/IP works, but rather to look at the design of its implementation under LINUX. The chapter therefore assumes that the reader is familiar with the C programming language as well as the basics of TCP/IP.

---

1   As secondary literature on the subject of TCP/IP, the books [Com91], [CS91], [Ste94], and [WE96] are suggested.

8.1   INTRODUCTION AND OVERVIEW

For the "normal" programmer, access to network services is available via sockets. Under LINUX, these have an extended functionality. The interface consists of the following C library routines:

```
int socket(int addr_family,int type,int protocol);
int bind(int s,struct sockaddr *address,int address_len);
int connect(int s,struct sockaddr *address,int address_len);
int listen(int s ,int backlog);
int accept(int s,struct sockaddr *address,int *address_len);
int getsockname(int s,struct sockaddr *address,int *address_len);
int getpeername(int s,struct sockaddr *address,int *address_len);
int socketpair(int addr_family,int type,int protocol,int fds[2]);
int send(int s,char *msg,int len,int flags);
int sendto(int s,char *msg,int len,int flags,struct sockaddr *to,int tolen);
int recv(int s,char *buf,int len,int flags);
int recvfrom(int s,char *buf,int len,int flags,struct sockaddr
                                         *from,int *fromlen);
int shutdown(int s,int how);
int setsockopt(int s,int level,int oname,char *ovalue,int olen);
int getsockopt(int s,int level,int oname,char *ovalue,int *olen);
int sendmsg(int s,struct msghdr *msg,int flags);
int recvmsg(int s,struct msghdr *msg,int flags);
```

All of these functions are based on the system call *socketcall* (see Section A.3). In addition, the system call *ioctl* on socket file descriptors enables network-specific configurations to be changed.

As the C library routine socket() returns a file descriptor, the usual I/O system calls such as *read* and *write*, are, of course, also applicable.

A computer can be connected to a network via a variety of hardware, including, for example, Ethernet cards and D-link adapters. The differences between these are hidden behind a unified interface, namely the network devices. The network devices assigned to Ethernet cards are called eth0, eth1, and so forth. The names for the devices handling SLIP and PLIP links are sl0, sl1, . . . and plip0, plip1, . . ., respectively.

There is no representation in the file system for these network devices. They cannot be set up in the /dev/ directory using the mknod command like "normal" devices. A normal device can only be accessed if the initialization function has identified the corresponding hardware.

8.1.1 The layer model of the network implementation

As communication with network components presents a fairly complex task, it uses a layer structure like the file system. The individual layers correspond to levels of abstraction, with the level of abstraction increasing from layer to layer, starting with the hardware.

When a process communicates via the network, it uses the functions provided by the BSD socket layer. This takes care of a range of tasks similar to those handled by the virtual file system and administers a general data structure for sockets, which we shall call BSD sockets. The BSD socket interface has been selected by virtue of its widespread use, which simplifies the porting of network applications, most of which are already quite complex.

Below this layer is the INET socket layer. This manages the communication end points for the IP-based protocols TCP and UDP. These are represented by the data structure `sock` which we will call INET sockets.

In the layers we have mentioned so far, no type distinction is as yet made between the sockets in the `AF_INET` address family. The layer that underlies the INET socket layer, on the other hand, is determined by the type of socket, and may be the UDP layer, TCP layer or the IP layer directly. The UDP layer implements the user datagram protocol on the basis of IP, and the TCP layer similarly implements the Transmission Control Protocol for reliable communication links. The IP layer contains the code for the Internet Protocol version 4. This is where all the communication streams from the higher layers come together. Sockets of other types are not included in this survey.[2] Below the IP layer are the network devices, to which the IP passes the final packets. These then take care of the physical transportation of the information.

True communication always takes place between two sides, producing a two-way flow of information. For this reason, the various layers are also connected together in the opposite direction. This means that when IP packets are received, they are passed to the IP layer by the network devices and processed. The interaction between the different layers is illustrated in Figure 8.1.

8.1.2 Getting the data from A to B

To better understand the interaction between the various parts of the network implementation, we shall follow the data which is sent through the network by process A to process B.

We assume that both processes have already created a socket and are connected to each other via `connect()` or `accept()`, and will restrict our survey to one TCP connection under LINUX. Data from process A is to be sent to process B. It is stored in a buffer of `length` pointed to by the `data` pointer. Process A contains the following fragments of code:

```
write(socket,data,length);
```

---

2 There are more socket types such as ATM, IPv6, AX.25 uvm.

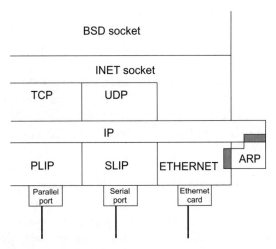

Figure 8.1: The layer structure of a network.

which is used to call the kernel code `sys_write()` (see Sections 6.2.9 and A.2), which is a component of the virtual file system. This tests for a number of conditions, including whether a write operation is entered into the file operation vector of the descriptor. To use the virtual file system, a socket provides the classical file operations in a vector.

The write operation for the BSD sockets is `sock_write()`, which only takes care of administrative functions. This searches for the socket structure associated with the inode structure. Then, the parameters of the write operation are transferred into a message structure. `sock_write()` then calls the send function `sock_sendmsg()`, passing parameters consisting of the pointer to the BSD socket data structure with the length of the data and an indication of whether it is permissible to block the function.

From the data component of the BSD socket that was passed to it, the function `inet_sendmsg()` extracts a pointer to the INET socket structure `sock`. In the present example, this structure contains the essential data used in the TCP and IP layers. The `prot` field in this structure refers to the operation vector of the TCP implementation. The `inet_sendmsg` calls this vector's send operation, `tcp_sendmsg()`, passing parameters consisting of the pointer to the INET socket, the pointer to the message structure, and the length of the data.

Up to now, the data has only passed through the different abstraction levels. In `tcp_sendmsg()`, the actual handling of communication aspects begins properly. First, a number of error conditions, such as the socket not being ready to send, are tested. Now with the `tcp_alloc_skb` function memory is allocated, which will later contain an `sk_buff` structure, the header, and the TCP segment. The `tcp_sendmsg()` function initializes the `sk_buff` structure. Now the data from the address space of the process is copied into the packet (see `copy_from_user()` in Section 4.1.2). The checksum is usually calculated after this. To optimize this process, a function `csum_and_copy_from_user()` is available which carries out both actions in one step.

If the length of the data exceeds the maximum segment size (MSS) they are divided into a number of packets. However, it is possible for short data blocks from a number of send operations to be collected together in one packet. Finally the `tcp_send_skb()` function is called. Here the sequence numbers for the TCP protocol are counted. Additionally, using a timer the function `tcp_transmit_skb()` is called. The TCP header is then inserted into the packet here. Then the TCP checksum is calculated and the function `ip_queue_xmit()` is called. In this function the IP routing now takes place along with the creation of the IP header. This is continued with ip_queue_xmit2(), ip_output(), ip_finish _output() and ip_finish_output2(). The last of these copies the MAC header from the header cache into the packet and finally calls `dev_queue_xmit()`.

A feature of LINUX is that all the headers are written to the memory in a linear sequence. In other TCP/IP implementations, the packet is stored as a vector of separate fragments.

The `dev_queue_xmit` function finally calls the `hard_start_xmit()` function of the machine. For a 3COM card, this points to the function `boomerang_start_xmit()`, which passes the data to the network adapter, which in turn sends it to the Ethernet.

We could say at this point that the data is halfway there. The data, embedded in an Ethernet packet, is received by a network card in the target computer. As before, we assume here that the adapter is a WD8013 card.

After receiving the Ethernet packet, the network card triggers an interrupt. This is dealt with by the `vortex_interrupt()` function. If the transfer via the Ethernet was completed without any errors, the `vortex_rx()` function will be called with a reference to the network device. This uses the DMA transfer operation to write the packet to a newly set up buffer, using, in our example, the `dev_alloc_skb()` function. As for the send function, this buffer includes space for the `sk_buff` structure, which is appropriately initialized after the transfer using the `eth_type_trans` function. Once this has been done, the function `netif_rx()` is called with the packet as argument. This adds the `input_pkt_queue` for the current CPU. All the functions for receiving packets described so far are executed within the interrupt. The soft interrupt is activated for the detection of packets using `netif_rx()`. The `net_rx_` function is now called by `do_softirq()` with the mask marker `setaction()`. The `do_softirq()` function is called after system calls and (normal) interrupts. The call is not made if an interrupt has interrupted another interrupt or `do_softirq()` itself. Further information on the soft IRQ mechanism is given in Section 3.2.3.

The `net_rx_action()` function puts the raw pointer of h and nh in the `sk_buff` structure at the beginning of the protocol packet, after the Ethernet header. The packet type in the Ethernet header then decides whether the receive function for the protocol is called. In the SLIP and PLIP protocols the type is not yet held in the packet header but is inserted directly at the beginning in the `protocol` field of the `sk_buf` structure.

In the case considered here, an IP packet has been received and the receive function `ip_rcv()` is called. This demonstrates the advantages of the union nh. In the soft interrupt routine, the raw pointer was set in the header of the protocol packet. The IP can now be accessed via the iph pointer provided by nh without the need to initialize it specially as it is identical to the raw pointer. The checksum of the IP packet is also checked here. Finally, ip_rcv_finish() is called.

In ip_rcv_finish() the exact aim of the packet is determined. For this, the ip_route_input() function is called, which enters its result in the dst field of the buffer. If they are available, the IP options of the packet are edited. The input function from the dst field is then called. In our case[3] this is ip_local_deliver(). If we are dealing with a fragment, the defragmentation is accomplished using the ip_defrag() function. .

This is continued with the ip_local_deliver_finish() function. The raw pointer in h and nh of the sk_buff structure is put at the end of the IP header and again points to the beginning of the header of the next protocol. This protocol is determined in the protocol field of the IP header. In our case this is TCP. Independently of this protocol, the corresponding protocol detection function is called; in the case of TCP this is tcp_v4_rcv(). This calls the __tcp_v4_lookup() function to determine, by reference to the sender and destination port numbers, the INET socket to which the TCP segment is addressed.

After a number of consistency tests tcp_rcv_established() enters the buffer tcp_copy_to_iovec() from the sk_buff in the memory of the detecting process. With tcp_rcv_established() we are dealing with an optimized function for the most commonly used method of execution. This means that the TCP socket is in an established condition and that the system call read() or rcvmsg() has been called and is still the active process. In the case where one of the preconditions of tcp_rcv_established() is not fulfilled, tcp_data() is called.

Here all the protocol options are checked in the conventional manner and the data at the socket is entered into the list of detected data. If fresh data has been received in the sequence of the data flow, the appropriate acknowledgment packets are sent after a delay and the INET socket's data_ready operation is called.

This wakes up all the processes waiting for an event at the socket. The delay with which the acknowledgments are sent is necessary to avoid sending superfluous packets over the network. Up to this point, all the actions related to receiving a packet have been carried out in the kernel, outside the program flow of any process. The processor time needed for this cannot be assigned to a process.

Process B wishes to receive the data sent by process A. To do so, it executes a read operation with the socket file descriptor.

```
read(socket,data,length);
```

This call is passed to a C library function via different abstraction levels and calls sys_read(), sock_read(), sock_recvmsg(), inet_recvmsg(), and tcp_recvmsg(). If the INET socket's receive buffer is empty the process is forced to block. However, blocking can be prevented by setting the O_NONBLOCK flag using *fcntl*. As

---

3 For IP packets that are to be processed further, dst field ip_forward() is entered.

mentioned in the previous paragraph, the process is woken up once data is received. After the process has been woken up, or if data is already present in the buffer on the read call, this is copied to the data address in the user area of the process's memory.

This completes the data's travels from process A to process B, which have led us through various layers of the operating system. The data has only been copied four times: from the user area of process A to the kernel memory, from there to the network card, from the network card in the second computer to the kernel memory and from there to the user area of process B. In the LINUX implementation of the TCP/IP code a great deal of care has been taken to avoid unnecessary copying operations.

The network implementation is very tightly interwoven: There is a wealth of mutually dependent functions, and it is not always easy to say where any of these belong. A glance at the sources shows that many of these functions are very long (more than 200 lines of source text), making them far from easy to follow. To be sure, the complexity of the C sources is a function of the subject matter; but it is a clear indication of the importance of good design in network implementation. In LINUX version 1.2, the interfaces between the layers were tailored to IP, but several improvements have been integrated into version 2.0.

With the transfer over to version 2.0, a few improvements have been integrated, and versions 2.2 and 2.4 have undertaken further generalizations. This development has further increased the complexity of the code.

It is widely believed that a network implementation is a balancing act between speed of operation and tidy structuring. We, however, do not consider these two aspects to be necessarily exclusive. Other areas of the kernel (such as the virtual file system) are proof of this.

8.2   IMPORTANT STRUCTURES

One way of achieving tidy structuring is the correct definition of the data structures forming the basis of any function in a network. This section therefore provides an introduction to the many different data structures in the LINUX network implementations.

8.2.1 The socket structure

The socket structure forms the basis for the BSD socket interface. It is set up and initialized with the system call *socket*. This section only deals with the characteristics of sockets in the AF_INET address family.

```
struct socket {
  socket_state        state;
```

The current state of the socket is stored in state. The most important states are SS_CONNECTED and SS_UNCONNECTED.

```
long                 flags;
struct proto_ops     *ops;
struct inode         *inode;
```

For a socket in the INET address family, the `ops` pointer points to the operation `inet_stream_ops` or `inet_dgram_ops`, where the specific operations for this address family are entered. `inode` is a reference back to the inode which belongs to this socket.

```
struct fasync_struct      *fasunc_list;
struct file               *file;
```

In `file` you will find a reference to the primary file structure which is associated with this socket.

However, this can give rise to certain problems during the asynchronous processing of files. Different file structures can refer to one and the same inode and as a result to the same BSD socket. If processes have selected asynchronous handling of this file, all the processes need to be informed about events. For this reason, they are held in `fasync_list`. The relationship between inodes and file structure is described in more detail in Sections 3.1.1 and 6.29.

```
struct sock          *sk;
```

The `sk` pointer points to the substructure of the socket corresponding to the address family. For `AF_INET`, this is the INET socket (see Figure 8.2). In LINUX, each file is described by an inode. There is also an inode for each BSD socket, so that there is one-to-one mapping between the BSD sockets and their respective inodes. Because, in contrast to previous versions of LINUX, the `sock` structure is already placed in the associated inode, no separate pointer is required, e.g., you can gain access to the inode for a BSD socket with the help of an `sk` pointer.

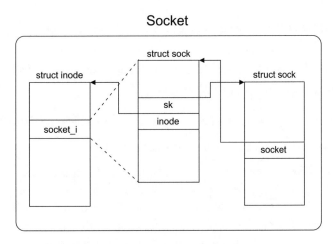

Figure 8.2: The socket and the relationship to its substructure.

```
struct wait_queue    *wait;
short                type;
unsigned char        passcred;
};
```

For `type`, `SOCK_STREAM`, `SOCK_DGRAM`, and `SOCK_RAW` are valid entries. Sockets of the `SOCK_STREAM` type are used for the TCP protocol, sockets of the `SOCK_DGRAM` type for the UDP protocol, and sockets of the `SOCK_RAW` type for sending and detection of IP packets.

8.2.2 The sk_buff structure – buffer management in the network

The task of `sk_buff` buffers is to manage individual communication packets.

```
struct sk_buff {
  struct sk_buff          *next, *prev;
  struct sk_buff_head     *list;
```

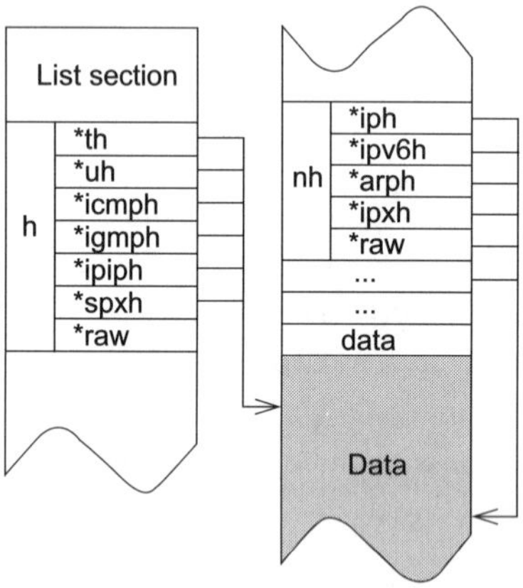

Figure 8.3:   The normal use for the `sk_buff` structure.

In exactly the same way as for the first two pointers in the structure, this pointer is required for linking in a circular list and various other lists.

```
struct sock          *sk;
```

The pointer `sk` points to the socket to which the buffer belongs (see Figure 8.4).

```
struct timeval       stamp;
```

`stamp` indicates when the packet was last transferred. However, the buffers are not only used when sending packets, but also when receiving them. When a packet is forwarded by the network devices to the higher layers of the network implementation, the function `netif_rx()` enters the current time in the structure `stamp`, using the kernel variable `xtime`, which is also updated by the timer interrupt

```
struct net_device    *dev
```

In the administration of network buffers, the identity of the network device by or via which a packet is sent or received is of great importance. A pointer to the device is therefore entered in dev.

```
union {
  struct tcphdr             *th;
  struct udphdr             *uh;
  struct icmphdr            *icmph;
  struct igmphdr            *igmph;
  struct iphdr              *ipiph;
  struct spxhdr             *spxh;
```

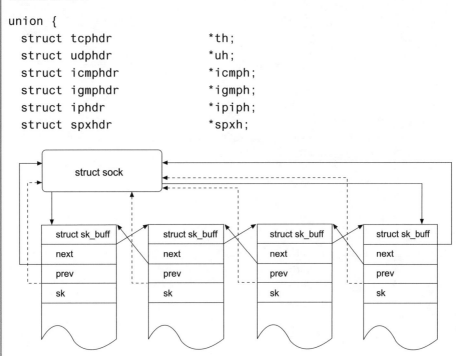

Figure 8.4: The normal localization of the sk_buff structures.

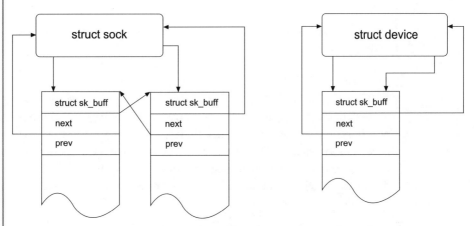

Figure 8.5: Transfer of a packet before calling the xmit function (the buffer is with the socket).

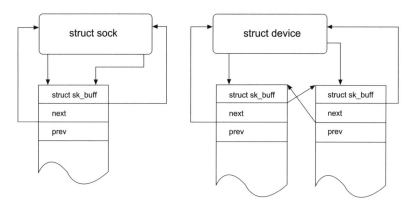

Figure 8.6: Transfer of a packet before calling the `xmit` function (the buffer is now in the device, e.g. `eth0`).

```
  unsigned char              *raw;
} h;
union {
  struct iphdr               *iph
  struct ipv6hdr             *ipv6h;
  struct arphdr              *arph;
  struct ipxhdr              *ipxh;
  unsigned char              *raw;
} nh;
union {
  struct ethhdr              *ethernet;
  unsigned char              *raw;
} mac;
```

This union, mentioned earlier, is generally used as a pointer to various header structures within the packet.

```
  struct dst_entry           *dst;
```

The `dst_entry` plays a central role in the processing of packets in the network implementation. If the route of a packet were to be determined, a corresponding entry would be left behind here. Among other things, this contains function pointers for the further processing of packets. Therefore, for a regularly used TCP connection, the entry from the INET socket can be used. This, then, also already contains the function pointers, which allow the quickest delivery of the packet. Therefore, we do not need to give a complicated description of the route.

```
  char                   cb[48];
  unsigned int           len, csum;
```

len gives us the length of the packet and csum contains the checksum, in case one is calculated.

```
volatile char          used;
unsigned char          cloned,pkt_type,ip_summed;
__u32                  priority;
atomic_t               users;
unsigned short         protocol,security;
unsigned int           truesize;
unsigned char          *head,*data,*tail,*end;

void (*destructor)(struct sk_buff *);
};
```

These elements are used in the management of the memory belonging to the structure. Unlike implementations before version 1.2, data need not necessarily be located directly after the structure, but rather in an individual memory block. This contains a reference counter which tells us how many buffers refer to it. It copies the sk_buff structure, increases the reference counter of the data, and sets cloned to 1 in the sk_buff structure.

Here are a few more remarks about the pointers: head always points to the start of the buffer's memory block, and end to the end. data refers to the start of the actual useful data in the packet. The area between head and data contains the header of the packet. The useful data is therefore found in the area between data and tail.

When using net filters, the structure contains a few further elements, which do not interest us here.

The administration of sk_buff structures normally uses doubly linked lists, so there is also a structure to implement a list header:

```
struct sk_buff_head {
  struct sk_buff         *next, *prev;
  __u32                  qlen;
  spinlock_t             lock;
};
```

So next then points to the start of the list and prev to the end. qlen indicates the number of elements in the list. The lock element is used to synchronize multiprocessors.

8.2.3 | The INET socket – a special part of the socket

It is in the INET socket structure that the network-specific parts of the socket are administered. This is required for TCP, UDP, and RAW sockets.

```
struct sock {
  struct sock                    *next;
  struct sock                    **pprev;
  struct sock                    *bind_next;
  struct sock                    **bind_pprev;
  struct sock                    *prev;
  int                            hashent;
```

To find an INET socket more quickly for a specific port, the INET sockets are also organized in different hash tables. The following pointers are used for this:

```
  __u32                          daddr;
  __u32                          saddr;
  __u32                          rcv_saddr;
  __u16                          dport;
  __u16                          sport;
  unsigned short                 num;
  struct dst_entry               *dst_cache;
  int                            bound_dev_if;
```

These fields contain the IP addresses and the port numbers of the INET socket. rcv_saddr indicates the address to which the INET socket is bound. dst_cache refers to a data structure that allows quicker processing of the packet. In the case where the INET socket is attached to a specific IP interface, bound_dev_if contains the interface index.

```
  rwlock_t                       dst_lock,
                                 callback_lock;
  atomic_t                       refcnt;
  socket_lock_t                  lock;
  wait_queue_head_t              *sleep;
```

sleep points to the head of a wait queue in which processes which have blocked during actions on this INET socket are saved.

```
  atomic_t                       rmem_alloc;
  atomic_t                       wmem_alloc;
  atomic_t                       omem_alloc;
  unsigned int                   allocation;
  int                            rcvbuf;
  int                            sndbuf;
  int                            wmem_queued;
```

Both variables wmem_alloc and rmem_alloc indicate how much memory is required by this INET socket. The first variable is for writing and the second is for reading on the INET socket. omem_alloc counts the memory which is not directly used for reading or writing (for example, for option processing of IP). In allocation, during the creation of the INET socket you can see in what order of priority the memory is required for this socket (see Figure 4.3). The values in `sndbuf` and `rcvbuf` are the upper limits for the memory requirements of the INET socket when writing or reading.

```
struct sk_buff_head        write_queue;
struct sk_buff_head        receive_queue;
```

`write_queue` contains a list of the packets still to be sent. The packets in the `receive_queue` list have already been detected by the protocol, but not yet delivered to the process.

```
unsigned char              reuse;

volatile char              dead,done,urginline,
                           keepopen,linger,destroy,
                           no_check,broadcast,
                           bsdism;
unsigned char              debug;
unsigned char              rcvtstamp;
unsigned char              userlocks;
unsigned long              lingertime;
```

These variables contain different flags and values that can be set for an INET socket.

```
int                        proc;
```

In `proc`, the ID of a process or a process group that should obtain a signal with the arrival of "out-of-band" data is stored.

```
struct sock                *pair;
```

Using the `accept()` protocol operation of the INET socket, a new `sock` structure is established.

```
struct {
        struct sk_buff     *head;
        struct sk_buff     *tail;
}                          back_log;
struct sk_buff_head        error_queue;
```

Packets that are defined for the INET socket, but cannot be inserted into the right list at the moment since a process is taking data from the socket at the same time are placed in `back_log`.

```
struct proto               *prot;
```

Here we see the operation vector for the protocol with which the INET socket is associated. Normally this would be the address of one of the following structures: `tcp_prot`, `udp_prot`, or `raw_prot`.

```
unsigned char                          shutdown;

union {
        struct tcp_opt af_tcp;
        struct raw_opt                 tp_raw4;
} tp_pinfo;

union {
        void                           *destruct_hook;
        struct unix_opt                af_unix;
        struct inet_opt                af_inet;
        struct packet_opt              *af_packet;
} protinfo;
```

Private data for each address family:

```
int                     err,err_soft;
volatile unsigned char  state,zapped;
```

With `err` we are dealing with an error indication that is similar to the `errno` variable in C. `state` indicates the condition of the INET socket.

```
unsigned short          ack_backlog,
                        max_ack_backlog;
__u32                   priority;
unsigned short          type,
                        family;
unsigned char           localroute,
                        protocol;
struct ucred            peercred;
int                     rcvlowat;
```

`type` and `family` are adopted by the necessary BSD socket structure `socket` and determine the type and family of the INET socket. With help from `localroute` it is indicated that the packet is only to be routed locally.

```
spinlock_t              timer_lock;
struct timer_list       timer;
struct timeval          stamp;
long                    rcvtimeo,
                        sndtimeo;
```

These two components of the structure are used in the administration of timers required for the implementation of TCP. As stamp is updated on receipt of each packet, this enables the time when the last packet was received to be determined precisely.

```
struct socket              *socket;
```

This pointer points to the associated BSD socket.

```
void                       *user_data;
void                       (*state_change)(struct sock *sk);
void                       (*data_ready)(struct sock *sk,
                           int bytes;
void                       (*write_space)(struct sock *sk);
void                       (*error_report)(struct sock *sk);
void                       (*backlog_rcv)(struct sock *sk,
                           struct sk_buff *skb);
};
```

The state_change() function is executed every time the status of the socket is changed. Similarly, data_ready() is called when data has been received, write_space() when the free memory available for writing has increased, and error_report() when an error occurs.

In the following description, the term "socket" is used to refer to the combination of a BSD socket and an INET socket (see Figure 8.2).

With the transfer over to LINUX version 2.4, further elements of the sock structure that were specific to IP are moved into the protocol-specific data structure inet_opt:

```
struct inet_opt
{
        int                ttl,
                           tos;
        unsigned           cmsg_flags;
```

These values are used during the creation of an IP header to fill the corresponding fields of the protocol head.

```
        struct ip_options  *opt;
```

opt is a pointer to a structure which contains the individual IP options used for this INET socket. These should be looked at with the formation of the IP protocol header.

```
unsigned char              hdrincl;
__u8                       mc_ttl;
__u8                       mc_loop;
unsigned                   recverr:1,freebind:1;
__u8                       pmtudisc;
```

```
int                     mc_index;
__u32                   mc_addr;
struct ip_mc_socklist   *mc_list;
};
```

The elements of the structure that begin with the mc_ prefix help to activate the IP multicast protocol.

8.2.4 Protocol operations in the proto structure

In LINUX, protocols such as TCP and UDP are accessed via an abstract interface. This consists of a number of operations and means that functions whose actions are the same for all protocols only need to be programmed once. This helps to avoid implementation errors and keeps the code as compact as possible.

```
struct proto {
  void                  (*close)(struct sock *sk, long timeout);
```

The close() function initiates the actions required to close a socket. For a TCP socket, for example, a packet with the necessary ACK and a FIN is sent.

```
  int                   (*connect)(struct sock *sk,
                              struct sockaddr *uaddr,
                              int addr_len);
  int                   (*disconnect)(struct sock *sk, int flags);
  struct sock *         (*accept)(struct sock *sk, int flags,
                              int *err);
```

connect() is to be implemented for all protocols, whereas accept() is only necessary for connection-free protocols. The semantics of connect() differs between connection-free and connection-oriented protocols. With connection-free protocols it is used to establish an address, which uses write requests as target addresses. However, connect() creates the connection for TCP.

```
  int                   (*ioctl)(struct sock *sk, int cmd,
                              unsigned long arg);
```

Among other things, with help from the ioctl function the amount of data of a TCP or UDP socket that has not been read or transferred can be determined, and debugging outputs switched on/off.

```
  int                   (*init)(struct sock *sk);
  int                   (*destroy)(struct sock *sk);
```

Important fields of the INET socket are initialized for this protocol implementation by the `init` function of the respective protocol. `destroy` carries out the functions that are necessary when unlocking the INET socket, such as unlocking memory, for example.

```
void              (*shutdown)(struct sock *sk, int how);
int               (*setsockopt)(struct sock *sk, int level,
                       int optname, char *optval,
                       int optlen);
int               (*getsockopt)(struct sock *sk, int level,
                       int optname, char *optval,
                       int *option);
```

The first function is used for TCP connection. A TCP connection can be aborted by this. Then two other functions implement `setsockopt()` or `getsockopt()` for the necessary protocol.

```
int               (*sendmsg)(struct sock *sk, struct msghdr *msg,
                       int len);
int               (*recvmsg)(struct sock *sk, struct msghdr *msg,
                       int len, int noblock, int flags,
                       int *addr_len);
int               (*bind)(struct sock *sk,
                       struct sockaddr *uaddr, int addr_len);
```

Considerable changes have been made to the protocol interfaces with the development of LINUX 1.2. All send and detect functions are replaced by `sendmsg` and `recvmsg`. The specific submission parameters are submitted by the `msghdr` structure. Besides this, since version 2.0 the `readv()` and `writev()` functions have been possible on sockets. With `bind()`, a socket is fixed to a certain address. This pointer is, so far, not used by any protocol.

```
int               (*backlog_rcv)(struct sock *sk,
                       struct sk_buff *skb);

void              (*hash)(struct sock *sk);
void              (*unhash)(struct sock *sk);
int               (*get_port)(struct sock *sk,
                       unsigned short snum);
```

The hash functions create a hash table of individual protocols, which means they are inserted and removed.

```
char              name[32];
int               inuse[NR_CPUS];
};
```

For fault tracing purposes, `name` holds the name of the associated protocol (for example, TCP). The other values are statistical in nature and are required for the SNMP.

The `proto` structure which has just been described can be regarded as an interface for protocols in the `AF_INET` family. A very similar structure describes the interface of the next layer above the BSD socket layer.

The name of this structure is `proto_ops`, and it is provided for each of the protocol families implemented. From version 2.2 upwards of LINUX these are `AF_INET`, `AF_INET6`, `AF_IPX`, `AF_X25`, `AF_UNIX`, and a few others.

8.2.5   The general structure of a socket address

Because sockets have to support different address formats for different address families, there is a general address structure containing the address family, the port number, and a field for addresses of different sizes. For Internet addresses, a special structure `sockaddr_in` is defined, which matches the general structure `sockaddr`.

```
struct sockaddr {
  unsigned short sa_family;        /* address family AF_xxx */
  char sa_data[14];                /* start of the protocol address */
};
struct sockaddr_in {
  short int sin_family;            /* address family */
  unsigned short int sin_port;     /* port number */
  struct in_addr sin_addr;         /* internet address */

  /* Fill bytes for the sockaddr structure */
  unsigned char __pad[__SOCK_SIZE__ - sizeof(short int)
                      - sizeof(unsigned short int)
                      - sizeof(struct in_addr)];
};
```

8.3   NETWORK DEVICES UNDER LINUX

As we have already seen, there is a great variety of hardware that can be used to connect computers. As a result, this hardware is controlled in many different ways. An abstract interface to the network hardware was introduced to enable the upper network layers to be implemented independently of the hardware used. This, of course, embodies a polymorphic approach to programming the operating system.

The data structure `net_device` controls an abstract network device. This is often referred to as a *network interface*, meaning the interface to the network rather than to the hardware.

```
struct net_device {
  char                          name[IFNAMSIZ];
```

In LINUX, every network device has a unique name. A reference to this name is held in name.

```
  unsigned long                 rmem_end;
  unsigned long                 rmem_start;
  unsigned long                 mem_end;
  unsigned long                 mem_start;
  unsigned long                 base_addr;
  unsigned int                  irq;
```

These elements describe the hardware of the device. The I/O address, which is important to the PC architecture, and the number of the interrupt associated with the device, are held in base_addr and irq respectively. The ranges rmem_start to rmem_end and mem_start to mem_end describe the device's receive and send memories. However, these parameters are tailored to Ethernet cards. For other devices, some of these fields in the structure are used with different semantics. For a SLIP device, base_addr holds the index to the corresponding SLIP structure.

```
  unsigned char                 if_port;
  unsigned char                 dma;
```

The hardware of some network devices uses DMA and communication with I/O ports for input and output. In version 1.2 of LINUX, the net_device structure therefore had to be expanded by the appropriate fields. In if_port, a note is made of in which port (AUI, TP, . . .) the card will be used.

```
  unsigned long                 state;
  struct net_device             *next;
```

state indicates the internal condition of the network devices. The network devices are managed in a list under LINUX. The kernel variable dev_base points to the first element in the list. For connections, next is used. With the help of the obvious name and the dev_get() function, a network device can be accessed in the kernel. This function sets whether the hardware required for this device is available, and initializes the net_device structure.

```
  int                           (*init)(struct net_device *dev);
  int                           (*uninit)(struct net_device *dev);
  void                          (*destructor)(struct net_device *dev);
```

As described in Section 2.3, before the kernel is compiled, which devices are to be tested for their presence can be specified. This includes network devices, and a static list of structures of the net_device type is therefore held in drivers/net/space.c. This list contains elements consisting only of the public section of the net_device structure, which runs from the start of the structure to the init component. The pointer dev_base points to the start of this list. By modifying this list it can now be determined which devices are tested for their presence during booting and which initialization functions are used. This is especially important for the different types of Ethernet card, as the separate card types are tested in sequence in the ethif_probe function.

If we turn once again to the sequence of actions when the kernel is started up, as described in Section 3.2.4, we see that this involves a call to sock_init(). The task of this function is to initialize the entire network part of the kernel. As part of this, the BSD sockets are set to their default settings, after which the dev_init() function is called.

This init initializes all the configured network devices by going through the list of network devices pointed to by dev_base(). The init function is called for each entry and fills the entire net_device structure with correct values, i.e., the function pointers.

```
struct net_device              *next_sched;
struct net_device              *master;
int                            ifindex,iflink;
unsigned long                  pkt_queue;
struct net_device              *slave;
```

The last two fields are required "load balancing." pkt_queue indicates the number of packets still to be edited and slave points to an additional network device which works as a slave device.

```
struct net_device_stats* (*get_stats)(struct net_device *dev);
struct iw_statistics* (*get_wireless_stats)
                            (struct net_device *dev);
```

net_device_stats is the respective statistic function of the device. It is used whenever statistical information is requested about the network device by another part of the kernel. With get_wireless_stats you can get specific information for network devices that do not use cable-connected media.

```
unsigned long                  trans_start, last_rx;
```

You will see when something was last sent (trans_start) or detected (last_rx) in these two fields. The units of time here are hundredths of a second, which are taken from jiffies.

```
unsigned short                 flags;
unsigned short                 gflags;
unsigned                       mtu;
```

These variables are used by the IP protocol. They can be modified using the system ifconfig (see Appendix B.7). The maximum size of a packet that can be transferred by this device is given in `mtu`, and is the size excluding the hardware header (for example, the header for Ethernet packets).

Using flags, the behavior of this can be modified. The possible values are summarized in Table 8.1.

```
unsigned short              type;
unsigned short              hard_header_len;
void                        *priv;
```

Table 8.1: Flags of the network devices

Flag	Description
IFF_UP	The network device can send and detect packets
IFF_BROADCAST	The address in `struct device` is valid and can be used
IFF_DEBUG	The debugger is switched on (momentarily not used)
IFF_LOOPBACK	The device sends all the submitted packets to their own computers
IFF_POINTOPOINT	Point-to point connection, with the protocol address of the remote station (SLIP, PLIP) held in `pa_dstaddr`
IFF_NOTRAILERS	Is always switched off, but is used in BSD systems for the alternative positioning of the header at the end of a packet
IFF_RUNNING	Operational resources are in use
IFF_NOARP	ARP is not used by this network device
IFF_PROMISC	The network device will receive all packets on the network, even those addressed to other devices
IFF_ALLMULTI	The network device will receive all IP multicast packets
IFF_MASTER	Master slave mode is activated: there is a slave for the device
IFF_SLAVE	This device is being used as a slave for another network device
IFF_MULTICAST	The hardware is capable of receiving IP multicast packets
IFF_PORTSEL	The hardware supports the setting of the card output port
IFF_AUTOMEDIA	The hardware automatically searches for the connected medium
IFF_DYNAMIC	The network device can change its address (for dialup)

The device type, which in effect means the hardware, is entered in `type`. At the present stage of development, however, all protocols use the type ARPHRD_ETHER, including SLIP and PLIP. The variable `hard_header_len` specifies the length of the protocol header on the hardware layer.

A pointer to a structure specially adapted to the device type can be placed under `priv`.

```
unsigned char              broadcast [MAX_ADDR_LEN],pad;
unsigned char              dev_addr [MAX_ADDR_LEN];
unsigned char              addr_len;
```

The field `dev_addr[]` contains the hardware address for the device. The `broadcast[]` field also holds an address, which could be termed the broadcast address. Packets with this destination address are received by all computers connected to the network. As the addresses are implemented as byte fields, they are type-independent. The variable `addr_len` indicates the length of the addresses, which is of course limited by `MAX_ADDR_LEN`. The values in these fields are entered when the device is initalized and cannot be changed.

```
struct dev_mc_list         *mc_list;
int                        mc_count;
int                        promiscuity;
int                        allmulti;
```

These elements were added for versions 1.2 and 2.0 of LINUX. The components `mc_list` and `mc_count` are used when implementing multicasting on the hardware layer. Many Ethernet cards support multicasting through their hardware. The number of entries is found in `mc_count`. Each element in the list describes exactly one IP multicast address. `promiscuity` and `allmulti` are measurements of how often the network device is set in a particular mode.

```
void                       *atalk_ptr,*ip_ptr,*dn_ptr,…;
```

In contrast to the previous versions of LINUX, the protocol-specific data is stored in individual substructures. The only surprise here is the use of typeless pointers.

```
struct Qdisc               *qdisc;
struct Qdisc               *qdisc_sleeping;
struct Qdisc               *qdisc_list;
struct Qdisc               *qdisc_ingress;
unsigned long              tx_queue_len;
```

These fields, which belong to the implementation of the packet wait queue, were introduced in version 2.2 of LINUX. For simple Ethernet devices, you first refer to `noop_qdisc` and set the default implementation when the device is activated. This is a simple FIFO action. `tx_queue_len` indicates the maximum length of the wait queue, which is, for example, 100 for the Ethernet.

```
spinlock_t                 xmit_lock;
int                        xmit_lock_owner;
spinlock_t                 queue_lock;
atomic_t                   refcnt;
int                        deadbeaf;
```

```
int                      features;
```

xmit_lock is used for the synchronization for the xmit functions; it replaces the tbusy mechanism. The ID of the CPU that holds the lock is stored in xmit_lock_owner.

```
int                      (*open)(struct net_device *dev);
int                      (*stop)(struct net_device *dev);
```

The operations open() and stop() should really be called start() and close(), which would describe their intention more precisely. After open() is called, packets can be sent via the network device, but the function does not initialize the addresses. The stop() function ends the transfer of packets and sets the addresses to NULL.

```
int    (*hard_start_xmit)  (struct sk_buff *skb,
                            struct net_device *dev);
int    (*hard_header)      (struct sk_buff *skb,
                            struct net_device *dev,
                            unsigned short type,
                            void *daddr, void *saddr,
                            unsigned len);
int    (*rebuild_header)   (struct sk_buff *skb);
```

The function hard_start_xmit() is hardware-dependent. Its parameters are set to the appropriate values when a particular card is detected. Its task is to send the packet waiting in the indicated buffer. The global function dev_queue_xmit() can be regarded as the buffered variant of hard_start_xmit(). If the device is not busy, dev_queue_xmit() calls hard_start_xmit() and attempts to transfer the packet straight away. Otherwise, the packet is added to one of the lists of packets waiting to be sent, depending on its priority. The hard_header() function writes the hardware protocol header to the buffer indicated, while rebuild_header() updates the buffer according to the data in the net_device structure pointed to by dev.

```
#define HAVE_MULTICAST
  void (*set_multicast_list)(struct net_device *dev);
```

set_multicast_list() is a function which supports recent developments in the internet. It enables a network device to receive packets that are not sent to the protocol address. The implementation for Ethernet cards uses their "promiscuous" mode, in which the cards receive all packets sent to the network.

```
#define HAVE_SET_MAC_ADDR
  int (*set_mac_address) (struct net_device *dev,
                          void *addr);
#define HAVE_PRIVATE_IOCTL
```

```
    int (*do_ioctl) (struct net_device *dev,
                          void *addr);
#define HAVE_SET_CONFIG
    int (*set_config) (struct net_device *dev,
                          struct ifmap *map);
```

The set_mac_address() allows you to set the network address of the hardware. Using the do_ioctl function, network devices can enable special configurations to be set from outside – with plip, for example, the value of the timeout can be set or read. More general settings of the hardware are possible using the set_config() function. This, for example, allows the number of the interrupt to be set.

```
#define HAVE_HEADER_CACHE
    int (*hard_header_cache)(struct neighbour *neigh,
                          struct hh_cache *hh);
    void (*header_cache_update)(struct hh_cache *hh,
                          struct net_device *dev,
                          unsigned char * haddr);
#define HAVE_CHANGE_MTU
    void (*change_mtu)(struct net_device *dev, int new_mtu);
```

The two cache functions are needed for the implementation of the routing cache. This has been added in LINUX version 2.0 in order to achieve an improved network processing speed. The change_mtu function is called when a user program changes the MTU of a network device.

```
    int                        watchdog_timeo;
    struct timer_list          watchdog_timer;
    int (*tx_timeout)(struct net_device *dev);
```

A transfer timer is set for the network devices using these three elements. watchdog_timeo tells us the timespan after which the function tx_timeout should be called.

```
    int (*hard_header_parse)(struct sk_buff *skb,
                          unsigned char *haddr);
    int (*neigh_setup)(struct net_device *dev,
                          struct neigh_parms *);
    int (*accept_fastpath)(struct net_device *,
                          struct dst_entry*);
};
```

The hard_header_parse function is introduced to allow the network device to hide the details of the low-level packet.

```
    struct module                        *owner;
```

With the introduction of a module pointer in this structure, the management of the modules is simplified and the network devices are maintained. Now you should not increase the module reference counter, but use `SET_MODULE_OWNER(X)` with a pointer to the `net_device` structure. In this way the reference counter is dealt with automatically. The trick with this is the empty definition of the macro in the case where we are not dealing with a module transfer.

```
struct in_device
{
        struct net_device        *dev;
        struct in_ifaddr         *ifa_list;
        struct ip_mc_list        *mc_list;
        unsigned long            mr_v1_seen;
        unsigned                 flags;
        struct neigh_parms       *arp_parms;
        struct ipv4_devconf      cnf;
};
```

8.3.1 | Ethernet

LINUX supports two groups of adapters for Ethernet. These include the classic Ethernet cards connected to the PC bus, and adapters linked to the PC via the parallel interface or the PCMCIA bus.

The network devices for the Ethernet cards are called "eth0", . . . , "eth3." This also applies to pocket adapters operated via the PCMCIA bus, which are included as a module. LINUX assigns cards to devices in the sequence in which the hardware is detected. During the startup, the kernel outputs a message on the cards detected and allocates them to the network devices. For modules, this output only takes place at the time of loading. Information on which cards and/or adapters LINUX supports can be found in the "Ethernet-HOWTO."[4] As cards compatible with the WD8013 and NE2000 cards are supported, a large number of inexpensive Ethernet adapters are available.

Let us take a close look at the Ethernet network devices. The Ethernet address of the associated network card is held in the field `dev_addr[]`. Every Ethernet adapter has a completely unique address. These addresses are 6 bytes long; an example, represented as text, would be 0:0:c0:9b:13:29. After the network device has been configured with an IP address, an entry in the ARP table is generated when the card is selected (see `ifconfig` in Appendix B.7).

A field in the hardware header of an Ethernet packet allows various types of Ethernet packet to be differentiated. There are types for IP, AR, IPX, and other protocols. The type determines which function the packet is passed to.

---

4 The "Ethernet-HOWTO" is located in the file docs / HOWTO / Ethernet - HOWTO on the CD-ROM accompanying this book.

The allocation of the packet types is carried out with the aid of a list. It is thus possible to carry out dynamic modifications on known packet types. For IP, for example, the list element is as follows:

```
static struct packet_type ip_packet_type = {
  htons(ETH_P_IP),
  NULL,
  ip_rcv,
  (void*)1,
  NULL
};
```

This entry contains both the Ethernet packet type and the associated receiving function. The first NULL indicates that no copies of packets of this type need to be made. Where there is a (void*) pointer, there can also be a pointer to special data. The final pointer is used for linking all the packet types in the list.

This list therefore represents the interface between the network devices and the separate protocols as far as the devices are concerned. Packets which do not match any of the types registered in the list are discarded.

8.3.2 SLIP and PLIP

Now let us turn to some more "exotic-looking" devices. The most significant difference between SLIP and PLIP is that one protocol uses the computer's serial interface for data transfer while the other transfers data via the parallel port. When we speak of the parallel interface here, we do not mean Ethernet pocket adapters but the "bare" interface.

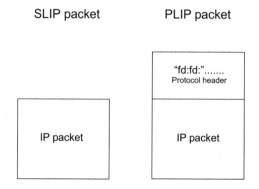

Figure 8.7: Relationship of SLIP and PLIP packets to IP packets.

PLIP enables a very powerful link to be set up between two computers. SLIP is the simplest way of connecting a computer or a local network to the internet via a serial link (a modem connection to a telephone network). SLIP and PLIP differ from Ethernet in that they can only transmit IP packets. For simplicity, SLIP does not even use a hardware header, nor does PLIP make great demands: It simply sets the hardware address to "fd:fd" plus the IP address and then uses the Ethernet functions for the protocol header (see Figure 8.7).

8.3.3 | The loopback device

The loopback device is used for communication with applications on the local computer using sockets in the INET address family. It can be implemented with little effort, as it immediately returns the packets to be sent to the upper layers. It can also be used to test network applications on a computer: this excludes the possibility of errors in the network hardware. The loopback device "lo" is generally assigned to the IP address 127.0.0.1.

8.3.4 | The dummy device

In the dummy device we encounter a rather exotic representation of network devices. It behaves, in fact, like any other device except that no real data transfer takes place.

You may well ask what use a network device of this sort is. It is mostly used to present a functioning network device to the higher-level areas of the network implementation when there is not actually one present. By the higher-level areas of the network implementation we also mean user processes.

8.3.5 | An example device

In this section we will show, using an Ethernet device, how to implement your own network devices. We will therefore diverge from the real hardware and concentrate on the essentials. Where hardware treatment is required will be pointed out to you.

The way in which a network device works is best described using a stream model, as with most other parts of the network implementation. Higher protocol layers send data to the device, which should then pass this on to the hardware. Also, the hardware detects data which has to be passed on to higher layers. The functions in the net_device structure show ways of viewing the higher layers in the network device.

For the Ethernet devices that are not loaded as a module, there is a central setup function (eth_setup()). Using this, it is possible to set the interrupt, the beginning of the I/O addresses, and the memory start and end for a particular ethX. The values are written for later access to the net_device structure. When implementing this as a module, the parameters can of course be chosen freely, subject to the general limitations of a module (see Chapter 9).

Before a device driver takes on its function, you should always check whether the appropriate hardware is available and function-capable. With network device drivers it has become natural to use an independent function (probe) for this job. This can then either be integrated in the initialization of the kernel, or called in the initialization function of the module. For this reason the macro module_init() has been introduced in LINUX version

2.4. This receives an `init` function as a parameter, which no longer has to be called an `init_module`. If the driver is integrated directly in the kernel this function will be called during startup. In the case where we are dealing with a module, on the other hand, this function is declared as a `module_init` (see Chapter 9).

Down stream

The functions which are required for the transport of data to the network are contained in the `net_device` structure and are dealt with separately. The role of the `probe` function is not only to get the hardware into a function-capable state, but also to cover the function pointer in the `net_device` structure. This should be returned completely initialized.

`open(dev)` Before using a network device, the `open` function is called, normally by `dev_open()`. By using `open`, the hardware and the driver are supposed to be brought into a working condition, which means, among other things, that the resources required for use (interrupts[5], . . .) are requested and covered. Also, it is a good strategy to switch on interrupt creation for hardware before the hardware recognition. In some circumstances, the function pointer in the `net_device` can also be modified. The result type of the function is an integer. A zero therefore indicates an error-free execution. Otherwise, negative error numbers are returned, such as -**EBUSY**.

`stop(dev)` In this function, the opposite actions to `open` are executed. The resources are released and interrupt creation switched off. After calling `stop`, no further data should be passed on by the network device to the upper protocol layers. The result type of the function is an integer. A zero therefore indicates success. Otherwise, negative error numbers are returned, such as -**EBUSY**. Normally, no errors should occur during shutdown.

`hard_start_xmit(skb, dev)` The `hard_start_xmit()` function is the key to the network device. It is called for every packet to be transferred, found in `skb`. Changes to the packet should no longer be made. The packet data should simply be submitted to the hardware or to the net. Which mechanism is used for this is left up to the user. Current options include DMA transfer, the shared memory of the card, or I/O ports. On top of this, the current value from `jiffies` is entered in `trans_start`, which indicates the beginning of the transfer. By using this you can establish whether or not a timeout occurred during the transfer. For other variables you use a private structure of the network device driver, which is noted in `priv` and defined separately for each device. After the successful transfer of a packet,

```
netif_wake_queue(dev);
```

should be used to hasten the sending of intermediately saved packets. In a DMA transfer, this should then be carried out during the following DMA interrupt.

---

5   When registering the ISR, we should indicate the pointer on our `net_device` structure as the data pointer.

set_multicast_list(dev) It is the role of this function to compare the mc_list of the driver structure with the hardware. For cards that have no multicast implementation, the promiscuous mode should be switched on or off. In this situation, like when opening the network device, the IFF_ALLMULTI and IFF_PROMISC flags of the driver structure should be taken into account and the card should be placed in the corresponding detection mode.

get_stats(dev) This function is especially used by the *Proc* file system to issue statistics for the network device. The implementation of the MIB (SNMP) for LINUX computers is accessing this file system.

Since you have to collect data during operation in order to calculate the values for the net_device_stats structure, you have the option of defining the structure as a private data field of the network device driver. The values in the statistic structure have to be counted at suitable points in the other functions.

do_ioctl(dev, addr) This function implements the ioctl calls on the driver. This is used for tasks which are not usually undertaken by the kernel, such as setting the MTU to non-standard values, the switching on of error messages, etc.

Up stream

There is no large interface for the transmission of data from the network to the upper protocol layers. The only function which is used there is netif_rx(). It receives an initialized sk_buff structure as a parameter, which contains the detected packet.

Because it is the network device driver's job to hide hardware differences from the rest of the kernel, there is of course no uniform interface for the hardware. The usual rules for device drivers apply here (see Chapter 7).

The connection of the hardware, with help from the interrupt, is a common scenario. The ISR is used for the interrupt of the net_device structure. It should be set to a value unequal to zero if the ISR is active, in order to prevent multiple calling of the ISR. This should be achieved by using the test_and_set_bit function, since a mutex is being dealt with here, which works for SMP. The further course of the function strongly depends on the hardware. In some circumstances, parts of the DMA treatment are implemented here. If the ISR has determined that a packet has been detected by the hardware, the following process should be implemented: An sk_buff structure is requested by the dev_alloc_skb() function. The size specified here indicates the size of the packet. The pointer to our net_device structure has to be entered into the dev field of the buffer. The packet data then has to be copied into the buffer, which is largely dependent upon the hardware (DMA, I/O, . . .). The protocol field of the buffer is then set – for Ethernet devices this is the returned value of eth_type_trans() using the buffer and our net_device pointer as a parameter. Now the buffer is ready and we call the netif_rx function with the buffer as a parameter. By doing so, the data flow is controlled and a few more statistical tasks now follow. `last_rx` from the `net_device` structure is set to the current value of `jiffies`. In addition, a few fields of the `net_device_stats` structure are brought up to date. If there is an error, these fields should be set to new values.

9 MODULES AND DEBUGGING

With each version, the LINUX kernel increases in size and scope. This occurs as much through the continual improvement and expansion of the kernel functionality as through the addition of new device drivers, file systems or emulations such as iBCS2. Because LINUX is a monolithic system, all device drivers and file systems used are integrated in the kernel. On the one hand, this means that with a change to the configuration the kernel has to be recompiled and, on the other, that even drivers and file systems that are rarely required occupy permanent memory. There is a further disadvantage for developers of new kernel code: After even the smallest change, a new kernel has to be created and installed, and the computer rebooted. These and many other reasons led to the development of modules. So the question now is: What are modules?

9.1 WHAT ARE MODULES?

From the kernel's point of view, modules consist of object code which is linkable and removable at runtime, usually comprising a number of functions (at least two). This object code is integrated into the kernel that is already running with equal rights, which means that it runs in system mode. The monolithic structure of the kernel is not changed: Unlike the micro kernel, the newly added functions do not run as processes in their own right. One advantage of implementing device drivers or file systems as modules is that only the documented interfaces can be used.

For the user, modules enable a small and compact kernel to be used, with other functions only being added as and when required. With the kernel daemon support of version 2.0, it is even possible to load modules automatically, without the user having to do this him/herself. As a further example we will mention the PCMCIA card manager.

The structure of the source code for the LINUX kernel is described in Section 2.1. The C files are organized in directories consisting of functional groupings of various kinds. During compilation, the functional subunits are collected in an object file, so that when the kernel is subsequently loaded as a whole there is no need to access every object file individually. These functional units can often be used as modules.

9.2   IMPLEMENTATION IN THE KERNEL

Now that we have seen the advantages of using modules, we will consider their implementation. For this, LINUX provides three system calls: *create_module*, *init_module*, and *delete_module*. A further system call is used by the user process to obtain a copy of the kernel's symbol table.

The administration of modules under LINUX makes use of a list which contains all the modules loaded. The form of the entries is shown in Section A.1. This list also contains the modules' symbol tables and references.

As far as the kernel is concerned, modules are loaded in two steps corresponding to the system calls *create_module* and *init_module*. For the user process, this procedure is divided into four phases:

- The process moves the content of the object file into its own address space. In a normal object file, the code and the data are arranged as if they started from address 0 after loading. To convert the code and data into a form in which they can actually be executed, the actual load address must be added at various points. This process is known as *relocating*. References to the required points are included in the object file. There may also be unresolved references in the object file. When the object file is analyzed, the size of the module is also obtained (see Figure 9.1).[1]

- The system call *create_module* is now used, firstly to obtain the final address of the object module and secondly to reserve memory for it. To do this, a structure `module` is entered for the module in the list of modules and memory is allocated. The return value gives us the address to which the module will later be copied (see Figure 9.1b).

- The load address received by *create_module* is used to relocate the object file. This procedure takes place in a memory area accompanying the process – that is, at this point the object module is still not at the right address, but is relocated for the loading address of the module in the kernel segment.

  Unresolved references can be solved using the kernel symbols, for which LINUX provides the system call *query_module*. Using this, it is possible to get the symbol table for each loaded module and the kernel. Note that there is no type information of any sort in the table, only addresses. Care must therefore be taken during the development of a module to ensure that the correct header files are included.

  To achieve the greatest possible degree of flexibility, the modules themselves can add symbols to the kernel's symbol table. This allows another module to use functions from one loaded earlier. This mechanism is known as *stacked module*. All the symbols exported by a module are collected in a separate symbol table (see Figure 9.1).

- Once the preliminary work is complete, we can load the object module. This uses the system call *init_module*, which is given a structure `module`. The `module`'s administration is entered in `init` and `cleanup` and LINUX now copies the object module into the kernel. The administration

---

1   You will find further particulars concerning the construction and use of object files in [Gir90] and [Elf].

function init() is called once the code and data have been installed, and the register function should also be called within this function.

The return value of init() determines whether or not the installation procedure is judged to have been successful. The second administration function cleanup() is called when the module is uninstalled, and initiates the relevant deregister function.

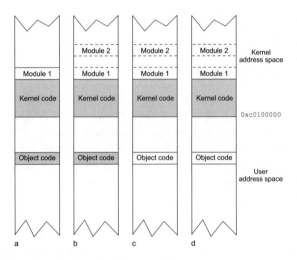

Figure 9.1: The address space when loading a module.

The symbol table for the kernel is defined in the files kernel/ksyms.c and arch/<arch>/kernel/<arch>_ksyms.c. Each exported function has an entry in the table symbol_table. The name of the function or variable in each case is transferred to module_symbol by the EXPORT_SYMBOL().

The module's own symbol table lists not only the symbols to be exported, but also references to symbols in the kernel which have been used by the module. This enables the mutual dependence of the modules to be gauged. As a result, a module which is still being used by another module will not be uninstalled.

An additional aid for avoiding problems when uninstalling modules after use is the USE_COUNT mechanism. If, for example, we have implemented a device driver and it has been loaded, the use counter will be incremented every time the module is opened and decremented every time it is closed. This means that when uninstalling the module we can find out whether it is still in use. It should also be mentioned that the locations where the use counter is changed are in some cases difficult or impossible to find.

As a final resort in particularly difficult cases, it is of course possible to increment the use counter as a one-off operation during the init function. This means that the module can never be removed.

The flexibility of modules does not only lie in the fact that they can be loaded dynamically. By using the system call *delete_module*, a module that has been loaded can be removed. Two prerequisites have to be met for this: there must be no references to the module and the module's use counter must have a value of zero. Before the module is released, the `cleanup` function registered during installation is called. In this function, dynamic resources requested during operation and in the `init` function can be released. For a device driver that is used by hardware, this means leaving the hardware in a condition which has no support from the device driver. In particular, the hardware should not trigger any more interrupts that are dealt with by the device driver, since this deregisters the interrupt treatment routine.

9.2.1 | Signatures of symbols

A common problem in module implementation is the module's dependence on the version of the kernel. Because of the continued rapid development of the LINUX kernel, exported structures and functions are continually changed. Therefore, for every new version of the kernel, all the modules should be recompiled to make sure that symbols are being used in accordance with their definitions. A way out of this dilemma is offered by symbol names containing a signature to the associated C object (the function or structure elements). A similar mechanism is used in C++: for example, for functions and namespaces.

In the LINUX kernel, a different model is used, in which the symbols to be exported are expanded to their full definitions and 32-bit checksums are calculated from the results, which are then added to the original symbol. Although this procedure is not unequivocal, the likelihood of a clash is sufficiently small. However, this mechanism must be included when configuring the kernel. This is achieved by answering "yes" to the question.

```
Set version information on all symbols for modules
```

The creation of this special symbol information is handled by the `genksyms` program, which is included in the module tools.

The `insmod` program included in this automatically tests for matching checksums when a module with signature information is loaded. This avoids the situation in which a module is loaded that is liable to call a function with the wrong parameters or access a structure whose definition has changed.

9.3 | THE MEANING OF OBJECT SECTIONS FOR MODULES AND KERNELS

The individual object sections (see [ELF] as well) and their functions are listed in the following.

.text   Here you find the executable code.

.data   Here you find initialized data for the code.

.bss   Here you find the un-initialized data.

.rodata   Here you find read-only initialized data.

.text.lock Because an optimistic procedure is normally chosen when loading the instruction pipe, the treatment of negative cases is removed from the normal instruction flow. They will end up in `.text.lock`. This is true for semaphores and the "spin locks" in SMP.

__ksymtab The contents of this section consist of a field of entries for the exported symbols of the module. The entries have the following structure:

```
struct module_symbol {
        unsigned long value;
        const char *name;
};
```

The `value` element contains the address of the symbol, and `name` refers to the name. The strings themselves are placed in the following section.

.kstrtab The strings for the exported symbols are found here. These correspond to the names of the exported symbols or, in the case where the signature is activated, the signed name of the symbol.

.fixup This section contains the treatment routines for illegal accesses from the kernel mode to the user space. They are implicitly created with the use of `copy_...` macros from `<asm/uaccess.h>`.

__ex_table To avoid usually unnecessary checking[2] for correct access in kernel mode to the user space, an optimistic approach is chosen. Every place in the code that can potentially create an incorrect access is entered into the exception table. In addition, the error treatment routine is entered for this code position (using the `copy_...` macros). When a forbidden access occurs, a memory fault is raised and the general treatment routine searches through the exception table and jumps to the special error treatment, which is noted in the table.

.modinfo Here we have a really innovative concept for the module under LINUX. General information about the module is placed in this section in character string form. The character strings have the format `<name>=<value>` and are terminated with a 0 byte. There are the firmly predefined names `author` (author of the module), `description` and `device` (implemented device). Further entries are concerned with the permitted transfer parameters, which can be sent along with the module during loading. They have the following format: `parm_<name>=<type>` and `parm_desc_<name>= <desc>`. The name relates to the supported module parameter. The parameter type is determined using the first format. The overall format is `[<min>[-<max>]]{b,h,i,l, s}[p]`. The minimum and maximum values are optional and are only necessary for fields. The current type is represented by a letter (see Table 9.1). The optional `p` at the end

---

2 Measurements produced a 99:1 ratio of correct to incorrect accesses.

indicates persistent module parameters. These are saved by `rmmod` when removing the module and then reset by `insmod` when loading it.

Table 9.1: Type codes for module parameters

b	byte
h	short
i	int
l	long
s	string

Table 9.2: Macros for modules

Macro	Functions of the macro
MODULE_AUTHOR(name)	Author of the module
MODULE_DESCRIPTION(desc)	Brief description of the module
MODULE_SUPPORTED_DEVICE(dev)	Device that is implemented by the module
MODULE_PARM(var, type)	A module parameter
MODULE_PARM_DESC(var, desc)	Brief description of the module parameter
EXPORT_SYMBOL(var)	Export the variables or functions
module_init(func)	Defines the func function for the module as the init function
module_exit(func)	Defines the func function for the module as the cleanup function

.text.init This section contains code which is only required during initialization. In normal use of the module, this code is no longer required and can therefore be removed. For this reason there is this additional code section, which can be removed after initialization.

.data.init Similarly to the previous section, there is data here that is only required during initialization.[3]

.setup.init A field from `kernel_param` structures is found in this section of the LINUX kernel. These are created by using the macro `__setup()`. The macro contains a string such as `"root="` as a parameter and a function for the evaluation of the kernel parameter.

---

3 In version 2.4 of LINUX, the release of the initial code is only supported for the kernel itself, but is actually planned for modules as well.

.initcall.init This section is a field and contains pointers to initialization functions that should be called at the start of the LINUX kernel. They are set up with the help of the macro __initcall(). The macro receives the function which is to be called (see Table 9.2). In the case where the file is not converted into a module, module_init() becomes an __initcall().

.data.init_task Here you find the init_task_union union for the i386 architecture. An individual section was selected to ensure the alignment at 8 Kbytes boundary.

.data.cacheline_aligned Data is packed in this section, which must have a suitable alignment corresponding to the CPU cache. This is particularly important for SMP computers.

.data.page_aligned corresponds to .data.cacheline_aligned, only this time data is aligned to the memory page borders.

The sections .comment and .note are not decisive for the functioning of modules and the kernel.

| 9.4 | PARAMETER TRANSFER AND EXAMPLES |

To make things clearer for the module programmer, C macros are offered, which support parameter transfer and generate the corresponding information for the .modinfo section in the LINUX *include* files. How these are used is shown in the following example. The export of symbols is also demonstrated:

```
#include <linux/module.h>
int register_hbsubmod(void *x)
{
  return 0;
}
/*
* Now set up the variables for the parameters. They can be pre-initialized
  */
static int hbdebug = 0;
static int io_addr[4] = { 0x300, 0, 0, 0 };
static char *init_string = zero;
/*
* When no functions of this module are required by other modules, please uncomment.
*/
/* EXPORT_NO_SYMBOLS;*/
```

```
/*
 * This module exports the function register _hbsubmod().
 */

EXPORT_SYMBOL (register_hbsubmod);

MODULE_AUTHOR ("Harald Boehme");
MODULE_DESCRIPTION ("Demonstration module of the usage of \
                    the MODULE-macros");
MODULE_SUPPORTED_DEVICE("hbdev");

MODULE_PARM (hbdebug, "i");
MODULE_PARM_DESC (hbdebug, "Debug level");

MODULE_PARM (io_addr, "1-4i");
MODULE_PARM_DESC (io_addr, "Up to four I/O-addresses");

MODULE_PARM (init_string, "s");
MODULE_PARM_DESC (init_string, "optional init-string");

int hb_init(void)
{
/* Initialization, calling register functions. */
}
void hb_cleanup(void)
{
/* Release resources, call deregister functions. */
}
module_init(hb_init)
module_exit(hb_cleanup)
```

The insmod module io_addr=0x300,0x308 init_string="foo" call initializes the io_addr field with the values 0x300 and 0x308 as well as the init_string pointer with the submitted string.

9.5 WHAT CAN BE IMPLEMENTED AS A MODULE?

As a rule of thumb, the aim should always be to use as few symbols or functions from the kernel or other modules as possible. In addition, there is the option to dynamically apply and then remove the module. It can be taken as a general rule that there should be a registering and deregistering function for the functions implemented by a module. This condition is met by a number of kernel elements; the best known example of this is offered by file system implementations, for which there are the functions `register_filesystem()` and `deregister_filesystem()`.

These satisfy all the conditions, including suitable points where the use counter can be administered. As described in Section 9.2, modules must be prevented from being removed while they are still in use. In file system implementations, this is relatively simple: A file system is in use if a file system of this type is mounted. During the mount procedure, the `read_super` function of the file system implementation is called, in which the counter can be incremented before a successful termination. The counterpart to the mount procedure is demounting, for which the function is `put_super()`.

Table 9.3 lists the functional units which can be implemented as modules. The registration and deregistration functions are given for each one.

Table 9.3: Functional units that can be used as modules

Unit	Functions
File system	`register_filesystem()` `unregister_filesystem()`
Blockdevice driver	`register_blkdev()` `unregister_blkdev()`
Signal device driver	`register_chrdev()` `unregister_chrdev()`
Network device driver	`register_netdev()` `unregister_netdev()`
PCMCIA device	`register_pccard_driver()` `unregister_pccard_driver()`
Exec-Domain	`register_exec_domain()` `unregister_exec_domain()`
Binary format	`register_binfmt()` `unregister_binfmt()`
Network protocol	`sock_register()`, `dev_add_pack()` and `register_netdevice_notifier()` `sock_unregister()`, `dev_remove_pack()` and `unregister_netdevice_notifier()`

9.6   THE KERNEL DAEMON

Apart from version 2.0 of LINUX, the kernel daemon has been discarded. One of the reasons for this is that System V IPC and UNIX domain sockets could not be implemented as modules themselves, because they are already required for the kernel daemon's function.

From the functions in the kernel that deal with the requirements of modules, only the `request_module()` remains. Its implementation creates a new process, which then executes the `modprobe` program with the corresponding module name.

9.7   SIMPLE DATA SWAPPING BETWEEN MODULES

During the development of modules you sometimes establish that other alternatives have to be taken into account for a certain part of the module. You then split the code into numerous modules (*stacked module*). To a certain extent, a wide function interface is not required. Since you have to exchange data between modules, you require some sort of interface. For this, LINUX 2.4 offers a new mechanism. With the help of the `inter_module_register()` and `inter_module_deregister()` functions, you can register or deregister a save area under a name.

On this basis, a module can produce data for other modules. Therefore the interface definition between modules is reduced by setting up a data structure.

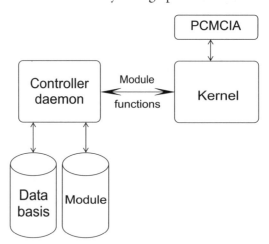

Figure 9.2:   Daemon for dynamic loading and unloading of modules.

Modules can now search for exported memory areas by specifying the name, with the help of the `inter_module_get()` and `inter_module_get_request()` functions. In the second variant, in the case where the name cannot be found, we attempt to load a module with a name given by the parameter. When you have finished accessing the saved area, use the `inter_module_put()` function to dereference the saved area and give the exporting module the chance to stop.

9.8   AN EXAMPLE MODULE

An interesting modular application is the PCMCIA card manager, which combines the dynamic characteristics of modules with those of the PCMCIA system. Just as a PCMCIA card is only slotted into the computer if its services are required, the PCMCIA card manager ensures that the modules for the card are loaded.

As a basis for this service a PCMCIA device is implemented. With its help, the PCMCIA card manager is informed of every status change in the PCMCIA hardware. In addition, this device allows the card identifier to be read. Using this identifier and the information in its database, the PCMCIA card manager is now able to load and remove modules.

Modules have also been chosen to implement the necessary basic functions in the kernel. There is a central module which contains the general standard for PCMCIA. A second module drives the PCMCIA controller chip. As there are two different types of the latter, there are also two different modules for this task. Finally, there is a module in which the interfaces are implemented: These include the character device for the PCMCIA device and the functions for the device drivers based on this system.

The function of the PCMCIA card manager can be described relatively simply. It opens the character devices associated with the individual sockets (PCMCIA inserts). Using these devices, the PCMCIA card manager can keep itself informed of status changes in the sockets. It also can obtain detailed information about the inserted cards.

The information important for its behavior is taken from the database, which is usually located in the `/etc/pcmcia/config` file and holds definitions for various devices. The definitions consist of the modules to be loaded and programs to be executed during the addition and removal of cards.

```
device "de650_cs"
  module "net/8390", "de650_cs"
  start "/etc/pcmcia/network start %d%"
  stop "/etc/pcmcia/network stop %d%"
```

The other part of the data detects various cards. Each of the PCMCIA cards contains an ASCII character string giving its name. By reference to this information, the various cards are assigned to the devices.

```
card "Accton EN2212 EtherCard"
  version "ACCTON", "EN2212", "ETHERNET", "*"
  bind "de650_cs"

card "D-Link DE-650 Ethernet Card"
```

```
    version "D-Link", "DE-650", "*", "*"
    bind "de650_cs"

card "GVC NIC-2000P Ethernet Card"
    version "GVC", "NIC-2000p", "*", "*"
    bind "de650_cs"
```

The drivers produced up to version 2.5.0 consist of Ethernet cards, memory cards, serial cards, modem cards, SCSI cards, and many others.

Furnished with all this information, the PCMCIA card manager does not have a great deal more to do. By means of `select()`, it waits for a change in any of the devices. If one occurs, it picks up the corresponding data from the device, then refers to the database to determine the appropriate actions, which it then carries out. This takes care of all the events and the manager can go back to waiting with `select()` until its services are required again.

9.9   DEBUGGING

Raley will a section of program code be free of bugs as soon as it is written. The program will usually need debugging, for which it will be loaded into a debugger such as `gdb` and run step by step until the error has been found. Unfortunately, some software cannot be debugged so easily. This includes real-time applications, (quasi) parallel processes, and software that runs without a host operating system. Again, unfortunately, the LINUX kernel (like all operating system kernels) matches all three of these conditions. It doesn't really need to be said that changes to an operating system kernel are equally – and particularly – liable to errors.

9.9.1   Changes are the beginning of the end

A useful general tip is: "Try not to change the kernel, because if you don't amend the LINUX kernel, you will not have to debug it and you will save yourself lots of problems." Simple though this statement is, it has a lot of meaning for the kernel programmer.

We have no wish to prevent people carrying out creative work on the LINUX kernel. However, anyone contemplating this should seriously ask him/herself whether the expansion that is planned really has any business in the kernel. It is often possible to implement it wholly or partially as an external program, or at least to divert some of the functions to an external process. A privileged process (that is, one with a UID of 0) can do practically anything a driver in the kernel can do. As often as not, communication with the hardware is only carried out via I/O ports, and a privileged process can do that too. This approach is used in the `svgalib` library, which takes care of controlling the graphic modes for various SVGA cards. Of course, there are also cases where this approach does not achieve the desired result.

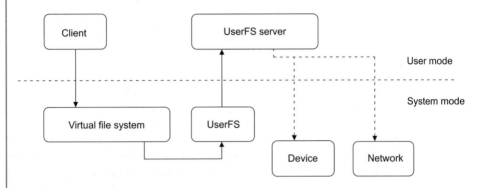

Figure 9.3: Functions of the user file system.

Device drivers communicating with the hardware via interrupts need, at the very least, support from the LINUX kernel, as this alone has the capacity to handle interrupts. Only really necessary functions are implemented in the kernel; the actual work should be handled by a normal process. The user file system is a rather good example of this approach. However, it is not a part of the standard kernel.

The logical grouping of data on a physical device is traditionally carried out in the operating system kernel, although strictly speaking this is not where it belongs. The *User* file system enables this set of functions to be located in an ordinary process. The kernel merely contains an interface for the queries, which are then forwarded to the process. One advantage is immediately obvious: The greater part of the code is in a normal process, which means that it can be debugged using the standard tools. A further advantage becomes apparent when we consider why the file system implementation has to access a hard disk or similar. The process can make any data available as a file system. Thus, in the current implementation of the user file system there is also an FTP file system, which accesses the data via the FTP protocol. This enables any FTP server to be made available to the user as if he/she were accessing it via NFS. There is one disadvantage of the *User* file system architecture that should not be ignored, however: Access to data is not particularly fast.

9.9.2 The best debugger – printk()

A test printout at a strategic point can save hours of debugging. Unfortunately, a little experience is required to find the right points.

For this reason, test printouts from a driver should be planned, even at the design stage: These are short but highly informative. When debugging the kernel, breakpoints can only be included if major changes are made to the kernel itself. Instead, we can make do with suitable test printouts at these points, for example by means of the `printk` function (see Appendix E).

Once again, an expansion of the GNU C compiler will be of excellent use here. This permits C pre-processor macros to be used with a variable number of arguments. A debugging macro can thus be defined along the following lines:

```
#ifdef DEBUG
#define MY_PRINTK(format, a...) printk(format, ## a)
#else
#define MY_PRINTK(format, a...)
#endif /* DEBUG */
```

Defined in this way, **MY_PRINTK** can be used in exactly the same way as the function `printk()`. However, it allows a decision of whether or not test printouts should be produced to be made during compilation. A second advantage is that it saves a lot of writing in comparison with ordinary C macros. If, in addition, the printouts are made dependent on a flag in the kernel, the process becomes even more dynamic. The flag then needs to be set by an external event: for this we can fall back on the `sysctl` interface (see Section A.1) or an `ioctl` command.

As described in Appendix A, only printouts with a level lower than the kernel variable `console_loglevel` are displayed on the console. As it is sometimes useful to have the information there as well, because the kernel crashes immediately afterwards or for some similar reason, the value of `console_loglevel` will need to be changed appropriately. There are a number of ways of doing this:

■ using the system call *syslog*;

■ direct modification of the variable.

When serious problems (traps) occur, the kernel automatically sets the level to the highest value, so that all messages appear on the console.

The user of modules should also be aware that direct manipulation of the variable `console_loglevel` is only possible in quite a roundabout way, as the associated symbol is not included in the global symbol table. This means that this external reference must be resolved using the map file `System.map` in the kernel, or else the symbol must be entered in the file `kernel/ksyms.c`.

9.9.3   Debugging with gdb

Finally, the LINUX kernel can also be debugged easily using the GNU debugger `gdb`. However, a number of conditions need to be met first. The kernel, or at least the area of the kernel to be debugged, must be compiled with debugging information. This calls for nothing more than replacing the line in the kernel central makefile

```
HOSTCFLAGS = -Wall -Wstrict-prototypes -O2 -fomit-frame-pointer
```

with

HOSTCFLAGS = -Wall -Wstrict-prototypes -O2 -g

The relevant area can then be compiled and the kernel relinked.

We can now run the debugger via

gdb /usr/src/linux/vmlinux /proc/kcore

As is evident from the command line, /proc/kcore is read by the debugger as the core file for the kernel. This enables all the structures in the kernel to be read, but no local variables. Unfortunately, it is not possible to change values or call kernel functions: The functions are restricted to the simple reading of values. Despite this, many errors can be tracked down. Unlike the use of standard core files, gdb reads the value from memory, which means that it is always the current, updated value that is given.

In addition, when using gdb you should note that you have to load the symbol table along with the modules into gdb. Therefore, the modules also have to be compiled with debug information. If you now wish to access the values from a loaded module, you have to load the symbols from the .o files of the module into the gdb. For this you need the loading address of the module in the current kernel. This is noted by insmod when loading the symbol table of the kernel. It can be found under __insmod_<module name>_S.text_L.... You will also find ..._S.data_... and ..._S.bss_... here. These values are submitted in gdb to the add-symbol-file function.[4] Now you can access the variables and functions from the module as usual.

---

4 An example for reloading a module in the gdb is: add-symbol-file awe_wave.0 0xc8828000 0xc882a760.

10 MULTIPROCESSING

Even though ever more advanced and faster processors are entering the market, there will always be applications that require even more processor power. In multitasking systems, a solution to this problem is to employ several processors in order to achieve true parallel processing of tasks. As in all truly parallel systems, performance does not increase in a linear manner according to the number of processors employed. Instead, it is the operating system that bears an increased responsibility to distribute all tasks among the processors in such a way that as few processors as possible hinder each other. This chapter deals with symmetric multiprocessing (SMP) which is supported by LINUX since version 2.0.

10.1 THE INTEL MULTIPROCESSOR SPECIFICATION

Most of the currently available multiprocessor main boards for PCs use Pentium II or Pentium III processors. The Pentium already has some internal functions which support multiprocessor operations, such as cache synchronization, interprocessor interrupt handling, and atomic operations for checking, setting, and exchanging values in main memory. Cache synchronization in particular greatly facilitates SMP implementation in the kernel.

Intel's multiprocessor specification MP 1.4 [SMP] defines the interaction between hardware and software in order to facilitate the development of SMP-capable operating systems and to make it possible for these systems to run on new hardware. The aim of the specification is to create a multiprocessor platform which is still 100% compatible with the PC/AT. It defines a highly symmetrical architecture in terms of:

Memory symmetry All processors share the same main memory. All physical addresses are the same. This means that all processors execute the same operating system, and all data and applications are visible to all processors and can be used or executed on every processor.

I/O symmetry All processors share the same I/O subsystem (including the I/O port and the interrupt controller). I/O symmetry allows reduction of a possible I/O bottleneck. However, some MP systems assign all interrupts to a single processor.

Figure 10.1 shows the hardware overview of a typical SMP system with two processors. Both are connected via the ICC (*Interrupt Controller Communications*) bus with one or more I/O-APICs (*Advanced Programmable Interrupt Controller*). Pentium processors have their own integrated local APIC. These local APICs, together with the I/O-APICs, constitute a unit which deals with the distribution of incoming interrupts.

One processor is preferred by the BIOS. This one is called the boot processor (BSP) and is used for system initialization. All other processors are called application processors (AP) and are initially halted by the BIOS. The MP specification defines a configuration structure which is filled in by the BIOS and informs the operating system about the existing MP system. The BIOS initially forwards all interrupts to the boot processor, so that single-processor operating systems see no difference and only run on the BSP.

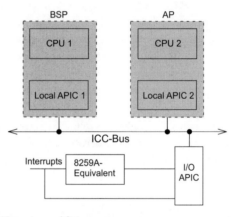

Figure 10.1: A typical SMP system with two processors.

10.2 PROBLEMS WITH MULTIPROCESSOR SYSTEMS

For the correct functioning of a multitasking system it is important that data in the kernel can only be changed by one processor so that identical resources cannot be allocated twice. In UNIX-like systems, there are two approaches to the solution of this problem. Traditional UNIX systems use a relatively coarse-grained locking; sometimes even the whole kernel is locked so that only one process can be present in the kernel. Some more advanced systems implement a finer-grained locking which, however, entails high additional expenditure and is normally used only for multiprocessor and real-time operating systems. In the latter, fine-grained locking reduces the time that a lock must be kept, thus allowing a reduction of the particularly critical latency time.

In the LINUX kernel implementation, various rules have been established. One of them is that no process running in kernel mode is interrupted by another process running in kernel mode, except when it releases control and sleeps. This rule ensures that large areas of the kernel are atomic with respect to other processes and thus simplifies many functions in the LINUX kernel.

A further rule establishes that interrupt handling cannot be interrupted by a process running in kernel mode, but that in the end control is returned back to this same process. A process can block interrupts and thus make sure that it will not be interrupted.

The last rule that is important for us states that interrupt handling cannot be interrupted by a process running in kernel mode. This means that interrupt handling will be processed completely, or at most be interrupted by another interrupt of higher priority.

In the development of the multiprocessor LINUX kernel, at first a decision was made to maintain these three basic rules, on the one hand to facilitate the first implementation, and on the other to allow a simple integration of already existing code. A single semaphore was used by all processes to monitor the transition to kernel mode. Each processor that has this lock can always enter kernel mode, for example for interrupt handling. As soon as the process no longer has the lock, it is no longer allowed to change to kernel mode.

This semaphore is used to ensure that no process running in kernel mode can be interrupted by another process. Furthermore, it guarantees that only a process running in kernel mode can block interrupts without another process taking over interrupt handling.

This design decision has resulted, however, in low performance of I/O-intensive applications because CPU time in kernel mode becomes a bottleneck. In LINUX version 2.2, a finer-grained locking was therefore introduced. Only this can ensure a higher parallelism and consequently a higher system performance. The current LINUX multiprocessor implementation achieves good performance for CPU-intensive processes which are in user mode most of the time, as well as processes with a large amount of I/O.

10.3 CHANGES TO THE KERNEL

In order to implement SMP in the LINUX kernel, changes have to be made to both the portable part and the processor-specific implementations.

10.3.1 Kernel initialization

The first problem with the implementation of a multiprocessor operation arises when the kernel is started. All processors must be started because the BIOS has halted all APs and initially only the boot processor is running. Only this processor enters the kernel starting function `start_kernel()`. After it has executed the normal LINUX initialization, `smp_init()` is called. This activates all other processors by calling `smp_boot_cpus()`.

After the SMP information and the required hardware setup has been checked, every processor is started by calling the `do_boot_cpu()` function.

But how can a processor be started? This is done by the APIC. It allows each processor to send other processors a so-called interprocessor interrupt (IPI). Furthermore, it is possible to send each processor an INIT (INIT IPI). On a Pentium processor, an INIT signal works like a reset, but the cache, FPU, and write buffer are also reset. Then, via its reset vector, the processor jumps into the BIOS. If the warm start flag was previously set in

CMOS and the warm start vector (0040:0067) was set to a real mode routine, the processor will then jump into that routine.

Furthermore, it is possible to send Pentium processors a STARTUP IPI. With this, the processor begins to execute a real mode routine at the address VV00:0000.[1]

Let us now go back to `smp_boot_cpus()`. After all remaining processors have been started, the variable `smp_num_cpus` contains the number of all currently running processors. Now, a separate idle task is created for each processor. This is necessary because in SMP operations the idle task must run in user mode in order not to block kernel mode for all other processors.

After the termination of `smp_init()` the boot processor generates the `init` task which finally calls `smp_commence()`. This function sets the `smp_commenced` flag, at which point all APs can run freely and process their separate idle tasks.

10.3.2 Scheduling

The LINUX scheduler shows only slight changes. First of all, the task structure now has a processor component which contains the number of the running processor or the constant `NO_PROC_ID` if no processor has been assigned as yet. The `last_processor` component contains the number of the processor which processed the task last.

Each processor works through the scheduler and is assigned a new task which is executable and has not yet been assigned to any other processor. Furthermore, the tasks that ran last are preferred. This can lead to an improvement in system performance if the internal processor caches still contain the data valid for the selected process.

10.3.3 Interrupt handling

Interrupts are distributed to the processors by the I/O-APIC. At the system start, however, all interrupts are only forwarded to the BSP. Each SMP operating system must therefore switch the APIC into SMP mode so that other processors can also handle interrupts (Exception: IPI). LINUX supports this operating mode, so that interrupts can be distributed to all available processors.

10.4 ATOMIC OPERATIONS

It is often sufficient to make sure that certain simple operations, such as increment, decrement, and tests, can be processed by variables atomically by all processors. A few problems, which arise due to the simultaneous execution of code in kernel mode, can be overcome in this way. Unfortunately, ANSI-C does not offer any options for expressing this portably. Therefore, atomic operations for the respective architectures are coded in the

---

1 The MP specification defines the precise algorithm of how APs are started. Among other things, one INIT IPI and two STARTUP IPIs are sent to Pentiums.

header file `asm/atomic.h`. Furthermore, these functions also have the properties to be atomic on single processors. This means that they are not interrupted by interrupts.

10.4.1 The atomic data type

Next, `asm/atomic.h` defines the "atomic data type":

```
typedef struct { volatile int counter; } atomic_t;
```

Variables of the `atomic_t` type are in the kernel and therefore not held in registers, but are otherwise equivalent to the scaled data type `int`.[2] This definition alone is not sufficient to guarantee atomic operations on this data type, since during the time between reading a value from memory and writing the value back, other processors could change the value.

10.4.2 Accessing the atomic data type

In order to access variables from atomic data types, the following functions or macros are defined:

```
atomic_t ATOMIC_INIT(int i);
int atomic_read(atomic_t *v);
int atomic_set(atomic_t *v, int i);
```

Although they are displayed here as functions, they are normally defined as macros on most architectures. `ATOMIC_INIT` gives the initial value allocation of an atomic variable.

Using `atomic_read()` a variable's value can be read. `atomic_set()` assigns a new value to the variable.

10.4.3 Changing and testing atomic variables

Now to the complicated functions:

```
void atomic_add(int i, atomic_t *v);
void atomic_sub(int i, atomic_t *v);
int atomic_sub_and_test(int i, atomic_t *v);
void atomic_inc(atomic_t *v);
void atomic_dec(atomic_t *v);
int atomic_dec_and_test(atomic_t *v);
```

These functions allow the value of an atomic variable to be changed by the addition or subtraction of a value. The `atomic_sub_and_test()` and `atomic_dec_and_test` functions also tell us whether, by subtracting the atomic variable, the value zero has been produced. In addition to this, some architectures support other functions, a few of which are listed here:

---

2 Due to its implementation, on the Sparc architecture only 24 bits are usable.

```
/* x86 */
void atomic_clear_mask (int mask, atomic_t *v);
void atomic_set_mask (int mask, atomic_t *v);
/* ALPHA, SPARC */
int atomic_add_return (int i, atomic_t * v);
int atomic_sub_return (int i, atomic_t * v);
int atomic_inc_return (atomic_t * v);
int atomic_dec_return (atomic_t * v);
```

10.5 SPIN LOCKS

The job of spin locks in the LINUX kernel is to make sure that critical code areas are only executed by one processor at any time. This protects the kernel code from unwanted parallel executions by other processors. An analysis of spin locks with regard to communication can be found in Section 5.1.

Spin locks are represented by the spinlock_t data type. An individual spin lock is defined for each area to be protected. This spinlock should be initialized using the macros SPIN_LOCK_UNLOCKED or spin_lock_init(), as the following examples show:

```
spinlock_t inode_lock = SPIN_LOCK_UNLOCKED;
/* or in a function */
spinlock_t lock;
void f()
{
  spin_lock_init(lock);
}
```

10.5.1 Access functions

The following functions and macros are used to protect an area with the help of a spin lock and are all displayed as function definitions so that they can be understood more easily:

```
/* without change to the interrupt condition */
void spin_lock(spinlock_t *lock);
void spin_unlock(spinlock_t *lock);
int spin_trylock(spinlock_t *lock);

/* local interrupts are switched off and then on again */
void spin_lock_irq(spinlock_t *lock);
void spin_unlock_irq(spinlock_t *lock);
```

```
/* local interrupts are switched off, the condition secured   */
void spin_lock_irqsave(spinlock_t *lock, int *flags);
void spin_unlock_irqrestore(spinlock_t *lock, int *flags);

/* Software interrupts are switched off and then on again */
void spin_lock_bh(spinlock_t *lock);
void spin_unlock_bh(spinlock_t *lock);
```

To enter a critical area, `spin_lock()` has to be called. If another processor is found in this area, the current processor is caught in the spin lock[3] until the other processor has left the critical area. In LINUX version 2.4 spin locks are not fairly implemented, which means that if two processors are waiting to enter a critical area, the processor which has been waiting the longest is not automatically admitted. If a processor leaves a critical area, `spin_unlock()` has to be called. If you forget to call this, the whole computer could quite easily freeze up since no other processor can enter the area after this.

Using `spin_trylock()` you can enquire whether an area can be entered. If the function returns the value 0, the area is in use. Otherwise, it is free. An additional `spin_lock` is no longer needed since `spin_trylock()` occupies the spin lock.

The functions described up until now do not change the interrupt flag of the local processor. This means that interrupts are treated further, if allowed, even if the processor is in the spin lock. Variations of this function also exist, which prohibit the interrupts on the local processor during its time in the spin lock until it has left the critical area.

10.5.2 Read-write spin locks

Read-write spin locks are a special type of spin lock that allow any number of reading processors to stay in a critical area. Writing functions have exclusive access to this area. Read-write spin locks are represented by the `rwlock_t` data type and have to be initialized by using the macros `RW_LOCK_UNLOCKED` or `rwlock_init()`.

For read access, the following functions and macros are used:

```
void read_lock(rwlock_t *lock);
void read_unlock(rwlock_t *lock);
```

whereas the following functions and macros are used for write access:

```
void write_lock(rwlock_t *lock);
void write_unlock(rwlock_t *lock);
```

In a similar way to the basic spin lock, the `*_irq()`, `*_irqsave()`, and `*_bh()` versions are also available.

---

3 A "trapped" processor has to endlessly "spin around in circles." Hence the name spin lock.

A SYSTEM CALLS

This appendix describes the implementation of all system calls in LINUX. With regard to architecture-dependent implementations, the emphasis[1] is on the LINUX system running on the Intel PC. A description of the other architectures is not possible for several reasons (including time, and the lack of documentation). A basic knowledge is given in the previous chapter. We also recommend you have a look at the corresponding source files of the kernel.

A precise distinction has to be made between the system call[2] and its corresponding kernel function. A system call is the transition of a process from user mode to system mode. In LINUX this is done by calling the interrupt 0x80, together with the register values. The kernel (in system mode) calls a kernel function out of the _sys_call_table. These functions, which begin with "sys_" in the source text, are described in the following sections. In the meantime, the return values of the system call are switched over to the type long. On the one hand, error information is transferred to the higher-valued bits and, on the other, this is essential for the porting on the Merced processor.

The conversion from a function used by a program to a system call is carried out in the C library. This allows, for example, several functions to be handled by a single kernel function, as is shown rather nicely by sys_socketcall(). Such functions have a typical characteristic: Parameters whose structure can vary are passed to the kernel function as unsigned long, which is then used as an address. In LINUX it is common to have commonly known system calls as library functions – which blurs the borderline between system calls and C library functions.

The kernel functions are divided into six groups: process management, file system, interprocess communication, memory management, initialization, and the rest (not implemented or not yet implemented system calls). The division can be found roughly expressed as follows: System calls whose source files can be found in the same subdirectory are described together in a group.

The description of a kernel function is structured similarly to a UNIX manual page: At the top left we find the name of the kernel function, at the top right, the origin of the corresponding system call (POSIX, BSD, SVR4). Below there is the name of the file in

---

1   If a system call is not available for another architecture, this is mentioned explicitly.
2   The question "What is a system call?" has been queried for a long while!

which the kernel function is implemented. If special header files are needed for the corresponding system call, these also are listed. The prototype of the function and the description follow. The interface provided by the C library and any peculiarities are described in the section on implementation.

The description finishes with a list of errors that can occur during execution of the kernel function.

A.1   PROCESS MANAGEMENT

The following calls access the kernel of each and every UNIX system, the scheduler, and process management. The foundations for this are described in Chapters 3 and 4.

System call	adjtime	4.3+BSD

File: kernel/time.c
```
#include <linux/timex.h>
long sys_adjtimex(struct timex *txc_p);
```

The sys_adjtimex() call allows the reading and setting of the kernel's time structures, or more precisely, of the variables beginning with "time_." As these control the timer, the system's temporal behavior can be controlled.[3] The timex structure is an extension of the timeval structure:

```
struct timex {
  unsigned int modes; /* function                              */
  long offset;        /* time offset (usec)                    */
  long freq;          /* frequency offset (scaled ppm)         */
  long maxerror;      /* maximum errors (usec)                 */
  long esterror;      /* estimated errors (usec)               */
  int status;         /* time status                           */
  long constant;      /* PLL time constant                     */
  long precision;     /* precise time (usec) (ro)              */
  long tolerance;     /* frequency fluctuation of the time     */
                      /* (ppm) (read only)                     */
  struct timeval time;/* system time (read only)               */
  long tick;          /* microseconds between two ticks        */
  long ppsfreq;       /* PPS frequency (scaled ppm) (ro)       */
  long jitter;        /* PPS jitter (us) (ro)                  */
  int shift;          /* interval duration (s) (shift) (ro)    */
  long stabil;        /* PPS stability (scaled ppm) (ro)       */
```

---

3 The commentated source text says: "to discipline kernel clock oscillator."

```
  long jitcnt;          /* jitter barrier overstepped      */
                        /* (counter) (ro)                  */
  long calcnt;          /* calibration interval (ro)       */
  long errcnt;          /* calibration error (ro)          */
  long stbcnt;          /* overstepping the stability barrier */
                        /* (counter) (ro)                  */
int    :32; int    :32; int    :32; int    :32; int    :32; int    :32;
int    :32; int    :32; int    :32; int    :32; int    :32; int    :32;
};
```

If modes is zero, the values are read. Otherwise they are written. For this, CAP_SYS_TIME has to be set. The following values can be entered in modes to set the values:

ADJ_STATUS – time_status is set.

ADJ_FREQUENCY – time_freq derives from txc.frequency.

ADJ_MAXERROR – time_maxerror is set.

ADJ_ESTERROR – time_esterror is set.

ADJ_TIMECONST – time_constant is set.

ADJ_OFFSET – If ADJ_OFFSET_SINGLESHOT is also set, the time_adjust value derives from txc.offset. Otherwise, time_offset is set to the value txc.offset << SHIFT_UPDATE and time_reftime to xtime.tv.sec. time_freq is recalculated.

ADJ_TICK – tick is set to txc.tick. For reasons of stability, the value txc.tick must not deviate more than 10 percent from the normal value (1000).

ADJ_OFFSET_SINGLESHOT – allows, together with ADJ_OFFSET, emulation of the well-known system call *adjtime*.

As the timer interrupt would disturb the settings, interrupts are disabled while copying. After copying, the txc structure is filled with the currently valid time_ values (offset contains the previously stored time_adjust value) and returned.

Implementation

The system call is converted with the syscall macro. Furthermore, the well-known system call *adjtime* is based on the function adjtimex(), as shown in the following (abridged) source:

```
int adjtime(struct timeval * itv, struct timeval * otv)
{ struct timex tntx;
  if (itv) {
        struct timeval tmp;
```

```
            tmp.tv_sec = itv->tv_sec + itv->tv_usec / 1000000L;
            tmp.tv_usec = itv->tv_usec % 1000000L;
            tntx.offset = tmp.tv_usec + tmp.tv_sec * 1000000L;
            tntx.mode = ADJ_OFFSET_SINGLESHOT;
    }
    else tntx.mode = 0;
    if (adjtimex(&tntx) < 0) return -1;
    return 0;
}
```

Errors

EPERM – a write access was attempted without superuser privileges.
EINVAL – a value in the txc structure is not valid.

System call	alarm	POSIX

File: kernel/sched.c kernel/itimer.c
```
unsigned long sys_alarm(unsigned int seconds);
```

sys_alarm() sets a timer (itimerval) to the value seconds. After the timer's expiry, the SIGALRM signal is triggered. When seconds equals zero, the timer is restarted.

If a previous alarm is still running, its remaining time (in seconds) is returned and the timer is restarted. The execution of the alarm is described in Section 3.2.1.

Implementation

The conversion is carried out by the syscall macro. This function is not available on Alpha machines.

System call	brk	

File: mm/mmap.c

```
unsigned long sys_brk(unsigned long brk);
```

sys_brk() changes the size of the used area of the data segment. It sets the value mm->brk of the task structure to new_brk. First, brk is rounded up to the beginning of the next page.

The function do_mmap() (see Section 4.2.2) organizes the required memory (vma areas) and sets the flags PROT_READ, PROT_WRITE, and PROT_EXEC as well as MAP_FIXED and MAP_PRIVATE. The new brk value is finally returned.

Implementation

The system call does not use the syscall macro for Intel systems, but instead skips directly over the assembler code to the interrupt 0x80. This system call is used for malloc(), to allocate memory. The memory required by malloc() is added to the current brk value.[4]

Error

ENOMEM – there is no memory available for a larger brk value.

System call	capget	POSIX
	capset	

File: kernel/capability.c

```
#include <linux/capability.h>
long sys_capget(cap_user_header_t header,
        cap_user_data_t dataptr);
long sys_capset(cap_user_header_t header,
        const cap_user_data_t data);
```

The functions sys_capget() and sys_capset() allow access to the rights (capabilities) of a process. The parameter header has the following structure:

```
typedef struct __user_cap_header_struct {
        __u32 version;       /* internal version number    */
        int pid;             /* PID of the desired process  */
} *cap_user_header_t;
```

If the transferred version (defined in capability.h) does not agree with that of the kernel, the kernel version is entered and an error is returned.

The second parameter (dataptr) has the following structure:

```
typedef struct __user_cap_data_struct {
        __u32 effective;         /* effective rights       */
        __u32 permitted;         /* permitted capabilities */
        __u32 inheritable;       /* inheritable capabilities */
} *cap_user_data_t;
```

This data contains the data for the setting of the new capabilities. In sys_capget() the capabilities of the pid process are saved in dataptr. If pid is equal to 0, then the capabilities of the current process are used. You can set the capabilities of a process using sys_capset(). Note the following: Capabilities of a process can only be limited and capabilities of foreign processes can only be changed if the process itself has the capability CAP_SETCAP. With limitations, it is the case that the new capability has to be a subset (smaller or equal to) and with:

4 The function used for this is called morecore(), which is simply a pointer to brk().

- inherited capabilities from the connected capabilities of the target process and the permitted capabilities of the current process,

- permitted capabilities from the connected capabilities of the target process and the permitted capabilities of the current process, and

- effective capabilities from the new permitted capabilities.

If a value less than zero is used for `pid` this has special effects: If `pid` is equal to -1, then the capabilities of all processes (excluding `init`) are set, otherwise the capabilities of all processes with the process group `pid`. For the upper tests, the current process is inserted as the target process.

Implementation

Both system calls are converted using the syscall macro.

Errors

`EINVAL` – if an incorrect version is inserted in header.
`EPERM` – if an unauthorized process wants to change foreign capabilities.
`ESRCH` – if the given process does not exist.

System call	exit	POSIX

File: `kernel/exit.c`
`long sys_exit(int error_code);`

The kernel function moves the bottom two bytes eight places to the left, and submits the value to `do_exit()`. This function releases all resources used by the process to the kernel and informs the affected processes.

The value status is returned to the parent process. The sequence is described in Section 3.3.3.

Implementation

The system call is converted into the kernel function without changing the parameters.

System call	clone	POSIX
	fork	LINUX
	vfork	

File: `arch/i386/kernel/process.c`

kernel/fork.c

```
long sys_clone(struct pt_regs regs);
long sys_fork(struct pt_regs regs);
long sys_vfork(struct pt_regs regs);
```

sys_fork() generates a new process (child process) as a copy of the current process (parent process). In order to be able to distinguish between parent and child processes, the PID of the child process is returned in the parent process, while a 0 is returned in the child process. In LINUX, copy-on-write is used so that only the page tables and the task structure are duplicated. A child process can only be generated if the resources of the father process (rlim[RLIMIT_NPROC]) and the system are not overstepped. The maximum number of processes (more precisely: the threads) are initialized with the following value when booting:

```
max_threads = num_physpages / (THREAD_SIZE/PAGE_SIZE) / 2;
```

The child process sends a SIGCHLD with exit() to the father process. In order to extend the semantics of the *fork* system call, LINUX provides a system call *clone*. By means of the regs registers, two parameters are submitted. In regs.ebx these are the flags and the signal. The signal is located in the lower two bytes and is passed to the parent process upon termination of the child. Interestingly enough, the signal is later masked out with 0xff, which would allow for up to 255 signals. The flags control the "nursery" of the new process:

CLONE_VM – Parent and child processes share the same memory pages. If this flag is not specified, the memory pages of the child are generated via copy-on-write.

CLONE_FS – Parent and child processes use the same file system structure (with the counter being incremented). Otherwise, the structure is copied.

CLONE_FILES – Parent and child processes use the same descriptors. Otherwise the file descriptors are copied.

CLONE_SIGHAND – Parent and child processes share the same signal handling routines. Otherwise, these structures are copied.

CLONE_PID – Parent and child processes share the PID.

CLONE_PTRACE – Parent and child processes share the ptrace() flags.

CLONE_VFORK – With the mm_release() of the parent process, the child process is woken up.

CLONE_PARENT – The parent and child process have the same father.

In the regs.ecx register there is a pointer which is used as the stack pointer of the child process. If it is zero, the stack pointer of the parent process is used. The implementation of the system calls is described in Section 3.3.3.

The system call *vfork* is, in principle, a calling of *clone* by which the flags CLONE_VFORK, CLONE_VM, and SIGCHLD are set internally.

Implementation

The conversion of *fork* is carried out via the syscall macro. The pt_regs structure of <asm/ptrace.h> contains these registers in their correct order which a system call puts on the stack. Therefore the kernel function can access them, although the call itself is has no parameters. The clone() call is also converted via the syscall macro.

Errors

ENOMEM – if sys_fork() cannot allocate any memory for the page table and the task structure.

EAGAIN – if there were no longer any free processes available.

System call	setpid	getuid	geteuid	POSIX
	getgid	geteuid	getegid	4.3+BSD
	getppid	getpgid	getpgrp	
	getsid	setuid	setgid	
	setreuid	setregid	setsid	
	setfsuid	setfsgid		

```
File:   kernel/sched.c
        kernel/sys.c

long sys_getpid(void);              long sys_getuid(void);
long sys_geteuid(void);             long sys_getgid(void);
long sys_getegid(void);             long sys_getppid(void);
long sys_getpgid(pid_t pid);        long sys_getpgrp(void);
long sys_getsid(pid_t pid);         long sys_setuid(uid_t uid);
long sys_setgid(gid_t gid);         long sys_setsid(void);
long sys_setfsuid(uid_t uid);       long sys_setfsgid(gid_t gid);
long sys_setreuid(uid_t ruid, uid_t euid);
long sys_setregid(uid_t rgid, uid_t egid);
long sys_setpgid(pid_t pid,pid_t pgid);
```

All these calls read (or set) identification numbers of the process. In the meantime, the numbers for the identification of users and groups have a size of 32 bits. For reasons of compatibility, the call responsible for this occurs again with the suffix 16 (e.g. sys_getuid16()), which then internally converts the value to 16 bits.

sys_getpid() and sys_getpgrp() determine the process identification (PID) and the process group (PGRP)[5] of the current process. sys_getpgid() returns the process group of an arbitrary process pid; if pid is zero, it returns its own group. The sys_getppid() function returns the process identification of the parent process (PPID).

The sys_getsid() function returns the session of the process pid.

The sys_getuid() returns the user identification (UID) and the sys_getgid() function to the group identification (GID) of the calling process. The effective user (EUID) and group (EGID) identifications are determined by the kernel functions sys_geteuid() and sys_getegid().

All these functions simply read the task structure of the calling process:

```
asmlinkage int sys_getpid(void)
{
        return current->pid;
}
```

sys_setpgid() sets the process group to pgid for the current process or one of its children. If pid is equal to zero, the value of the calling process will be used and if pgid is zero, the value pid is used. The PGRP can only be changed for the individual process or for a child process if the child process is in the same session and did_exec is set (see Section 3.1.1).

In both cases a leader has to be defined anyway, and there has to be a process that already possesses the given PGRP. It cannot be in another session though.

The functions sys_setreuid() and sys_setregid() manipulate the UID and EUID as well as the GID and EGID of a process. If ruid is greater than -1, the UID is set to this value. As well as this, if the calling process has the privileges CAP_SETUID the UID or EUID is set to ruid. ruid is then saved as the new UID (but not set). Otherwise an error is returned. If euid is greater than -1, the EUID is set to this value.

In order to set the EUID to euid one of the following conditions has to be met in the privilege CAP_SETUID: UID, EUID, or SUID is equal to euid. Then the EUID is set. Otherwise, an error is returned. If ruid or euid is equal to -1 and is not equal to UID, the SUID of the process is set to the value of the EUID. If no error has occurred, the function finally sets FSUID to EUID and the UID to the value noted. When setting the UID, the limit RLIMIT_NPROC is checked. If SECURE_NO_SETUID_FIXUP is set in the kernel in the secure bits, the process privileges are set (see Appendix E).

Therefore, a user with no superuser privileges can only exchange effective and normal (real) IDs. setreuid(geteuid(),getuid()) performs the exchange; if the call is repeated, the original values are restored. The same applies for the calling of setregid(), only it deals with the group rather than the user ID and the last two steps (limit and privileges) are removed. sys_setuid() sets the UIDs of a process to uid. In the case where the process contains the CAP_SETUID privilege, these are UID, EUID, SUID, and

---

5 There is also the name PGID for the process group (e.g. with *ps*).

FSUID. Otherwise, only FSUID and EUID are set, provided uid is equal to UID or SUID. With a change to UID, RLIMIT_NPROC is tested again, and the privileges are used. As an equivalent for the setting of the process GIDs there is the function sys_setgid(). The functions are the SVR4 counterparts to the set calls above, which come from the world of BSD. You have to bear in mind that there is no possibility of resetting a EUID once it has been changed, as is possible with sys_setreuid(). The return value is zero upon successful execution and a negative value in the event of an error.

The functions sys_setfsuid() and sys_setfsgid() set FSUID and FSGID.

This is (for the setting of the UIDs) only allowed, if either UID, EUID, SUID, or FSUID is equal to uid or the privilege CAP_SETUID is set. For the setting of the GID, one of the first four conditions must apply. When setting the FSUID from 0 to another value, the privilege CAP_MASK is erased; when setting to 0 all privileges apart from CAP_MASK are erased. The old IDs are respectively returned.

sys_setsid() makes the call process the process session leader. It sets SESSION and PGRP to PID, the leader component of the tsk structure to 1 and deletes its controlling channel. If there is a process that is already the session leader, an error is returned (PGRP is equal to the PID of the current process). The return value is the new PGRP.

Implementation

Owing to the simplicity of the functions, the conversion of the system calls is carried out via the syscall macro.

The well-known system calls seteuid, setegid, and setpgrp are provided by LINUX as library functions. The conversion is shown taking seteuid() as an example:

```
int seteuid(uid_t uid)
{
        return setreuid(-1, uid);
}
```

Errors

EINVAL – if an invalid PID, PGID, and so on are passed to a function.
EPERM – if the function used is not allowed. Generally, only the superuser may
   change or process data. Normal users can only change their group and user IDs.
ESRCH – if no processes are found by sys_setpgid().

System call	getpriority	4.3+BSD
	setpriority	

File: kernel/sys.c
```
#include <linux/time.h>
#include <linux/resource.h>
```

```
long sys_getpriority(int which, int who);
long sys_setpriority(int which, int who, int niceval);
```

The kernel functions `sys_getpriority()` and `sys_setpriority()` adminster the priorities for the scheduling.

`sys_getpriority()` is used for calls. The `which` parameter specifies whether the priority of a process, a process group, or a user is called. In `who`, the value is specified. The following values are allowed for `which`:

`PRIO_PROCESS` – the value in `who` specifies a PID.

`PRIO_PGRP` – the value in `who` specifies a PGRP.

`PRIO_USER` – the value in `who` specifies a UID.

If zero is specified for `who`, the kernel uses the value of the calling process. All processes are searched to find out whether they match the specified values (`proc_sel()`). If more than one entry has been found (process group) the return value is the highest value found. The priority found is still scaled to the interval [0; 40] and then returned. In this way, the macro of earlier versions is eliminated by giving a valid negative return value.

The `sys_setpriority()` function sets the priority for the processes selected via `which` and `who`, where `niceval` must be between [-20; 20]. The priority is scaled to time-slice units and assigned to all processes found. For the allocation, either the UID of the process found has to be equal to the UID or EUID of the current process, or the the privilege `CAP_SYS_NICE` has to be set.

Implementation

While `setpriority()` simply uses the syscall macro, the `getpriority()` call assembles the interrupt 0x80 by hand and calculates the mirroring at `PZERO` in order to make the return value of `getpriority()` match the value passed to `sys_setpriority()`.

This is a dangerous exception! It is possible that the library function `getpriority()` returns -1 without an error having occurred. In this case, for the purpose of error checking, not only the return value, as is normally done in UNIX, but also `errno` should be tested.

Errors

`ESRCH` – if no matching process could be found for `which` and `who`.
`EINVAL` – if an invalid value is specified for `which`.
`EPERM` – if in `sys_setpriority()` the EUID of the specified process is not equal to the EUID of the calling process.
`EACCES` – if a non-privileged user wants to increase the priority.

System call	ioperm	iopl	LINUX

File: `arch/i386/kernel/ioport.c`

```
int sys_ioperm(unsigned long from,
  unsigned long num, int turn_on);
int sys_iopl(unsigned long unused);
```

These calls can only be used with the CPA_SYS_RAWIO privilege. The bits of the port access rights are set by `sys_ioperm()`, that is, num bits beginning with the address from are set to the value turn_on. The value 1 means full access to the port (read and write) and 0 means no access. Only the first 1,023 (32*IO_BITMAP_SIZE) ports can be set.

In order to access all 65,536 ports under LINUX, for example for the X server, the system call *iopl* is provided. The corresponding kernel function `sys_iopl()` regards unused as a pointer to a `pt_regs` structure and carries the value `regs->ebx` as the I/O privilege level of the process. Normally, only two of the four possible levels are used: level 0 and level 3.

Implementation

Both system calls work with the syscall macro.

Errors

EINVAL – if a negative value has been specified for num, from+num is greater than 1,023 or level is greater than 3.

EPERM – if the calling process is not authorized.

System call	kill	POSIX

File: `kernel/exit.c`
```
#include <signal.h>
long sys_kill(int pid, int sig);
```

`sys_kill()` sends the signal sig to a process or a process group, or more precisely to the siginfo structure. The whole structure can be found on page 306.

```
typedef struct siginfo {
  int si_signo;
  int si_errno;
  int si_code;
  union { … } _sifields;
} siginfo_t;
```

The function sets si_sino to sig, si_errno to 0, and si_code to the value SI_USER. The _kill structure of the union is filled with the values of the current process. If pid is greater than zero, the signal is sent to the process with the PID pid. If pid is zero, the signal is sent to the process group of the current process. If pid is less than -1, the signal is sent to all processes of the process group pid.

In POSIX, the behavior of kill (-1, sig) is not defined. In LINUX, the signal is sent to all processes with a PID greater than 1 (except the current one).

Implementation

The system call is converted via the syscall macro.

Errors

EINVAL – if sig is not valid.
ESRCH – if the process or the process group pid does not exist.
EPERM – the privileges of the calling process do not allow the signal to be sent.

System call	modify_ldt	LINUX

File: arch/i386/kernel/ldt.c
```
#include <linux/ldt.h>
int sys_modify_ldt(int func, void *ptr, unsigned long bytecount);
```

In the course of the implementation of WINE it became necessary to emulate the internal functions of MS Windows. This includes the manipulation of the local descriptor table. This is the task of the system call *modify ldt*. Being a part of the task structure, this table can be manipulated quite easily.

If func is equal to zero, the local descriptor table of the current process is read. If it does not yet possess a table, the default table {0, 0} is provided. The required size can be set with the bytecount parameter. If the table is smaller, only the table of size LDT_ENTRIES*LDT_ENTRY_SIZE is read.

The return value is the actual size of the table; ptr is a pointer to the structure desc_struct:

```
struct desc_struct {
        unsigned long a,b;
}
```

In order to change an entry in this table, func must be 1 or 0x11. Then ptr is a pointer to the structure modify_ldt_ldt_s:

```
struct modify_ldt_ldt_s {
  unsigned int entry_number; /* Index of searched entries */
  unsigned long base_addr;
  unsigned int limit;
  unsigned int seg_32bit:1;
```

```
  unsigned int contents:2;
  unsigned int read_exec_only:1;
  unsigned int limit_in_pages:1;
  unsigned int seg_not_present:1;
  unsigned int useable:1;
};
```

bytecount must indicate the size of the structure. The specified structure is described in the table of the current process. If this does not yet possess a local descriptor table, a table is initialized. It is also possible to delete an entry (by entering 0).

Implementation

The C library does not provide an interface to this system call. Users must proceed in the same way as specified for sys_sysinfo() (see page 321).

Errors

ENOSYS – func is invalid.
EINVAL – ptr is 0 (for reading) or incorrectly set (for writing).

System call	create_module	delete_module	LINUX
	init_module	query_module	
	get_kernel_syms		

File: kernel/module.c

```
unsigned long sys_create_module(char *name, unsigned long size);
long sys_init_module(const char *name_user,
            struct module *mod_user);
long sys_delete_module(char *name);
long sys_query_module(const char *name_user, int which,
            char *buf, size_t bufsize, size_t *ret)
long sys_get_kernel_syms(struct kernel_sym *table);
```

The sys_create_module() function allocates memory for a module. The size of the required memory is specified by size. The call generates an instance of the module structure, where name is the name of the module. The following values of the structure are set: the name, the size (number of pages), the start address of the memory allocated for the module, and the status (to MOD_UNINITIALIZED). All other values are initialized with NULL.

```
struct module {
  unsigned long size_of_struct;    /* size of the module    */
```

```
struct module *next;                    /* the next module        */
  const char *name;                     /* name of the module     */
  unsigned long size;                   /* module size            */
union
{
  atomic_t usecount;                    /* use counter            */
  long pad;
} uc;                                   /* structure size         */
unsigned long flags;                    /* flags (AUTOCLEAN etc.) */
unsigned nsyms;                         /* number of symbols      */
unsigned ndeps;                         /* number of dependencies */
  struct module_ref *deps;              /* list of modules        */
  struct module_ref *ref;               /* point to myself        */
  struct module_symbol *syms;           /* symbol table           */
  init (*init)(void);                   /* init function          */
  void (*cleanup)(void);                /* erase function         */
  const struct exception_table_entry *ex_table_start;
  const struct exception_table_entry *ex_table_end;
  const struct module_persist *persist_start;
  const struct module_persist *persist_end;
  int (*can_unload)(void);
};
```

If a module of the same name already exists, an error is returned, otherwise the return value is the address of the memory allocated in the kernel address space. sys_init_module() loads the module and activates it. code is the address where the module is loaded, and codesize is its size in bytes. This must not exceed the value stored in module->size. If the loaded module does not end on a page address, the remainder is initialized with 0. In addition, the module must possess the CAP_SYS_MODULE privilege. After the module has been loaded, its own initialization routine init() is called and the status is set to MOD_RUNNING, and the module is now activated. sys_delete_module() removes modules. If name is specified, that particular module is released. In addition to this, the process must possess the CAP_SYS_MODULE privilege.

There must be no references to the module, and its usage counter must be 0. If the module is running (MOD_RUNNING), its own clean-up function is called and the status is set to MOD_DELETED. The module can then be removed by a call to free_modules(). If no name is specified, the function searches the list of all modules and tries to release all modules that are no longer in use.

To receive information on one (or all) modules, there is the sys_query_module() function. In name we have the searching module. If this is NULL, the (static) start of the module list (&kernel_module) is used. The precise function depends upon which:

0 – it only checks whether name is a valid module name.

QM_MODULES – The names of all modules are saved to the address buf one by one. The size of buf must be contained in bufsize. If there is not enough space for all names, as much as possible is copied and the missing space entered in ret.

QM_DEPS – The names of all the modules to which this module refers are given in buf. If there is no space, the above applies.

QM_REFS – The names of all the modules which refer to this module are given in buf. If there is no space, the above applies.

QM_SYMBOLS – Copies the symbol of the module in buf. Therefore, the following applies for the symbol number n: At the buf+n position there is the address of the symbol and at buf+(buf+n+1) the name of the symbol.

QM_INFO – The most important information of the module is written to the buf address as the module_info structure.

```
struct module_info
{
  unsigned long addr;        /* address of the module  */
  unsigned long size;        /* size of the module     */
  unsigned long flags;       /* flag of the module     */
  long usecount;             /* use counter            */
}
```

sys_get_kernel_syms() allows access to the symbol table. It copies the symbol table to the location referenced by table and returns the number of known symbols. First, the call checks whether there is enough memory for writing following the address. Therefore, the size of the table is normally determined by means of a call to get_kernel_syms(0), then the necessary memory is allocated, after which get_kernel_syms() is called again.

Errors

EBUSY – if the initialization routine fails or an attempt is made to remove a module that is still in use.

EEXIST – if the module name already exists. This error can be returned by sys_create_module().

ENOENT – if the module name does not exist. This error message is possible with sys_init_module() and sys_delete_module().

ENOMEM – if with sys_create_module() there is not enough free memory.

EPERM – if a non-privileged user uses one of these system calls.

ENOSPC – if the missing size cannot be returned.

System call   **nanosleep**   LINUX

File: `kernel/sched.c`
`long sys_nanosleep(struct timespec *rqtp, struct timespec *rmtp);`

The increased clock frequency of today's CPUs allows more precise time structures.

This kernel function allows the halting of the current process on a nanosecond level. The required period of time is specified in `rqtp`:

```
struct timespec {
        long tv_sec;            /* seconds                 */
        long tv_nsec;           /* nanoseconds             */
};
```

Provided that SCHED_OTHER is not set, a period of up to 2 ms is delayed by the process itself in a short `for` loop. Otherwise, the pause is converted into `jiffies` and entered as the process's `timeout`, after which the scheduler is called. If the `timeout` has not yet expired after re-entering the function, the remaining time is returned in `rmtp`.

Errors

EINVAL – if a negative period of time or more than 1,000,000,000 nanoseconds were specified.

EINTR – if a period of time remains.

System call   **nice**   4.3+BSD

File: `kernel/sched.c`
`long sys_nice(long inc);`

`sys_nice()` sets the priority of the current process. As priorities are measured in time slices, some conversions are needed. The new priority is obtained by subtracting `inc` from the old priority. This means that the higher the value of `inc`, the lower the priority of the process after the execution of the call. Only processes with the CAP_SYS_NICE privilege are allowed to specify negative values for `inc` and thus increment the priority . A simultaneous changing of the value by `setpriority()` is not taken into consideration at the moment.

First of all, however, the new priority is set to `inc` and limited to a maximum of 40, and then it is scaled to one time slice [0,2*DEF_PRIORITY]. Then the new priority is subtracted from the old one, and the resulting value is limited to the interval [1, DEF_PRIORITY*2] and assigned to the process. `sys_nice()` does not use `sys_setpriority()`. The reason for this is that `sys_nice()` has been implemented earlier.

Implementation

The system call is converted via the syscall macro.

Errors

EPERM – if a non-privileged user specifies a negative value for inc.

System call	pause	POSIX

File: `arch/i386/kernel/sys i386.c`
```
int sys_pause(void);
```

The `sys_pause()` function is a very simple system call. It sets the status of the current process to `TASK_INTERRUPTIBLE` and calls the scheduler. With this, the process voluntarily relinquishes control. It can only continue to work if it is woken up by a signal. The function returns `ERESTARTNOHAND`; this error message is changed into `EINTR` by the routine `ret_from_sys_call`.

Implementation

The system call is converted via the syscall macro.

System call	personality	LINUX

File: `kernel/exec domain.c`
```
#include <personality.h>
long sys_personality(unsigned long personality);
```

The LINUX kernel supports several execution environments, called *exec-domain*.

During booting, the kernel generates the first exec domain (filled with LINUX-specific data); all others can be loaded at a later stage via modules. A domain has the following structure:

```
struct exec_domain {
  char *name;
  lcall7_func handler;
  unsigned char pers_low, pers_high;
  unsigned long * signal_map;
  unsigned long * signal_invmap;
  struct module * module;
  struct exec_domain *next;
};
```

The values `pers_low` and `pers_high` are not, as one might think, the higher and lower byte values of `personality`, instead they represent a (numerical) upper and lower limit for the operating system located in `personality`. The `personality` parameter is divided into two areas. The upper word contains flags for known bugs,[6] the lower word contains the operating system. The values can be found in the header file `<linux/personality.h>`.

By means of `sys_personality()`, a certain domain can now be set, or the current domain can be interrogated. If all bits in `personality` are set (`0xffffffff`), the current value is returned. Otherwise, a domain that matches `personality` is sought. For this, the lower 2 bytes of `personality` must be between the low and high values. If no domain is found, the kernel issues an error message with the level `KERN_ERR`.

This domain is entered, together with `personality`, in the task structure of the current process. The counter of the old domain (`usecount`) is decremented, and that of the new domain is incremented. The return value is the old value of `personality`.

Errors

`EINVAL` – there is no domain that matches `personality`.

System call	prctl	LINUX

File: `kernel/sys.c`

```
int sys_prctl(int option, unsigned long arg2, unsigned long arg3,
              unsigned long arg4, unsigned long arg5)
```

This call is designed for the manipulation of a process. The precise option depends upon `option`:

`PR_GET_PDEATHSIG` – returns the `pdeath` signal of the processor.

`PR_SET_PDEATHSIG` – `arg2` is entered as the `pdeath` signal of the processor. As the name suggests, a process receives this signal if its father dies.

`PR_GET_DUMPABLE` – returns the `dumpable` flag of the processor.

`PR_SET_DUMPABLE` – `arg2` is entered as the `dumpable` flag of the processor.

Errors

`EINVAL` – if an invalid value is submitted.
`EBADF` – if an invalid descriptor is used.
`EMFILE` – if a descriptor is no longer free for `sys_prctl()`.

6 It is more correct to talk, not of bugs, but rather of the properties of the respective operating systems. An example is the `STICKY_TIMEOUTS` flag, see page 354 also.

System call	ptrace

File: `arch/i396/kernel/ptrace.c`

`#include <linux/ptrace.h>`

`long sys_ptrace(long request, long pid, long addr, long data);`

By means of the system call *ptrace*, a process can monitor the execution of another process. This system call is used, for example, in the implementation of debug algorithms. A process in whose task structure the PT_PTRACED flag is set is stopped on a signal. It halts, and its parent process is informed via the system call *wait*. The memory of the halted process can then be read and written to. The parent process can make the child process continue.

It is first tested whether the request is P_TRACEME. If this is the case and in the case where the PT_PTRACED bit is already set in the flag of the task structure, an error is returned. Otherwise the bit is set and return 0 is called.

In `pid`, the PID of the desired process is given. Of course, not just any process can be supervised. Generally you should not touch `init` as other properties are dependent upon the desired request. The value in `request` determines the precise meaning of the call:

PTRACE_TRACEME – The process sets the flag PT_PTRACED. The parent process is requested to monitor the process. If this flag is already set, an error occurs.

PTRACE_ATTACH – Sets the PT_PTRACED flag in the process specified by `pid`. For this, one of the following conditions must be met: `pid` is not the PID of the current process, the UID (GID) of the current process must match the UID, EUID, or SUID (GID, EGID, or SGID) of the desired process, or the child is "willing" (`dumpable`). Furthermore, the CAP_SYS_PTRACE privilege must be set and PF_TRACED can not be set yet. If all these obstacles have been surmounted, the flag is set, the current process becomes a father of the child and sends it the SIGSTOP signal.

PTRACE_PEEKTEXT, PTRACE_PEEKDATA – Reads a word (`long`) from the address `addr`. The value is saved in `data` and returned. As yet, there is no distinction between text and data segments.

PTRACE_PEEKUSR – Reads an address from the address `addr` from the `user` structure of the process. The value is saved in `data` and returned.

PTRACE_POKETEXT, PTRACE_POKEDATA – Writes the value contained in data to the address `addr`.

PTRACE_POKEUSR – Writes the value contained in `data` to the address `addr` of the user structure. Great care is taken to ensure that no register or task structure information is overwritten. Only a few debug registers are allowed.

PTRACE_SYSCALL, PTRACE_CONT – Continues processing the child process. With PTRACE_SYSCALL, the PT_TRACESYS flag is set. This causes the processing to stop after the return of the next system call. With PTRACE_CONT, this flag is deleted. Then the contents of data are entered into the exit code of the child and it is woken up. Finally the *trap* flag[7] is deleted.

PTRACE_KILL – Sends a SIGKILL signal to the child process. In addition, the trap flag is deleted.

PTRACE_SINGLESTEP – The PT_TRACESYS flag is deleted. The trap flag is set instead and data is set as the exit code.

PTRACE_DETACH – Releases the process stopped by PTRACE_ATTACH. The PF_TRACED and PT_TRACESYS flags of the task structure are deleted, and the process is woken up, data is entered as the exit code, the original father is re-entered as the parent process, and finally the trap bit is deleted.

PTRACE_GETREGS – The contents of the register (EBX, ECX, EDX, ESI, EDI, EBP, EAX, DS, ES, FS, GS, ORIG EAX, EIP, CS, EFLAGS, ESP, and SS) are written one after the other to the address data.

PTRACE_SETREGS – After the address data, 17 long values are read and the register of the process is written. To prevent more extensive manipulation the values are subject to some control.

ORIG_EAX – This register cannot be set.

FS, GS – The value cannot be zero and the two bottom bits cannot be set.

DS, ES – The value cannot be zero and both bottom bits cannot be set. Bits above 0xffff are not displayed.

SS, CS – The bottom two bits cannot be set. Bits above 0xffff are not displayed.

EFLAGS – Before writing, the bits above FLAG_MASK are not displayed, and the value is superimposed by the flags that have just been set (OR connection).

PTRACE_GETFPREGS – The contents of the FPU register (user_i387_struct) are written to the address data. If the supervising process does not use an FPU, an empty FPU is simulated.[8] The values are read from the i387_union of the thread structure.

PTRACE_SETFPREGS – The user_i387_struct structure is read from the data address and is written into the thread structure of the i387_union.

PTRACE_GETFPXREGS – With this, the structure user_fxsr_struct is used. Otherwise, this instruction corresponds to the request PTRACE_GETFPREGS.

PTRACE_SETFPXREGS – The structure user_fxsr_struct is read from the address data and is written into the i387_union of the thread structure.

---

7 The flag (also called single step) is found in the Eflags register of the processor. If it is set, and a SIGTRAP is sent to the controlled process, it carries out exactly one instruction.

8 For the registers CWD, SWD, and TWD the values 0xffff037f, 0xffff0000, and 0xffffffff are entered.

Implementation

Because the value of the data parameter is not used in the peek calls but is nevertheless placed on the stack (for the interrupt), the C library provides a secure pointer by placing a dummy value on the stack.

```c
int ptrace(int request, int pid, int addr, int data)
{
  long ret; long res;
  if (request > 0 && request < 4) (long *)data = &ret;
        __asm__ volatile ("int $0x80"
                 :"=a" (res)
                 :"0" (SYS_ptrace),"b" (request), "c" (pid),
                 "d" (addr), "S" (data));
  if (res >= 0) {
        if (request > 0 && request < 4) {
                errno = 0; return (ret);
} return (int) res;
}errno = -res; return -1;
}
```

Errors

EPERM – if no sys_ptrace() can be executed for the process specified by pid or there is one already running.
ESRCH – if the process specified by pid does not exist or PT_PTRACED is not set.
EIO – if an invalid value is specified for request.

System call	reboot	LINUX

File: kernel/sys.c
```c
long sys_reboot(int magic1, int magic2, int cmd, void * arg);
```

sys_reboot() boots the system or enables booting via the key combination Ctrl + Alt + ←. The parameters magic1 and magic2 are fixed. They must be set to 0xfee1dead and 672274793, 85072278, or 369367448.[9] The precise function depends on cmd. If cmd equals

LINUX_REBOOT_CMD_RESTART then for all processes which have been entered in the reboot_notifier_list list, notify_call() is called with SYS_RESTART as a parameter. Finally, the architecture-dependent function machine_restart() is called which reboots the computer.

9 If these numbers seem a little strange to you, you should look at them hexadecimally.

LINUX_REBOOT_CMD_HALT then for all processes which have been entered into the
reboot_notifier_list list, notify_call() is called with SYS_HALT as a parameter. Finally, the architecture-dependent function machine_halt() is called.

LINUX_REBOOT_CAD_ON then booting is enabled by Ctrl + Alt + ⏎.

LINUX_REBOOT_CAD_OFF then booting is switched off by Ctrl + Alt + ⏎.

LINUX_REBOOT_POWER_OFF then for all processes which have been entered into the
reboot_notifier_list list, notify_call() is called with SYS_POWER_OFF as
parameter. Finally, the architecture-dependent function machine_power_off() is
called. If *Advanced Power Management* is configured, it is used here.

LINUX_REBOOT_RESTART2 then for all processes which have been entered into the
reboot_notifier_list list, notify_call() is called using SYS_RESTART as a
parameter. Finally, the architecture-dependent function machine_restart() is called,
which reboots the computer.

There is a command at the address arg which is executed on the reboot of the computer.
With Intel machines, however, this function is not implemented. Make sure that
sys_reboot() does not call sys_sync()!

Implementation

The system call is converted via the syscall macro.

Errors

EINVAL – if an invalid value is specified for one of the parameters.
EPERM – if a non-privileged user calls the function.

System call	rt_sigreturn	rt_sigaction	LINUX
	rt_sigprocmask	rt_sigpending	
	rt_sigtimedwait	rt_sigqueuinfo	
	rt_sigsuspend		

```
File: arch/i386/kernel/signal.c
  kernel/signal.c
#include <linux/signal.h>
long sys_rt_sigreturn (unsigned long __unused);
long sys_rt_sigaction (int sig, const struct sigaction *act,
            struct sigaction *oact, size_t sigsetsize);
long sys_rt_sigprocmask (int how, sigset_t *set,
            sigset_t *oset, size_t sigsetsize);
```

```
long sys_rt_sigpending (sigset_t *set, size_t sigsetsize);
long sys_rt_sigtimedwait (const sigset_t *uthese, siginfo_t
        *uinfo, const struct timespec *uts, size_t sigsetsize);
long sys_rt_sigqueueinfo (int pid, int sig, siginfo_t *uinfo);
long sys_rt_sigsuspend (sigset_t *unewset, size_t sigsetsize);
```

These system calls are scheduled for the treatment of real-time signals. Depending on the type of system call, there will be differences to "normal" versions. The most important difference is that the new functions work with a signal range of 64 signals. According to POSIX, additional information can be transmitted with these signals, e.g., the PID of the sending process. This data is held in the siginfo structure:

```
typedef struct siginfo {
  int si_signo; int si_errno; int si_code;
union {
  int _pad[SI_PAD_SIZE];
  struct {                        /* for SIGKILL                */
     pid_t _pid;                  /* PID of the sender          */
     uid_t _uid;                  /* UID of the sender          */
} _kill;
  struct {                        /* for POSIX timers           */
     unsigned int _timer1;
     unsigned int _timer2;
} _timer;
  struct {                        /* for POSIX signals          */
     pid_t _pid;                  /* PID of the send            */
     uid_t _uid;                  /* UID of the sende           */
     sigval_t _sigval;            /* signal information         */
} _rt;
  struct {                        /* for SIGCHLD                */
     pid_t _pid;                  /* PID of the child           */
     int _status;                 /* exit code                  */
     clock_t _utime;              /* time in user mode          */
     clock_t _stime;              /* time in system mode        */
} _sigchld;
  struct {                        /* for SIGFPE, SIGSEGV, SIGBUS */
  void *_addr;                    /* address                    */
} _sigfault;
  struct {                        /* for SIGPOLL                */
        int _band;                /* POLL_IN, POLL_OUT, POLL_MSG */
        int _fd;                  /* file descriptor            */
     } _sigpoll;
```

```
    } _sifields;
} siginfo_t;
```

With rt_sigaction(), rt_sigpending(), and rt_sigsuspend() there is no difference to the old functions. The function rt_sigreturn() works like the "normal" sigreturn(), except that the values sas_ss_sp and sas_ss_size of the calculated frame are assumed by the task structure. In rt_sigprocmask(), only SIG_BLOCK and SIG_UNBLOCK are implemented as functions; a SIG_SETMASK has no effect.

There is no equivalent for rt_sigtimedwait(). Using this, a process can wait for the arrival of a signal from a set. The set is given in uthese and the waiting time in uts. With the arrival of a signal, its number is returned and the information from the signal queue of this signal is saved in uinfo.

If the timer runs without a break, it returns the EAGAIN function, otherwise the EINTR is returned. The rt_sigqueueinfo() function that sends a real-time signal to the process is also new. Therefore pid is the target process, sig the signal, and uinfo is the additional data that is to be passed on to pid. The function tests whether the value si_code in uinfo is less than zero, since nobody is permitted to send signals "as a kernel."

Errors

EFAULT – if the copying of a structure takes place inside or outside of the user address space fails.

EINTR – if the process is interrupted at sys_rt_sigtimedwait() with a non-blocked signal.

EPERM – if an incorrect signal code is used at rt_sigqueueinfo().

System call	sched_getparam	sched_getscheduler	LINUX
	sched_setparam	sched_setscheduler	

File: kernel/sched.c
```
long sys_sched_getparam(pid_t pid, struct sched_param *param);
long sys_sched_setparam(pid_t pid, struct sched_param *param);
long sys_sched_getscheduler(pid_t pid);
long sys_sched_setscheduler(pid_t pid, int policy,
        struct sched_param *param);
```

A process can control its handling by the scheduler. The parameters (only one up to now) are combined in a structure:

```
struct sched_param { int sched_priority; };
```

The function sys_sched_getparam() returns the basic priority of real-time processes (rt_priority) of the process pid in the param structure.

sys_sched_setparam() enters the submitted value as the rt_priority of the process pid and calls the scheduler. The value must be between 0 and 99. A non-privileged process (CAP_SYS_NICE) may only change its own priority.

The sys_sched_getscheduler() returns the scheduler tactics for the process. The scheduler has three tactics:

SCHED_OTHER – The rt_priority of these processes is 0. Therefore they receive a normal value when the priority is recalculated.

SCHED_FIFO – Small, time-critical processes. They get a priority bonus of 1,000.

SCHED_RR – Big, time-critical processes. When their counter has expired, they are inserted at the very back of the scheduler's process list.

With sys_sched_setscheduler(), a process can change its tactics and its rt_priority value. If policy is negative, the old value is maintained. The priority must also correspond to the tactics; only the superuser is allowed to assign time-critical tactics.

Errors

EPERM – if a normal user attempts to change another process.
ESRCH – if the process pid could not be found.
EINVAL – if an invalid parameter is passed.

System call	sched_rr_get_interval sched_get_priority_max sched_get_priority_min	sched_yield	LINUX

File: kernel/sched.c

```
long sys_sched_get_priority_min(int policy);
long sys_sched_get_priority_max(int policy);
long sys_sched_yield(void);
long sys_sched_rr_get_interval(pid_t pid,
        struct timespec *interval)
```

The get_priority functions return the upper and lower boundaries of the rt_priority values of the individual scheduler tactics. With sys_sched_yield(), a process can acquiesce in its fate. It enters SCHED_YIELD in its policy value and is inserted at the end of the list of running processes and treated by the scheduler accordingly.

The function sys_sched_rr_get_interval() returns the fixed value of 150 milliseconds.

Errors

EINVAL – If incorrect tactics were passed on.

System call	setdomainname

File: `kernel/sys.c`

```
long sys_setdomainname(const char *name, int len);
```

The function `sys_setdomainname()` overwrites the domain name with the name specified in `name`. The name does not have to terminate with a zero byte: This is entered by the function itself.

Implementation

The system call *setdomainname* is converted via the syscal macro. The system call *getdomainname* is implemented in the C library. A call to `__uname()` is made and the domain name is read. The return value is 0.

```
int getdomainname(char *name, size_t len)
{
  struct utsname uts;
  if (name == NULL) {
  errno = EINVAL; return -1;
}
  if (__uname(&uts) == -1) return -1;
  if (strlen(uts.domainname)+1 > len) {
  errno = EINVAL; return -1;
}
  strcpy(name, uts.domainname);
  return 0;
}
```

Errors

EINVAL – if in `getdomainname()` the string supplied by `sys_uname()` points to
NULL if it is greater than `len` or if `sys_setdomainname()` `len` is too big.
EPERM – if a non-privileged user calls `sys_setdomainname()`.

System call	getgroups	POSIX
	setgroups	

File: `kernel/sys.c`
`#include <linux/types.h>`

```
long sys_getgroups(int len, gid_t *groups);
long sys_setgroups(int len, gid_t *groups);
```

The functions `sys_getgroups()` and `sys_setgroups()` allow several group privileges for a process to be read and set. The groups are part of the task structure (see Section 3.1.1).

`sys_getgroups()` provides the groups in which the meaning of the parameters is somewhat illogical. If `len` is 0, only the number of groups is returned. If `len` is smaller than 0 or smaller than the number of groups, the call returns `EINVAL`. Otherwise, the groups of processors are written to the address groups.

`sys_setgroups()` sets the group capabilities. It is only possible to set all groups at once, as the old groups are overwritten. The number of groups is given by `len`, which is found in `groups`. This call can only execute a process with the `CAP_SETGID` privilege.

Implementation

Both system calls are converted via the syscall macro.

Errors

`EINVAL` – if in `sys_setgroups()` the value `len` is greater than NGROUPS.
`EPERM` – if a non-privileged user calls `sys_setgroups()`.

System call	sethostname	4.3+BSD
	gethostname	

File: `kernel/sys.c`
```
long sys_sethostname(char *name, int len);
long sys_gethostname(char *name, int len);
```

This function allows a write access to the computer name. The first function, `sys_sethostname()`, enters `name` as the host name (`nodename`) of the computer and can only be executed by a process with the `CAP_SYS_ADMIN` capability. If successful, zero is returned. `sys_gethostname()` reads the `nodename` of the computer and returns it in `name`.

Implementation

The system call *sethostname* is converted via the syscall macro. The system call *gethostname* is implemented in the C library and makes use of `__uname()`.

```
int gethostname(char *name, size_t len)
{
```

```
        struct utsname uts;
        if (name == NULL)
{
        errno = EINVAL; return -1;
        }
        if (__uname(&uts) == -1) return -1;
        if (strlen(uts.nodename)+1 > len)
{
        errno = EINVAL; return -1;
}
        strcpy(name, uts.nodename);
        return 0;
}
```

Errors

EINVAL – if in sys_sethostname() the string name points to NULL, or the size
indicated in len exceeds __NEW_UTS_LEN. The value is defined as 64 in
<linux/utsname.h>.

EPERM – if an unauthorized process has called sys_sethostname().

System call	getitimer
	setitimer

File: kernel/itimer.c
```
#include <linux/time.h>
long sys_getitimer(int which, struct itimerval *value);
long sys_setitimer(int which, const struct itimerval *value,
        struct itimerval *ovalue);
```

These functions allow better time monitoring of a process than sys_alarm() does.
Three special timers can be programmed for the current process, specified by which.

ITIMER_REAL – refers to real time. The alarm is updated each time a process is triggered in
the scheduler and, on expiry, provides a SIGALRM.

ITIMER_VIRTUAL – is the time during which the process is active but is not in a system call
(system mode). The alarm is updated by the do_timer() routine and, on expiry, provides SIGVTALRM.

ITIMER_PROF – indicates the total time the process is running. After expiry of the alarm, a
SIGPROF is sent. Together with the previous timer, this makes it possible to distinguish
between the time consumed in system mode and that consumed in user mode.

The times are indicated in the following structure:

```
struct itimerval {
        struct timeval it_interval;              /* interval  */
        struct timeval it_value;                 /* initial value*/
};
struct timeval {
        long tv_sec; long tv_usec;
};
```

sys_getitimer() returns the current value for the alarm set in which sys_setitimer() sets the alarm specified in which to value. The old value is returned in ovalue. When it is first started, the timer is set to the value it_value. When the timer has expired, a signal is generated and from now on the alarm is reset to the value it_interval, as described in Section 3.2.5. The alarm may be triggered slightly later than the specified time: This depends on the system clock. Generally, the delay is 10 milliseconds.

Under LINUX, generation and sending of signals are separate things. Thus it is possible that under a pathologically heavy load a SIGALRM is sent before the process has received the signal of the previous cycle. The second signal is then ignored.

Implementation

Both system calls are converted via the syscall macro.

Errors

EFAULT – if value or ovalue are invalid pointers.
EINVAL – if which is invalid.

System call	getrlimit	4.3+BSD
	setrlimit	
	getrusage	

File: kernel/sys.c
```
#include <linux/resource.h>
long sys_getrlimit(unsigned int resource, struct rlimit *rlim);
long sys_setrlimit(unsigned int resource, struct rlimit *rlim);
long sys_getrusage(int who, struct rusage *usage);
```

sys_getrlimit() reads the size of a resource of the current process and saves it in rlim. The setting is possible by means of the function setrlimit(). The rlimit structure is defined in linux/ressource.h:

```
struct rlimit {
```

```
        int rlim_cur; /* Softlimit */
        int rlim_max; /* Hardlimit */
};
```

There are two limits for a process: the *soft limit* (current limit) and the *hard limit* (upper limit). A non-privileged process can set the soft limit to an arbitrary value between zero and the hard limit, and it can lower the hard limit to the soft limit. A lowering of the hard limit cannot be undone. A process with the CAP_SYS_RESOURCE privilege can set the limits to anything (up to RLIMIT_NOFILE), since for the value RLIMIT_NOFILE, NR_OPEN is the upper limit. The following values are defined as resource in <asm/resource.h> (the initialization for the soft and hard limits are in brackets):

RLIMIT_CPU – maximum CPU time (the sum of utime and stime of the process) in milliseconds (LONG_MAX, LONG_MAX)

RLIMIT_FSIZE – maximum file size (LONG_MAX, LONG_MAX)

RLIMIT_DATA – maximum size of the data segment used, initialized by (LONG_MAX, LONG_MAX)

RLIMIT_STACK – maximum stack size (_STK_LIM, _STK_LIM)

RLIMIT_CORE – maximum size of a core file (0, LONG_MAX)

RLIMIT_RSS – maximum memory size for arguments and environment (RSS) (LONG_MAX, LONG_MAX)

RLIMIT_NPROC – maximum number of child processes; the lower limits are (MAX_TASKS_PER_USER, MAX_TASKS_PER_USER)

RLIMIT_NOFILE – maximum number of open files (NR_OPEN, NR_OPEN)

RLIMIT_MEMLOCK – maximum memory size a process can block (LONG_MAX, LONG_MAX)

RLIMIT_AS – maximum address space (LONG_MAX, LONG_MAX)

If the value of a resource is RLIM_INFINITY, there is no restriction. A process that exceeds its current soft limit is aborted. Both calls return 0 upon successful execution. While the above functions administer the environment of a process, the sys_getrusage() provides information about the process itself. The individual values are defined in the rusage structure:

```
struct rusage {
        struct timeval ru_utime;    /* user time           */
        struct timeval ru_stime;    /* system time         */
        long ru_maxrss;             /* max. RSS            */
        long ru_ixrss;              /* size of shared RSS  */
        long ru_idrss;              /* size of unshared RSS */
        long ru_isrss;              /* stack size          */
```

```
        long ru_minflt;              /* number of minor faults */
        long ru_majflt;              /* number of major faults */
        long ru_nswap;               /* swap operations        */
        long ru_inblock;             /* block input operations */
        long ru_oublock;             /* block output operations*/
        long ru_msgsnd;              /* messages sent          */
        long ru_msgrcv;              /* messages received      */
        long ru_nsignals;            /* signals received       */
        long ru_nvcsw;               /* voluntary context changes */
        long ru_nivcsw;              /* involuntary context changes*/
};
```

The function does not, however, fill the complete structure. Only the values for ru_utime and ru_stime, together with the indication for the memory pages (minor faults, major faults, and swap operations), are filled in. If the value RUSAGE_SELF is specified for who, the information refers to the process itself. Data about child processes is obtained by specifying RUSAGE_CHILDREN. All other values for who supply the sum of both values.

Implementation

Both system calls are converted via the syscall macro.

Errors

EINVAL – if the limit functions are called with an invalid resource value or if the who value in sys_getrusage() is invalid.
EPERM – if a non-privileged user calls sys_setrlimit().

System call	signalstack	POSIX

File: arch/i386/kernel/signal.c
        kernel/signal.c
#include <linux/signal.h>
int sys_sigaltstack(const stack_t *uss, stack_t *uoss);

This function allows for the manipulation of the process signal stack. If uoss is unequal to NULL, then the old data is returned here. The stack_t structure has the following structure:

```
typedef struct sigaltstack {
        void *ss_sp; /* pointer to the stack */
        int ss_flags; /* flags */
        size_t ss_size; /* stack size */
```

} stack_t;

Two values are possible as flags:

SS_ONSTACK – The stack pointer and stack size are entered into the task structure. It is important here that the new pointer does not point to the old stack and that the new stack is larger than MINSIGSTKSZ.

SS_DISABLE – NULL is entered as the pointer and 0 as the size. uss cannot, however, be NULL.

Implementation

The system call is converted by the syscall macro.

Errors

EFAULT – if a copy of the values fails.
EINVAL – if SS_ONSTACK is set.
ENOMEM – if a new stack size is too small.
EPERM – if the new stack pointer is inside the old stack.

System call	signal	sigaction	POSIX
	sigpending	sigsuspend	
	sgetmask	setmask	
	sigprocmask	sigreturn	

File: kernel/signal.c
         arch/i386/kernel/signal.c

```
#include <signal.h>
unsigned long sys_signal(int signum, __sighandler_t handler);
int sys_sigaction(int signum, const struct old_sigaction *new,
        struct old_sigaction *old);
long sys_sgetmask(void);
long sys_ssetmask(int newmask);
long sys_sigpending(sigset_t *buf);
int sys_sigsuspend(int restart, unsigned long oldmask,
        unsigned long set);
long sys_sigprocmask (int how, const sigset_t *set,
        sigset_t *old_set);
int sys_sigreturn(unsigned long __unused);
```

The sys_signal() function sets the handling routine for the signum signal. The handler routine can be a user-defined function or a macro taken from <signal.h>. The following is possible:

SIG_DFL – Default handling of the signal is carried out.

SIG_IGN – The signal is ignored.

The handling routine is entered in the sigaction structure of the current process. The flags SA_ONESHOT and SA_NOMASK are set and all other values are initialized with 0. If sucessful, the address of the old routine is returned, otherwise a negative (-1) is returned. For the SIGKILL and SIGSTOP signals, no new handlers can be implemented, and the signal number must be lower than 32 (set in the source text).

According to POSIX 3.3.1.3, the following applies: If SIG_IGN is specified as a routine, any signal still pending is deleted (except for SIGCHLD). If the routine is SIG_DFL, the signal is deleted if it is not one of SIGCONT, SIGCHLD, or SIGWINCH.

In both cases, it does not matter whether the signal is blocked or not. This is handled by the recalc_sigpending() function, which is called after the new routine is entered.

The function sys_sigaction() is the up-to-date and extended version of sys_signal() (both use do_sigaction()). It is used to specify the routine for the signal more precisely. In new, the new routine is defined.

If old is different from NULL, the old routine is returned. The sigaction structure is defined as follows:

```
struct sigaction {
    __sighandler_t sa_handler; /* signal handling routine     */
    old_sigset_t sa_mask;      /* mask for the blocked signals */
    unsigned long sa_flags;    /* flags                        */
    void (*sa_restorer)(void); /* routine, that should be called
                                * after sa_handler             */
};
```

The flags have the following importance:

SA_NOCLDSTOP – With a SIGSTOP signal, the father is not informed by the SIGCHLD signal.

SA_SIGINFO – For a return from the routine, a stack with the rt_sigframe structure is used instead of sig_frame.

SA_ONSTACK – The task structure signal stack is used as the return stack.

SA_RESTART – If a system call is interrupted by the arrival of the signal (regs->eax == ERESTARTSYS), EINTR is returned.

SA_NODEFER – After the first signum signal, this bit is set in the sa_mask.

SA_RESETHAND – After the arrival of the signal, the handler is reset to SIG_DFL.

SA_NOMASK – Like SA_NODEFER.

SA_ONESHOT – Like SA_RESETHAND.

SA_RESTORER – sa_restorer() is used as a reverse function.

For setting and calling up the signal mask of blocked signals, the functions are sys_sgetmask() and sys_ssetmask(). The first function returns the mask of the first 32 signals[10] (current->blocked.sig[0]), and the second deletes SIGKILL and SIGSTOP from the passed mask and enters them in the task structure (blocked.sig[0]).

sys_sigpending() checks whether there are blocked signals pending for the process. The signals are stored in buf; the return value is 0.

With the functions sys_sgetmask() and sys_ssetmask(), blocking of the signals can be toggled. sys_sigsuspend() makes it possible to set a signal mask and stop the process in a single action. The process is set to sleep until an unblocked signal arrives. If only the mask for blocking signals has to be set, the sys_sigprocmask function can be used. The how parameter specifies how the new signal mask should be used:

SIG_BLOCK – The signals that are set in the signal mask are blocked. The new mask is super-imposed on the old mask using |=.

SIG_UNBLOCK – The signals set in the signal mask are deleted. The new mask is superim-posed on the old mask using & = ˜.

SIG_SETMASK – The signal set mask is taken over as the signal mask for the current process.

The call first deletes the signal bits for SIGKILL and SIGSTOP from the passed mask. If old_set is different from NULL, the old mask is returned.

The sys_sigreturn() function organizes the return from a signal interrupt. It is called internally in order to return to system mode after a signal handling routine. In order for each signal to be handled, a frame is generated on the stack of the process which ensures that the system call *sigreturn* is triggered.[11] The function is not called if a restore handler is set with *sigaction*.

Implementation

The functions sys_signal(), sys_sigprocmask(), sys_sgetmask(), and sys_ssetmask are not available on Alpha machines. Curiously enough, the library function signal() does not work with the system call *signal*, but is based on *sigaction*.

```
__sighandler_t signal (int sig, __sighandler_t handler)
{
  int ret;
  struct sigaction action, oaction;
```

10 More precisely, the first _NSIG_BPW signals are informed.

11 For this purpose, all important registers and the machine code (!) that triggers *sigreturn* are put on the stack as a frame.

```
    action.sa_handler = handler;
    __sigemptyset (&action.sa_mask);
    action.sa_flags = SA_ONESHOT | SA_NOMASK | SA_INTERRUPT;
    action.sa_flags &= ~SA_RESTART;
    ret = __sigaction (sig, &action, &oaction);
    return (ret == -1) ? SIG_ERR : oaction.sa_handler;
}
```

The remaining calls work with the syscall macro, whereas for sys_sigreturn() there is no external interface.

Errors

EINVAL – if an invalid signal number is used.
EFAULT – if the handling routine is bigger than the permitted process size (TASK_SIZE).
EINTR – if the process returns from sys_sigsuspend().

System call	sysctl	POSIX

File: kernel/sysctl.c
#include <linux/sysctl.h>
int sys_sysctl(struct __sysctl_args *args);

In a few cases, it is practical to have a standarized interface for kernel system variables which have to be adjusted to the running time or have to be watched. The sys_sysctl() function allows extensive administration of system-relevant information. This information is held in internal tables and mapped onto /proc/sys. To use this function, the question: Sysctl support? has to be answered with "yes" during the configuration of the kernel.

Before the actual function description, a few more executions should be added to the internal data structure. For every file (and every directory) in /proc/sys, there is a table with the following structure:

```
struct ctl_table {
  int ctl_name;                   /* binary ID              */
  const char *procname;           /* text ID for /proc/sys  */
  void *data;                     /* data area              */
  int maxlen;                     /* size of the file area  */
  mode_t mode;                    /* write/reader rights    */
  ctl_table *child;               /* next table             */
  proc_handler *proc_handler;     /* function for text output */
  ctl_handler *strategy;          /* function for I/O       */
  struct proc_dir_entry *de;      /* /proc control block    */
  void *extra1;
```

```
  void *extra2;
};
```

The decision of whether a `ctl_table` entry should be displayed as a directory or as a file is given by the child component. If child is the same as `NULL`, we are dealing with a leaf node. If a pointer is submitted to a field of the `ctl_table`, we are dealing with a directory. In this way, table fields can be hierarchically encapsulated. A `NULL` entry concludes a table field.

When accessing a variable mirrored in the *Proc* file system a handler routine undertakes the formatting (`proc_handler`) as well as the evaluation of the data.

The strategy routine (`strategy`) is called with all write and read accesses and should save the correct treatment of value changes. If, for example, a cache size is modified, this routine can undertake the administration of memory space. The following semantics apply for the strategy function: If this process was successful, zero is returned and the normal process is continued. Any other value is returned immediately. A value less than zero corresponds to an error and a value greater than zero means that the actual work (the reading as well as the writing) is carried out by the `strategy` function.

With the `mode` component, the access entitlement can be adjusted in the rwxrwxrwx notation,[12] just as with normal files. In the network interface (`net/core/sysctl_net_core.c`), for example, the leaf nodes are defined for a few system variables:

```
#include <linux/sysctl.h>
extern __u32 sysctl_wmem_max;
extern __u32 sysctl_rmem_max;
...
ctl_table core_table[] = {
        {NET_CORE_WMEM_MAX, "wmem_max", &sysctl_wmem_max,
        sizeof(int), 0644, NULL, &proc_dointvec},
        {NET_CORE_RMEM_MAX, "rmem_max", &sysctl_rmem_max,
        sizeof(int), 0644, NULL, &proc_dointvec},
...
{ 0 }
};
```

`proc_dointvec` is the default treatment routine for integer variables or integer fields. A few treatment routines can be integrated here, which undertake the indication and illustration of particular modes or values, such as "on" or "off," or illustrate special data types. The different network parameters are then summarized in directories in superior network systems (`net/sysctl_net.c`):

```
#include <linux/sysctl.h>
extern ctl_table core_table[];
```

12 So mode=0644 means writing entitlement for root; all other bits are only adjusted for reading.

```
ctl_table net_table[] = {
        {NET_CORE, "core", NULL, 0, 0555, core_table},
        ...
        {0}
};
```

In order to deregister or deregister these tables with the kernel, the following functions are available:

```
struct ctl_table_header * register_sysctl_table(ctl_table * table,
                            int insert_at_head);
void unregister_sysctl_table(struct ctl_table_header * table);
```

The tables create dynamic lists. At the start of the system, eight[13] of these lists are placed in the kernel and they are managed in root_table_header:

CTL_KERN – kernel and control structures

CTL_VM – VM management

CTL_NET – network

CTL_PROC – process information

CTL_FS – file systems

CTL_DEBUG – debugging

CTL_DEV – devices

CTL_BUS – information about the bus (ISA, etc.)

After the explanation of the data structure we now come to the effects of the function. It is controlled by the __sysctl_args structure.

```
struct __sysctl_args {
        int *name;          /* name of the information     */
        int nlen;           /* area of the information     */
        void *oldval;       /* pointer to the old value    */
        size_t *oldlenp;    /* length of the old value     */
        void *newval;       /* pointer to the new value    */
        size_t newlen;      /* length of the new value     */
        unsigned long __unused[4];
};
```

The name parameter indicates which information should be accessed. The values possible for this are given in <linux/sysctl.h>; a short extract now follows:

KERN_OSTYPE – a string: the operating system

---

13 If no network is configured, then only seven lists are laid out.

KERN_OSRELEASE – a string: the version

KERN_VERSION – a string: the compile information

KERN_NODENAME – a string: the host name

KERN_DOMAINNAME – a string: the domain name

VM_SWAPCTL – a structure: the parameter of the swapping process

VM_FREEPG – three numbers: the values of the free-page steps

VM_BDFLUSH – structure: the parameter bd_flush() process.

   The function searches through all the tables until it finds the one with the ID (name) that is being searched for. If this table has a successor and a strategy function, this is executed, otherwise the default strategy is used. This first checks the access privileges (if oldval is not equal to zero the read privilege is required; if newval is not equal to zero, the write privilege is required). Then the table-specific strategy function is executed (if one is defined). Finally, the function saves the old value and its size in oldval and oldlenp if both are unequal to zero. If newval and newlen are both unequal to 0, the memory area addressed by newval of size newlen is entered into the table as the new value.

Implementation

The C library does not provide an interface. The kernel function does not check for superuser privileges either!

Errors

EFAULT – if the copying of the values fails.
ENOPERM – if access privileges prohibit the operation.
ENOTDIR – if no table was found for name.

System call	sysinfo	LINUX

File: kernel/info.c
```
#include <linux/sys.h>
#include <linux/kernel.h>
int sys_sysinfo(struct sysinfo *info);
```

   sys_sysinfo() provides information about the system load. The data is returned in the following structure:

```
struct sysinfo {
  long uptime;                /* seconds since start        */
  unsigned long loads[3];     /* load 1, 5, and 15 min. ago */
```

```
unsigned long totalram;    /* size of RAM memory          */
unsigned long freeram;     /* free RAM memory             */
unsigned long sharedram;   /* size of shared memory       */
unsigned long bufferram;   /* size of buffer memory       */
unsigned long totalswap;   /* size of swap memory         */
unsigned long freeswap;    /* free swap memory            */
unsigned short procs;      /* number of running threads   */
unsigned long totalhigh;   /* size of user memory         */
unsigned long freehigh;    /* size of free user memory    */
unsigned int mem_unit;     /* page size                   */
char _f[20-2*sizeof(long)-sizeof(int)];   /* fill bytes   */
};
```

sys_sysinfo provides a generally accessible method for obtaining system information. This is simpler and less risky than reading /dev/kmem (whereby the values five, ten, and eleven are filled with zero).

Implementation

This system call is not supported by the C library. In order to use it, a file sysinfo.c with the following contents should be created:

```
#include <unistd.h>
_syscall1( int , sysinfo , struct sysinfo *, s)
```

This corresponds to the process of implementing a system call as described in Section 3.3.4.

Errors

EFAULT – if the pointer to info is invalid.

System call	syslog

File: kernel/printk.c
```
long sys_syslog(int type, char *buf, int len);
```

sys_syslog() administers the log book of the system and sets the log level. The log book is a memory area in the kernel which is 8 Kbytes in size and is filled by the printk() function (see Appendix E). The log level is the priority level for the behavior of the printk() function. Only the messages whose priority is higher than the log level are displayed by printk() on the console.

```
#define LOG_BUF_LEN 8192
static char log_buf[LOG_BUF_LEN];
```

There are three variables for the access:

```
unsigned long log_size = 0;
  static unsigned long log_start = 0;
  static unsigned long logged_chars = 0;
```

The first variable describes the size of the log book, which can vary between 0 and LOG_BUF_LEN. The second indicates the beginning of the current message. With the access operation (log_start+log_size) & (LOG_BUF_LEN-1) we thus arrive at the last position of the current entry. The overall number of characters in the log book is saved in logged_chars.

The precise functioning of syslog can be specified in type using the following values:

0   closes the log book. This is not implemented. The return value is 0.

1   opens the log book. This is not implemented. The return value is 0.

2   reads len characters from the log book from the position log_start onwards. For this, the log_size variable is evaluated. If the book is empty (log_size equals 0) this call blocks until a process has left an entry and then reads it. log_size is decremented by the number of characters actually read.

3   reads entries from the log book in the memory buf of length len. This function does not block. len is first checked against the sizes LOG_BUF_LEN and logged_chars and (if greater) is set to this value.

4   like 3, also deletes the call of the log book by setting logged_chars to 0.

5   deletes the log book.

6   sets the log level for the printk() function to 1. Only messages of the highest priority are displayed on the console.

7   sets the log level for the printk() function to the default value (7).

8   sets the log level for the printk() function to the value of len, which in this case must be between 0 and 9.

The return value is the number of characters actually read (in cases 2, 3, and 4) or 0.

Implementation

There is no conversion in the C library. Linking is possible with the following file:

```
#include <unistd.h>
_syscall1( int , syslog , int, type, char *, buf, int, len)
```

Errors

EPERM – if a non-privileged user calls `sys_syslog()` with a type other than 3.
EINVAL – if buf is NULL or `len` is negative.

System call	time	stime	POSIX
	gettimeofday	settimeofday	SVR4
			4.3BSD

File: kernel/time.c
```
#include <time.h>
long sys_time(int *t);
long sys_stime(const time_t *t);
long sys_gettimeofday(struct timeval *tv,
        struct timezone *tz);
long sys_settimeofday(struct timeval *tv,
        struct timezone *tz);
```

sys_time() saves the time passed since January 1st, 1970, 0.00 a.m., in seconds in t, and returns it using the macro CURRENT_TIME.

sys_stime() sets the system time, more precisely xtime.tv_sec, to the value specified in t.

xtime.tv_usec is set to 0. This function can only execute a process which has the corresponding privileges (CAP_SYS_TIME). It returns 0 when sucessful, and a negative number in the event of an error.

sys_gettimeofday() and sys_settimeofday() allow a more exact time management.

tv is the same structure as the one specified in sys_setitimer():

```
struct timeval {
  long tv_sec;                  /* seconds              */
  long tv_usec;                 /* microseconds         */
};
tz is a time zone:
struct timezone {
  int tz_minuteswest;
  /* minutes west of Greenwich */
  int tz_dsttime;
  /* uses summer time */
};
```

The sys_settimeofday() function is, as for sys_stime() only allowed for authorized processes (CAP_SYS_TIME). If tv or tz is set to NULL, the corresponding system value does not change. At the first call[14] with `tz` set, the CMOS clock is changed to UTC. For the setting of `tv` values, the interrupts are disabled and `time_status` is set to `TIME_BAD`. The system call returns 0 if successful. The functionality of the underlying timer is described in Section 3.1.6.

Implementation

All four system calls are converted via the syscall macro.

Errors

`EFAULT` – if the copying of data from the user to the address field (or vice versa) fails.
`EPERM` – if the process calling `sys_stime()` or `settimeofday` does not have `CAP_SYS_TIME` privileges.
`EINVAL` – if an invalid value (time zone, and so on) is specified.

System call	times	POSIX

File: `kernel/sys.c`
```
#include <linux/times.h>
long sys_times(struct tms *buf);
```

`sys_times()` writes the time used by the current process and its children into the structure `buf`. The structure `tms` is defined in `<linux/times.h>` as follows:

```
struct tms {
  time_t tms_utime;          /* user time                    */
  time_t tms_stime;          /* system time                  */
  time_t tms_cutime;         /* user time of children        */
  time_t tms_cstime;         /* system time of children      */
};
```

`sys_times()` returns the `jiffies` of the system.

Implementation

The system call is converted via the syscall macro.

Errors

`EFAULT` – if copying the values does not work.

---

14 This should happen as early as possible in order not to confuse other programs possibly running. Usually, a script in `/etc/rc` is used.

System call	uname	POSIX

File: `kernel/sys.c`
```
#include <linux/utsname.h>
long sys_newuname(struct new_utsname *buf);
```

`sys_uname()` returns information about the system. The information can then be found in `buf`. The structure `utsname` appears as follows:

```
struct utsname {
  char sysname[65];         /* operating system name       */
  char nodename[65];        /* computer name               */
  char release[65];         /* operating system release    */
  char version[65];         /* operating system version    */
  char machine[65];         /* processor type              */
  char domainname[65];      /* computer domain             */
};
```

The release is the current state of development of the system (e.g. 2.4). The version is the number of existing kernel configurations together with the time of the most recent compilation (`#95 Sat Dec 4 05:08:15 GMT 1999`).

For reasons of compatibility, there are another two simplified versions: The first one (`old_utsname`) does not have the domain; the second (`oldold_utsname`) limits the entry lengths to 9 bytes (POSIX defines entries for the structure that are only 8 bytes long (plus the space for the zero byte)).

Implementation

The system call is converted via the syscall macro.

Errors

EFAULT – if `buf` is NULL.

System call	vm86	LINUX

File: `arch/i386/kernel/vm86.c`
```
#include <linux/vm86.h>
int sys_vm86(unsigned long subfunction,
        struct vm86plus_struct * v86);
```

The `sys_vm86()` function sets the process in the virtual 8086 mode. To control this, the register set of the 8086, regs can be used:

```
struct vm86plus_struct {
        struct vm86_regs regs;    /* register sentence        */
```

```
            unsigned long flags;
            unsigned long screen_bitmap;
            unsigned long cpu_type;
            struct revectored_struct int_revectored;
            struct revectored_struct int21_revectored;
            struct vm86plus_info_struct vm86plus;
};
```

The precise way of working of the function controls the parameter subfunction. If subroutine is the same as one of the following five values, vm86 is interpreted as an integer number irqnumber.

VM86_GET_AND_RESET_IRQ – If irqnumber is between 3 and 5 and the entry vm86_irqs[irqnumber] is the current process, this is changed to the bit belonging to this number in irqbits and the old value is returned.

VM86_GET_IRQ_BITS – The irqbits are returned.

VM86_REQUEST_IRQ – irqnumber is interpreted as ((sig<<8)|(irq & 255)), and both values extracted. The process must have the CAP_SYS_ADMIN privilege, sig must be a valid signal, and irq must lie between 3 and 15.

Then the irq_handler() function is entered as the interrupt treatment routine, and in vm86_irqs[irq], sig is entered as the signal, and the current process will be returned as the task irq.

VM86_FREE_IRQ – If the irqnumber interrupt is between 3 and 15 and the vm86_irqs[irqnumber] entry is the current process, the accompanying interrupt treatment routine is deleted, vm86_irqs[irqnumber].tsk is set to 0, and the bit in irqbits is deleted.

VM86_PLUS_INSTALL_CHECK – The call returns zero. Because old versions do not recognize this parameter, it allows a version query.

Otherwise, a pt_regs structure is read from this address and entered as a register for the process. Before this, the Eflags register is checked so that the protected mode is unchanged.

The function stores the current stack of the kernel and then jumps into virtual mode. The call is used by the DOS emulator.

Implementation

The system call is converted via the syscall macro.

Errors

EPERM – if the stack has already been stored.

System call	wait4	4.3+BSD
	waitpid	POSIX

File: kernel/exit.c
```
long sys_waitpid(pid_t pid, unsigned int *stat_addr,
        int options);
long sys_wait4(pid_t pid, unsigned int *stat_addr,
        int options, struct rusage *ru);
```

sys_wait4() waits for the process indicated by pid to terminate. In addition, the function writes the exit code to the address stat_addr, and information about resources used by the process is written into the structure ru. The following values are possible:

__WCLONE – Only processes generated with clone() are waited for.

WUNTRACED – The stopped processes in which PF_PTRACE is not set are also considered.

WNOHANG – sys_wait4() does not block.

The function queries all child processes in a loop to check whether one of them matches PID. If pid

> 0, wait4() waits for the child process with PID equal to pid.

= 0, wait4() waits for each child process whose PGRP matches the PGRP of the calling process.

= -1, wait4() waits for all child processes.

< -1, wait4() waits for each child process whose PGRP is equal to pid.

If no process was found, sys_wait4() is returned if WNOHANG was set. Otherwise, the scheduler is called and the loop is entered again.

sys_wait4() returns when the process (that is being waited for) terminates or is a zombie, if WNOHANG is set, or if a non-blocking signal was received. The return value is a negative number if there is an error, the PID of the terminated process, or 0 (with WNOHANG).

sys_waitpid() waits for the process pid with the specified options options.

The sys_waitpid() function is only still provided for compatibility reasons and could well be implemented in the C library sys_wait4() in future versions.

```
asmlinkage long sys_waitpid(pid_t pid,
  unsigned int * stat_addr, int options)
{
return sys_wait4(pid, stat_addr, options, NULL);
}
```

The exact interplay between sys_wait4(), sys_exit(), and the scheduler is described in Section 3.3.3.

Implementation

The system calls *wait4* and *waitpid* are converted via the syscall macro. The function `waitpid()` is not available on Alpha machines. `wait()` is no longer provided as a system call, but as a libray function (in `unistd.h`).

```
static inline pid_t wait(int * wait_stat)
{
return waitpid(-1,wait_stat,0);
}
```

Errors

ERESTARTSYS – if WNOHANG is not set and the process receives a non-blocking signal or a SIGCHLD.

ECHILD – if the child process pid does not exist.

A.2   THE FILE SYSTEM

The following system calls establish a connection with the file system. Because of the existence of a virtual file system in LINUX, the transition from the user to the kernel is just an intermediate step of the real work involved.

Nearly all system calls execute a parameter check first and then call the corresponding inode or file operation of the file system implementation. All system calls that possess a path parameter use the open_namei() function. This function determines the inode belonging to the name and is described in detail in Section 6.2.3.

System call	access	POSIX

File: `fs/open.c`
```
#include <unistd.h>
long sys_access(const char *filename, int mode);
```

The sys_access() function checks whether a user has the access rights mode for the file filename. In mode, only the last three bits can be set; possible values are:

S_IROTH – if the file can be read.

S_IWOTH – if the file can be written to.

S_IXOTH – if the file can be executed.

For access to the file system, sys_access() does not use the effective UID and GID, but the ones that are copied into the FSUID and FSGID for the access test. If the current UID for this is not equal to 0, all process privileges are deleted for the test (cap_clear()).

If the inode operations provide a `permission` component, this function is used in the determination of the access privileges. Otherwise `inode->i_mode` is used with UNIX privileges.

Implementation

The conversion is simply carried out via the syscall macro.

Errors

EINVAL – if the rights specified in `mode` are invalid or the `filename` does not exist.
EROFS – if the write right is checked for a read-only file system.
EACCESS – if access with the specified rights is not permitted.

System call	bdflush	POSIX

File: `fs/buffer.c`
```
long sys_bdflush(int func, long data);
```

The kernel function `sys_bdflush()` organizes the writing out of blocks marked as "dirty" in the buffer cache. The LINUX kernel administers the buffer cache by means of two tables (among other things):

```
#define NR_LIST 3
static struct buffer_head * lru_list[NR_LIST] = {NULL, };
int nr_buffers_type[NR_LIST] = {0,};
```

The first table contains pointers to doubly linked lists, each of which contains a class of blocks. A class can be, for example, `BUF_SHARED` or `BUF_LOCKED`. The second table contains the number of blocks in the corresponding list.

The pointer `lru_list[BUF_DIRTY]` points to the list administered by `bdflush()`, which contains the blocks not yet written out of the memory. The number of blocks in this list is contained in `nr_buffers_type[BUF_DIRTY]`. A block is administered by means of the structure `buffer_head` and appears as follows:

```
struct buffer_head {
  struct buffer_head * b_next;       /* pointer to the next entry*/
  unsigned long b_size;              /* block size              */
  unsigned long b_blocknr;           /* block number            */
  kdev_t b_dev;                      /* device                  */
  kdev_t b_dev;                      /* device                  */
  unsigned long b_rsector;           /* position of the buffer  */
  struct buffer_head * b_this_page;/* buffer of the current page*/
  unsigned long b_state;             /* status bitmap           */
```

```
    struct buffer_head * b_next_free;
    unsigned short b_count;              /* number of users       */
    char * b_data;                       /* pointer to data block  */
    unsigned long b_flushtime;           /* last time written      */
    unsigned long b_lru_time;            /* last time used         */
    struct wait_queue * b_wait;
    struct buffer_head ** b_pprev;
    struct buffer_head * b_prev_free; /* list of buffers          */
    struct buffer_head * b_reqnext;   /* request list             */
    void (*b_end_io)(struct buffer_head *bh, int uptodate);
    void *b_dev_id;
};
```

In order to control swapping, there is a structure that contains the necessary parameters.

```
static union bdflush_param {
  struct {
        int nfract;          /* activation threshold in percent*/
        int ndirty;          /* max. number of blocks to be swapped
                              * out in one cycle            */
        int nrefill;         /* number of free blocks that are
                              * loaded by means of refill_
                              * freelist                    */
        int nref_dirt;       /* activation threshold        */
        int dummy1;
        int age_buffer;      /* aging time for data blocks  */
        int age_super;       /* aging time for metablocks
                              * (directories and so on)     */
        int dummy2;
        int dummy3;
} b_un;
unsigned int data[N_PARAM];
} bdf_prm = {{40, 500, 64, 256, 15, 30*HZ, 5*HZ, 1884, 2}};
```

As well as the default values, the kernel also sets the minimum and maximum values.

```
static int bdflush_min[N_PARAM] =
                { 0, 10, 5, 25, 0, 100, 100, 1, 1};
static int bdflush_max[N_PARAM] =
                {100,5000, 2000, 2000, 100, 60000, 60000, 2047, 5};
```

The process can only be executed by a process with the CAP_SYS_ADMIN capability. If the argument func is greater than 1, all marked blocks are written out. Different behavior happens where func is greater than 1. The number of the parameter is therefore (func-

2)>>1. An even value[15] of func means that the parameter is filled with the value contained in data, whereas an odd value yields the reading of the parameter. During writing a check is made as to whether data lies between the minimum and maximum parameters that have been established.

Implementation

The C library does not provide an interface for converting the system call into the kernel function.

Errors

EPERM – only processes with the CAP_SYS_ADMIN capability can execute the function.
EINVAL – the value for func or data is invalid.

System call	chdir		POSIX
	fchdir		

File: fs/open.c
```
long sys_chdir(const char *path);
long sys_fchdir(unsigned int fd);
```

sys_chdir() sets the current working directory to the directory specified in path. It determines the inode belonging to path and enters it in the fs->pwd component of the task. sys_fchdir() works in the same way, except that by using the file descriptor passed the function can determine the inode somewhat more easily.

Implementation

Both system calls use the syscall macro.

Errors

ENOTDIR – if path is not a directory.
EBADF – if fd is invalid.
ENOENT – if there is no inode for path.
EACCES – if no exception rights are set for the directory.

System call	chmod	fshmod	POSIX
	chown	fchown	
	lchown		

---

15 For example, 2 is written parameter 0; 3 is read 0; 4 is written parameter 1; etc.

File: fs/open.c

```
#include <linux/types.h>
#include <linux/stat.h>
long sys_chmod(const char *filename, mode_t mode);
long sys_fchmod(unsigned int fildes, mode_t mode);
long sys_chown(const char *filename, uid_t owner, gid_t group);
long sys_fchown(unsigned int fd, uid_t owner, gid_t group);
long sys_lchown(unsigned int fd, uid_t owner, gid_t group);
```

sys_chmod() sets the capabilties of the file filename to the capabilities specified in mode. Bits that are higher than S_ISUID (for example, S_IFIFO) are first masked out in order to prevent manipulation. If mode is set to -1, the current access rights remain unchanged; only ctime is reset. In sys_fchmod(), a file descriptor is specified instead of the name.

sys_chown() changes the owner and group of a file in owner and group. The call sys_fchown() has the same function, except that a descriptor is specified. sys_lchown() works the same as sys_chown(), apart from one difference: If filename is a symbolic link, it is closed.

If the UID or GID of the file is changed, the correspondingly set S-bit is deleted (S_ISGID only with the set S_IXGRP). With all three of these functions, the quotas of the new users are correspondingly updated (transferred). All five calls update their inode information using the notify_change() function.

Implementation

All five system calls work with the syscall macro.

Errors

ENOENT – if the file does not exist.
EROFS – if the file system is read-only.
EPERM – if the file is labeled as IS_IMMUTABLE or as IS_APPEND.
EDQUOT – if the quotas of the new owner do not allow the operation.

System call	chroot

File: fs/open.c

```
long sys_chroot(const char * filename);
```

sys_chroot() sets the directory filename as root directory for the calling process. The call determines the inode belonging to filename and checks whether it is a directory and whether the EXECUTE bit is set. If the process then still has CAP_SYS_CHROOT rights, the directory is entered as fs->root in the task structure.

Implementation

The conversion is carried out via the syscall macro.

Errors

EPERM – if a non-privileged user executes the call.
ENAMETOOLONG – if the specified name is too long.
ENOENT – if the directory does not exist.
ENOTDIR – if a part of the path is not a directory, but a file.

System call	dup	dup2	POSIX

File: fs/fcntl.c
```
long sys_dup(unsigned int filedes);
long sys_dup2(unsigned int oldfd, unsigned int newfd);
```

sys_dup() and sys_dup2() generate a copy of the file descriptor. Afterwards, both descriptors point to the same file structure. A set close_on_exec flag is deleted. sys_dup() returns the first free descriptor for the copy. sys_dup2() uses newfd as a copy. If newfd is not yet free, the corresponding file is closed. Both system calls are mapped onto the dupfd() function.

Implementation

The conversion of both system calls is carried out via the syscall macro.

Errors

EBADF – if an invalid file descriptor is used.
EMFILE – if there is no free file descriptor in sys_dup().

System call	execve		POSIX

File: fs/exec.c
```
arch/i386/kernel/process.c
int sys_execve(struct pt_regs regs);
```

sys_execve() executes a new program. The necessary parameters can be found in the register structure. Thus regs.ebx contains a pointer to the filename of the program, regs.ecx a pointer to the arguments to be passed to the specified program, and regs.edx the address of the environment in which the process should be running.

The function `pt_regs` receives the register stack as the argument in the kernel. Because these are, of course, different for each individual architecture, the function (that is, an interface to do_execve(), the current function) is found in the architecture directory.

The file `filename` must be a binary file whose format is known to LINUX or a script. `sys_execve()` analyzes the `filename` file, goes through the list of configured binary formats (plus `kmod`, if configured), and tries to call the file with the `load_binary` function.

The program called with `sys_execve()` completely blots out the calling process, which means that text and data segments plus stack and BBS are overwritten with those of the loaded program. The program takes over the PID of the calling process and its opened file descriptors. Pending signals are deleted. In the event of an error, a negative number is returned; there is no return value upon success. The implementation of the call is described in Section 3.3.3.

If the current process is executed with `ptrace()`, the system call *execve* returns a `SIGTRAP` signal after successful completion.

Implementation

The structure `pt_regs` in `<asm/ptrace.h>` contains one image of the registers on the stack which are deposited there during a system call before the kernel function is called. LINUX supports several binary formats, and each format has its own function for loading binaries. The name of the program (which might be an interpreter with a script as an argument) and the register (see Section 3.3.3) are submitted to these.

The normal system calls such as *execl* or *execv* are implemented as library functions. With `execv()`, the current environment is passed to the actual system call, whereas in `execvp()` the command name is looked for in the current path and a new argument is put together. In the case of functions with argument lists such as `execl()`, the submitted argument list is copied into a vector.

Errors

`EACCESS` – if the filename is not a normal file.
`EPERM` – if the file system has been mounted with `MS_NOEXEC`.
`ENOEXEC` – if no file identification (magic number) or no shell could be found after #!.
`E2BIG` – if there is no free memory in the kernel to sumbit arguments and the environment.

System call	fcntl	POSIX

File: `fs/fcntl.c`
      `net/inet/sock.c`
`#include <fcntl.h>`
`long sys_fcntl(unsigned int fd, unsigned int cmd,`
      `unsigned long arg);`

The system call `sys_fcntl()` modifies the properties of an opened file `fd`. The corresponding operation is specified by `cmd`:

F_DUPFD – The file descriptor `fd` is duplicated in `arg`. This corresponds to the functioning of `sys_dup2()`. If successful, the new file descriptor is returned.

F_GETFD – Reads the `close-on-exec` flag of the specified file descriptor.

F_SETFD – If the lowest bit of `arg` is evaluated, the `close-on-exec` flag of the specified file descriptor is used, otherwise it is deleted.

F_GETFL – The flags of the descriptor are returned. The flags are the same as described in `sys_open()`.

F_SETFL – Sets the flags to the value specified in `arg`. Internally, only `O_APPEND`, `O_NDELAY`, `FASYNC`, and `O_NONBLOCK` are set. The flags and their semantics are the same as in `sys_open()`. If the file has been created as an append-only file and `O_APPEND` is not specified in the flags (that is, it has to be deleted), the function reacts with an error message. Upon modification of the `FASYNC` flag, the file operation `fasync()` is called.

F_GETLK, F_SETLK, and F_SETLKW – Set or read the locks of a file. The functionality and use of file locking is described in detail in Section 5.2.2.

F_GETOWN – Returns the PID (PGRP) of the process that uses the socket `fd`. Process groups are returned as negative values! The value can be found in `f_owner` of the file structure.

F_SETOWN – Enters `arg` as the PID in the `f_own` structure for the given file descriptor. Otherwise, `uid` and `euid` of the structure are set to the values of the current process.

F_GETSIG – Returns the signal that is activated with an IO error in accordance with POSIX (found in the `f_owner` structure).

F_SETSIG – Enters `arg` as a signal in the `f_owner` structure.

If the file descriptor `fd` is connected to a socket, the call is shown on the corresponding function for sockets.

Implementation

The conversion is carried out via the syscall macro.

Errors

EBADF – if `fd` is not a descriptor of an opened file.

EINVAL – if a negative or excessively large value has been specified for `arg` in the case of F_DUPFD, or if the process has already reached its maximum number of open files, or if an invalid value has been specified for `cmd`.

EPERM – if there are no rights for F_SETOWN.

System call	flock	POSIX

File: fs/locks.c
long sys_flock(unsigned int fd, unsigned int cmd);

This function is used to administrate locks on files. If several locks exist for one file, they are put in a list. For this purpose, each inode contains a reference to a file_lock structure:

```
struct file_lock {
    struct file_lock *fl_next;    /* list of all locks for this*/
                                  /* inode                     */
    struct list_head fl_link;     /* list of all locks         */
    struct list_head fl_block;    /* list of all blocked
                                  *processes                   */
    fl_owner_t fl_owner;          /* files of the locking
                                  * processes                  */
    unsigned int fl_pid;          /* locking process           */
    wait_queue_head_t fl_wait;    /* queue for all blocked
                                  * processes                  */
    struct file *fl_file;
    unsigned char fl_flags;
    unsigned char fl_type;
    loff_t fl_start;              /* start of the lock         */
    loff_t fl_end;                /* end of the lock           */
    void (*fl_notify)(struct file_lock *);/* release-Callback */
    void (*fl_insert)(struct file_lock *);/* insert-Callback */
    void (*fl_remove)(struct file_lock *);/* erase-Callback */
    struct fasync_struct * fl_fasync;
    union {
      struct nfs_lock_info nfs_fl;
  } fl_u;
};
```

The function always works in the same way on the whole of the file. Subordinate functions can be locked specifically by using instructions from file areas. For cmd, the following values are possible:

LOCK_SH – The file is locked for read access.

LOCK_EX – The file is locked for write access.

LOCK_UN – All locks are removed. All processes that entered a waiting loop by accessing the lock are woken up.

LOCK_MAN – A mandatory lock. SMB accesses are simulated with this.

Implementation

The conversion is carried out in two steps. First of all the kernel function is called via the syscall macro. If this fails, an attempt is made to use sys_fcntl().

Errors

EBADF – The descriptor is invalid.
EINVAL – The cmd value is invalid.
ENOLCK – No further entry can be made in the list.
EBUSY – The F_POSIX flag is set.

System call	getcwd	LINUX

File: fs/dcache.c
```
long sys_getcwd(char *buf, unsigned long size);
```

This call saves the current work directory in buf. If this is erased, "(deleted)" is attached. size indicates the size of the submitted buffer. If the path string is longer, an error is returned.

Errors

ENOENT – if the determination of the directory fails.
ERANGE – if the path is longer than size.
EFAULT – if the copying into the buffer buf fails.

System call	ioctl	4.3+BSD

File: fs/ioctl.c
```
#include <fs/ioctl.h>
long sys_ioctl(unsigned int fd, unsigned int cmd,
               unsigned long arg);
```

The sys_ioctl() function manipulates the parameters of a device. This function is mainly used to control device drivers. The first parameter is an opened descriptor of the corresponding file.

The requireq function is specified in the argument cmd. Macros and definitions for the use of this call are found in <linux/ioctl.h>. Some functions are permitted for all file descriptors:

FIOCLEX – The `close_on_exec` flag is set.

FIONCLEX – The `close_on_exec` flag is deleted.

FIONBIO – If the value specified by the address `arg` is equal to 0, the `O_NONBLOCK` flag is deleted, otherwise it is set.

FIOASYNC – As with `FIONBIO`, the `O_SYNC` flag is set or deleted. The synchronization flag has not yet been implemented, but is dealt with for reasons of completeness.

These four functions are handled by the call itself; all others are passed on to the `ioctl` functions of the file system, either to the function `file_ioctl()` if `fd` refers to a regular file, or to the file operation `ioctl()` (see Section 6.2.9). The `file_ioctl()` function deals with the following commands:

FIBMAP – Reads the block with the number `arg` from the file and saves it to the address `arg`.

FIGETBSZ – Saves the size of the superblock to the address `arg`.

FIONREAD – Enters the number positioned in `arg` as the position of the file pointer.

Implementation

The system call is converted via the syscall macro.

Errors

EBADF – if `fd` is invalid.
ENOTTY – if `fd` does not refer to a character-oriented device or the `cmd` used is not supported by the device `fd`.
EINVAL – if `cmd` or `arg` is invalid.

System call	link	unlink	POSIX
	rename	rmdir	
	symlink		

File: `fs/namei.c`

```
long    sys_link(const char *oldname, const char *newname);
long    sys_rename(const char *oldname, const char *newname);
long    sys_rmdir(const char *name);
long    sys_symlink(const char *oldname, const char *newname);
long    sys_unlink(const char *name);
```

`sys_link()` and `sys_symlink()` create references (hard links) and symbolic references (soft links) with the name `newname`, which refer to `oldname`.

First, both parameters are copied into the kernel address space (for runtime reasons), and then the do_link() function is called with the two names. Symbolic links are not used as names! The function do_link() creates the reference and initializes the quota structure for the directory in which the reference is applied. For files which are labeled as S_APPEND or S_IMMUTABLE no references can be created.

The sys_symlink() function copies both oldname and newname and calls do_symlink(). This works like do_link(), but does not carry out a check for oldname.

sys_rename() re-creates the file under the name newname and deletes the old file. A file which is labeled as S_APPEND can not be renamed.

Finally, the quota structures for oldname and newname are initialized.

The sys_unlink() function decrements the link counter for the name file and erases the file if the counter is 0. sys_rmdir() works similarly to sys_unlink(), but removes the directory.

These kernel functions are converted into the corresponding inode operations after the necessary rights have been tested.

Implementation

The system calls are converted via the syscall macro.

Errors

EACCESS – if the directory has no execution rights.

ENOENT – if oldname does not exist or the path name is invalid.

ENOTDIR – if an error appears when converting the file name into a dentry structure (no inode or the inode operation lookup() is found).

EPERM – if the file inode does not permit the link, newname is invalid, or the file system does not support the operation.

EROFS – we are dealing with a read-only file system.

EBUSY – no mount points could be erased.

EXDEV – if oldname and newname are not in the same file system in sys_link().

System call	lseek	POSIX
	llseek	

File: fs/read write.c
```
#include <linux/types.h>
long sys_lseek(unsigned int fd, off_t offset, unsigned int origin)
long sys_llseek(unsigned int fd, unsigned long offset_high,
                unsigned long offset_low, loff_t * result,
                unsigned int origin);
```

sys_lseek() sets a new current position in the file (file->f_pos) relative to offset and origin (2 – from the end of file, 1 – from the current position). LINUX first tries to use the llseek() function of the file system to which the file belongs.

If this does not possess an llseek function, the kernel calculates the new position itself. The new absolute address is returned. The current position and file size are then easily determined:

```
pos = lseek(fd, 0, 1); size = lseek(fd, 0, 2);
```

The sys_llseek() function positions in large files. To do this, a new offset of type long long is put together from offset_high and offset_low.

```
offset = ((loff_t) offset_high << 32) | offset_low;
```

If the file system supports an llseek() inode operation, this is called. Otherwise, the function tries to calculate the new position itself. This function returns 0 if successful. The new position is saved in result.

Implementation

While the system call *lseek* is converted via the syscall macro as usual, there is only a restricted implementation in the C library for sys_llseek() on Intel computers.

```
loff_t __llseek (int fd, loff_t offset, int origin);
```

Errors

EBADF – if fd is invalid.
EINVAL – if origin is greater than 2 or if the calculation of the new position produces a value < 0.

System call	mount	SVR4
	umount	

File: fs/super.c
```
int sys_mount (char * dev_name, char * dir_name, char * type,
        unsigned long new_flags, void * data);
int sys_umount(const char *name, int flags);
```

sys_mount() mounts the file system located on the block device dev_name in the directory dir_name. It is important that the process has the CAP_SYS_ADMIN capability. type contains the type of the file system, for example ext2. The new_flags control the mounting process and the properties of the mounted file system.

MS_RDONLY – The file system is read-only.

MS_NOSUID – SUID and SGID bits are ignored.

MS_NODEV – Access to device files is prohibited.

MS_NOEXEC – Execution of files is prohibited.

MS_SYNCHRONOUS – Write accesses are immediately executed on disk.

MS_REMOUNT – The flags of an already mounted file system are modified (*remount*).

S_QUOTA – When creating or erasing an inode, the quota structure is updated.

S_APPEND – The O_APPEND flag must be set when opening files for writing.

S_IMMUTABLE – The files and their inodes must not be modified.

MS_NOATIME – When accessing a file the *access time* is not actualized.

MS_NODIRATIME – When accessing a directory, its *access time* is not updated.

MS_MGC_VAL – Indicates the more recent version of the system call *mount*. Without this signature in bits 16 to 31, only the first four options are evaluated.

data is a pointer to an arbitrary structure of maximum size PAGE_SIZE-1 which may contain file-system-specific information.[16]

With MS_REMOUNT, no type and device have to be indicated. In this case, the call just updates the information contained in new_flags and data.

sys_umount() removes the file system. The directory, as well as the device, can be given as the name. It writes back to the superblock and releases the file system's device. MNT_FORCE can then be submitted as the flag, and then the superblock function umount_begin() is called (as long as it is implemented).

Implementation

Both system calls are converted via the syscall macro.

Errors

EPERM – no superuser privileges.
ENODEV – no file system is known for type.
EACCES – dev_name is not a device.
ENOTBLK – dev_name is not a block device or does not provide a file operation.
ENXIO – the major number of the device is invalid.
EBUSY – a process is running in the directory or the directory is already mounted.
ENOTDIR – dir_name is not a directory.
EINVAL – read_super() has failed or dev_name is not mounted.

---

16 This data is applied in the u union of the superblock, see Section 6.2.1.

System call	nfsservctl	LINUX

File: `fs/filesystems.c`
        `fs/nfsd/nfsctl.c`
`int sys_nfsservctl(int cmd, void *argp, void *resp);`

This call controls the work of the NFS daemon. It can be configured as a module. For this, during the conversion of the kernel, `CONFIG_NFSD_MODULE` must be activated, otherwise the call returns the error `ENOSYS`.

The actual `handle_sys_nfsservctl()` function can be found in `nfsctl.c`. The transfer can be made either as a delegation or as a preprocessor macro.

The pointer `argp` points to a `nfsctl_arg` structure, the pointer `resp` to an `nfsctl_res` structure.

```
struct nfsctl_arg {
        int ca_version; /* safety parameter */
        union {
                struct nfsctl_svc        u_svc;
                struct nfsctl_client     u_client;
                struct nfsctl_export     u_export;
                struct nfsctl_uidmap     u_umap;
                struct nfsctl_fhparm     u_getfh;
                struct nfsctl_fdparm     u_getfd;
                unsigned int             u_debug;
        } u;
union nfsctl_res {
        struct knfs_fh           cr_getfh;
        unsigned int             cr_debug;
};
```

The `cmd` parameter indicates, as always, the precise function:

`NFSCTL_SVC` – Creates a new server; the port number and the number of desired threads are given. Returns the value 0 upon success.

`NFSCTL_ADDCLIENT` – Creates a new client. Returns 0 if successful.

`NFSCTL_DELCLIENT` – Erases the given client. Returns 0 if successful.

`NFSCTL_EXPORT` – Exports the given file system. Returns 0 if successful.

`NFSCTL_UNEXPORT` – Ends the exporting of the given file system. Returns 0 if successful.

`NFSCTL_GETFH` – Fills `resp` with the value of the file, which is described in `addr.u.u_export` using device and inode number.

NFSCTL_GETFD – Fills `resp` with the value of the file that is labeled with the path input in `addr.u.u_export`.

Implementation

The system call is converted by the syscall macro.

Errors

`EINTR` – if an unblocked signal is reached.
`EFAULT` – if the values cannot be copied.

System call	creat	open	POSIX
	mkdir	mknod	4.3+BSD
	close		SVR4

File: `fs/open.c`
        `fs/namei.c`

```
#include <linux/types.h>
long sys_close (unsigned int fd);
long sys_creat (const char *file_name, int mode);
long sys_mkdir (const char *file_name, int mode);
long sys_mknod (const char *file_name, int mode, dev_t dev);
long sys_open (const char *file_name, int flag, int mode);
```

   `sys_open()` opens a file indicated by `file_name` for the operations specified by `flag`. The possible values for `flag` are:

O_RDONLY – The file is opened for reading only.

O_WRONLY – The file is open for writing only.

O_RDWR – Both reading and writing are possible.

O_CREAT – The file is created if it does not exist. The third parameter, `mode`, must be specified. `mode` is then combined with umask (`˜umask & mode`).

O_EXCL – An error is returned if O_CREAT is specified and the file already exists. With this, a simple lock mechanism can be implemented.

O_NOCTTY – The terminal specified in `file_name` becomes the *controlling terminal*. This flag is not implemented.

O_TRUNC – If the file exists and is writeable, it is set to size 0.

O_APPEND – Data of subsequent write operations is appended to the file.

O_NONBLOCK – Operations on the file do not block.

O_NDELAY – Is mapped to O_NONBLOCK.

O_SYNC – Modifications to the file in (buffer) memory are immediately written to the device. This operation is only implemented for block devices and files of the *Ext2* file system.

sys_creat() does exist as a system call, but the kernel calls sys_open() with the corresponding flags.

```
asmlinkage int sys_creat(const char * pathname, int mode)
{
  return sys_open(pathname, O_CREAT | O_WRONLY | O_TRUNC, mode);
}
```

The sys_close() function closes the file descriptor fd. Any existing file locks (i_flock) are deleted.

After checking the rights, sys_mkdir() creates the directory file_name by using the inode operation mkdir(). sys_mknod() creates a pseudo file with mode specifying the type and access rights of the pseudo file to be created. Directories cannot be created using this function, and FIFOs can only be created by authorized users (CAP_SYS_ADMIN). For device files, dev contains the device number.

Implementation

All five system calls work with the syscall macro. The system call *mkfifo* is implemented in the C library by means of mknod():

```
int mkfifo(const char path, mode_t mode)
{
        return mknod (path, mode | S_IFIFO, 0);
}
```

Errors

EMFILE – if too many files are open.

EACCESS – if the directory has no exectution rights.

ENFILE – if no free file descriptors are available to the system or the process. Both values are defined in <linux/fs.h>.

EEXIST – if a file is to be created that already exists as a directory.

EISDIR – if a directory is to be opened that cannot be read or if the flags O_CREATE or O_TRUNC are set with sys_open().

ENOENT – if the path name is invalid.

EPERM – if the inode of the file does not permit the requested operation.

System call	pipe	POSIX

File: `arch/i386/kernel/sys i386.c`
```
int sys_pipe(unsigned long * fildes);
```

    `sys_pipe()` creates two descriptors and writes them in a field addressed by `fildes`. `fildes[0]` is opened for read operations and for write operations, provided that the process has two free descriptors available.

Implementation

The system call is converted via the syscall macro. Because other architectures use the stack registers as arguments for the kernel functions, the function has been moved to the architecture-dependent directory.

Errors

`EMFILE` – if there are no free descriptors in the system.
`ENFILE` – if there are no free descriptors for the process.
`EINVAL` – if `fildes` is invalid.

System call	pivot_root	POSIX

File: `fs/super.c`
```
long sys_pivot_root(const char *new_root, const char *put_old)
```

    The `sys_pivot_root()` function carries `new_root` as the new root directory of the current process. The old root directory is moved behind `put_old`. To be able to call this function, the entitlement `CAP_SYSADMIN` is required.

    The following conditions apply to the `new_root` and `put_old` parameters: They must be directories, `new_root` and `put_old` cannot be in the same file system as the current root directory, and `put_old` must be below `new_root` in the file system.

    If the current root directory is not a mount point (for example `/nfs/my_root`), then not the directory, but the mount point is moved to `put_old`.

    Finally, all processes whose root or current directory points to `old_root` are set to `new_root`.

Errors

`EBUSY` – if `new_root` or `put_old` is the root directory of the specific process.
`EINVAL` – if `put_old` is not within `new_root`.

ENOENT – if new_root is deleted, but (a dead) directory is still open, or if either new_root or put_old is a directory.

EPERM – if a non-privileged process calls a function.

System call	poll	SVR4

File: fs/select.c
```
#include <linux/time.h>
#include <linux/types.h>
long sys_poll(struct pollfd * ufds,
        unsigned int nfds, int timeout);
```

This system call is the equivalent of the system call select(). Instead of submitting three fields (one for each condition), one field is used, which includes the descriptor and the condition.

```
struct pollfd {
        int fd;             /* descriptor           */
        short events;       /* event to be supervised */
        short revents;      /* event occurring      */
};
```

In contrast to select(), the events remain unchanged. The polling occurs in an endless loop. In an inner loop, the file operation f_op->poll is called for every file, and the result is connected to events (OR connection) and is entered in revents. After running through the inner loop, it checks whether a revents has changed (using a flag), whether the timeout given in timeout has run out, or whether a signal exists. If this is the case, the loop is interrupted and the number of changed revents is returned.

Three settings are possible as timeouts:

timeout < 0 – The timeout is set to infinity.

timeout == 0 – The call checks the descriptors and returns immediately.

timeout > 0 – The value is converted from milliseconds into jiffies and entered as the timeout for the process.

Implementation

The system call is converted by the syscall macro.

Errors

EINTR – if a non-blocked signal arrives.
EFAULT – if the values cannot be copied.

System call	quotacl	LINUX

File: kernel/dquot.c

```
#include <linux/sys.h>
#include <linux/quota.h>
long sys_quotactl(int cmd, const char *special,
        int id, caddr_t addr);
```

This kernel function represents the entry point of the quota program. Currently, only disk quotas are considered; for process quotas, use of rlimits is probably the most suitable way.

The quotas look as follows:

```
struct dquot {
  unsigned int dq_id;                   /* for which ID (uid, gid) */
  short dq_type;                        /* type                    */
  kdev_t dq_dev;                        /* device                  */
  short dq_flags;                       /* flags                   */
  short dq_count;                       /* reference counter       */
  unsigned long dq_referenced;          /* number of accesses      */
struct vfsmount *dq_mnt;                /* VFS mount point         */
struct dqblk dq_dqb;                    /* usage                   */
struct wait_queue *dq_wait;             /* processes waiting for
                                         * a quota change          */
struct dquot *dq_prev, *dq_next;
struct dquot *dq_hash_prev, *dq_hash_next;
};
struct dqblk {
__u32 dqb_bhardlimit;         /* hard limit of usable blocks   */
__u32 dqb_bsoftlimit;         /* soft limit of usable blocks   */
__u32 dqb_curblocks;          /* current number of blocks      */
__u32 dqb_ihardlimit;         /* hard limit of usable inodes   */
__u32 dqb_isoftlimit;         /* soft limit of usable inodes   */
__u32 dqb_curinodes;          /* current number of inodes      */
time_t dqb_btime;             /* time limit for a soft
                               * excess (blocks)               */
time_t dqb_itime;             /* time limit for a soft
                               * excess (inodes)               */
};
```

The time limits have meanings. For example, in response to queries, the expiry time of the limit is usually given in seconds. Limits are set by entering the value in the vfsmount structure of the device. The value is used as the interval for updating the limit (new expiry = current time + internal). In addition, the following structure is used for administration:

```
struct dqstats {
  __u32 lookups;
  __u32 drops;
  __u32 reads;                  /* number of quotas read        */
  __u32 writes;                 /* number of quotas written     */
  __u32 cache_hits;
  __u32 pages_allocated;        /* number of pages occupied     */
  __u32 allocated_dquots;       /* quotas used                  */
  __u32 free_dquots;            /* quotas free                  */
  __u32 syncs;                  /* number of sync operations    */
};
```

The `cmd` contains the command and the type of the call. It can be put together via the `QCMD (cmd, type)` macro.[17] When processed, `cmd` is broken down into `cmds` and `type`. If no `cmd` is given, `QUOTA_SYSCALL` is entered. The parameters have the following meaning (if not specified otherwise):

`cmds` – precise function of the call

`type` – detail of whether `id` is a UID or GID or the index of the `dq_mnt` array

`special` – the desired device

`id` – the id that the quotas refer to.

Most functions can only be executed if the process has the `CAP_SYS_RESOURCE` capability. Exceptions to this are `Q_SYNC` and `Q_GETSTATS` (anyone can call these functions) as well as `Q_GETQUOTA` (the UID or GID (depending on type) must be the same as `id`).

`Q_GETQUOTA` – Supplies the quotas and their present usage. A non-authorized process may only call its own quotas.

`Q_GETSTATS` – addr is a pointer to a `dqstats` structure. However, only the number of used and free quotas is entered.

`Q_RSQUASH` – The value `addr` is entered in place of `type` in the `rsquash` field of the `dev` device.

`Q_SYNC` – A sync is executed on the list of quotas.

`Q_QUOTAON` – Enables the quotas for a file. `addr` holds the name of the file in which the quota values are saved (as `dqblk` structures); `type` is used as an index for the `mnt_quotas` array.

---

17 The macro is defined as `(((cmd)<<SUBCMDSHIFT) | ((type) & SUBCMDMASK))`.

Q_QUOTAOFF – Disables the quotas. With `type=-1`, all `mnt_quotas` quotas are disabled for the device.

The next three functions are treated in an extra subfunction. First we try to find the dquot structure (hash function), defined by `dev`, `id`, and `type`. If one does not exist, one is created and initialized. Otherwise, `cache_hits` is increased. `addr` is used as a pointer to a dqblk structure.

Q_SETQLIM – If `id>0`, all limits are set to the level submitted.

Q_SETUSE – The `curinodes` and `curblocks` values are set and if the soft limit is exceeded, the time limits are also updated.

Q_SETQUOTA – Combines the effect of the last two flags.

If `id==0` in the subfunction, the expiry times for the new structure are set (to the submitted values).

Implementation

The C library does not provide a syscall macro; the quota package must be used instead.

Errors

`EINVAL` – if `type` is greater than `MAXQUOTAS`.
`EPERM` – if an unauthorized process attempts to change other quotas or call a privileged command.
`ENOTBLK` – if `special` is not a block device.
`ESRCH` – if no matching quota structure could be found.

System call	write	POSIX
	read	

File: `fs/read write.c`
```
#include <linux/types.h>
long sys_read(unsigned int fd, char * buf,unsigned int count);
long sys_write(unsigned int fd, char * buf,unsigned int count);
```

`sys_read()` tries to read `count` bytes from the file `fd`. The bytes are filed in the memory `buf`. The system call `sys_write()` works with the same parameters, except that the bytes are written in the buffer. First we attempt to lock the corresponding area. It is important for an obligatory locking that the file has set the `IS_ISGID` bit, but not the `S_IXGRP` bit.

The number of bytes actually read or written is returned. In the case of EOF or an unsucessful locking, 0 is returned, and in the event of an error, a negative number. The corresponding file operations are the last to be called.

Implementation

Both system calls work with the syscall macro.

Errors

EBADF – if fd is invalid or the file has been opened incorrectly.
EINVAL – if there are no read or write rights for the file.

System call	readv	POSIX
	writev	

File: fs/read write.c
```
#include <linux/types.h>
#include <linux/uio.h>
long sys_readv(unsigned long fd, const struct iovec * vector,
        long count)
long sys_writev(unsigned long fd, const struct iovec * vector,
        long count)
```

Both functions read (or write) data via a file descriptor. The differences between the read/write functions is the type of buffers submitted. The iovec structure looks as follows:

```
struct iovec {
  void *iov_base;           /* pointer to a memory area   */
  __kernel_size_t iov_len;  /* size of memory area        */
};
```

The number of buffers is held in count, the upper limit being UIO_MAXIOV. The areas are checked one after the other for readability or writeability, their lengths are added, and the resulting area is checked for a lock (FLOCK).

If fd refers to a socket, the socket operations are used, otherwise the file operations are used. With sys_readv(), the buffers are filled one after the other through reading from the descriptor. Using sys_write() they are written one after the other into the descriptor.

If the file operations (see Section 6.2.9) offer no readv() or writev() operations, the buffers are processed one after the other with normal read() or write() calls.

The number of bytes actually read or written is returned. 0 is returned in the case of EOF, and a negative number in the event of an error.

Implementation

Both system calls work via the syscall macro.

Errors

EBADF – if fd is invalid or the file has been opened incorrectly.
EINVAL – if an invalid parameter has been submitted.

System call	pread	POSIX
	pwrite	

File: fs/read write.c
```
#include <linux/types.h>
long sys_pread(unsigned int fd, char * buf,
        size_t count, loff_t pos);
long sys_pwrite(unsigned int fd, const char * buf,
        size_t count, loff_t pos);
```

Both functions read (or write) data about a file descriptor. The difference between the well-known write-read functions is that it is not the current position that is used, but pos. The current position remains unchanged: The call carries out an lseek() on the new position, reads (or writes) count characters, and finally executes an lseek() on the old position.

The number of read or written bytes is returned, 0 in the case of EOF and a negative number in the event of an error.

Errors

EBADF – if fd is invalid or the file has been opened incorrectly.
EINVAL – if an invalid parameter has been submitted.

System call	readdir	POSIX
	getdents	LINUX

File: fs/readdir.c
```
int old_readdir (unsigned int fd, void * dirent,
                unsigned int count)
long sys_getdents(unsigned int fd, void * dirent,
                unsigned int count)
```

The old_readdir() function fills the structure to which dirent refers, with the data of the fd directory. The count parameter is ignored. The structure looks as follows:

```
struct linux_dirent {
        unsigned long              d_ino;
        unsigned long              d_off;
        unsigned short             d_reclen;
        char                       d_name[1];
};
```

LINUX forwards the call to the operations of the virtual file system by calling the appropriate file operation (see Section 6.2.9). The new improved sys_getdents() function has become available. It also introduces a new structure:

```
struct getdents_callback {
        struct linux_dirent * current_dir;
        struct linux_dirent * previous;
        int count;
        int error;
};
```

The function reads several entries, as long as the sum of their sizes (calculated from the offset of the current name and its length) does not exceed the value of count. The difference between count and the size of the entries actually read is returned.

Implementation

The system call sys_readdir() is mapped on old_readdir() in entry.S. Both system calls are used by the library function readdir(). The old old_readdir() call is called if no sys_getdents() is available. Both kernel functions are directly jumped into via the 0x80 interrupt.

Errors

EBADF – if fd is invalid.
ENOTDIR – if no sys_readdir() file operation exists.

System call	readlink	POSIX

File: fs/stat.c
```
long sys_readlink(const char *path, char *buf, int bufsize);
```

The sys_readlink() function reads the path to which a symbolic link refers.

A maximum of bufsize characters are stored in the buffer buf by the corresponding inode operation. No zero bit ("\0") is appended to the end of buf. The function returns the length of the path for this.

Implementation

The system call is converted via the syscall macro.

Errors

EINVAL – if bufsize is negative, the call is not supported by the file system or path is
   not a reference.
ENOENT – if path does not exist.

System call	select	4.3+BSD

File: fs/select.c
```
#include <linux/time.h>
#include <linux/types.h>
long sys_select(int n, fd_set *inp, fd_set *outp,
        fd_set *exp, struct timeval *tvp)
```

The sys_select() functions allows the multiplexing of input or output operations.
The time interval is coverted to jiffies and entered as the timeout of the process. The
process sleeps after the call until one of the descriptors in inp, outp, or exp or the time
span tvp has elapsed. The descriptors are therefore created as bit fields. The parameter n
contains the length of the bit field.

The functions return the number of available descriptors. If in personality the
STICKY_TIMEOUTS flag is set, tvp is also updated.

Several macros are defined for use:

FD_ZERO (*fdset*) – deletes all bits in *fdset*.

FD_CLR (*fd*, *fdset*) – deletes the descriptor *fd* in *fdset*.

FD_SET (*fd*, *fdset*) – sets the descriptor *fd* in *fdset*.

FD_ISSET (*fd*, *fdset*) – checks the descriptor *fd* in *fdset*. Returns a value unequal to 0
   if *fd* is set.

Implementation

The system call is converted via the syscall macro.

Errors

EBADF – if there is an invalid descriptor in one of the fields.
EINTR – if a non-blocking signal has been received.
EINVAL – if n is negative.

ENOMEM – if there is not enough memory for internal tables in the kernel.

System call	stat	newstat
	fstat	newlstat
	lstat	newfstat

File: `fs/stat.c`

```
#include <linux/stat.h>
long sys_stat (const char *file_name, struct old_stat *buf);
long sys_fstat (unsigned int fd, struct old_stat *buf);
long sys_lstat (const char *file_name, struct old_stat *buf);
```

 sys_stat(), sys_fstat(), and sys_lstat() return a filled data structure which contains information about the submitted file. There is a new structure (stat) that is defined in <asm/stat.h>. The old structure does not contain the fill bits and the values st_blocksize and st_blocks. With this new structure, the functions work with "new_."

```
struct stat {
    unsigned short st_dev;          /* device                */
    unsigned short __pad1;          /* fill size             */
    unsigned long st_ino;           /* inode                 */
    unsigned short st_mode;         /* access rights         */
    unsigned short st_nlink;        /* number of hard links  */
    unsigned short st_uid;          /* UID of owner          */
    unsigned short st_gid;          /* GID of owner          */
    unsigned short st_rdev;         /* device type           */
    unsigned short __pad2;          /* fill size             */
    unsigned long st_size;          /* size in bytes         */
    unsigned long st_blksize;       /* block size            */
    unsigned long st_blocks;        /* occupied blocks       */
    unsigned long st_atime;         /* time of last access   */
    unsigned long __unused1;        /* fill size             */
    unsigned long st_mtime;         /* time of last change
                                     * (file)                */
    unsigned long __unused2;        /* fill size             */
    unsigned long st_ctime;         /* time of last change
                                     * (inode)               */
    unsigned long __unused3;        /* file size             */
    unsigned long __unused4;        /* file size             */
    unsigned long __unused5;        /* file size             */
    unsigned int st_gen;            /* file size             */
};
```

sys_stat() returns the data for the file_name file. For references there is sys_lstat(); this function returns the data for the symbolic link itself. sys_fstat() is identical to sys_stat(), using a descriptor fd instead of a name.

All three calls determine the inode of the object submitted and call the kernel function cp_old_stat(). This reads most of the data from the inode. The new functions use cp_new_stat(). If the file system does not support st_blocks and st_blksize, these are determined by means of a simple algorithm.

Implementation

The system calls are converted via the syscall macro.

Errors

EBADF – if fd is invalid.
ENOENT – if file_name does not exist.

System call	statfs	SVR4
	fstatfs	

File: fs/open.c
```
#include <linux/vfs.h>
long sys_statfs(const char *path, struct statfs *buf);
long sys_fstatfs(unsigned int fd, struct statfs *buf);
```

The sys_statfs() function returns the information about the file system on which the file path is located. In sys_fstatfs() a descriptor is specified instead of the name. The structure buf is defined in the architecture-dependent statfs.h:

```
struct statfs {
  long    f_type;            /* type of file system        */
  long    f_bsize;           /* optimum block size         */
  long    f_blocks;          /* number of blocks           */
  long    f_bfree;           /* total number of free blocks */
  long    f_bavail;          /* free blocks for user       */
  long    f_files;           /* number of inodes           */
  long    f_ffree;           /* number of free inodes      */
  fsid_t f_fsid;             /* file system ID             */
  long    f_namelen;         /* max. filename length       */
  long    f_spare[6];        /* not used                   */
};
```

Fields which are not defined in the file system are set to -1. The data is read using superblock operations (see Section 6.2.3).

Implementation

The system call is converted via the syscall macro.

Errors

EBADF – if fd is not a valid descriptor.
EFAULT – if buf points to an invalid address.
ENOSYS – if no superblock operation is available.

System call	sync		SVR4
	fsync	fdatasync	4.3+BSD

File: fs/filemap.c

```
long sys_sync(void);
long sys_fsync(unsigned int fd);
long sys_fdatasync(unsigned int fd);
long sys_msync(unsigned long start, size_t len, int flags);
```

sys_sync() writes all information stored in the memory, such as buffers, superblocks, and inodes, to the disk. The functon always returns 0. The function works via fsync_dev() with 0 as a parameter. This means that all block devices are to be synchronized.

The sys_fsync() function writes the data stored in memory of the file fd. To do this, it calls fsync() and also locks access to the file using the inode semaphore. The sys_fdatasync() function has the same function as sys_fsync(), only the semaphore is not set. The sys_msync() function synchronizes the functions, which are displayed in the given memory area. First, the displayed areas are synchronized (calling vm_ops-> sync). With this, if MS_INVALIDATE is not set the file is written back memory page by memory page. If the MS_SYNC flag is then set the DEntry of the file is synchronized.

Implementation

Both system calls are converted via the syscall macro.

Errors

EBADF – if no file can be determined for fd.
EINVAL – if the file does not have any file operations or sync operations.

EFAULT – if the interval [start;start+len] contains areas in which no file is displayed (a sync is executed for the remainder anyway).

System call	sysfs	SVR4

File: fs/super.c

```
long sys_sysfs(int option, unsigned long arg1,
unsigned long arg2);
```

The sys_sysfs() function returns information about the file systems known to the kernel by reading the file_systems list. The option argument specifies the required function:

1 – The call returns the index of the specified file system. arg1 contains this name.

2 – The name of the specified (index-ten) file system is returned.

arg1 is the index, the name is put in arg2.

3 – The call returns the number of known file systems.

Implementation

There is as yet no interface in the C library.

Errors

EINVAL – if option, index, or name are invalid.

System call	truncate ftruncate	4.3+BSD

File: fs/open.c

```
long sys_truncate(const char *path, unsigned long len);
long sys_ftruncate(unsigned int fd, unsigned long len);
sys_truncate() shortens or lengthens the file path to the size of len bytes.
sys_ftruncate() carries out the same operation for the file behind fd.
```

The prerequisites are that it is not a directory and that the inode flags allow modification (shortening). Furthermore, there must be no lock on the area that is to be changed.

The quotas of the inode are updated, the corresponding inode operation is carried out, and ctime is updated. If the file is mapped into the memory, the corresponding memory area is modified.

Implementation

Both system calls are converted via the syscall macro.

Errors

EACCES – if the file path has no write access or is a directory.
EROFS – if the file is located in an IS_RDONLY file system.
EPERM – if the file is located in an IS_IMMUTABLE or IS_APPEND file system.
EBADF – if an invalid descriptor is used in sys_ftruncate().
ENOTDIR – if a part of path is not a directory.
ENOENT – if the file does not exist.

System call	uselib	LINUX

File: fs/exec.c
```
long sys_uselib(const char *library);
```

sys_uselib() selects a shared library for the current process. The file is opened with sys_open(), after which an attempt is made to execute the load_shlib() for each registered binary format. The first successful attempt terminates the call. It is important that both read and execution rights are set for the library file.

Implementation

The system call is converted via the syscall macro.

Errors

ENOEXEC – if no matching binary format could be found for library.
EACCES – if library cannot be read.

System call	umask	POSIX

File: kernel/sys.c
```
int sys_umask(int mask);
```

sys_umask() sets the mask for the access rights of a file. The value mask & S_IRWXUGO (0777) is used as a new mask. The old mask is returned. This mask is used in open_namei() when creating a file. The mode specified there is swapped with umask:

```
mode &= S_IALLUGO & ~current->fs->umask;
```

Implementation

The system call is converted via the syscall macro.

System call	ustat	LINUX

File: fs/super.c
```
long sys_ustat(dev_t dev, struct ustat * ubuf);
```

The call fills the ustat with the information of the superblock, which has entered dev as the device. This structure is architecture-dependent; its i386 source has the following structure:

```
struct ustat {
  long f_type;              /* magic number of the file system*/
  long f_bsize;             /* block size                      */
  long f_blocks;            /* number of blocks                */
  long f_bfree;             /* number of free blocks           */
  long f_bavail;            /* number of free and unreserved
                             * blocks                          */
  long f_files;             /* number of files                 */
  long f_ffree;             /* number of free inodes           */
  __kernel_fsid_t f_fsid;   /* ID (unused until now)           */
  long f_namelen;           /* max. name length                */
  long f_spare[6];          /* unused                          */
};
```

Implementation

Both system calls use the syscall macro.

Errors

EINVAL – if dev is an invalid device.
ENOSYS – if no statfs() exists for the superblock.

System call	utime	POSIX

File: fs/open.c
       fs/attr.c
```
#include <utime.h>
long sys_utime(char *filename, struct utimbuf *buf);
```

sys_utime() sets the time stamps for the file filename to the values specified in buf. The structure buf is defined as follows:

```
struct utimbuf {
  time_t actime;
  time_t modtime;
};
```

Both time specifications are in UNIX seconds, corresponding to sys_time(). With the execution, sys_utime() is set to CURRENT_TIME. If buf is NULL, all values are set to (CURRENT_TIME). The values are only set if the UID of the inode is the same as the FSUID of the process or if CAP_FOWNER is set.

Implementation

The system call is converted via the syscall macro.

Errors

ENOENT – if the file filename does not exist.
EROFS – if the file system of the file is labeled as *read only*.
EACCES – if the inode of the file cannot be changed.

System call	vhangup	LINUX

File: fs/open.c
long sys_vhangup(void);

sys_vhangup() executes a *hangup* for the current terminal. The call is, for example, used by init in order to provide users with a clean login terminal on which processes are not active. If successful, the call returns 0. To call this, the process has to have the CAP_SYS_TTY_CONFIG capability.

The called function tty_vhangup() is implemented in drivers/tty_io.c. In this, all processes that work with the terminal are woken up, the current session is closed, and the corresponding tty value of all processes is set to -1.

The function is only carried out if the current process actually possesses a terminal (current->tty).

The "v" in the name of the system call stands for *virtual*. This does not mean, however, that a hangup is simulated, but that this call is used for the virtual terminals.

Implementation

The system call is converted via the syscall macro.

Errors

EPERM – if a non-privileged user calls `sys_vhangup()`.

A.3	COMMUNICATION

There are only two system calls for communication. This may, at first sight, seem somewhat strange, but nevertheless, the entire gamut of commonly used system calls is available in the form of library functions.

Originally, the idea was to simplify the implementation through this summary. However, when it comes to putting the right parameters on the stack, things quickly become unfathomable. The usual system calls, such as *semget*, are therefore provided as library functions.

System call ipc	LINUX

```
File: arch/i386/kernel/sys i386.c
#include <linux/ipc.h>
int sys_ipc (uint call, int first, int second,
         int third, void *ptr, long fifth);
```

`sys_ipc()` allows full use of the SVR4 interprocess communication by means of a call. Because of a few differences between the individual architectures this call has drifted into the `arch` directory.

All system calls that work with message queues, shared memory, or semaphores are mapped to this system call. Since the implementation of the call is not exactly optimal, the individual calls are found as already finished kernel functions in the `ipc/` directory; however, they are not yet interchangable.

The parameter `call` specifies the exact function; in addition, the `IPCCALL (version,call)` macro can be used to hide a version number in `call`. The call values are defined in `<asm/ipc.h>`:

SEMOP – Function corresponds to `semop()`.

SEMGET – Function corresponds to `semget()`.

SEMCTL – Function corresponds to `semctl()`.

MSGSND – Function corresponds to `msgsnd()`.

MSGRCV – Function corresponds to `msgrcv()`. If `version` is equal to 0, an old `msgbuf` structure is ended and the parameters are converted.

MSGGET – Function corresponds to `msgget()`.

MSGCTL – Function corresponds to msgctl().

SHMAT – Function corresponds to shmat(). If version is equal to 1, iBCS2 is run and then tests whether FS and DS point to the same segment.

SHMDT – Function corresponds to shmdt().

SHMGET – Function corresponds to shmget().

SHMCTL – Function corresponds to shmctl().

The remaining parameters must be set accordingly to the specification of call. If during kernel compilation no CONFIG_SYSVIPC has been set, this call returns -ENOSYS.

Implementation

The library, of course, provides the usual functions for interprocess communication. They are mapped onto the library function ipc() which is defined via the syscall macro. The example below illustrates the implementation of the system call *semget()*:

```
int semget (key_t key, int nsems, int semflg)
{
        return __ipc (SEMGET, key, nsems, semflg, NULL);
}
```

Errors

EINVAL – if an invalid value is specified for call.

System call	socketcall	LINUX

File: net/socket.c
```
#include <linux/socketcall.h>
long sys_socketcall(int call, unsigned long *args);
```

Just as there is one system call for SVR4-IPC, there is a call that allows the entire programming of the sockets. The sys_socketcall() function makes it possible, by specifying a parameter, to implement all normal calls as library functions. The programming of the conversion of the args parameter shows the contrast between optimized and readable code.

The parameter call specifies the exact functionality. The following macros are defined in <linux/net.h>:

SYS_SOCKET – Function corresponds to socket().

SYS_BIND – Function corresponds to bind().

SYS_CONNECT – Function corresponds to connect().

SYS_LISTEN – Function corresponds to listen().

SYS_ACCEPT – Function corresponds to accept().

SYS_GETSOCKNAME – Function corresponds to getsockname().

SYS_GETPEERNAME – Function corresponds to getpeername().

SYS_SOCKETPAIR – Function corresponds to socketpair().

SYS_SEND – Function corresponds to send().

SYS_RECV – Function corresponds to recv().

SYS_SENDTO – Function corresponds to sendto().

SYS_RECVFROM – Function corresponds to recvfrom().

SYS_SHUTDOWN – Function corresponds to shutdown().

SYS_SETSOCKOPT – Function corresponds to setsockopt().

SYS_GETSOCKOPT – Function corresponds to getsockopt().

SYS_SENDMSG – Function corresponds to sendmsg().

SYS_RECVMSG – Function corresponds to recvmsg().

The required parameters must be set in args according to the specification of call.

Implementation

As with the IPC calls, the well-known socket functions are also called via the C library. As an example, we present socket(); the other functions are implemented in practically the same way.

```
static inline
_syscall2(long,socketcall,int,call,unsigned long *,args);
int sys_socket(int family, int type, int protocol)
{
        unsigned long args[3];
        args[0] = family; args[1] = type; args[2] = protocol;
        return socketcall(SYS_SOCKET, args);
}
```

Errors

EINVAL – if an invalid value is specified for call.

MEMORY MANAGEMENT

The next group describes the system calls for memory management. There are only a few calls, although this area is one of the most important in multitasking systems. On the other hand, the work connected with administration of memory is far from trivial, and the less (disruptive) influences there are, the more safely the system runs.

System call	madvise	LINUX

File: `mm/filemap.c`
```
#include <linux/mman.h>
long sys_madvise(unsigned long start, size_t len,
        int behavior)
```

With these functions, an application can influence the management of the virtual memory area. You can therefore adjust it so that, during access, the whole area is read first. The kernel only uses these adjustments as pointers; however, the correct process is not affected if another strategy is used. The memory area is addressed by the start address `start` and the size `len` and the desired strategy located in `behavior`. Possible values for this are:

`MADV_NORMAL` – During access, the whole cluster is read, which leads to a certain read-ahead and read-behind. This is the normal method.

`MADV_RANDOM` – During access, the system only reads the requested data. This method is useful if it is unlikely that the appliction will read more data.

`MADV_SEQUENTIAL` – During access, all pages of the area are read at once and then released as soon as possible afterwards.

`MADV_WILLNEED` – The application instructs the kernel to pre-read a few pages. This is only possible if the area relates to a displayed file.

`MADV_DONTNEED` – The application no longer accesses the area; the kernel can therefore release the affiliated resources. The kernel "throws" the resources away. Anyone requiring *dirty pages* should use `sys_msync()`.

For the conversion of the second and third strategies, a flag is entered in the `vm_flags` of the virtual memory area.

Errors

`EACCES` – if `start` plus `len` is less than 0 or `behavior` is invalid or if the application attempts to release locked or divided pages.

`ENOMEM` – if an address is not mapped into the given area or does not belong to the address space of the processor at all.

EIO – if an error occurs when setting out or removing a page.

EBADF – if the virtual memory area exists, but does not relate to a file.

EAGAIN – if a kernel resource is not available.

System call	mincore	LINUX

File: `mm/filemap.c`

```
asmlinkage long sys_mincore(unsigned long start, size_t len,
        unsigned char * vec);
```

sys_mincore() determines the status of the memory pages of the current process. The pages to be investigated are indicated by the [start, start + len] address interval. Their status is laid out in the vec vector. If the bottom bit of a byte is 1, the page is found in memory, or more precisely, it is located in the page cache and is valid. The start address must be a page border.

Because the condition of the pages can be changed by parallel memory requirements, the information is not valid for long. A guarantee can only be made for locked pages.

Errors

EFAULT – if vec points to an invalid address.

EINVAL – if addr does not lie on a page boundary or len is smaller than 0.

ENOMEM – if the [addr, addr + len] area contains invalid addresses or areas for the process that are not displayed.

EAGAIN – if the saving of the result in vec fails due to memory requirement.

System call	mmap munmap	4.3+BSD

File: `arch/i386/kernel/sys i386.c`
        `mm/mmap.c`

```
#include <linux/types.h>
#include <linux/mman.h>
long old_mmap(struct mmap_arg_struct *arg);
long sys_mmap2(unsigned long addr, unsigned long len,
        unsigned long prot, unsigned long flags,
        unsigned long fd, unsigned long pgoff);
long sys_munmap(unsigned long addr, size_t len);
```

old_mmap() displays a file in the memory. The old prefix has its foundations in the type of parameter transfer. With this, the function of the buffer is transferred to a field of values as the parameter. Correspondingly:

```
struct mmap_arg_struct {
  unsigned long addr;        /* address in the main memory    */
  unsigned long len;         /* size of area                  */
  unsigned long prot;        /* access rights to be entered   */
  unsigned long flags;       /* flags to be entered           */
  unsigned long fd;          /* file descriptor               */
  unsigned long offset;      /* offset in the file            */
};
```

The following values can be used as access rights:

PROT_EXEC – Pages can be executed.

PROT_READ – Pages can be read.

PROT_WRITE – Pages can be written to.

The parameter flags specifies the type and treatment of memory pages; the last four flags are LINUX-specific.

MAP_FIXED – The precise address must be used, and addr must be a multiple of the page size.

MAP_PRIVATE – Changes only affect the memory.

MAP_SHARED – Changes in the memory also affect the file.

MAP_ANONYMOUS – No file is mapped.

MAP_GROWSDOWN – The memory area is oriented towards the bottom (stack).

MAP_DENYWRITE – Direct write access to the file yields -ETXTBSY.

MAP_EXECUTABLE – The mapped memory area is marked as a library.

MAP_LOCKED – The memory area is locked.

MAP_NORESERVE – Before mapping, it is not tested whether enough memory is free.

In Intel systems the file descriptor is checked (except with MAP_ANONYMOUS), and the MAP_EXECUTABLE and MAP_DENYWRITE are masked out before the do_mmap2() function itself is called. sys_mmap() does the same as this, only here the parameters are transferred individually.

sys_unmap() swaps the file out and releases the memory used.

Implementation

The system call *sys_mmap()* is mapped to old_mmap() with Intel systems. The system call *munmap()* simply uses the syscall macro.

Errors

EACCES – if the values specified in the flags do not match the rights of the specified file.

EBADF – if no file is opened.

EINVAL – if an invalid value has been specified for the flags, or the sum of address and length exceeds the permitted process memory, or MAP_FIXED has been specified and the address addr is not a page boundary.

ENOMEM – if the address (with MAP_FIXED) is not available.

System call	mprotect	LINUX

File: mm/mprotect.c

```
#include <linux/types.h>
#include <linux/mman.h>
long sys_mprotect(unsigned long addr, size_t len,
        unsigned long prot);
```

This function allows the access protection for mapped areas to be modified at a later stage. The area is defined by the address addr, which must lie on a page boundary, and the size len. For prot, the values PROT_READ (for reading), PROT_WRITE (for writing), and PROT_EXEC (for execution) are allowed.

As the selected area must lie within the vma zones belonging to the process, the area that contains the start address is determined first. The rights are re-entered, and the old values are overwritten. After this, all further areas are modified via the linked list until the whole length of len has been reached.

Implementation

The system call is converted via the syscall macro.

Errors

EFAULT – if there is no matching vma zone.

EBADF – if a parameter is invalid.

EACCES – if prot contains an invalid value.

EINVAL – if the sum of addr and len exceed the permitted process memory.

System call	mremap	

File: mm/mremap.c

```
#include <linux/mman.h>
unsigned long sys_mremap(unsigned long addr,
        unsigned long old_len, unsigned long new_len,
```

```
unsigned long flags)
```

This function allows the size of a mapped memory area to be changed. The start address addr must lie on a page boundery. old_len specifies the old size, new_len the new size. The old area must not exceed the limit of a virtual memory area.

When the area is reduced, the freed area is mapped out with do_nmap(). When a locked memory area is increased, the process resources must not be exceeded. If there is enough space free up to the beginning of the next virtual memory area, the old area is enlarged. If the MREMAP_MAYMOVE flag is not set, an error is returned; otherwise, a new area of the required size is created, and the old area copied and released. The return value is the (new) address of the memory area.

Implementation

The C library does not provide an interface.

Errors

EINVAL – if addr does not lie on a page boundary.
EFAULT – if no virtual memory area can be found for the specified address or the size is spread over more than one area.
EAGAIN – if the RLIMIT_MEMLOCK process resource is exceeded.
ENOMEM – if there is not enough memory available for an increase.

System call	msync	POSIX

File: mm/filemap.c
```
long sys_msync(unsigned long start, size_t len,
int flags)
```

This function changes the flags of a mapped memory area. Its beginning is specified by start, its size by len. If no mapped area can be found at that location, an error is returned. As this call takes the local memory management peculiarities into account, it is extremely architecture-dependent. The following values can be specified as flags:

MS_SYNC – The cache buffer is written back and changes to the kernel segment are transferred to the user segment.

MS_ASYNC – The cache buffer is written back and a sync() call is sent to the inode of the mapped inode.

MS_INVALIDATE – The cache buffer is written back and the occupied areas are released.

Implementation

The system call is converted via the syscall macro.

Errors

EINVAL – one of the passed parameters is invalid or a part of the specified area is not mapped.

EFAULT – no virtual memory area can be found for `start`.

System call	sendfile	POSIX

File: `mm/filemap.c`

```
#include <linux/capability.h>
long sys_sendfile(int out_fd, int in_fd,
off_t *offset, size_t count);
```

If you wish to write data from one file[18] to another, this function is more suitable than a combined read/write function since the call runs completely in the kernel and therefore no data is copied between the different address spaces.

The function reads count bytes in the `in_fd` file from the offset position and writes them in `out_fd` in the current positions. Otherwise the normal read and write limits apply (no locks, etc.). Because of the address space (in contrast to `sys_read()`), the file operation `readpage()` is used instead of the inode operation `read()`.

Implementation

The system call is converted via the syscall macro.

Errors

EBADF – if a file descriptor is invalid.

EINVAL – if no `readpage` operation exists for the file.

EIO – if a read error occurs.

System call	swapon swapoff	LINUX

File: `mm/swapfile.c`

```
long sys_swapon (const char * specialfile, int swap_flags);
long sys_swapoff (const char *file);
```

---

18 A file can also be a device!

sys_swapon() switches the *swap* on. The file or block device specialfile is used as memory space. The SWAP_FLAG_PREFER flag can be set in swap_flags. The last three bytes are then interpreted as a priority, which fixes the sequence during the use of many swaps. If no priority is given, a static variable is read, which is automatically decremented with each access.

The call can only be executed by a process with the CAP_SYS_ADMIN privilege and can only be executed once for each specialfile. In total, a maximum MAX_SWAPFILES can be used at one time.

If sucessful, 0 is returned and a note is written to the console. Interestingly, when calling this function, you can receive the message Unable to start swapping: out of memory :-). The reason for this is that the kernel allocates a page before the initialization.

sys_swapoff() then switches the evacuation process off again. This call can also only be executed by a process having the CAP_SYS_ADMIN capability.

Implementation

Both system calls are converted via the syscall macro.

Errors

EPERM – if a non-privileged user calls the function.
EINVAL – if file exists, but is not a file or block device.
EBUSY – if file is already being used as the swap.
ENOMEM – if no memory is free. Two memory pages are required in the kernel for the initialization with sys_swapon().

A.5   ALL THAT REMAINS

Here we find the system calls which have not been implemented. However, in order to be able to work with programs and configuration scripts (such as the well-known configure from the world of GNU), a common interface has been implemented.

System call	acct	afs_syscall	
	break	ftime	idle
	lock	mpx	phys
	prof	profil	stty
	gtty	ulimit	

File: kernel/sys.c

These system calls are not implemented. When called, they return sys_ni_syscall().

```
asmlinkage long sys_ni_syscall(void)
{
        return -ENOSYS;
}
```

Implementation

The implementation is carried out via the syscall macro.

B KERNEL-RELATED COMMANDS

This chapter deals with *kernel-related* commands: in other words, with commands that use special properties of the LINUX kernel or operate directly with the kernel. As this is a rather elastic definition, we have made the decision to describe only the commands that have either been mentioned in the previous chapters or thematically belong to them.

Many programs, however, exist in different versions. Reasons for this are the large number of different distributions, and the widespread use of the freely available LINUX system. For this appendix we have selected programs that use special features of LINUX.

Some programs have versions that cooperate with the *Proc* file system. The advantages of such programs are the increased security and independence of the kernel. Thus, for example, the ps command (originally procps) does not need to access kernel memory (/dev/kmem) at all.

B.1   free – OVERVIEW OF THE SYSTEM'S MEMORY

The free program indicates the occupation of the available memory, differentiating between RAM and the swap memory. The display shows the total, used, and free sizes. Free also indicates, for the RAM area, the parts used as shared memory and as buffers. The following switches can be used:

-b values are displayed in bytes.
-k values are displayed in Kbytes.
-m values are displayed in megabytes.
-o in addition, a line displays the size of (free) RAM memory without (with) buffer memory.
-t a line of total sizes is displayed.
ssec free repeats its input every sec. sec can be specified as *float* in microsecond resolution.
-V The version is output.

```
$ free
              total      used      free    shared   buffers    cached
Mem:          30956     30512       444     15792      9372      9136
-/+ buffers:             12004     18952
Swap:         34236      4176     30060
```

This program works with the *Proc* file system. It reads the file `meminfo` and formats the result:

```
$ cat /proc/meminfo
          total:      used:      free:    shared:   buffers:  cached:
Mem:    31698944   31227904     471040   16183296   9584640  9351168
Swap:   35057664    4276224   30781440
```

B.2   ps – OUTPUT OF PROCESS STATISTICS

The ps command gives a synopsis of the process running in the system. This synopsis is only a "snapshot"; for continuous monitoring, top should be used.

In LINUX, the ps command reads its data from the *Proc* file system. As a result, it runs independently from the kernel version, and does not need special privileges or S bits. The options may begin with a minus sign "-", but this is not compulsory. The following options are available:

-O   The output is sorted. Several keys can be specified:

G   The sorting key is the TPGID.

J   The sorting key is the time spent in user mode (including the total time spent by the children).

K   The sorting key is the time spent in user mode.

M   The sorting key is the number of major faults of the process.

N   The sorting key is the number of major faults of the process and its children.

P   The sorting key is the PPID.

R   The sorting key is the size of unswapped memory.

S   The sorting key is the size of repeatedly used memory.

T   The sorting key is the start time.

U   The sorting key is the UID.

c   The sorting key is the command line.

f   The sorting key is the F field.

g   The sorting key is the PGRP.

j   The sorting key is the time spent in system mode (including the total time spent by the children).

k   The sorting key is the time spent in system mode.

m   The sorting key is the number of minor faults of the process.

n   The sorting key is the number of minor faults of the process and its children.

o   The sorting key is the SID.

p   The sorting key is the PID.

r   The sorting key is the RSS field.

s   The sorting key is the size of the physically occupied memory.

t   The sorting key is the TTY name.

u   The sorting key is the user name.

v   The sorting key is the sum of occupied virtual memory areas.

y   The sorting key is the priority of the process (nice value).

-S   *CPU time* and *page faults* are the values of the child process added.

-X   Stack and register occupation is displayed.

-a   Processes of other users are also displayed.

-c   The command name currently present in the task structure is displayed.

-e   In addition, the environment of the processes is displayed.

-f   The output is formatted like a tree, and in the process, child processes form the branches (see pstree at the end of the section).

-h   No headline is displayed.

-j   In addition, PPID, PGID, TPGID, and UID are displayed.

-l   A detailed display is generated.

-m   Memory data is generated.

-n   For the USER and WCHAN fields, the numeric values are displayed (UID and addresses).

-o   The output is not sorted.

-p   Memory-oriented values are not displayed in bytes, but in pages.

-r   Only running processes are displayed.

-s   In addition, set signal masks are displayed.

-u   User name and percentage of CPU and memory usage are displayed.

-v   In addition, virtual memory data is displayed.

-w   The complete command line of the process is displayed. If this option is not set, ps truncates the display to make it fit on one line; this option can be specified several times!

-x   Only processes without a controlling terminal are displayed.

-txx   Only processes connected to the terminal xx, are displayed.

All running processes or (if specified) a comma-separated list of PIDs are evaluated. According to the option that is used, ps has a different display format. Table B.1 shows a summary of the output of the individual options. The columns represent the option indicated, the rows the data displayed. The simple call of ps is the first (empty) column. Only one of the options j, l, s, u, v, m, and X can be specified at any one time. The options a, x, S, r, and n work in combination with the other options and do not modify the display format. The TTY, PID, and COMMAND rows have been omitted, as they are always output. The individual fields have the following meaning:

ALARM alarm timer of the process

BLOCKED the signal mask of signals blocked by the process

CATCHED the signal mask of the signals handled by the process

COMMAND the command line of the process

%CPU the ratio of system time (`stime`) and user time (`utime`)

DRS the RSS of the data segment

DSIZ size of the data segment

DT the number of data library pages accessed

EIP the EIP register

ESP the ESP register

FLAGS the flags of the process, now left-aligned

IGNORED the signal masks of signals ignored by the process

LIB the memory size of used shared libraries

LIM memory limit of the process; if no limit is set, xx is displayed.

MAJFLT number of page access faults leading to the corresponding pages being loaded from hard disk

%MEM memory occupied by the process (RSS) in proportion to existing memory (RAM only)

MINFLT number of page access faults where the requested page is already in the memory

NI the (converted) `priority` value of the process

NR see FLAGS

PAGEIN number of page access faults leading to the corresponding pages being loaded from hard disk (same as `MAJFLT`)

PGID process group of the process

PID process PID

PPID process PPID

PRI the (converted) `counter` value of the process

RSS size of the program in memory (in Kbytes)

SHRD size of the shared memory

SIGNAL signal received by the process (`task->signal`)

SID process SID

SIZE virtual memory size; the sum of virtual memory areas occupied

STACK start address of the stack

START start time of the process

STAT status of the process, with the following meaning:

   D process sleeps and cannot be woken up by a signal

   R process is active

   S process sleeps, but can be woken up by a signal

   T process is halted or runs with `ptrace`

   Z process is in zombie state

   Additional information can follow:

   W process has no pages in memory (RSS=0), but is not a zombie

   < `task->nice` is less than 0

   N `task->nice` is greater than 0

SWAP the swap memory used (in Kbytes); the -p option displays the size in pages
TIME the running time of the process
TMOUT the timeout set for the process
TPGID the process group for the process owning the terminal
TRS the RSS part of the text segment
TSIZ the size of the text segment
TTY the terminal connected to the process
UID the process EUID
USER the name belonging to process UID
WCHAN the current kernel routine the process is executing.

Table B.1: Options of the ps program

	u	j	s	v	m	l	X		u	j	s	v	m	l	X
ALARM							x	PPID		x				x	
BLOCKED			x					PRI						x	
CATCHED			x					RSS	x				x	x	
%CPU	x							SHRD						x	
DRS					x			SIGNAL			x				
DSIZ				x				SID		x					
DT					x			SIZE	x				x	x	
EIP						x		STACK							x
ESP						x		START	x						
FLAGS						x		STAT	x	x	x	x		x	x
IGNORED			x					SWAP					x		
LIB					x			TIME	x	x	x	x		x	x
LIM				x				TMOUT							x
MAJFLT					x			TPGID		x					
%MEM	x		x					TRS					x		
MINFLT					x			TSIZ				x			
NI						x		UID	x	x				x	
NR							x	USER	x						
PAGEIN					x			WCHAN						x	
PGID		x													

Normally, only the address is displayed. In order to obtain a reasonable display of the field, the `psupdate` program must be called. This generates a file `psdatabase` in the `etc` directory containing the kernel functions and their addresses in the kernel. Thus, `ps` can display the name of the function, not just its address.

For a graphic display of the process tree, there is the `pstree` program. It displays, starting with `init`, all processes in a tree structure, for example:

```
init-+-5*[agetty]
     |-amd
     |-crond
     |-gpm
     |-inetd-+-2*[in.rshd-tcsh-xterm-tcsh-vim]
     |               |-in.rshd-tcsh-xterm-tcsh
     |               |-nmbd
     |               '-smbd
     |-kflushd
     |-klogd
     |-kswapd
     |-lpd
     |-4*[nfsiod]
     |-rpc.mountd
     |-rpc.nfsd
     |-rpc.portmap
     |-4*[rsh]
     |-sendmail
     |-syslogd
     |-tcsh-startx-xinit-+-X
     |                                           '-fvwm-+-GoodStuff
     |                                                  |-xbiff
     |                                                  |-xload
     |                                                  '-xterm-tcsh
     |-timed
     |-update
     '-ypbind
```

B.3   top – THE CPU CHARTS

Similarly to `ps`, the `top` program provides an overview of the running system. However, `top` runs in a loop and displays a new overview every five seconds.

`top` has the following options:

d *xxx* top waits xxx seconds between its output. The interval may be a floating point number with microseconds of resolution.

q the waiting time is 0 seconds. With root privileges, the priority is set to -10, in order to avoid collisions with kswapd.

c instead of the command name, the whole command line is displayed.

S the displayed time is the total time of the process and its children. CTIME is (unfortunately) not displayed with the command line parameter.

i processes whose status is S or Z are not displayed.

s top runs in secure mode. Thus, the following interactive commands are no longer available: k (*kill*), r (*renice*) and s (*sleeping time*).

A call with the option -q lets top repeat the output without waiting. If the user is a superuser, the program runs with the highest possible priority.

While running, the program can be controlled by inputting commands. The following keys may be pressed:

Ⓜ The processes are sorted by %MEM.

Ⓟ The processes are sorted by %CPU.

Ⓢ The program displays the total time (including child processes, cumulative mode).

Ⓣ The processes are sorted by [C]TIME.

Ⓦ The current settings are saved in the file ~/.toprc.

Ⓒ Toggles between display of command name and entire command line.

Ⓕ The displayed fields can be modified.

Ⓗ A brief overview of the supported commands is output.

Ⓘ The processes in the *idle* status are displayed.

Ⓚ The user can send a signal to a process. The PID of the process and the signal are queried.

Ⓘ Switches on or turns off the display of *uptime* information (first line).

Ⓜ Switches on or turns off display of *free* information (fourth and fifth lines).

Ⓝ or # Modifies the number of processes displayed.

Ⓞ Modifies the order of the fields displayed.

Ⓠ Quits the program.

Ⓡ Sets a new priority for a process.

Ⓢ Allows the user to modify the time span between updates.

Ⓣ The display of process statistics (second and third lines) is switched on or off.

A mixture of uptime, free, and ps is output. In addition, a synopsis of all processes and the CPU load are displayed. The display is sorted in decreasing order of priority.

```
10:44am up 1:01, 5 users, load average: 0.02, 0.06, 0.09
55 processes: 52 sleeping, 1 running, 0 zombie, 2 stopped
CPU states: 4.1% user, 3.6% system, 7.7% nice, 92.3% idle
Mem: 30956K av, 30424K used, 532K free, 24636K shrd, 4164K buff
Swap: 34236K av, 0K used, 34236K free 10840K cach
```

PID	USER	PRI	NI	SIZE	RSS	STAT	%CPU	%MEM	TIME	COMMAND
352	magnus	18	0	688	688	R	5.5	2.2	0:01	top
107	root	5	0	5952	5952	S	1.8	19.2	1:39	X
111	root	2	0	1592	1592	S	0.4	5.1	0:04	xterm
1	root	0	0	520	520	S	0.0	1.6	0:01	init
2	root	0	0	0	0	SW	0.0	0.0	0:00	kflushd
3	root	-12	-12	0	0	SW<	0.0	0.0	0:00	kswapd

At the beginning, some indications are given as to the current state of the system. The first line contains times and system load analogous to uptime. The second line shows the number of processes, differentiating between the individual states. The third line gives information about the CPU time used (in percentages) for processes in user mode, for processes in system mode and with a negative nice value, as well as for the idle process.

The remaining fields correspond to the homonymous fields of the free (see Section B.1) and ps (see Section B.2) commands. They are, therefore, not explained in further detail.

B.4   init — PRIMUS INTER PARES

The init process with process number 1 is often called the parent of all processes. In LINUX, this is *not* the case, as this function is exercised by the *idle* process, but it is still called as such out of habit and also in the source.

The features described here refer to the program in version 2.75 which is compatible with System V. Its task is a controlled initialization of the system and the management of the start processes for the individual run levels. Several configurations can be specified in this file indicating different run levels. It is configured by means of the file /etc/inittab.

A run level is a predetermined software configuration of the system. The start processes are managed in a special structure as follows:

```
typedef struct _child_ {
  int flags;                /* entry status              */
  int exstat;               /* exit status               */
  int pid;                  /* process PID               */
  time_t tm;                /* last start time point     */
  int count;                /* starts in last 2 min.     */
  char id[8];               /* inittab-Id (clear)        */
  char rlevel[12];          /* run level                 */
  int action;               /* action (see below)        */
  char process[128];        /* command line              */
  struct _child_ *new;      /* new entry (new inittab)   */
```

```
    struct _child_ *next;        /* reference to next entry        */
} CHILD;
```

init is controlled by the file /etc/inittab. The file contains individual lines, each of which trigger an action for a predetermined event. A comment line begins with a #.

name:level:action:command

the individual elements have the following meaning:

name This is a label that defines the line clearly.

Old *init* versions (a.out and similar that were compiled with libraries before version 5.2.18) only allow two characters.

Warning: for *getty* or *login* processes, the name must match the end of the corresponding tty. The reason for this is that the name is used as an utmp entry – otherwise, *accounting* would not work (another reason for the limited size: The entry cannot exceed the size of utmp.ut_id).

level One or more run level(s) (a maximum of eleven) of the system. Possible values are the numbers 0 to 9 and the characters S, A, B, and C, where init does not distinguish between upper and lower case. The value S stands for single user mode. If the indication of the level is omitted, the action of the process is activated with each change of the run level. The level field is ignored for the *action* fields sysinit, boot, and bootwait.

action This tells the process when to execute the program specified by command. The following actions are recognized:

boot The command is executed once when the system is booted. The process does, however, wait for it to terminate, but continues evaluating the inittab file.

bootwait The command is executed once when the system is booted, and init waits for it to terminate; the file /etc/rc is usually executed in this way.

ctrlaltdel The command is started when Ctrl + Alt + ←[1] are pressed.

initdefault The level used when the system is booted. If this line is omitted, init asks for the level on the console when the system is booted. The *command* entry is ignored.

kbrequest The command is executed when a predetermined key combination is pressed. For this, KDSIGACCEPT must be configured in the source.

off Nothing is executed.

once The program is started once at the beginning of the level.

ondemand The program is always executed each time init changes to the corresponding run level. Usual levels for onedemand are A+, B+, and C+.

powerfail As powerwait, however, *init* does not wait for it to terminate.

powerfailnow The command is executed when the signal SIGPWR occurs and the entry L is found in /etc/powerstatus (for example, almost empty battery packs in laptops).

powerokwait The command is executed when the main power is restored (the signal SIGPWR and the entry "O" in /etc/powerstatus). Usually shutdown -c is called.

---

1 Also known as the "hacker's claw" or Three Finger Salute.

powerwait The command is executed when the `init` process receives the SIGP signal. With this signal, uninterruptible power supplies (UPS) indicate a main failure. Normally, a `shutdown` is executed.

respawn After it has terminated, the program is normally executed again. A classic candidate for this is `getty`.

sysinit The command is executed when the system is booted. These entries are executed before `boot` and `bootwait`.

wait The command is started once at the beginning of the level and `init` waits for the process to terminate.

command Here we find a UNIX command. A parameter instruction is possible. If the command begins with a plus sign, it is not entered in the files `wtmp` and `utmp`.

The processing of the file is carried out in the routine `read_inittab()`. It performs the following tasks: It reads the file `/etc/inittab`, creates a new child list, and terminates and starts the necessary processes. Reading the file is the easiest part; the file is read and decoded line by line. "#" is used as a run level for SYSVINT and the value "*" is used for BOOT and BOOTWAIT. A shell call is entered as the last entry. All children are managed in the list `newFamily`, and the old children are managed in `family`. If there are entries with the same ID in both lists, the new child is entered as `new` in the old. The list is read and built up at the same time. Finally, a double loop is run, and all unnecessary processes under `family` are completed. Therefore we send them a SIGINT the first time and a SIGTERM the second time. A question has still to be answered: What are the unnecessary processes?

These are all children that do not have a `new` entry or whose action field has changed, OneDemand entries in single user mode, and children that have set RUNNING in their flags. In the case of the remaining children, we copy flags, the PID, and the exit status into the new entry and by doing so we save the old values. After running the loop twice, we update the `wtmp` and `utmp` entries for the processes that have been completed. Thus, in principle, everything has been finished. Now we open the old list `family` again, set the pointer to `newFamily` and delete[2] the file `initrunlvl`. This is, depending on the configuration, under `/etc/` or `/var/log`.

If the `init` program is called, it first checks whether it has been called as `init` or as `telinit`. We will consider the second case later on.

```
if (getpid() == INITPID || !strcmp(p, "init.new") ||
!strcmp(p, "sh"))
{
```

The command line is examined for available parameters and `init boot` is entered as a command name. When the `init` process has been started, it opens a pipe with the fixed STATE_PIPE descriptor. If this pipe already exists, this is a reboot and we can read the old values from the pipe and then pass to `init_main()`.

---

2   If the file is a link, it is not deleted, but the file at which the link points is set to size 0.

```
if (check_pipe(STATE_PIPE)) {
        [...]
        reload = 1;
        init_main();
}
```

If the pipe does not yet exist, we must evaluate the arguments of the command line:

```
[...]
maxproclen = strlen(argv[0]) + 1;
  for(f = 1; f < argc; f++) {
  if (!strcmp(argv[f], "single") ||
      !strcmp(argv[f], "-s"))
  dfl_level = 'S';
  else if (!strcmp(argv[f], "-a") ||
  !strcmp(argv[f], "auto"))
  putenv("AUTOBOOT=YES");
  else if (!strcmp(argv[f], "-b") ||
  !strcmp(argv[f], "emergency"))
  emerg_shell = 1;
  else if (strchr("0123456789sS", argv[f][0]) &&
  strlen(argv[f]) == 1)
  dfl_level = argv[f][0];
  /* "init u" in the very beginning makes no sense */
  if (dfl_level == 's') dfl_level = 'S';
  maxproclen += strlen(argv[f]) + 1;
}
  maxproclen--;
  argv0 = argv[0];
  argv[1] = NULL;
  setproctitle("init boot");
  init_main(dflLevel);
}
```

The function `init_main()` undertakes the main part of the work. In the process it has to distinguish between the first start of `initv` at the boot of the system and a restart. The following code is only executed when `reload` is not set.

Because a debugging of the `init` process is not possible because of the (quite sensible) features of the system call *ptrace*, the flag **INITDEBUG** can be set during the conversion. By doing so, the program code that executes a `fork()` at this point is activated, allowing it to be monitored.

---

3 The kind of key combination depends on the configuration of the keyboard; further information in the
   kbd packages.

```
#if INITDEBUG
  if ((f = fork()) > 0) {
      while(wait(&st) != f) ;
      [...]
}
#endif
```

Then the kernel is informed that by pressing the key combination Ctrl + Alt + ← we would like to obtain a `SIGINT` signal and with a special key combination[3] a `SIGWINCH` signal. We ignore all signals the first time.

```
init_reboot(BMAGIC_SOFT);
if ((f = open(VT_MASTER, O_RDWR | O_NOCTTY)) >= 0) {
    (void) ioctl(f, KDSIGACCEPT, SIGWINCH);
    close(f);
} else
    (void) ioctl(0, KDSIGACCEPT, SIGWINCH);
/*
 *      Ignore all signals.
 */
for(f = 1; f <= NSIG; f++) signal(f, SIG_IGN);
```

Thus the part that is only executed during the boot is completed. At this point we enter the handling routine for the ALARM, HUP, INT, CHLD, PWR, WINCH, USR1, STOP, TSTP, CONT, and SEGV signals:

```
SETSIG(sa,    SIGALRM,      signal_handler);
SETSIG(sa,    SIGHUP,       signal_handler);
SETSIG(sa,    SIGINT,       signal_handler);
SETSIG(sa,    SIGCHLD,      chld_handler);
SETSIG(sa,    SIGPWR,       signal_handler);
SETSIG(sa,    SIGWINCH,     signal_handler);
SETSIG(sa,    SIGUSR1,      signal_handler);
SETSIG(sa,    SIGSTOP,      stop_handler);
SETSIG(sa,    SIGTSTP,      stop_handler);
SETSIG(sa,    SIGCONT,      cont_handler);
SETSIG(sa,    SIGSEGV,      segv_handler);
```

The routine `signal_handler()` sets the signal in a global bit mask `got_signals()`; the routines `cont_` and `stop_handler()` create a semaphore, and `segv_` provides an output via `syslog()` and lands in an endless loop. The `chld` handler is a bit more complex. It determines which child has died using the PID. Then it enters the signal in `exstat` and sets ZOMBIE in the `flags`. If the child has a new entry, both values are also set.

---

3 The kind of key combination depends on the configuration of the keyboard; further information in the kbd packages.

Now we distinguish between first start and the restart. In the first case, the standard inputs and outputs as well as the standard error outputs are closed, and the console is initialized via SetTerm(). The values (speed and flags) are read from the file /etc/ioctl.save, if it exists. The program enters itself as the leader of a new process group and initializes a PATH variable.

As well as this, the *utmp* file is created again – and says4 "Hello."

```
close(0); close(1); close(2);
if ((s = getenv("CONSOLE")) != NULL)
        console_dev = s;
SetTerm(0); setsid();
if (getenv("PATH") == NULL) putenv(PATH_DFL);
(void) close(open(UTMP_FILE, O_WRONLY|O_CREAT|O_TRUNC, 0644));
Log(L_CO, bootmsg);
```

For systems with special safety requirements, it is also possible to start a shell via the sulogin program before *anything* is done, by issuing -b. sulogin asks for the root password and starts a shell (which can be set via SUSHELL) – by default the one written in /etc/passwd or /bin/sh. When the shell is completed, the normal boot process continues.

```
if (emerg_shell) {
  SETSIG(sa, SIGCHLD, SIG_DFL);
      if (spawn(&ch_emerg, &f) > 0) {
        while(wait(&st) != f)
                ;
        }
  SETSIG(sa, SIGCHLD, chld_handler);
}
```

The boot process appears as follows: first, init reads its inittab configuration file.

```
runlevel = '#';
read_inittab();
```

By doing so, the part that is only executed by booting the system is exited. All signals are unblocked during a reboot. Then all the required processes are started.

```
} else {
    /* Reboot: signals unblocked and then further*/
    log(L_CO, bootmsg);
    sigfillset(&sgt);
    sigprocmask(SIG_UNBLOCK, &sgt, NULL);
}
  start_if_needed();
```

4 The function Log() issues the string over the syslog daemon or the console.

After all necessary processes have been started, `init` enters a loop in which the transitions from the start (`runlevel='#'`) are made into normal operations by booting (`runlevel='*'`).

If no more processes are running and no signals are received, the control FIFO is checked.

```
while(1) {
  boot_transitions();
  for(ch = family; ch; ch = ch->next)
  if ((ch->flags & RUNNING ) && ch->action != BOOT ) break;
  if (ch != NULL && got_signals == 0) check_init_fifo();
```

Using this pipe (`/dev/initctl`) `init` can also be controlled. Programs (`telnetd`) can enter requests in the file and thus trigger various actions.

A request has the following structure:

```
struct init_request {
int magic;                    /* magic number                */
int cmd;                      /* kind of request             */
int run level;                /* new runlevel                */
int sleeptime;                /* time between TERM and KILL   */
char gen_id[8];               /* not used                    */
char tty_id[16];              /* TTY name without /dev/tty    */
char host[MAXHOSTNAMELEN];    /* host name                   */
char term_type[16];           /* terminal type               */
int signal;                   /* signal to be sent           */
int pid;                      /* and its receiver            */
char exec_name[128];          /* program to be executed      */
char reserved[128];           /* future extensions           */
};
```

Up to now, however, only four kinds of request are known:

INIT_CMD_RUNLVL – The new `sleeptime` is entered and then changed to the desired level.

INIT_CMD_POWERFAIL – The new `sleeptime` is entered and the commands belonging to the POWERFAIL action are started.

INIT_CMD_POWERFAILNOW – The new `sleeptime` is entered and the commands belonging to the POWERFAILNOW action are started.

INIT_CMD_POWEROK – the new `sleeptime` is entered and the commands belonging to the POWEROK action are started.

The next function has the following background: If `init` notes that *respawn* processes are to be called very often during a short period of time (ten times within two minutes), an error is assumed and the `inittab` entry is deactivated for five minutes. This prevents unnecessary system loads in case of an incorrect `inittab` entry. `fail_check()` reactivates the entries after five minutes.

```
fail_check();
```

If `init` receives a signal, depending on the kind of signal, the processes specified in `inittab` are activated. Most signals are processed not when the signal is met, but by setting the signal number to a bit mask and then centrally evaluating it.

SIGALRM Nothing happens.

SIGCHLD A child process has terminated. The flags `RUNNING`, `ZOMBIE`, and `WAITING` are deleted and the `utmp` and `wtmp` files updated.

SIGHUP `init` tries to read the new run level `/etc/initrunlvl`. If it does not exist, the old level is used again. In addition, the inittab file is re-read and all "sleepers" (`fail_cancel()`) are woken.

SIGINT The program belonging to `ctrlaltdel` is activated.

SIGPWR The file `/etc/powerstatus` is read and deleted. The `do_power_fail()` function activates the appropriate commands.

SIGUSR1 The `/dev/initctl` control pipe is closed and opened again.

SIGWINCH The program belonging to `kbrequest` is activated.

When the signals received are processed, the necessary processes are started and the loop is nearing its end:

```
        /* process signals */
        process_signals();
        /* start the processes */
        start_if_needed();
    } /* while */
} /* init_main() */
```

Thus the `init_main()` function is complete. Now back to the case that `init` or `telinit` is called to change the run level. This is only permitted for the superuser. After the compulsory syntax check, two strategies are employed. First, a request is assembled and written to the control FIFO. This attempt is encapsulated by an `alarm()` to avoid blocking.

```
signal(SIGALRM, signal_handler);
alarm(3);
if ((fd = open(INIT_FIFO, O_WRONLY)) >= 0 &&
write(fd, &request, sizeof(request))
== sizeof(request)) {
close(fd); alarm(0); return 0;
}
```

If this attempt fails, the "traditional" way is used: the new run level is saved in the file `/etc/initrunlvl` and a `SIGHUP` is sent.

The program `telinit` is a link to `init`. It is used to change the run level from the command line. The following arguments can be specified:

`0–6` Change to the specific run level.

`a–c` Only those processes are executed that have the specified run level in inittab.

`Qq` The inittab file is re-read.

`Ss` The system changes to the single user mode.

`Uu` `init` is executed (with `execl()`) again.

`-t` *sec* With the option `-t` *sec* the waiting time between the signals `SIGTERM` and `SIGKILL` can be changed. The default is 20 seconds.

B.5   shutdown – SHUTTING DOWN THE SYSTEM

The `shutdown` program safely shuts the system down. All users are warned and `login` is blocked.

`shutdown [-t` *sec*`] [-rkhncfF] [-i` *level*`] [-g]` *time* [*message*]

The following options can be used:

-a   The access control is activated.

-c   A running `shutdown` is aborted. Obviously, no time can be indicated; a message is, however, possible.

-f   No `fsck` is executed during the startup of the system (*fast reboot*).

-F   No `fsck` is executed in any case during the startup of the system.

-g   Time specification according to the old syntax.

-h   After shutdown, the system halts.

-i   The system changes into the run level indicated.

-k   The shutdown is simulated, and only the corresponding messages are issued.

-n   No use is made of `init`; instead, `shutdown` shuts the system down itself. The option is only possible with `-h` or `-r`.

-r   Is rebooted after shutdown.

-t*sec*   The program waits *sec* seconds between the sending of the signals `SIGTERM` and `SIGKILL` to all processes.

time   The time at which `shutdown` shuts the system down.

message   This message is issued to all users when `shutdown` is called.

The argument *time* has two different formats. It can be indicated in the form of *hh:mm* (%d:%2d), where *hh* stands for hours and *mm* for minutes. Or the format is *+m*, where *m* is the number of minutes. The specification *now* is an alias for +0.

When called, `shutdown` first of all sets its UID to its effective UID. If the UID is not 0 after this, the program aborts. It only works with root-rights. The command line parameters are then evaluated.

If the /etc/shutdown.allow file is available and can be read, and the use of access control was activated, the file is read. Within this there are the users that can shut the system down. If this file is not present, only the superuser has the right to shut the system down. The length of this file is limited to 32 lines. All users are identified and compared with the authorized users. Remote users are excluded. Users are recognized by their login names. Root is implicitly authorized (but not as a remote user).

In addition to this, an attempt is made to determine the process number of an already running shutdown from the /etc/shutdownpid file. If a shutdown is already running and the -c option is set, the shutdown that is running is completed by being sent a SIGINT.

If the option is not set, and a process with this PID is available, the program aborts. Now the file is created, its own PID is stored, and all signals except SIGINT blocked. When shutdown receives a SIGINT, it deletes all files it has created and calls exit(0). The program changes to the root directory. If the option -f was indicated, the file /fastboot is created, and with the option -F the file /forcefsck is created.

As a last step, the time is evaluated. If it is now or +0, the function shutdown() is called immediately. Otherwise, the program waits and, fifteen minutes after the download, begins to issue warnings. As well as this, the login is blocked creating the /etc/nologin.

The shutdown() then goes into the required run level. It issues a last warning. If the option -k is set, all created files are deleted and the program is exited.

With -n (without the deviation via init) all processes are exited in the usual manner (SIGTERM plus SIGKILL), the script /etc/rc.d/rc.halt is executed (if present), and finally the system is halted (or rebooted). Otherwise, shutdown() assembles a command line and calls the init program. Using the option -h this leads to a transition into run level 0, and with option -r into run level 6. If none of the options are specified, the system changes into run level 1. This may possibly lead to a nasty surprise: some old inittab files sometimes contain the line "x1:6:wait:/etc/rc.d/rc.6". Thus, after a shutdown -r, one finds oneself in front of the X login, instead of the computer booting.[5]

B.6 strace – MONITORING A PROCESS

The detection of errors in programs is a tiresome business. Often there is a desire to have a summary of all system calls executed, together with their parameters. This is exactly what strace provides.

```
strace [ -dffhiqrtttTvVxx ] [ -a column ] [ -e expr ]
        [ -o filename ] [ -p pid ]
        [ -s strsize ] [ -u username ]
        command
strace -c [ -e expr ] [ -O overhead ]
            [ -S sortby ] command
```

---

5 Note: Imitation not exactly recommended.

The strace program monitors the execution of the command *command*. It registers system calls and signals. Output is made using the standard error output, or in the case of the option -o, in a file.

Each output line contains a system call, its arguments (in parentheses), and the return value. In the case of an error (return value == -1) the error number is given as a symbolic name, together with its description (for example "EINVAL(Invalid Argument)"). Signals are indicated by their names.

Arguments are output, if possible, in readable form. Pointers to structures are dereferenced and their components and contents indicated in curly brackets. Pointers to strings are also dereferenced and the string is displayed in quotation marks. Non-printable characters are output as escape sequences, as is usual in C, while curly brackets are used for structures, and arrays are indicated by square brackets.

In order to control monitoring more precisely, there is a multitude of options. Thus it is possible, for example, to restrict monitoring to certain system calls or to follow child processes generated by fork().

The following options are possible:

-c   strace generates a time statistic for each system call and outputs them at the end.

-d   strace works in debugging mode and outputs information itself.

-f   If a monitored process generates children by means of fork(), these are monitored in their turn.

-ff   works together with -o *filename*. Each child process writes its output into the file *filename.pid*, where *pid* is the child's PID. The option -f is switched on in addition.

-h   Help about usage is displayed.

-i   At the beginning of each line, the instruction pointer (EIP) is output.

-q   Information on halting and releasing processes is suppressed. This is done automatically, if the output is not redirected to a file. This option is meaningful only if used in conjunction with -f or -p *pid*, as only then are processes controlled by means of ptrace(PTRACE_ATTACH,pid,data); see also page 302).

-r   For each system call, the time passed since the previous call is output in seconds and microseconds.

-t   Each line begins with the current time in the format HH:MM:SS.

-tt   In addition, microseconds are output.

-ttt Each line begins with the current time in seconds and microseconds.

-T   The time used by the system call is displayed, measured between call and return.

-v   All complex data, such as argument vectors and structures, are displayed to their full extent. Otherwise, only the first components or characters are shown.

-V   strace displays its version number.

-x   Non-printable characters in strings are output in hexadecimal format.

-xx   All characters in strings are output in hexadecimal format.

-a *column* The return value of the system call is written in the column *column*; the default is 40.

-e *expr* Here, an expression *expr* can be specified, which controls the trace procedure more precisely. The expression has the following format:

[*type*=] [!]*value1* [,*value2*]...

the type can be trace, abbrev, verbose, raw, signal, fault, read or write depending on the type; the value can be a name or a number. The default type is trace. An exclamation mark negates the value. An example: -e open, which corresponds to -e trace=open, only traces the open() calls – as opposed to -e trace=!open, where all calls are traced except open(). In addition, there are two special cases: all and none.

abbrev=*set* Influences the display of individual components of large structures. The -v option sets abbrev=none. The default is all.

faults Erroneous memory access attempts are displayed as well. This option works only with SystemV!

raw=*set* Displays the arguments of the calls specified in *set* uncoded in hexadecimal format.

read=*set* For all read operations on the file descriptor *set*, a dump is output in both ASCII and hexadecimal format.

signal=*set* Only the signals specified in *set* are traced. The default is all.

trace=*set* Only the calls specified in *set* are traced. The default is all. The following classes can be specified as *set*:

file All system calls are traced that belong to the file system. These are:

```
access(), acct(), chdir(), chmod(), chown(),
chroot(), creat(), execve(), link(), lstat(),
mkdir(), mknod(), mount(), open(), readlink(),
rename(), rmdir(), stat(), statfs(), swapon(),
symlink(), truncate(), umount(), unlink(),
uselib(), utime()
```

ipc All system calls are traced that belong to the IPC (SystemV). These are:

```
msgctl(), msgget(), msgrcv(), msgsnd(), semctl(),
semget(), semop(), shmat(), shmctl(), shmdt(),
shmget()
```

network All system calls are traced that belong to network communication. These are:

```
accept(), bind(), connect(), getpeername(),
getsockname(), getsockopt(), listen(), recv(),
recvfrom(), recvmsg(), send(), sendmsg() sendto(),
setsockopt(), shutdown(), socket(), socketpair()
```

process All system calls are traced that belong to process administration. These are:

```
_exit(), fork(), waitpid(),
execve(), wait4(), clone()
```

signal All system calls are traced that belong to signal handling. These are:

```
pause(), kill(), signal(), sigaction(),
siggetmask(), sigsetmask(), sigsuspend(),
sigpending(), sigreturn() und sigprocmask()
```

verbose=*set* controls the display of arguments for system calls as pointers or as dereferenced structures. For *set*, the structures are displayed to their full extent, for the remainder, only the pointers as hexadecimal addresses. The default is all.

write=*set* For all write operations on the file descriptor *set*, a dump is output in both ASCII and hexadecimal formats.

-o *filename* The output is redirected to the file *filename*, or, with -ff set, to the file *filename.pid*.

-p *pid* The process *pid* has to be monitored.

-O *Overhead* Through the monitoring of system calls, an overhead is generated that distorts the statistics with -c. The value, heuristically determined by the program itself can be corrected here. The precision may be checked by the user him/herself by determining the system time used by the program to be monitored with the time program and comparing it with the values determined by -c. The overhead value is indicated in microseconds.

-s *strsize* By default, only the first 32 characters of strings are output. This can be changed by using this option.

-S *sortby* The table obtained with -c is sorted by the *sortby* column. Possible values are time, calls, name, and nothing. The default is time.

A final example:

```
# strace sync
execve("/bin/sync", ["sync"], [/* 32 vars */]) = 0
sync() = 0
_exit(0) = ?
```

B.7   CONFIGURING THE NETWORK INTERFACE

The network interface is configured by ifconfig. Normally, it is executed whilst the system is being rebooted and sets the parameters of the network devices.

ifconfig [*interface* [[*options* ...] *address*]]

If ifconfig is called without parameters, the current configuration of the network interface is displayed. Otherwise, the interface with the specified *options* parameters is configured to the IP address *address*. The following parameters are allowed:

interface The name of the interface (for example, lo or eth0).

up   The interface is activated. If a new address is specified (see below), this option is set implicitly.

down The interface is switched off.

metric *N* The parameter sets the interface metrics to the value N. It should be set to 0.

mtu *N* The parameter sets the maximum packet size.[6] For Ethernet cards, a value between 1,000 and 2,000 is suitable, for SLIP a value between 200 and 4,096.

[-]arp The use of the ARP protocol is switched on or off. If preceded by a minus sign(-), the protocol is switched off.

[-]trailer This option is ignored by LINUX.

broadcast *aa.bb.cc.dd* The address is entered as the broadcast address for the interface.

dstaddr *aa.bb.cc.dd* Sets the specified address for a point-to-point connection (PPP) as "another end." This option is currently not supported.

netmask *aa.bb.cc.dd* The value is entered as a network mask for the interface.

B.8   traceroute – ARIADNE'S PATHS IN THE INTERNET

The internet is a worldwide conglomeration of extremely different networks. This makes the occurrence of connection problems unavoidable. In order to look more deeply into such problems as "network unreachable" the traceroute program has been developed.

traceroute [-dnrv] [-m *max'ttl*] [-p *port#*] [-q *nqueries*]
[-s *src'addr*] [-t *tos*] [-w *wait*] host [data size]

traceroute traces the route of UDP packets from source to destination. The destination address can be specified as a computer name or IP address. The program uses two techniques to trace the route of packets: a time stamp (a small TTL value [7]) and an invalid port address.

The first technique finds the route to the destination computer. Each gateway in the internet that receives an IP packet decrements a TTL value and when it has reached 0, sends back an ICMP packet of the type ICMP_TIMXCEED. When it starts, traceroute sends its packets with a TTL value 1 and increments it with each ICMP_TIMXCEED message received. In addition, when traceroute receives the packet, it displays a status line for the gateway:

8 bnl-pppl.es.net (134.55.9.33) 516 ms 687 ms 771 ms

The line contains the TTL value, the name of the computer that originated the message, its IP address, and the transmission times (traceroute always sends three packets).

When the UDP packet has reached the specified destination, the destination computer sends back an ICMP packet of the type ICMP_UNREACH. The reason for this is that traceroute uses packets that contain an invalid port number (33.434) in order to generate this error. The program uses the following options:

-d The debug flag is set in the sock structure. This causes more information to be displayed.

6 MTU – Maximal Transfer Unit.
7 TTL – Time To Life.

-m *ttl* ttl is used as the maximum time stamp. This allows the range to be preset. The default value is 30.

-n The program only displays the IP address and not the domain name of the destination computer.

-p *port* port sets the port number used. The default value is 33,434.

-q *nqueries* The number of packets to be sent per computer, usually three packets.

-r traceroute tries, by going round the route tables, to deliver the packet directly. This is achieved by setting the localroute flag in the sock structure. If the destination cannot be reached directly, an error message is returned.

-s *addr* *addr* is used as address for the source. An internet address must be specified, and not a domain name. If a computer has more than one address, this may be used to change the sender's address. If the specified value is invalid for the machine, an error is returned.

-t *tos* Enters *tos* into the IP packet as *type of service*. Values between 0 and 255 are allowed; additional information can be found in the IP specification.

-v All packets that have been received are displayed, not only those returned with TIME_EXCEEDED and UNREACHABLE.

-w *n* Sets the waiting time for the answer to *n* seconds. The default is 5. If no ICMP packet is received within the specified waiting time, an asterisk (*) is displayed for the corresponding tests.

An example[8] for the execution of a traceroute call:

```
# ./traceroute ice3.ori.u-tokyo.ac.jp
traceroute to ice3.ori.u-tokyo.ac.jp (157.82.132.65),
       30 hops max, 40 byte packets
  1 delta.informatik.hu-berlin.de (141.20.20.19) 6 ms 4 ms 4 ms
  2 141.20.20.9 (141.20.20.9) 4 ms 4 ms 4 ms
  3 192.2.6.2 (192.2.6.2) 98 ms 41 ms 33 ms
  4 Berlin1.WiN-IP.DFN.DE (188.1.132.250) 653 ms 549 ms 1037 ms
  5 ipgate2.WiN-IP.DFN.DE (188.1.133.62) 856 ms 669 ms 559 ms
  6 usgate.win-ip.dfn.de (193.174.74.65) 466 ms 392 ms 506 ms
  7 ppp1-frg.es.net (192.188.33.9) 2288 ms 2964 ms 1057 ms
  8 umd2-ppp12.es.net (134.55.12.162) 361 ms 1375 ms 1441 ms
  9 umd1-e-umd2.es.net (134.55.13.33) 1669 ms 2334 ms *
 10 ppp1-umd.es.net (134.55.6.34) 1421 ms 1346 ms 1477 ms
 11 llnl-ppp1.es.net (134.55.5.97) 1970 ms 1440 ms *
 12 * ames-llnl.es.net (134.55.4.161) 1255 ms 2781 ms
 13 ARC5.NSN.NASA.GOV (192.203.230.12) 2499 ms 2353 ms 2223 ms
 14 132.160.252.2 (132.160.252.2) 2417 ms 1798 ms *
 15 tko3gw.tisn.ad.jp (133.11.208.3) 1738 ms 1141 ms 1053 ms
 16 uts4gw.tisn.ad.jp (133.11.210.2) 1575 ms 1505 ms 1498 ms
```

8 If you really want to know: 132.160.252.2 is a computer in Hawaii.

```
17  ncgw.nc.u-tokyo.ac.jp (133.11.127.127) 1740 ms 1677 ms 1170 ms
18  hongogw.nc.u-tokyo.ac.jp (130.69.254.3) 1222 ms * *
19  nakanogw.nc.u-tokyo.ac.jp (157.82.128.2) 1380 ms 594 ms 680 ms
20  origw1.nc.u-tokyo.ac.jp (157.82.128.65) 1770 ms 2006 ms 1650 ms
21  origw3.nc.u-tokyo.ac.jp (157.82.129.3) 2669 ms 854 ms 1254 ms
22  * ice3.ori.u-tokyo.ac.jp (157.82.132.65) 1262 ms *
```

traceroute inserts an exclamation mark (!) in the output of the time duration to indicate problems.

! The port cannot be reached (ICMP_UNREACH_PORT), and the returning ttl value is less than 2.

!F Fragmentation is needed (ICMP_UNREACH_NEEDFRAG).

!P A protocol error occurred (ICMP_UNREACH_PROTOCOL).

!H The computer is unreachable (ICMP_UNREACH_HOST).

!N The network is unreachable (ICMP_UNREACH_NET).

!S Use of the source address failed (ICMP_UNREACH_SRCFAIL).

B.9   CONFIGURING A SERIAL INTERFACE

The setserial program (version 2.12) sets or reads the parameter and flags of a serial interface. With this, port number and IRQ can be modified. If an already occupied IRQ is specified, setserial returns the error message Device busy.

```
setserial [ -abqvVW ] device [ opt [ arg ] ] ...
setserial -g [ -abv ] device1 ...
```

The following options can be specified:

-a   All parameters of the device are displayed.
-b   The default settings (port, IRQ, and UART) are displayed.
-g   A list of devices can be specified.
-q   No display is generated with -W set.
-v   After setting the device, its new data is displayed.
-V   The program only displays its version number.
-W   Tries to find all unused interrupts (and displays them with -va).

The following options may be specified, if necessary. Numbers can be specified in several formats (decimal, octal, or hexadecimal). A ^ in front of an option negates it.

[^]auto_irq During auto-configuration an attempt was made to establish the IRQ.

[^]callout_nohup If the device was opened as *callout*, no hangup() is executed when it is closed (only if ASYNC_CALLOUT_NOHUP was configured).

[^]fourport Configures the port as AST Fourport.

[^]pgrp_lockout Only one process group can access the cua port, others are locked out.

[^]sak The *secure attention key* is used.

[^]session_lockout Only one session group can access the cua port, others are locked out.

[^]skip_test During auto-configuration, the UART type is tested.

[^]split_termios *dialin* and *callout* devices use different termios entries (only if ASYNC_SPLIT_TERMIOS was configured).

autoconfigure The kernel tries to configure the device automatically.

base *base* See baud_base.

baud_base *baud base* This option sets the baud rate.

close_delay *number* Sets the waiting time of the process if it closes the device. The value is specified in hundredths of seconds.

closing_wait2 *number* This option is no longer supported by the kernel! Originally, it meant the waiting time of the process after closing the device.

closing_wait *number* Time during closure of the device in which the process may still accept data (only if ASYNC_CLOSING_WAIT_NONE was configured).

divisor *divisor* This sets the divisor for the baud rate. The divisor is used when the option spd_cust is set and the port is set to 38.4 kbaud.

get_multiport Displays the configuration of multi-port devices.

hup_notify The getty program is notified about the hangup and close of the port.

irq *number* The program sets the IRQ to the specified number, where *number* is a value between 0 and 15.

port *number* The program sets the port to the specified number.

set_multiport Allows multi-port devices to be configured. The parameters must be passed via port[n], mask[n], and match[n].

spd_cust The baud rate is calculated as *baud base=divisor*.

spd_hi The baud rate is set to 57.6 kbaud if the application using the device requires 38.4 kbaud.

spd_normal The default baud rate of 38.4 kbaud is used.

spd_vhi The baud rate is set to 115.2 kbaud, if the application using the device requires 38.4 kbaud.

termios_restore The terminal settings are restored after blocking is released.

uart *type* The parameter sets the UART type used. Supported types are 8250, 16450, 16550, 16550A, and none. When FIFOs are to be used, the type 16550A must be specified, as the other types do not support this or only do so incorrectly. The specification none switches the port off.

In LINUX, on x86 computers, serial interfaces cannot share an IRQ (only special hardware, such as the AST FourPort, supports this). By default, 38 ports, ttyS0 to ttyS38, are initialized in the file drivers/char/serial.c.

If other configurations are required, they can be activated by a call to setserial in /etc/rc.local. The setting of a new IRQ is not that easy, because most IRQs are already occupied. The use of IRQ 5, which is normally responsible for LPT2, has proved to be useful. Other possibilities are 3, 4, and 7, or if the card supports 16 bits, IRQs 10, 11, 12, and 15. By default, the IRQ9 is mapped to IRQ2.

To obtain the data, the device is read using an `ioctl` call.

```
void getserial(char *device, int fd)
{
  struct serial_struct serinfo;
  if (ioctl(fd, TIOCGSERIAL, &serinfo) < 0) {
        perror("Cannot get serial info");
        exit(1);
}
  printf("%s, Type: %s, Line: %d, Port: 0x%.4x, IRQ: %d\n",
        device, serial_type(serinfo.type),
        serinfo.line, serinfo.port, serinfo.irq);
}
```

The port number and the interrupt are set by an `ioctl` call. This call also tests whether the specified port or interrupt is already occupied, and returns an error message. When specifying the port number, special attention should be paid, as specifying an incorrect number can crash the computer.

B.10 CONFIGURING A PARALLEL INTERFACE

Just as there is a program to configure the serial interfaces, there is also one for the parallel ports: `tunelp` (version 1.5). It is mainly used for printer configuration. The following options are available as parameters:

```
tunelp device [-i irq | -t time | -c chars | -w wait | -a [on|off]]
| -o [on|off]] | -C [on|off]] | -r | -s | -q [on|off]]
```

`-a [on|off]` This allows the user to specify whether the printer should abort the printing process when an error occurs. If one sits at the printer oneself, this might be more convenient, as errors can be remedied immediately. If this is not the case, however, the print spooler should deal with this, terminate the job, and send a message to the user. The choice is yours, the default is `off`.

`-C [on|off]` If this option is set, the driver defines the printer as *online* and ignores all error messages. This is useful for the printers that can also accept data in offline status.

`-c chars` The value *chars* specifies the number of attempts to output a character on the printer port. 120 is a good value for most printers. The default setting is `LP_INIT_CHAR`, as some printers take a bit more time. For very fast printers (HP-Laserjet), a value of 10 makes more sense.

-i *irq* This sets the interrupt to be used. If the port does not use interrupts (polling), this specification aborts the printing process. `tunelp -i 0` re-creates the polling, and the printer should work again.

-o `[on|off]` Prior to printing, the device is opened and a status check is made

-q `[on|off]` This option can be combined with all other ones. If it is set, at the end of the output it displays whether the control works via IRQ (plus number) or polling.

-r Sends a reset to the device.

-s Displays the status of the device. This option switches -q to *off*.

-t *time* This specifies how long the device driver should wait for the parallel interface after -c *char* attempts. The interface is initialized with the value `LP_INIT_TIME`. If printing needs to be carried out as fast as possible and the system load plays no role, this value can be set to 0. If printing speed plays no role and the printer is slow, 50 is a good value which, in addition, puts very little load on the system. The instruction is given in hundredths of seconds.

-w *wait* This is the wait time for the *strobe* signal, which is a *busy waiting* signal. Most printers only require an extremely short signal, therefore this value is initialized with 0 (`LP_INIT_WAIT`). Apart from the use of corresponding printers, increasing this value allows for a longer printer cable.

LINUX administers printers in a table. The BIOS supports up to four printers. In reality this will hardly ever happen. Therefore, only three entries are initialized.

```
struct lp_struct lp_table[LP_NO];
```

B.11   BUILDING A DIRECTORY TREE

The LINUX file systems are administered by using the commands `mount` and `umount`. They are used to mount and unmount file systems. The programs included in version 2.5m have the following parameters:

```
mount [-hV]
mount -a [-nfrvw] [-t vfstypes]
mount [-nfrvw] [-o options] special | node
mount [-nfrvw] [-t vfstype] [-o options] special node
umount -a [ -t type ]
umount special | node
```

Without parameters, `mount` displays the list of all currently mounted file systems. Otherwise it tries, by means of the system call *mount*, to mount the file system present on the *special* device at the mount point *node*. If *special* or *node* is not specified, the missing information is read from the file /etc/fstab. The `mount` options have the following meaning:

-a An attempt is made to mount all file systems specified in the /etc/fstab file. If the
   -t option is also set, this attempt is made only for file systems of a specified type.

-f The mounting of the file system is simulated. Together with the -v option, this makes
   it possible to check which actions the mount program would execute.

-h Help about usage is displayed.

-n The file /etc/mtab is not modified. This is necessary when the etc/ directory is
   located on a CD.

-o *options* The -o option specifies the mount options *options*, separated by a comma (,).
   These are often very specific; the following options are valid for all file systems:

   defaults This is the default option. It corresponds to the options:
       rw,exec,suid,dev,async,auto,nouser
   [no]auto The device is (is not) included in the mount -a call.
   [no]dev The use of device files on this file system is (is not) allowed.
   [no]exec Execution of binaries of the mounted file systems is (is not) allowed.
   remount A file system is remounted. Usually, this option is used to enter new flags (for
   example, to change from ro to rw).
   ro The file system is mounted read-only.
   rw The file system is mounted read and write.
   [no]suid When executing binaries of mounted file systems any set S bits are interpreted
   (or ignored).
   [a]sync All input and output operations on this file system are executed synchronously
   (asynchronously).
   [no]users Normal users can (cannot) mount this device. This option implies noexec,
   nosuid, and nodev, if not set otherwise.

   Further mount options of individual file systems are described later.

-r The file system is mounted read-only.
-w The file system is mounted read and write.
-t *type* The file system to be mounted is of the given type *type*. If no type is specified or
   -a is set, mount() tries to recognize the type by reading the superblock. If the specified
   special "device" contains a colon (:), it is automatically assumed that the file system
   is of the NFS type. With the additional -a option, several file systems can be specified,
   separated by commas (,). In this case, the type can also be prefixed with the string "no."
   Thus, for example, the command

   mount -a -t nomsdos,nonfs

   mounts all the file systems contained in the fstab file which are neither of the
   MSDOS or nfs type.

-v The program generates detailed output to inform users about its actions.
-V Displays the version of the program.

The umount program removes mounted file systems from the file system tree. It recognizes the -a and -t options with semantics similar to the ones described above.

The file /etc/fstab has a simple structure. Comment lines begin with a hash sign (#). The other lines contain four fields, separated by *white space* (spaces and tabs), of the form:

special   node   type   option

Here, all fields are compulsory, so that for an omitted device or mount point none has to be specified defaults for default options. In addition to file systems, the file also indicates swap devices and files. In this case, the type is swap, and the entry is ignored by mount and umount.

Both programs modify the /etc/mtab file, so that this file normally describes the current state of the file system tree. When this file is write-protected or located on a write-protected file system (CD), the option -n must be specified and the file /proc/mounts must be used!

A string specified with the -o option or contained in the /etc/fstab file is checked by mount for the mount flags (see Table 6.1), and the remaining mount options are passed as parameters to the system call *mount*. An exception to this is the NFS, in which first a connection to the remote computer is established, and then the already interpreted mount options together with the socket file descriptor are passed to the system call in the structure nfs_mount_data.

Mount options of the *Ext2* file system

bsddf If this option is specified, the system call *statfs* removes the number of blocks needed for the structures of the *Ext2* file system from the total number of free blocks. This is the default behavior of the *Ext2* file system.

check=*Value* This option specifies how many safety tests the *Ext2* file system should perform during its normal operation. none switches all tests off, whereas the default normal checks at each mount/remount whether the number of free inodes or blocks entered in the inodes or block bitmaps correspond to the values in the superblock. The strict option additionally checks at each allocation or release of a data block whether the corresponding block number describes a data block.

debug This option activates the debug mode of the *Ext2* file system. At each mount/remount operation, the file system issues a message containing its version number together with the parameters of the currently mounted file system, such as block size and number of block groups.

errors=*action* This option defines the behavior of the file system in the event of an error being detected. In the default setting continue, the error is merely signaled. The remount-ro setting mounts the file system after an error in read-only mode, so that a possible error cannot spread out and e2fsck can be used. The panic setting halts the LINUX kernel when an error with a panic message occurs.

grpid, bsdgroups When this option is set, all files generated are assigned the ID of the directory in which they are created. With the default setting nogrpid the new files are assigned the group identification of the directory, but only if the group S-bit is set.

minixdf In contrast to the bsddf option, the system call *statfs* returns the total number of blocks on the underlying device.

nocheck corresponds to the option check=none.

nogrpid, sysvgroups Newly created files and directories contain the group identification of the directory and not those of the process in the group S-bit of the directory. In addition, newly created directories are also assigned the group S-bit. This option is the default.

resgid=*gid* The GID of the group whose user may also occupy the reserved blocks. If none of the options is set, only the superuser may access the reserved blocks.

resuid=*uid* The UID of the user who, as well as the superuser, may occupy the reserved blocks.

sb=*block number* The number of the block in the device that should be read as the superblock. By default, block 1 is read. If all 8,912 blocks of the superblock are saved, the numbering starts from 1 Kbyte blocks onwards.

quota, usrquota, noquota, grpquota These options are recognized but ignored.

Mount options of the MS-DOS file system (FAT)

sys_immutable Files or inodes cannot be modified.

[no]dots Files bearing the hidden attribute receive one (or none) dot (.) in front of their names. The default is nodots.

dotsOK=[yes|no] See [no] dots.

blocksize=[512|1024] Sets the sector size of the MS-DOS file system. This is normally 512 bytes. As MS-DOS 3.0 could only handle partitions of a maximum of 65,536 sectors, some partition managers set the sector size to 1,024 bytes, thus allowing access to partitions of up to 64 Mbytes. In order to access such partitions, the parameter blocksize=1024 must be set.

debug Activates the debug mode.

fat=[12|16] Specifies whether the file system to be mounted has a 12- or a 16-bit FAT. As the size of the FAT can normally be deduced from the number of clusters on the file system, it should not be necessary to use this parameter.

quiet As the MS-DOS file system does not normally support either a change of owner of the inode or all the UNIX access rights, these operations return the error EPERM. Setting the quiet option suppresses this error message; in other words, the operations appear to be executable.

check=type Activates various grades of filename checking.

r[elaxed] Upper case and lower case letters are treated the same, long filenames are shortened, and spaces are allowed.

n[ormal] as relaxed, but filenames must not contain any character contained in the bad_chars[] field (that is, *?<>|"). This is the default setting.

s[trict] as normal, but forbidden characters also include those contained in the bad_if_strict[] field (that is, +=,;) .

conv=*type* Switches the conversion of MS-DOS text files on and off.

auto Conversions are carried out by "unknown" file types. These are files whose extension can be found in ascii_extensions[]. Because one or the other extension is practically always missing, programs that operate on such files with lseek() may react rather ungracefully. Thus, care[9] must be taken!

binary No conversion takes place. This is the default.

text This setting converts all files, removing all CR characters when reading, and jumping to the end of the file when the end-of-file character ^Z (ASCII 0x1a) is encountered. When writing the file, all newline characters are converted back into the usual MS-DOS combination.

gid=*gid* The group of the owner of all files. By default, this is 0.

showexec Only files with extensions .exe, .com, or .bat are assigned an *executable* flag.

uid=*uid* Since MS-DOS does not recognize owners of files, if this option is set, the MS-DOS file system displays the owner uid for all files. By default, 0 is entered.

umask=*umask* Uses the specified umask (octal!) to calculate the access rights for all files. If this option is omitted, the umask of the process that called the *mount* system call is used.

Mount options of the ISO file system

norock Deactivates the use of the *Rock Ridge Extensions*.

check=*typ* Activates various grades of the filename checking:

r[elaxed] Upper case letters are converted into lower case before access takes place. This option is only sensible in combination with norock and map=normal .

s[trict] No conversions are carried out.

cruft This option masks the highest 8 bits of the file length, as some CD-ROM manufacturers use them to store additional information. As a consequence, however, no files longer than 16 Mbytes can be read. This option is automatically set for (presumably) defect CDs. These include CDs with a capacity greater than 800 Mbytes and a *volume number* unequal to 0 or 1.

map=[normal|off] Toggles naming conventions for CD-ROMs that do not possess *Rock Ridge Extensions*. By default, normal is set, which converts all filenames into lower case and semicolons into full stops. The suffix ";1" is removed. In the off position names are not converted.

conv=[auto|binary|text|mtext] Since LINUX 1.3.54 this option has been ignored.

block=[512|1024|2048] Sets the block size used for CD-ROM access. The ISO file system sets it to 1,024 by default.

9 In contrast with the older LINUX versions, which recorded the binary extensions in the field bin_extensions(), in version 2.4 these extensions have to be converted. By doing this, the risk of converting a binary file incorrectly is greatly reduced.

mode=*value* Sets the file access rights for all files if the media does not contain *Rock Ridge Extensions*. By default, the value is set to S_IRUGO, therefore the read rights for all users are entered.

uid=*uid* The user identification number of the owner of all files. By default, the value is 0.

gid=*gid* The group of the owner of all files. By default, 0 is entered.

unhide Also hidden files are displayed.

Mount options of the HPFS

uid=*uid* The user identification number of the owner of all files. By default, 0 is entered.

gid=*gid* The group of the owner of all files. By default, this is 0.

umask=*umask* Uses the specified *umask* to calculate the access rights for all the files. If this option is omitted, the umask used is that of the process that called the mount.

case=[lower|asis] Switches the name conversion on and off. In the default setting lower, filenames are converted into lower case; in the asis setting, they are left as they are.

conv=*type* Switches the conversion of files on and off. In the default setting *binary*, no conversion takes place. In the text setting, all files are converted, converting the *Carriage Return Linefeed* sequence into the UNIX newline. In the auto setting, whether the first block of the file to be read is a text or a binary file is checked by means of heuristics. The remainder of the file is then converted.

nocheck Mounting is not aborted if errors occur during the consistency check.

Mount options of the NFS

acdirmax=*n* The maximum time span in seconds in which attributes of directories are saved intermediately before updated information is fetched from the NFS server. The default is 60.

acdirmin=*n* The minimum time span in seconds in which attributes of directories are saved intermediately before updated information is fetched from the NFS server. The default is 30.

acregmax=*n* The maximum time span in seconds in which attributes of regular files are saved intermediately before updated information is fetched from the NFS server. The default is 60.

acregmin=*n* The minimum time span in seconds, in which attributes of regular files are saved intermediately before updated information is fetched from the NFS server. The default is 3.

actimeo=*n* The options acregmin, acregmax, acdirmin, and acdirmax are set to the specified value.

addr=*n* this option is ignored.

mounthost=*n* The name of the computer in which the mount daemon is running.

mountport=*n* The port number of the mount daemon.

mountprog=*n* A different RPC program is to be used. The default is 100,005, the normal RPC mount number.

mountvers=*n* This number is presented to the mount daemon of the remote computer as an RPC version.

namlen=*n* The query of filename lengths of the remote file system has only been supported since version 2 of the RPC mount protocol. This detail is used as a specification for older servers.

nfsprog=*n* A different RPC program is to be used for linking to the remote NFS daemon.

nfsvers=*n* This number is given to the NFS daemon of the remote computer as an RPC version.

port=*n* The number of the UDP port for connection to the NFS server. The default is the standard NFS port 2049.

retrans=*n* The number of minor timeouts and retransmissions before a major timeout is triggered. The default is 3. After this, the operation is aborted or the message "server not responding" is displayed.

retry=*n* The number of attempts of a HUHU. The default value is 10,000.

rsize=*n* The number of bytes the NFS uses when reading the files from an NFS server. The default is 1,024, but a better value would be 8,192.

timeo=*n* The time in tenths of a second, before data is retransmitted after the first RPC timeout. The default is seven-tenths of a second. Each time another RPC timeout occurs, this time is doubled, until the maximum of 60 seconds or a major timeout is reached.

[no]ac The noac option prohibits the intermediate saving of attributes of files and directories. This leads to a higher workload for the server, but it is very important when several NFS clients actively write to a file system on the server at the same time. The default is ac with the values set by acregmin, acregmax, acdirmin, and acdirmax.

[no]bg If mounting leads to a timeout, bg tries to continue mounting in the background. The default is fg or nobg.

[no]cto The nocto option prohibits the requesting of attributes after creating a file. The default is cto.

[no]fg If mounting leads to a timeout, the fg option displays an error message. The default is fg or nobg.

[no]hard If an NFS operation has a major timeout, the hard option displays the message "server not responding" on the console and tries to continue the operation. This is the default.

[no]intr If an NFS operation has a major timeout and the file system has been mounted hard, the intr option allows the operation to be interrupted by signals. In this case the error EINTR is returned to the calling program. The default is nointr, which means that interruption of NFS operations is not allowed.

[no]posix A file system mounted with the posix option behaves according to the POSIX specifications. Default is noposix.

[no]soft If an NFS operation has a major timeout, the soft option returns an error from the calling program. The nosoft default or hard continues the NFS operation indefinitely, if necessary.

[no]tcp The TCP protocol is used for communication. Default is UDP.

[no]udp UDP is used for communication. Several NFS servers only support this protocol.

wsize=*n* The number of bytes the NFS uses when writing to files on an NFS server. The default is 1,024, but 8,192 would be a better value.

THE *PROC* FILE SYSTEM

This appendix describes the individual components of the *Proc* file system which is normally mounted under /proc in LINUX. Some system utilities, such as ps, rely on this. The path is firmly provided in their sources. The main task of the *Proc* file system is to provide, in a simple way, information about the kernel and the processes. The sometimes cryptic ioctl calls are avoided, and information is made as readable as possible.

The single files and directories are normally generated when reading actually takes place (system calls *open* and *readdir*) and therefore always contain the current status of the LINUX system.

The root directory of the *Proc* file system has the inode number 1 and each existing process possesses a subdirectory. In order to guarantee a clear allocation, the name of this subdirectory is the process ID itself. In this subdirectory we find the files containing process-related information. In addition to this, the root directory contains the following subdirectories and files. The inode numbers of the individual files are defined as enumeration constants in the file <linux/proc_fs.h> and correspond to the specified order.

C.1 THE /PROC/ DIRECTORY

bus/ This directory contains the files of the bus system. Generally, this is the description of the PCI bus.

cmdline The command line that was submitted to the kernel during startup.

```
root=/dev/hdc2 delay=700 BOOT_IMAGE=vmlinuz
```

cpuinfo This file contains the parameters of the processor recognized during system boot (file arch/i386/kernel/setup.c).

processor	: 0	*Number of the processor*
vendor_id	: GenuineIntel	*Manufacturer*
cpu family	: 5	*CPU type*
model	: 2	*Model*

model name	: Pentium 75 -200	*Model name*
stepping	: 5	*Stepping*
cpu MHz	: 100.230096	*Internal CPU time*
fdiv_bug	: no	*Does it calculate properly?*
hlt_bug	: no	*Does it stop properly?*
f00f_bug	: yes	*f00f bug?*
coma_bug	: yes	*Cyrix coma bug?*
fpu	: yes	*FP unit present?*
fpu_exception	: yes	*Does exception 16 work?*
cpuid level :	: 2	*Maximum cpuid level*
wp	: yes	*WP bit in the supervisor mode?*
flags	: fpu vme de pse tsc msr mce cx8	
		Processor features
bogomips	: 39.94	*Bogomips value*

devices This file contains information about registered device drivers. It may be used by the MAKEDEV script in order to achieve consistency in the /dev/ directory. The first column contains the major number of the device driver, followed in the second column by the name that was given during the registration of the device.

```
Character devices:
1        mem
2        pty
3        ttyp
4        ttyS
5        cua
7        vcs
128      ptm
136      pts
162      raw

Block devices:
2        fd
3        ide0
8        sd
22       ide1
```

dma The occupied DMA channels can be read from this file:

```
1:   SB16 (8bit)
4:   cascade
5:   SB16 (16bit)
```

filesystems This file contains the available (or currently loaded) file system implementations of the LINUX kernel. The name of each file system that has been registered with the function `register_filesystem()` is output. If the file system does not need a device, the name is preceded by the string "nodev."

```
        ext2
nodev   proc
nodev   nfs
        iso9660
nodev   autofs
nodev   devpts
        vfat
```

ide This directory contains the descriptions of the IDE controller in the system and the affiliated devices.

interrupts This file contains the number and names of hardware interrupts received. It indicates the number of the interrupts received for each CPU, the interrupt controller being used, as well as the name of the device driver that deals with the interrupt. Finally, the number of the non-masked interrupts that have occurred (NMI) as well as the number of the waiting cycles are indicated in the interprocessor interrupts (IPI).

```
        CPU0        CPU1
0:      6598        6763     IO-APIC-edge     timer
1:      0           2        IO-APIC-edge     keyboard
2:      0           0        XT-PIC           cascade
8:      1           0        IO-APIC-edge     rtc
9:      155         158      IO-APIC-level    eth0
12:     7           2        IO-APIC-edge     PS/2 mouse
13:     1           0        XT-PIC           fpu
14:     847         759      IO-APIC-edge     ide0
15:     4           0        IO-APIC-edge     ide1
NMI:    0
ERR:    0
```

iomem This file contains a list whose memory is occupied by hardware drivers or by the kernel. The start and end addresses of the area occupied and the name of the hardware are indicated.

```
00000000-0009ffff  :        System RAM
000a0000-000bffff  :        Video RAM area
000c0000-000c7fff  :        Video ROM
000c8000-000cbfff  :        Extension ROM
000f0000-000fffff  :        System ROM
00100000-03ffffff  :        System RAM
```

```
00100000-001e963f :        Kernel code
001e9640-001faacb :        Kernel data
e0000000-e1ffffff :        S3 Inc. Vision 968
e4000000-e40000ff :        NCR 53c860
```

ioports This file contains the I/O ports occupied with request_region().

```
0000-001f :   dma1
0020-003f :   pic1
0040-005f :   timer
0060-006f :   keyboard
0080-009f :   dma page reg
00a0-00bf :   pic2
00c0-00df :   dma2
...
```

kcore The kcore file contains a core of the kernel. This allows the debugging of the kernel during runtime. This can take place using

```
# gdb /usr/src/linux/vmlinux /proc/kcore
```

The size of this file equals the size of main memory plus the page size.

kmsg When selected, this file provides the kernel messages that have not yet been read via the system call syslog (see page 322). A side-effect of the selection is that the messages read from the log ring buffer are removed, so a kernel message can only be read once. Therefore, the selection of the file should not occur while the syslogd daemon is running. Also, the file is only readable for root.

ksyms This file contains all symbols exported by the kernel, with the address, the name and (perhaps) the mode instructions. These kernel symbols can be used by the module. The file only exists if CONFIG_MODULES has been configured.

```
c485299c packet_command_texts [ide-cd]
c48528c4 sense_key_texts [ide-cd]
c4852728 ide_cdrom_init [ide-cd]
...
```

loadavg During the reading of this file, the values of average system load for the last 1.5 and 15 minutes will be provided. These values are updated during each timer interrupt. In addition, the number of running processes, their total, and the PID of the last active process are displayed. The kernel function used is loadavg_read_proc().

```
0.14  0.12  0.05  2/57  242
```

locks The reading of this file gives the current file locks:

```
1: BROKEN ADVISORY WRITE 72 03:42:8072 0 2147483647
01f88d98 00000000 00000000 00000000 00000000
```

Each line contains inode number of the file, followed by a colon, the flags, the lock, its type (READ or WRITE), the PID of its owner, and then the major and minor numbers of the device on which the file is located, as well as the inode number (separated by a colon) and the start and end position of the lock. This is followed by the address of the lock itself, the previous and following list, and the previous and following lock. If processes wait for this lock, they will be issued in the following lines; the line begins with `<nr>:  ->` and the rest is as in the previous line.

malloc This file allows the monitoring of the kmalloc() and kfree() operations. If CONFIG_DEBUG_MALLOC has not been configured, this file does not exist.

md If *Multiple device driver support* (CONFIG_BLK_DEV_MD) has been configured, this file contains the statistics of use.

meminfo This file contains the number of all users and free bytes of the main memory and the swap area. In addition to this, it contains the size of the memory shared by more than one process together with the size of cache memory, similar to the free command, but indicates the size in bytes instead of Kbytes.

```
          total:      used:    free: shared:   buffers:  cached:
Mem:    64958464  56840192  8118272 31260672   5582848   35291136
Swap:   33021952     77824 32944128
MemTotal:      63436 kB
MemFree:        7928 kB
MemShared:     30528 kB
Buffers:        5452 kB
Cached:        34464 kB
SwapTotal:     32248 kB
SwapFree:      32172 kB
```

modules This file contains information about the single modules loaded, their size and their state. This file exists only if CONFIG_MODULES has been configured.

```
serial          17300       1       (autoclean)
nfs             32132       1       (autoclean)
nfs             32132       1       (autoclean)
lockd           28104       1       (autoclean) [nfs]
sunrpc          49884       1       (autoclean) [nfs lockd]
nls_iso8859-1    2012       6       (autoclean)
nls_cp437        3536       6       (autoclean)
vfat            13484       6       (autoclean)
fat             23988       6       (autoclean) [vfat]
```

mounts The file (corresponds to mtab in the previous versions) contains a list of currently mounted file systems.

```
/dev/root / ext2 rw 0 0
/dev/hdc3 /usr ext2 rw 0 0
none /proc proc rw 0 0
/dev/hda1 /dos/c vfat rw 0 0
/dev/hda5 /dos/d vfat rw 0 0
/dev/hdb5 /dos/e vfat rw 0 0
/dev/sdb5 /dos/f vfat rw 0 0
/dev/sdb6 /dos/g vfat rw 0 0
murdock:(pid79) /nfs nfs rw,rsize=1024,wsize=1024,acregmin=1,
        acregmax=1,acdirmin=0,acdirmax=0,intr,
        addr=pid79@murdock:/nfs 0 0
/dev/sda4 /dos/z vfat rw 0 0
/dev/cdrom /mnt iso9660 ro 0 0
```

net/ This directory contains some files that describe the status of the network layer. For more detailed information refer to Section C.2 and Chapter 8.

partitions This file contains information about the partitions of all block devices: the major and minor number of the device, its size, and name.

major	minor	#blocks	name
8	0	98304	sda
8	4	98288	sda4
8	16	4233600	sdb
8	17	1	sdb1
8	21	2096451	sdb5
8	22	2096451	sdb6
3	0	1251936	hda
3	1	52384	hda1
3	2	1	hda2
3	5	1197472	hda5
3	64	1251936	hdb
3	65	1	hdb1
3	69	1247872	hdb5
22	0	833616	hdc
22	1	32255	hdc1
22	2	32256	hdc2
22	3	769104	hdc3

pci Here we find information about the occupation of the (old) PCI slots. If the kernel has not been configured for PCI, information is usually given under /proc/bus/pci. This file only exists in the case where *Backward-compatible /proc/pci* has also been set.

```
PCI devices found:
  Bus 0, device 0, function 0:
```

```
        Host bridge: Acer Labs M1531 Aladdin IV (rev 178).
        Slow devsel. Master Capable. Latency=32.
    Bus 0, device 2, function 0:
        ISA bridge: Acer Labs M1533 Aladdin IV (rev 180).
        Medium devsel. Master Capable. No bursts.
    Bus 0, device 4, function 0:
        VGA compatible controller: S3 Inc. Vision 968 (rev 0).
        Medium devsel. IRQ b.
        Non-prefetchable 32 bit memory at 0xe0000000 [0xe0000000].
    Bus 0, device 5, function 0:
        SCSI storage controller: NCR 53c875 (rev 3).
        Medium devsel. IRQ 9. Master Capable. Latency=64.
        Min Gnt=17.Max Lat=64.
        I/O at 0x6400 [0x6401].
        Non-prefetchable 32 bit memory at 0xe4000000 [0xe4000000].
        Non-prefetchable 32 bit memory at 0xe4001000 [0xe4001000].
    Bus 0, device 11, function 0:
        IDE interface: Acer Labs M5229 TXpro (rev 32).
        Medium devsel. Fast back-to-back capable.
        IRQ f. Master Capable. Latency=64.
        Min Gnt=2.Max Lat=4.
        I/O at 0xf000 [0xf001].
```

rtc If *Enhanced Real Time Clock Support* (CONFIG_RTC) has been configured, this file contains the RTC values.

scsi This directory contains the files (beginning with inode number 256) that contain information on the individual devices. If the kernel has not been configured for SCSI, this directory is empty. Otherwise there is a scsi file that contains the instructions of the controller, and there is a subdirectory for each (configured) device.

```
Host: scsi0 Channel: 00 Id: 05 Lun: 00
Vendor: IOMEGA      Model: ZIP 100      Rev: E.08
Type: Direct-Access                ANSI SCSI revision: 02
Host: scsi0 Channel: 00 Id: 06 Lun: 00
Vendor: IBM         Model: DCAS-34330W Rev: S65A
Type: Direct-Access                ANSI SCSI revision: 02
```

self/ This directory contains information about the process accessing the *Proc* file system. It is identical to the directory that bears the process's PID. For more detailed information refer to Section C.3.

slabinfo This file contains an overview of all cache objects used. The name of the cache, the number of the entries currently used and their total number are output.

If SLAB_STATS has been set in mm/slab.c SLAB_STATS, statistics on the access are also output.

```
slabinfo - version: 1.0
kmem_cache          27    42
tcp_tw_bucket        0    42
tcp_bind_bucket     28   127
tcp_open_request     0    63
skbuff_head_cache    5    75
sock                86    99
filp               465   504
signal_queue         0     0
buffer_head       8348  8358
mm_struct           48    62
...
```

smp The file contains information on the individual CPUs in SMP systems. For this file, SMP_PROF must be configured.

stat This provides general LINUX kernel statistics.[1]

cpu 7191 0 1542 341934	*Jiffies in user, nice, system mode, and idle process*
cpu0 7191 0 1542 341934	*For the respective CPU*
disk 102 6118 4 0	*Number of disk requests*
disk_rio 102 3586 4 0	*Read accesses per disk*
disk_wio 0 2532 0 0	*Written accesses per disk*
disk_rblk 108 7146 8 0	*Read sectors per disk*
disk_wblk 0 5064 0 0	*Written sectors per disk*
page 19588 5865	*Memory pages mapped and deleted*
swap 1 0	*Swap pages mapped and deleted*
intr 421905 350667 23464 0 0 41434 0 2 0 0 92 0 0 0 1 6225 20	
...	
	Sum and number of interrupts
ctxt 244058	*Number of context switches*
btime 841823772	*UNIX boot time*
processes 473	*PID of the current process*

swaps Contains the data about the single swap areas.

Filename	Type	Size	Used	Priority
/dev/hdc1	partition	32248	148	-1

sys/ This directory contains information controlling the most important algorithms of the kernel. For more details refer to Section C.4.

---

1 With IDE devices, the indicators per disk refer to the first four controllers; with SCSI devices they refer to the first four devices.

sysipc/ This directory contains information describing the messages, semaphores, and shared memory areas used in the system.

tty/ This directory contains information describing the terminals and their drivers.

uptime This file indicates the time in seconds since the startup of the system and the time used by the idle process.

```
501.05 344.11
```

version The file version represents the variable linux_banner, and results, for example, in an output of the form:

```
linux version 2.4.2 (root@murdock) (gcc version 2.96)
#1 Sat Feb 3 01:24:03 CET 2001
```

C.2   THE NET/ DIRECTORY

This directory contains files that describe the state of the LINUX network layer. The files have inode numbers starting with 128. For more detailed information refer to Chapter 8. The individual files are:

arp displays the content of the ARP table in readable form.

IP address	HW type	Flags	HW address	Mask	Device
141.20.22.210	0x1	0x2	08:00:5A:C7:10:24	*	eth0
141.20.22.203	0x1	0x2	00:00:C0:1B:E2:1B	*	eth0
141.20.22.204	0x1	0x2	00:00:C0:34:DE:24	*	eth0

dev This file contains the available network devices, together with their statistics. Because of the output length the table is divided in two.

Inter- face	Receive bytes	packets	errs	drop	fifo	frame	compressed	multicast
lo:	252822	1710	0	0	0	0	0	0
eth0:	196448	1734	0	0	0	47	0	778

Inter- face	Transmit bytes	packets	errs	drop	fifo	colls	carrier	compressed
lo:	252822	1710	0	0	0	0	0	0
eth0:	27846	116	0	0	0	0	0	0

dev_mcast gives an output of the multicast lists of all network devices. The index and name of the device, the UID and GID of its user, as well as the hardware address are written in full.

2	eth0	1	0	01005e000001
3	dummy0	1	0	01005e000001

dev_stat provides data for network use. The first number is the number of the last packets that were lost. Forwarding between high-speed interfaces and Fast switching have to be configured for the further versions.

```
00000000 00000000 00000000 00000000 00000000
```

netlink provides details about the netlink sockets. The address, the protocol, the PID and the groups, the size of the memory used, the address of its callback, and the number of references are ouput.

```
sk          Eth   Pid   Groups     Rmem   Wmem   Dump       Locks
c1135740    0     0     00000000   0      0      00000000   2
```

netstat provides the net statistics for SNMP purposes.

```
TcpExt:  SyncookiesSent SyncookiesRecv SyncookiesFailed EmbryonicRsts
         PruneCalled RcvPruned OfoPruned
TcpExt:  0 0 0 0 26 96 616
```

packet This file provides information about the individual sockets of the packet driver, the address of the socket, the number of references, the type, the protocol number, the index of the network devices, the running flag, the read memory previously allocated, as well as the UID and the inode number of the socket inode.

```
sk      RefCnt        Type    Proto Iface R      Rmem   User   Inode
```

raw provides information about opened RAW sockets.

```
sl local_address  rem_address   st tx_queue rx_queue   tr tm->when   retrnsmt
       uid     timeout    inode
0: 00000000:0001  00000000:0000  07 00000000:00000000  00:00000000  00000000
         0          0 0
1: 00000000:0006  00000000:0000  07 00000000:00000000  00:00000000  00000000
         0          0 0
```

route This file contains the routing table in an unfamiliar form. The route program gets its information from this file.

Iface	Destination	Gateway	Flags	RefCnt	Use	Metric	Mask	MTU	Win	IRTT
eth0	C01D148D	00000000	01	0	0	0	C0FFFFFF	1500	0	0
lo	0000007F	00000000	01	0	2	0	000000FF	3584	0	0
eth0	00000000	C11D148D	03	0	0	1	00000000	1500	0	0

rt_cache contains information about the routing cache.

Iface	Destination	Gateway	Flags	RefCnt	Use	Metric	Source
MTU	Window	IRTT	TOS	HHRef		HHUptod	SpecDst
lo	C21D148D	C21D148D	80000000	6	29	0	C21D148D
3924	0300	00	2	1		C21D148D	
lo	C21D148D	C21D148D	80000000	0	1633	0	E31D148D
0	00	00	-1	0		C21D148D	
lo	C21D148D	C21D148D	80000000	0	65	0	C31D148D
0	00	00	-1	0		C21D148D	

snmp This file contains the MIBs (Management Information Bases) for the SNMP protocol.

sockstat This file displays the number of proto structures for the single socket types.

```
sockets: used 79
        TCP: inuse 25 highest 33
        UDP: inuse 15 highest 16
        RAW: inuse 2  highest 3
```

tcp provides information about opened TCP sockets. The output is in the same format as raw.

udp provides information about UDP sockets. The output is in the same format as raw.

unix provides information about each open UNIX domain socket, such as path, status, type, flags, protocol, and reference counters.

Num	RefCount	Protocol	Flags	Type	St	Inode	Path
00ecddfc:	00000002	00000000	00000000	0001	01	1015	/dev/log
00ecda04:	00000002	00000000	00000000	0001	03	1014	

C.3   THE SELF/ DIRECTORY

The process directories and the self/ directory have the following structure, in which the respective inodes have the *PID* << 16 + *specified value*.

status [+3] This file contains the characteristics of the process (in short form).

Name:	xman				*command name*
State:	S (sleeping)				*process status*
Pid:	120				*its PID*
PPid:	108				*its PPID*
Uid:	15216	15216	15216	15216	*its [ESF] UID*
Gid:	15200	15200	15200	15200	*its [ESF] GID*
FDSize:	256				*max. number of file descriptors*
Groups:	15200				*its groups*
VmSize:	2296 kB				*size of VM areas*

VmLck:	0 kB	*locked VM areas*
VmRSS:	308 kB	*RSS size*
VmData:	500 kB	*data segment (without stack)*
VmStk:	24 kB	*stack segment*
VmExe:	40 kB	*loaded program*
VmLib:	1620 kB	*loaded libraries*
SigPnd:	00000000	*pending signals*
SigBlk:	00000000	*mask of blocked signals*
SigIgn:	80000000	*mask of ignored signals*
SigCgt:	00000000	*mask of received signals*
CapInh:	00000000ffffefff	*inherited rights*
CapPrm:	0000000000000000	*allowed rights*
CapEff:	0000000000000000	*effective rights*

mem [+4]   While the device /dev/mem represents the physical memory before address
conversion, this mem file represents the linear address space of the corresponding process.

It is generally not possible to write to this file, because owing to the lack of tests,
it would be possible to write to the memory of the LINUX kernel itself. It is,
however, possible to enable writing by removing the macro definition of mem_write in
the file fs/proc/mem.c.

cwd [+5]   This is a link to the PID directory of the process in the *Proc* file system.

root [+6]   The root directory of the process can be reached via this link (see also chroot
on page 333).

exe [+7]   This is a link to the executable file.

fd/ [+8]   In this directory we find an entry with the name of the file descriptor for each
file opened by the process. The link points to the opened file.

Because both standard input (0) and output (1) are located here, programs which, for
example, do not want to read from the standard input can be persuaded to do so by making
them read from the file /proc/self/fd/0.

This can, however, lead to problems, because no searching is possible in the files of this
directory.

environ [+9]   This file contains the current environment of the process. The individual
entries are issued without a hyphen. If the whole process is taken out or if it is a zombie,
the file is then empty.

cmdline [+10]   In a similar way to the environ file, this file contains the process's
command line.

stat [+11]   This file provides more detailed information about the process, for example:

```
 185    (bash)     S    1  185  185  1028  330  256  699
 615         542  2458   28   10   34    20   18    0    0
               0       16669      1990656        320  4294967295
     134512640  134956915  3221225072  3221224492  1074512521
```

0	65536	3686404	260128507	3222375209
0	0	17	0	

The file lists the individual values of the process's task structure in order,[2] thus providing the user with a complete state description of the process.

As the individual single entries are generally evaluated in programs (see `ps` in Section B.2) they are listed in `scanf()` format. If an entry is the value of a component of the task structure, the name of the component is added in brackets.

The individual entries of the file are:

%d   the process Id (`pid`)

(%s)   the name of the executable file in brackets (also visible when the process is taken out)

%c   the process status (`state`; "R" for *running*, "S" for *interruptable sleeping*, "D" for *uninterruptable sleeping or swapping*, "Z" for *zombie*, "T" for *traced* or *stopped*, and "W" for *swapped*)

%d   the PID of the parent process (`p_pptr->pid`)

%d   the process group (`pgrp`)

%d   the SID of the process (`session`)

%d   the terminal used by the process (`kdev_t_to_nr()`)

%d   the process group owned by the terminal

%lu   the flag of the process (`flags`)

%lu   the number of minor faults[3] (`min_flt`) incurred by the process

%lu   the number of minor faults (`cmin_flt`) incurred by the process and its children

%lu   the number of major faults[3] (`maj_flt`) incurred by the process

%lu   the number of major faults (`cmaj_flt`) incurred by the process and its children

%ld   the number of jiffies (`times.tms_utime`) the process used in process mode

%ld   the number of jiffies (`times.tms_stime`) spent in kernel mode

%ld   the number of jiffies (`times.tms_cutime`) the process and its children spent in user mode

%ld   the number of jiffies (`times.tms_cstime`) the process and its children spent in kernel mode

%ld   the maximum number of jiffies the process can run in a time slice

%ld   the UNIX nice value (`priority`) used to calculate a new value for `counter`

0   the value in jiffies before triggering a timeout (`timeout`)

%lu   the value of the interval timer (`it_real_value`)

%ld   the start time of the process (`start_time`) in jiffies since the start of the system

%u   the size in bytes of the memory accessible to the process

%u   the number (`mm->rss`) of pages of the process currently in physical memory

%u   the maximum number (`rlim[RLIMIT_RSS].rlim_cur`) of memory pages for the process which may be present in memory at the same time

2 For better readability the output is lightly formatted.

3 A minor fault is an error in accessing memory pages which is handled without accessing external media. A major fault, on the other hand, must be dealt with by accessing external media.

%lu   the start address (mm->start_code) of the text segment

%lu   the end address (mm->end_code) of the text segment

%lu   the start address (mm->start_stack) of the stack

%lu   the current stack pointer[4] of the process

%lu   the current instruction pointer[4] of the process

%lu   the signal vector[5] (signal) of the received signals

%lu   the signal vector (blocked) of the blocked signals

%lu   the signal vector of the ignored signals

%lu   the signal vector of the signals equipped with handling routines

%lu   the address of the kernel function the process is in

%lu   the number of swap operations (nswap)

%lu   the number of swap operations of the children (cnswap)

%d   the exit signal (exit_signal)

%d   the CPU in which the task is running (processor)

statm [+12] The memory information of the process is saved here. Determining these
values takes some time, therefore they are not included in the stat file.

```
220 143 60 4 0 139 12
```

%d   the total number of memory pages used (*size*)

%d   the number of memory pages (*resident*) currently in the physical memory

%d   the number of memory pages (*share*) the process shares with other processes

%d   the number of text pages (*trs*) currently in physical memory

%d   the number of library pages (*lrs*) currently in the physical memory

%d   the number of data pages (*drs*) including written library pages and the
stacks currently in the physical memory

%d   the number of library pages (*dt*) that have been accessed

maps   [+15] Here we find information about the virtual address areas (see also vm_area
structures in Section 4.2.2) of the process. For each virtual address area the following are
specified: start and end addresses, access rights and offset in the mapped file, identified
by the major and minor number of the device together with the inode number as well
as the name of the file. The access rights are indicated in the usual UNIX notation
(rwxsp) where additional flags indicate whether the area is shared (s) or private (p). If
a virtual memory area is mapped anonymously, the inode number is 0.

```
08048000-0807d000    r-xp    00000000    16:02  4077    /bin/tcsh
0807d000-08081000    rw-p    00034000    16:02  4077    /bin/tcsh
08081000-080b5000    rwxp    00000000    00:00  0
40007000-40008000    rw-p    00000000    00:00  0
...
```

4 During the determination of parameters the process is in kernel mode so that the current values ESP and EIP are
also calculated and point to the user segment. As the EIP, one usually gets an address in the C library.

5 The signal vector is a 32-bit number, in which each signal is represented by a bit. Because of the restriction to 32,
the output has become obsolete.

C.4   THE SYS/ DIRECTORY

The subdirectories of the /proc/sys directory allow the reading of information relevant to the system. This information is held in internal tables and mapped to /proc/sys. The inode numbers begin with 4,096. Some files are writeable, therefore the corresponding parameters can be altered in the kernel during runtime. In the following they are indicated with [w].

fs/ This directory contains data and settings to do with the file system.

dentrystate Values of the dentry_stat structure: the total number of the DEntries, the number of free DEntries, the maximum age in seconds, the number of the pages required by the system, and two filler entries.

```
0      2834   45    0     0     0
```

dquotmax[w] The maximum quota number (NR_DQUOTS).

```
0
```

dquotnr The current number of the quotas and free quotas.

```
0      0
```

filemax[w] The maximum number of file descriptors (NR_FILES).

```
4096
```

filenr Number of the file descriptors used, free descriptors, and the maximum number of open descriptors.

```
216    3      4096
```

inodenr[w] Current number of inodes and free inodes.

```
3072   2802
```

inode-state Values of the inodes_stat structure (inode-nr and five filler values).

```
3072   2802   0     0     0     0     0
```

supermax[w] Maximum number of superblocks (NR_SUPER).

```
256
```

supernr Current number of superblocks.

```
5
```

kernel/ This directory contains information on the kernel and its control structures.

random/ This subdirectory contains files that allow access to the number randomizer.

boot_id a 128-bit (16*8 byte) random number calculated when the system was started.

e7b2d9c0-aa0d-4a5b-bc74-f6954cc8024b

entropy_avail Degree of possibility of the numbers.

0

poolsize[w] Size of the entropy pool.

512

read_wakeup_threshold[w] Lowest limit of entropy. If it is exceeded, all processes that have called random_read() (for example, reading a random device) are woken up.

8

write_wakeup_threshold[w] Upper limit of entropy. If it is exceeded, all processes waiting by means of random_poll() are woken up.

128

uuid A 128-bit (16*8 byte) random number which is calculated for each new selection.

2f532b1d-4df7-4296-89fe-c4009f64c885

acct The control of process management. When the free memory (for the log files) drops below the second value, the management deactivates, and when the free memory exceeds the first value, it is deactivated again. The third value is the monitoring frequency in seconds. This file exists only if BSD Process Accounting was activated.

4   2   50

ctrl-alt-del 1 indicates that Ctrl+Alt+Del starts the machine again, 0 indicates that the SIGINT signal is sent to the process with the PID 1.
domainname The domain name of the system.
hostname The computer's name.
modprobe The path of the program which loads modules.
osrelease The version of the kernel.
ostype The name of the operating system.
panic The timeout after a panic message.
printk The current log level, the default level, the minimal and maximum log level.
version Compiler information during kernel compilation.

net/ Depending on the network configuration, this directory may contain the most varied subdirectories and files. There is one subdirectory for each network subsystem (corresponds to a device).

vm/ This directory does not contain any data about the current memory occupation, but contains control parameters of processes responsible for memory management.

bdflush[w] The control parameter of the bd_flush() process.

40 500 64 256 500 3000 500 1884 2

buffermem[w] The control parameters for rewriting the used memory pages (minimal, normal, and maximum size).

2   10   60

freepages[w] The three levels for free memory. The first number is the absolute lowest.   If the free memory drops under the third (second) number, the (intensive) swap process starts.

128   256   384

kswapd[w] The control parameters of the Kswap daemon (calculation base for the number of swap attempts, minimal number of attempts, swap cluster size).

512   32   32

overcommit_memory[w] controls vm_enough_memory(). If this value is unequal to 0, 1 is always returned.

0

pagecluster[w] The number of common pages.

4

pagecache[w] Control parameters of the page processes (like buffermem).

2   15   75

pagetable_cache[w] The minimal and maximum size for the page-table cache.

25   50

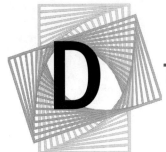

D THE BOOTING PROCESS

The proper way of starting up the LINUX kernel has already been described in Chapters 2 and 3. There are, however, several different methods of making the kernel start. The simplest one is to write the complete kernel to a floppy disk, starting with sector 0, using the command

```
# dd if=zImage of=/dev/fd0,mm
```

and then boot from the floppy disk. A much more elegant way of booting LINUX is via the LINUX loader (LILO).

D.1 CARRYING OUT THE BOOTING PROCESS

In a PC, booting is carried out by the BIOS. After the Power-On *Self Tests* (POST) have terminated, the BIOS tries to read the first sector of the first floppy disk: the boot sector. If this fails, the BIOS tries to read the boot sector from the first hard disk. More recent BIOS versions can invert this sequence and boot directly from the hard disk. As most BIOS systems do not have SCSI support, SCSI adapters must provide their own BIOS if SCSI disks are used for booting. If no valid boot sector can be found, the original PC starts its built-in ROM-BASIC, or a message appears saying "NO ROMBASIC."

The booting of an operating system generally proceeds in several steps. As there is not much room for code in the boot sector, this normally loads a second loader, and so on, until the actual operating system kernel is completely loaded.

As Figure D.1 shows, the structure of a boot sector is relatively simple; its length is always 512 bytes (so that it can be saved on either a floppy disk or a hard disk).

The disk parameters are only significant for MS-DOS. It is important that the code starts at offset 0 and that the boot sector is terminated by the *magic number*.

Booting from floppy disk is relatively simple, because each floppy disk has exactly one boot sector: the first sector. This is followed by arbitrary data. Booting from a hard disk is slightly more difficult because it is divided into partitions. The BIOS, however, knows nothing about this; it therefore loads, as it would with a floppy disk, the first sector, which is called the *master boot record* (MBR).

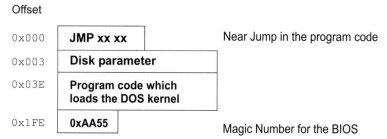

Figure D.1: The MS-DOS boot sector.

The MBR must therefore have the same structure, that is, the code should start at offset 0, and the magic number 0xAA55 should be found at offset 0x1FE. At the end of the MBR, the partition table is saved. This always has four entries, as shown in Figure D.2.

Offset	Length	
0x000	0x1BE	**Code which loads and starts the boot sector of the active partition**
0x1BE	0x010	**Partition 1**
0x1CE	0x010	**Partition 2**
0x1DE	0x010	**Partition 3**
0x1EE	0x010	**Partition 4**
0x1FE	0x002	**0xAA55**

Figure D.2: The structure of the master boot record and the extended partition table.

A partition table entry consists of 16 bytes and is structured as shown in Figure D.3.

A hard disk can thus be divided into four partitions: These are called primary partitions. If they are not enough, an extended partition can be set up.

This contains at least one logical drive. As there evidently have been no plans to introduce any further structure at this point, the structure of the first sector of an extended partition corresponds to that of the MBR. The first partition entry of this extended partition table contains the first logical drive of this partition. The second entry is used as a pointer, if further logical drives exist. It points behind the first logical drive, where there is again a partition table with an entry for the next logical drive. The single entries of the logical drives are thus chained in a linked list: Theoretically, an extended partition could contain an arbitrary number of logical drives. The first sector of each primary or extended partition contains a boot sector with the structure described above. As booting can only be carried out from one of these partitions, the boot flag determines the active partition.

Size

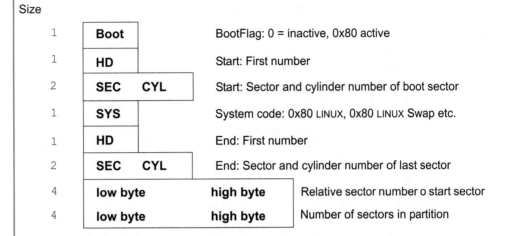

1	**Boot**		BootFlag: 0 = inactive, 0x80 active
1	**HD**		Start: First number
2	**SEC**	**CYL**	Start: Sector and cylinder number of boot sector
1	**SYS**		System code: 0x80 LINUX, 0x80 LINUX Swap etc.
1	**HD**		End: First number
2	**SEC**	**CYL**	End: Sector and cylinder number of last sector
4	**low byte**	**high byte**	Relative sector number o start sector
4	**low byte**	**high byte**	Number of sectors in partition

Figure D.3: The structure of a partition entry.

Originally, there were only primary partitions: Therefore fdisk under MS-DOS and most of the equivalent programs can only activate those partitions. The code in the MBR must therefore only carry out the following operations:

■ determining the active partition,

■ loading the boot sector of the active partition, using the BIOS,

■ jumping into the boot sector at offset 0.

The number of bytes in the MBR are more than sufficient to do this. Because, as described above, in principle each partition contains a boot sector, and furthermore, the structure of any second hard disk which may be present is similar to that of the first disk, a multitude of replacements for the standard MS-DOS MBR have come about: boot managers.

They all have in common the fact that they either substitute the MBR with their own code or occupy the boot sector of an active partition. To boot LINUX, most will use the LINUX loader LILO.

D.2 LILO — THE LINUX LOADER

The LILO boot sector contains room for one partition table. Therefore, LILO can be installed both in a partition and in the MBR. LILO possesses the full functionality of the standard MS-DOS boot sector but it can also boot logical drivers or partitions in the second hard disk. LILO can also be used in combination with another boot manager, which makes a large number of installation variants available.

D.2.1 | LILO started by MS-DOS MBR

If there is at least one primary LINUX partition[1] on the first hard disk, LILO can be installed there. After this partition is activated, the boot process proceeds as follows:

■ The BIOS loads the MBR.

■ The MBR loads the boot sector of the active partition, the LILO boot sector.

■ The loader boots LINUX or another operating system.

A de-installation is also very simple: another partition is activated.

Because no data is altered outside the LINUX partition (except for the boot flag), this is the "safest" variant.

D.2.2 | LILO started by a boot manager

This approach is recommended if you do not wish to renounce your old boot manager or if LILO is incapable of booting a foreign operating system. Depending on the capabilities of the other boot manager, there are some more "places" for the LILO installation.

■ If the boot manager can boot extended partitions, this is an ideal place for LILO.

■ If the boot manager can boot partitions on the second disk, LILO can be installed in one of these.

■ Some boot managers can even boot logical drivers, in which case LILO could be installed in one of these.

However, the following should be observed:

■ The installation programs of several operating systems[2] write their own MBR to disk without checking; this could destroy the other boot manager.

■ Repartitioning could destroy the boot sector of the extended partition, in which case LILO would have to be reinstalled.

A de-installation strongly depends on the boot manager used: Either the LILO boot partition used must be deregistered, or the boot manager itself can be used to boot each existing partition. The repartitioning or formatting of partitions removes both LINUX and LILO.

D.2.3 | LILO in the master boot record

If all of LINUX is on the second hard disk and there is no extending partition on the first one, then LILO must be installed in the MBR. This overwrites the existing MBR. Therefore, before beginning such an installation, one should make a backup of the old MBR (which also contains the partition table). Various DOS utilities can be used for this. Under LINUX, a backup is easily made by:

---

1 Not a swap partition, as in this the first sector is used as well!

2 An example of this is the installation of some versions of MS-DOS.

```
# dd if=/dev/hda of=/backup/MBR bs=512 count=1
```

Using

```
# dd if=/backup/MBR of=/dev/hda bs=446 count=1
```

the MBR is written back without the partition table. If the old partition table is also to be restored, the parameter to substitute is `bs=512`.

But beware! By doing this, the new partition table can be easily destroyed!

D.2.4 LILO files

The LILO files are normally located in the `/boot/`[3] directory, the configuration file `lilo.conf` in `/etc/`. The map file contains the actual information needed to boot the kernel and is created by the map installer `/sbin/lilo`. For any LILO installation, the configuration file must be adapted to personal requirements.

The configuration file

In principle, the configuration file consists of variable assignments. Each line contains either a flag variable or a variable assignment. Flag variables are simple denominators; variable assignments consist of the name of the variable, followed by an equals sign and the value of the variable. In addition, the configuration file is subdivided into boot configurations using special variable assignments, each of which boots either a kernel or another operating system. The following variables are global for all LILO configurations.

`boot=`*device* indicates which device (or which disk partition) shall contain the boot sector. If boot is not present, the boot sector is put in the current root device.

`compact` activates a mode in which LILO tries to carry out requests for neighboring sectors by means of a single request to the BIOS. This reduces loading times drastically, above all when booting from a floppy disk.

`delay=`*tenths* indicates the time in tenths of a second that LILO waits for a key to be pressed before the first boot configuration is booted. If delay is not specified, LILO boots immediately.

`linear` causes LILO to generate linear addresses instead of the usual sector `/head/cylinder` addresses. Linear addresses do not depend on the geometry of the device.

`install=`*boot sector* installs the indicated boot sector instead of the standard book sector `/boot/boot.b`.

`disktab=`*disktab* indicates the path of the *disktab* file (which contains the geometry data of special disks) if it is not in `/boot/disktab`.

`map=`*map file* specifies the path of the map file.

---

3 In older LILO versions also in `/etc/lilo/`.

message=*file* indicates the path of a file whose contents should be displayed as a startup message during booting. If message is not specified, the message "LILO" appears. As this startup message is inserted into the map file, the map installer /sbin/lilo must be started after each modification.

verbose=*level* specifies the debug level for LILO. Levels 0 (no message) to 5 (all status messages) are allowed.

backup=*backup file* indicates the name of the file in which the previous boot sector is stored. Otherwise, /boot/boot. *device* number is chosen.

force-backup=*backup file* as backup, but the file is overwritten if it already exists.

prompt forces the input of a boot configuration via the keyboard, which means LILO no longer boots the first boot configuration specified.

timeout=*tenths* sets a timeout value, within which keyboard input must have taken place, otherwise the first configuration is booted. Analogously, the input of a password becomes invalid if too much time passes between two inputs. By default, this value is infinite.

serial=*Port, bps parity bits* sets the parameters for the serial interface if LILO is to accept input from this. If one of the components *bps, parity,* or *bits* is omitted, the subsequent parameters must also be omitted. *Port* selects one of the four (default) serial interfaces; 0 corresponds to COM1 or /dev/ttyS0. Supported baud rates range from 100 to 9,600 bps; the default is 2,400 bps. All parity settings (n none, e even, and o odd) are supported as well as 7- or 8-bit data. The default setting is serial=0,2400n8.

ignore-table instructs LILO to ignore corrupt partition tables.

fix-table allows LILO to adapt the sector/head/cylinder addresses to linear addresses in each partition. Normally, a partition starts at a cylinder boundary; other operating systems might, however, change this. As LILO can only write its boot sector on partitions in which both addresses are the same, incorrect 3D addresses can be corrected with fix-table. This does not, however, guarantee that these corrections are permanent; therefore a repartitioning that keeps to cylinder boundaries is preferable.

password=*password* sets a password for all boot configurations.

restricted loosens the password restriction. Passwords only have to be given if one wants to pass additional boot parameters to the kernel.

optional allows one of the kernels indicated in a boot configuration to be missing. If optional is not specified, the map installer aborts with an error message.

Each boot configuration for a LINUX kernel begins with the assignments

```
image=kernel
    label=name
```

image must contain the path of the kernel to be booted, and label the name with which the kernel can be selected at the LILO prompt. If image is specified as a device, such as /dev/fd0, the range in which the kernel can be found has to be indicated using range=*range*

The range must be specified either as `start sector-end sector` or as `start sector + length`, for example:

```
image=/dev/fd0
  label=floppy
  range=1+512
```

Variable assignments within a boot configuration have a kind of local effect. The following assignments are possible:

append=*string* submits the character string to the kernel as a boot parameter. This allows, for example, hardware parameters to be passed to LINUX device drivers (see Section 7.4.3).

literal=*string* is like `append`, but the string is passed exclusively! As this might lead to the loss of vital settings, `literal` cannot be specified globally.

ramdisk=*size* overwrites the kernel's default for the size of the RAM disk.

read-only indicates the root file system to be mounted as read-only.

read-write similar to above.

root=*device* specifies the name of the device on which the root file system is to be found.

vga=*mode* overwrites the kernel's default video mode. Possible modes are `normal`, `extended`, and `ask`. In addition, the number of the default video mode can be specified.

Boot configurations of other operating systems are started with

```
other=device
  label=name
```

other describes the device (or the partition) on which the boot sector of the foreign operating system is to be found. The following variables can be set for foreign operating systems:

loader=*loader* specifies the loader's path to be used for booting the operating system. The default is `/boot/chain.b`. In addition, the LILO distribution contains the following loaders:

os2 d.b – can boot OS/2 from the second hard disk.

any d.b – attempts, before booting the operating system from the second hard disk, to invert the first and second hard disk in order to boot operating systems located in the second hard disk.

table=*device* specifies the device on which the partition table for the operating system to be booted can be found. If `table` is not specified, LILO does not pass information about the partition table to the boot sector of the foreign operating system.

unsafe switches off the checking of the operating system which is to be booted. This switch should only be used when a configuration is to be booted from a floppy disk.

Without this switch, the boot disk would have to be inserted into the disk drive every time the map installer starts running.

The disktab file

The disktab file contains the information about the geometry of the device from which LILO is to boot. Normally, this information can be obtained from the device driver, so a disktab file is only needed if this does not work. In this case, LILO outputs the error message

```
geo_query_dev HDIO_GETGEO (dev …)
```

or

```
HDIO_REQ not supported for your SCSI controller.
Please use /boot/disktab
```

In this case the geometry data must be input manually:

```
# /boot/disktab - LILO parameter table
#
# This table contains the geometry parameters for SCSI and
# IDE disks, which cannot be recognized automatically.
# Entries in this table overwrite recognized parameters!
#
# Dev. BIOS Secs/ Heads/ Cylin- Part.
# num. code track cylin. ders offset
# (optional)
#0x800   0x80   32      64      202 0 #  /dev/sda
```

These fields have the following meaning:

0x800 The device number as a combination of the major and minor numbers.

0x80 The BIOS code or this drive. 0x80 is the first hard disk in the system, 0x81 the second, and so on. The whole physical device, not single partitions, is considered as one unit!

32, 64, 202 The geometry data: number of sectors per track, number of heads and number of cylinders.

0 The start of the partitions in relative sectors beginning with sector 0 of the hard disk. As this information can also be read from the partition table, this specification is optional.

D.2.5 | LILO boot parameters

If, during the booting of LILO, Ctrl, ⇧, or Alt is pressed, if caps or Scroll were set, or the directive prompt is entered, LILO switches to interactive mode. To select a boot configuration, the name, defined as *label*, must be input. Pressing the ⬚ key shows all available boot configurations. In addition, as with the start of a program from the shell, parameters can be submitted. These parameters yield a command line which LILO submits to the kernel during startup. Some of the parameters are used by the kernel and the device drivers. Later on, parameters containing an equals sign "=" are inserted into the environment of the `init` program; the others are submitted as parameters.

The following boot parameters are recognized by the kernel and/or the `init` program:

`root=`*device*
`ro` and `rw` mount the root file system explicitly read-only or read/write.
`debug` all kernel messages are output on the system console.
`vga=`*video mode* selects the kernel's default video mode.
`S` tells the `init` program that LINUX is to be started in single user mode.
`reserve=`*port address, range,...* prohibits hardware recognition on the I/O addresses from *port address* to *port address+range*. Normally, hardware is recognized by the drivers via the writing and reading of magic values on port addresses. This can, with hardware that by chance occupies the same ports, lead to anything from undefined behavior to a complete crash of the system.[4] Therefore, `reserve=0x300,8` prohibits the kernel from searching for hardware at these addresses (see Section 7.2.3).

A further description of the boot parameter of the LINUX version 2.4 can be found in the kernel sources in the file `Documentation/kernel-parameters.txt`.

The command line always adds the parameter `BOOT_IMAGE=`*label* to LILO as well as the word `auto` if the first boot configuration was booted automatically. The submission of the command line to the kernel is very easy: LILO writes the magic number `0xA33F` to the physical address `0x9000:20` and to the offset of the address of the command line relative to `0x9000:0` after `0x9000:22`.

D.2.6 LILO startup messages

During the booting process the loader issues the message "LILO." If the loading process has been aborted, the characters that were output up to that moment can be used to diagnose the error. Some of these error messages should, however, not occur because they can only be caused by destroying LILO or by a faulty BIOS.

`no message` No part of LILO has been loaded. LILO has not been installed or the partition containing LILO is not active.
`L`*number* The first step of the loader has been loaded and started up, but the second step could not be loaded. The two digit-error number indicates the problem (see Section D.2.7). This may be caused by a physical error on the hard disk or floppy disk or by incorrect geometry (wrong parameter in `disktab`).

4 Especially in ISA architecture, in which only 10 bits of the port address are on the bus, this can lead to "unwanted," overlaps. This is also the reason why S3 cards apparently occupy the port address of the four serial interfaces.

LI The first step of the loader has been able to load the second step, whose processing then failed. This can be caused by incorrect geometry or by repositioning the file `boot.b` without having reinstalled the loader.

LIL The second step of the loader has been started, but cannot read the descriptor tables from the map file. This error indicates a physical defect or incorrect geometry.

LIL? The second step of the loader has been loaded to an incorrect address. This behavior is because of the same reasons as with `LI`.

LIL- The descriptor table is faulty. This error indicates incorrect geometry or a repositioning of the file `map` without having reinstalled the loader.

LILO All parts of the loader were loaded.

D.2.7 Error messages

If the BIOS signals an error while LILO loads the kernel, the error number is displayed.

0x00 *Internal error*

This error is generated by the read sector routine when an internal inconsistency is detected. The probable cause of the error is an incorrect map file.

0x01 *Illegal instruction*

This error message describes an internal LILO message which should not occur.

0x02 *Address label not found*

An error occurred while reading the media.

0x03 *Disk is write protected*

This error message should not occur.

0x04 *Sector not found*

This error is caused by incorrect geometry data. If the boot disk is a SCSI disk, the kernel does not recognize the geometry data or the disktab file is faulty. In rare cases, this error is also generated by the `compact` flag.

0x06 *Change line active*

This error is normally caused by opening and closing the disk drive door during the booting process.

0x08 *DMA overflow*

This error message occurs if there is an error while programming the DMA controller using LILO. This should not occur.

0x09 *DMA exceeds 64 Kbyte limit*

This error message occurs if there is an error while programming the DMA controller using LILO. This should not occur.

0x0C *Invalid media*

This error message is caused by defective media. It should not occur, however.

0x10 *CRC error*

The data on the media is faulty. A reinstallation of LILO might help (to rewrite the sector). If this error occurs when booting from a hard disk, the list of sectors which contain errors should be updated by using `fsck`.

0x20 *Controller error*

This error message occurs if there is an error while programming the floppy controller using LILO. This should not occur.

0x40 *Seek error*

This error message indicates a boot-media problem.

0x80 *Timeout*

The disk drive is not ready. The drive door might be open.

Generally, especially when booting from a floppy disk drive, it is a good idea to repeat the boot process, if no other possible cause for the error has been explicitly indicated.

E USEFUL KERNEL FUNCTIONS

There are some tasks in kernel programming that have to be carried out repeatedly. Unfortunately, in the LINUX kernel we cannot use the convenient C library that offers solutions to these tasks. Nevertheless, there is a plethora of functions in the LINUX kernel that facilitate developers' work.

We shall take a closer look at these functions here, in order to avoid reimplementations in future development work on the LINUX kernel. Knowledge of these functions also helps with reading and understanding the kernel sources. Many of these functions have been presented in previous chapters and are therefore only mentioned briefly.

Kernel function			
	close ()	dup ()	execve ()
	exit ()	open ()	setsid ()
	wait ()	write ()	

The kernel also provides a range of functions known as system calls. These can be used (with the already known functionality) in the kernel and work via the syscall macro.

Kernel function		
	set_bit	clear_bit ()
	change_bit ()	test_and_set_bit ()
	test_and_clear_bit ()	_test_and_change_bit ()
	__constant_bit_bit ()	__test_bit ()
	find_find_zero_bit ()	find_next_zero_bit ()
	ffz ()	

These functions are programmed as inline functions in the file `<asm/bitops.h>`. Depending on the architecture, they are assembler or C functions. They provide elementary bit operations. Bit 0 is the lowest bit of addr, bit 32^1 the lowest bit of addr+1.

```
inline int set_bit (int nr, void * addr);
inline int clear_bit (int nr, void * addr);
inline int change_bit (int nr, void * addr);
```

---

1 This is obviously true for 32-bit architectures.

```
inline int test_and_set_bit (int nr, volatile void * addr);
inline int test_and_clear_bit (int nr, volatile void * addr);
inline int test_and_change_bit (int nr, volatile void * addr);
inline int __constant_test_bit (int nr,
        const volatile void * addr);
inline int __test_bit (int nr, volatile void * addr);
inline int find_first_zero_bit (void * addr, unsigned size);
inline int find_next_zero_bit (void * addr, int size, int offset);
inline unsigned long ffz (unsigned long word);
```

The set_bit() function sets bit nr at the address addr. The function clear_bit() deletes bit nr at the address addr and change_bit() inverts it. test_and_set_bit() simply tests whether the bit is set or not. If bit nr previously had the value 0, the functions return 0, otherwise they return a value unequal to 0.

The find_first_zero_bit() function searches an area for a zero bit. The range starts with address addr and is size bits long. The function find_next_zero_bit(), on the other hand, searches the range starting from an offset offset. The function ffz() searches for the first free bit in the word value and returns its position. The behavior of the function is not defined if the value does not contain[2] a zero bit. This must therefore be tested in advance. All three functions return the position of the bit found.

Kernel function	iget ()	iput ()

These two functions, implemented in fs/inode.c, allow access to a specific inode structure.

```
struct inode * iget (struct super_block * sb,unsigned long ino);
void iput (struct inode * inode);
```

The iget() function supplies the inode described by sb and the inode number ino and simultaneously updates the hash table (increases the reference counter or enters it again). The inodes obtained with iget() have to be released with iput(). This function decrements the reference counter by 1 and releases the inode if the counter is 0.

Kernel function	sprintf() vsprintf()

To place different data in a string, C uses the sprintf() function. As kernel programming has to be carried out independently of the C library, it is rather useful that the kernel sources provide such a function.

```
int sprintf(char * buf, const char *fmt, …);
```

2 The i386 version returns 0.

The iget() function merely transforms its arguments into variable argument lists and calls vsprintf(). The return value is the number of characters written to buf. The function vsprintf() carries out the transformation itself.

```
int vsprintf(char *buf, const char *fmt, va_list args);
```

The string fmt contains two kinds of characters: normal characters which are simply copied, and conversion instructions which trigger transformation and output of the following argument. Each conversion instruction begins with a percentage sign and ends with a conversion sign. Between these, the following items can be placed in the specified order:

Control character – One or more characters in arbitrary order, which modify the conversion. The following characters are possible:

A space. If the first character is not a sign, a space is inserted.

- The converted argument is output ranged left.

+ If the number is greater than zero, a + is submitted.

\# Numbers are output in one of several formats. If the octal format is specified, the number is preceded by a 0; in hexadecimal format, it is preceded by 0x or 0X.

0 The number field is filled with zeros.

Number – Sets the minimum field width.

Dot (full stop) – Separates field width from the accuracy.

Number – The accuracy: this establishes the maximum number of characters to be output from a string, or the number of digits to be output after a decimal point.

Letter – h indicates short arguments and 1 or L indicates long arguments.

The conversion characters are specified by the following list:

c – Type int. The character arg is output.

s – Type char *. The character string arg is output up to byte "\0" or the required precision.

p – Type void *. The address arg is output in hexadecimal format.

n – Type int. The argument arg is a pointer to an integer (with h) or a long (with 1) in which the number of characters output so far is saved.

o – Type int. The number arg is output in octal format (with no leading 0).

x – Type int. The number arg is output in hexadecimal format (in lower case letters and with no leading 0x).

X – Type int. The number arg is output in hexadecimal format (in upper case letters and with no leading 0X).

d, i – Type int. The number arg is output signed.

u – Type int. The number arg is output unsigned.

Finally, the string buf is terminated with a zero byte and the number of characters actually written to buf is returned.

Kernel function	printk()

No one who has ever written extensive pieces of software will deny the usefulness of control and debug messages. Since LINUX has also become such a piece of software, it obviously must not lack a function to provide these messages. To offer and enhance the possibilities of an ordinary `printf()`, the kernel provides the function `printk()`.

```
int printk(const char *fmt, …);
```

The parameters are submitted to the `printk()` function in the same way as `printf()`. In addition, the first position can be taken by a macro which specifies the importance (called the "level" in the following) of the message. The following macros are available:

```
#define KERN_EMERG "<0>"      /* System no longer usable        */
#define KERN_ALERT "<1>"      /* Action to be terminated at once */
#define KERN_CRIT "<2>"       /* Critical condition             */
#define KERN_ERR "<3>"        /* Error                          */
#define KERN_WARNING "<4>"    /* Warning                        */
#define KERN_NOTICE "<5>"     /* Normal, but noteworthy         */
#define KERN_INFO "<6>"       /* Information                    */
#define KERN_DEBUG "<7>"      /* Debug level                    */
```

If no level is specified, the default level is entered. The default level is normally[3] `KERN_WARNING`.

Messages that are output with `printk()` are stored first in the log book, in a 16 Kbyte memory, and secondly, depending on their levels, are written to the console:

```
#define LOG_BUF_LEN (16384)
static char log_buf[LOG_BUF_LEN];
unsigned long log_size = 0;
static unsigned long log_start = 0;
static unsigned long logged_chars = 0;
```

The first variable describes the size of the log book; it can vary between 0 and `LOG_BUF_LEN`. The second variant indicates the start of the current message. With an access to `(log_start+log_size) & (LOG_BUF_LEN-1)` we can therefore obtain the last position of the current entry. The total number of characters in the log book can be found in `logged_chars`.

In what follows, we describe how the function is processed. First, `printk()` saves the flags of the processor and blocks all interrupts. The string passed (and any parameters

---

3 It goes without saying that other levels can be fixed as the default. If "debug" is located in the LILO boot parameters, the default log level is set to 10.

contained in it) are copied into a 1,024-byte internal buffer. There is no overflow check, and a longer string can therefore cause the kernel to crash. The first three characters are kept free for a level to be inserted later if required.

```
spin_lock_irqsave(&console_lock, flags);
va_start(args, fmt);
i = vsprintf(buf + 3, fmt, args);
                    /* hopefully i < sizeof(buf)-4 */
buf_end = buf + 3 + i;
va_end(args);
```

Now the messages are output. If no level was specified at call time, KERN_INFO is inserted as the level first.

```
for (p = buf + 3; p < buf_end; p++) {
    msg = p;
    if (msg_level < 0) {
        if ( p[0] != '<' || p[1] < '0' ||
            p[1] > '7' || p[2] != '>') {
            p -= 3;
            p[0] = '<';
            p[1] = default_message_loglevel + '0';
            p[2] = '>';
        } else
            msg += 3;
        msg_level = p[1] - '0';
    }
```

Now the message is written into the memory area allocated for this in the kernel – the *system's log book*. Since this memory is defined as a circular buffer, writing restarts at the beginning when the size is exceeded.

```
        for (; p < buf_end; p++) {
            log_buf[(log_start+log_size) & (LOG_BUF_LEN-1)] = *p;
            if (log_size < LOG_BUF_LEN)
                log_size++;
            else {
                log_start++;
                log_start &= LOG_BUF_LEN-1;
            }
            logged_chars++;
            if (*p == '\n') {
                linefeed = 1; break;
            }
        }
    }
```

Of course, the number of characters written is also counted. If a `printk()` call contains several messages, separated by '\n,' these are treated separately.

Now the message is written to the console. Only messages that are sufficiently important (with a priority above the log level) are output. The log level can be changed with the system call *syslog* (see page 322). While p now points to the end of the current message, msg still points to the beginning.

```
if (msg_level < console_loglevel && console_drivers) {
    struct console *c = console_drivers;
    while(c) {
        if ((c->flags & CON_ENABLED) && c->write)
            c->write(c, msg, p - msg + line_feed);
        c = c->next;
    }
}
```

When the current message is finished, a new priority has to be determined.

```
        if (linefeed) msg_level = -1;
}
```

Finally, the flags are put back on the stack and all processes which are blocked by reading from an empty log book are woken up.

```
        spin_unlock_irqrestore(&console_lock, flags);
        wake_up_interruptible(&log_wait);
        return i;
}
```

The number of characters written into the log book is returned.

Kernel function	panic()

The `panic()` function is a `printk()` with the fixed priority KERN_EMERG. The kernel function `sys_sync()` is also called, provided that the affected process is not the *Swap Task*, or the CPU is not in an interrupt handling routine. Then the function waits for `panic_timeout` seconds is waited for again and finally the computer is restarted.

```
NORET_TYPE void panic(const char * fmt, …);
```

Kernel function	memcpy()	bcopy()	memset()
	memcmp()	memmove()	memscan()

These functions handle memory areas. Generally these are areas consisting of character strings which are not terminated by a zero byte. None of the following functions checks for overflow conditions. These functions are similar to the string handling functions.

Generally, the same algorithms are implemented, the difference being that an additional length indication is needed.

```
void * memset(void * s,char c,size_t count);
```

The `memset()` function fills the area addressed by s of size `count` with the character c.

```
void * memcpy(void * dest,const void *src,size_t count);
char * bcopy(const char * src, char * dest, int count);
```

Both functions have the same effect: the area `dest` is filled with the first count characters of `src`.

```
void * memmove(void * dest,const void *src,size_t count);
```

This function copies `count` characters from the start of the area `src` into the `dest` area. It is, however, somewhat more intelligent than the previous function. It checks whether the copying could overwrite the source (destination address lower than source address), then starts copying at the end of the area.

```
int memcmp(const void * cs,const void * ct,size_t count);
```

The function `memcmp()` compares two memory areas of maximum count characters. The return value is a number greater than, equal to, or less than zero, depending on whether `cs` is lexicographically greater than, equal to, or less than `ct`.

```
void * memscan(void * addr, unsigned char c, size_t size);
```

The `memscan()` function searches `size` characters in the area `addr` for the character c. The address of the first occurrence is returned.

Kernel function	register_chdev()	unregister_chrdev()
	register_blkdev()	unregister_blkdev()

Both register functions register a device driver in the kernel. The first registers a character device driver, the second a block device driver.

```
int register_chrdev(unsigned int major, const char * name,
                    struct file_operations *fops);
int unregister_chrdev(unsigned int major, const char * name);
int register_blkdev(unsigned int major, const char * name,
                    struct file_operations *fops);
int unregister_blkdev(unsigned int major, const char * name);
```

The parameters are the same in both cases. They specify how and under which name the device has to be registered.

`major` – the desired major number of the device
`name` – the symbolic name, for example `"tty"` or `"lp"`

fops – the address of the `file_operations` structure

The driver is entered into the corresponding table in the kernel, with its major number as the index. If the major number is 0, the last free entry is used, and its index returned. If there is no free entry in the table or the major number is already occupied, the function returns `-EBUSY`.

The `unregister` functions terminate the driver's registration by entering `NULL` in the table.

Kernel function	register_binfmt()	unregister_binfmt()
	register_exec_domain()	unregister_exec_domain()
	register_filesystem()	unregister_filesystem()

These functions register and deregister binary formats and file systems in the kernel. In contrast to device drivers, the number of these formats is arbitrary, because they are not managed in a table but in lists. If an attempt is made to register the same format twice in the kernel, the function returns `-EBUSY`.

```
int register_binfmt(struct linux_binfmt * fmt);
int unregister_binfmt(struct linux_binfmt * fmt);
```

The `register_binfmt()` function registers a binary format in the kernel by entering it into the list of known formats. A binary format has the following structure:

```
struct linux_binfmt {
  struct linux_binfmt * next;
  struct module *module;
  int (*load_binary)
  (struct linux_binprm *, struct pt_regs * regs);
  int (*load_shlib)(int fd);
  int (*core_dump)(long signr, struct pt_regs * regs);
};
```

A known binary format can be removed using `unregister_binfmt()`.

```
int register_exec_domain(struct exec_domain *it);
int unregister_exec_domain(struct exec_domain *it);
```

The `register_exec_domain()` function registers a new exec domain in the kernel. A domain can be removed using `unregister_exec_domain()`. An exec domain has the following structure:

```
struct exec_domain {
  char *name;
  lcall7_func handler;
  unsigned char pers_low, pers_high;
```

```
unsigned long * signal_map;
unsigned long * signal_invmap;
struct module *module;
struct exec_domain *next;
};
int register_filesystem(struct file_system_type * fs);
int unregister_filesystem(struct file_system_type * fs);
```

These functions register and deregister a file system type in the kernel. The submitted structure looks as follows:

```
struct file_system_type {
char *name;
int fs_flags;
struct super_block *(*read_super)
      (struct super_block *, void *, int);
struct file_system_type * next;
};
```

Kernel function	register_serial()	unregister_serial()
	register_netdev()	unregister_netdev()

These functions register devices that are different from "normal" UNIX devices.

```
int register_serial(struct serial_struct *req);
int unregister_serial(int line);
```

Normally, the number of serial devices of a computer is fixed and does not vary during operations. This function is only of interest for owners of a PCMCIA interface (laptop owners), as it is used to add a serial port at runtime. The structure is entered into the rs_table[] and its index is returned. If no suitable port can be found in the table, the first free unknown port is occupied. Registration is terminated with unregister_ serial(). The line parameter determines the port to be deregistered. If this is still connected to a terminal, it is closed (using tty_hangup()).

```
int register_netdev(struct device *dev);
void unregister_netdev(struct device *dev);
```

These functions register and deregister abstract networks. Working with these functions is not easy because of the size of the device structure. For a more precise description, refer to Section 8.3.

Kernel function	tty_register_driver()
	tty_unregister_driver()

```
int tty_register_driver(struct tty_driver *driver);
int tty_unregister_driver(struct tty_driver *driver);
```

These functions register a new TTY driver in the kernel. When registering a kernel, an internal call is made to `register_chrdev()`. In `driver`, we find the major number and its name; the standard TTY operations are entered as file operations. If the driver does not yet possess a function to output a single character, the registering function inserts one. The driver is unregistered with `tty_unregister_driver()`. If the driver is still in use, `-EBUSY` is returned.

Kernel function	strcpy()	strncpo()	strchr()
	strcat()	strncat()	strspn()
	strcmp()	strncmp()	strpbrk()
	strlen()	strnlen()	strtok()

The functions listed here provide most of the routines known from the C library. They are defined as generic C functions in the `lib/string.c`, and as optimized inline assembler functions in `<asm/string.h>`.

```
char * strcpy(char * dest,const char *src);
char * strncpy(char * dest,const char *src,size_t count);
```

The `strcpy()` function copies the string `src` to `dest`, including the zero byte. The strings should not overlap, and the target string should have sufficient capacity. The function `strncpy()` works in the same way, but only copies the first `count` characters. If `src` (including the zero byte) is shorter than `count`, only `src` is copied. Both functions return the pointer to `dest`.

```
char * strcat(char * dest, const char * src);
char * strncat(char *dest, const char *src, size_t count);
```

The `strcat()` function appends a copy of the string `src` to the string dest. The `strncat ()` function appends a maximum of `count` characters of the string `src` to the string `dest`.

```
int strcmp(const char * cs,const char * ct);
int strncmp(const char * cs,const char * ct, size_t count);
```

The `strcmp()` function compares the string `src` character by character with the string `ct` over the length of `cs`. The return value is a number greater than, equal to, or less than zero, depending on whether `cs` is lexicographically greater than, equal to, or less than `ct`. The function `strncmp()` compares a maximum of `count` characters.

```
char * strchr(const char * s,char c);
```

The `strchr()` function returns a pointer to the first occurrence of the character `c` in the string `s`. If the character is not found, a `NULL` pointer is returned.

```
size_t strlen(const char * s);
size_t strnlen(const char * s, size_t count);
```

The `strlen()` function returns the number of characters in `s`, excluding the zero byte whereas `strnlen()` returns the minimum string length and `count`. This function is used by `vsprintf()` for formatting strings.

```
size_t strspn (const char *s, const char *accept);
char * strpbrk (const char * cs,const char * ct);
```

The `strspn()` function returns the size of the first part of `s` that does not contain characters from `accept`. The function `strpbrk()` returns a pointer to the position in `cs` where the first occurrence of a character from `ct` is found.

```
char * strtok (char * s,const char * ct);
```

The `strtok()` function returns the first character string (token) of the string `s` which does not contain characters from `ct`. Repeated calls of the function with a `NULL` pointer for `s` divide the string into a sequence of character strings.

Kernel function	simple_strtoul()

```
unsigned long simple_strtoul(const char *cp,
            char **endp,unsigned int base);
```

The eternal problem of converting a string into a number is handled by this function. The string `cp` contains the number to be converted, `base` contains the base of the number system to be used. If it contains a 0, the function tries to determine the base automatically. The default is base 10; but if `cp` begins with "0," base 8 is used and if it begins with "0x," basis 16 is used. Then `cp` is read character by character, until a character no longer fits into the number system, and is then converted. The remaining string is saved in `endp`, and the calculated result is returned.

Kernel function	verify area()

```
int verify_area(int type, const void * addr,
            unsigned long size);
```

This function checks whether an operation type is allowed on a memory area identified by the address `addr` and the size `size`. Two operations are possible: `VERIFY_WRITE` as type tests whether the write access is allowed; `VERIFY_READ` checks for read access.

Kernel function	get_user()	put_user()
	copy_to_user()	copy_from_user()

The first two functions allow access to the data contained in the user address memory. The size of the pointer is self-determined. The macro `get_user()` reads the value x from the address `ptr`, and `put_user()` writes it.

To copy larger data areas, the copy functions are used. They copy a data area of the size `size` from the kernel address memory in the user address memory (`to`) or vice versa.

Kernel function	suser()	fsuser()

These two functions check whether a process has superuser privileges or superuser privileges with respect to the file system. Both are simple functions in the header file `<linux/sched.h>` of the form:

```
extern inline int suser(void)
{
  if (!issecure(SECURE_NOROOT) && current->euid == 0) {
    current->flags |= PF_SUPERPRIV; return 1;
  }
  return 0;
}
```

New programs should check the rights of the process and use the function `capable()` to do so!

Kernel function	capable()

Now, using this function, one can check whether a particular right has been set for the current process.

```
#define cap_raised(c, flag) ((c) & (1 << (flag)))
extern inline int capable(int cap)
{
  if (cap_raised(current->cap_effective, cap)) {
    current->flags |= PF_SUPERPRIV;
    return 1;
  }
  return 0;
}
```

Kernel function	cap_emulate_setxuid()

This function is called if one of the UIDs[4] of the actual process changes. If this is the case, the rights are altered. We can distinguish three cases:

---

4 UIDs mean either uid, euid, or suid here.

1 Previously, at least one UID was 0 and now all UIDs are unequal to 0. Then all allowed and effective rights are deleted.

2 The EUID changes from 0 to another value. If so, all effective rights are deleted.

3 The EUID changes from a value unequal to 0 to 0. If so, the allowed rights are written as effective rights.

Kernel function	add_wait_queue()	remove_wait_queue()

The management of wait queues is not a complicated issue. But it must be ensured that no two processes or interrupts modify a wait queue at the same time. The following functions must be used for access.

```
inline void add_wait_queue(struct wait_queue ** p,
        struct wait_queue * wait);
inline void remove_wait_queue(struct wait_queue ** p,
        struct wait_queue * wait);
```

The first function puts the entry `wait` into the wait queue p (as the first entry), the second function removes it. Both functions occur atomically.

Kernel function	up()	down()

```
extern inline void up(struct semaphore * sem);
extern inline void down(struct semaphore * sem)
```

These two functions allow synchronization between processes via a semaphore:

```
struct semaphore {
  atomic_t count;
  int sleepers;
  struct wait_queue_head_t wait;
};
```

The down() function checks whether a semaphore is free (greater than or equal to 0) and decrements it if successful. Otherwise, the process enters itself in a waiting queue and blocks until the semaphore is free again.

The up() function does nothing but increment the semaphore by 1. If the value of the semaphore was previously negative, a wake_up() is executed on the associated waiting queue.

Kernel function	list_add()	list_del()	list_empty()
	list_entry()	list_splice()	

In LINUX version 2.2 most data structures, dynamically created, were switched over to a generic list implementation. This switch-over guarantees that list operations, such as the addition or the removal of objects, are automatically carried out in the correct way.

The generic list implementation supports doubly chained lists and is based on the structure list_head. It contains, respectively, a pointer to the previous and the next element of a list.

```
struct list_head {
  struct list_head *next, *prev;
};
```

This structure is used to build both the start points (anchors) and the elements of a list. At first, the macro LIST_HEAD defines an empty list. The list is empty since both the first and the last element point at the anchor.

```
#define LIST_HEAD (name) \
  struct list_head name = { &name, &name }
```

In a similar way, the macro INIT_LIST_HEAD initializes a predefined anchor of type struct list_head *:

```
#define INIT_LIST_HEAD (ptr) do { \
  (ptr)->next = (ptr); (ptr)->prev = (ptr); \
} while (0)
```

The addition of elements uses list_add(). It adds the new element after the head element. There, head can be also the anchor of the list. The function list_del() removes the element entry from the list. As this is a doubly chained list, its anchor does not have to be known.

```
void list_add(struct list_head *new, struct list_head *head);
void list_del(struct list_head *entry);
```

It is also possible to replace an element in a list with another element. The function list_splice() is used to do this. It replaces the element list with the element head.

```
void list_splice(struct list_head *list, struct list_head *head);
```

To create a characteristic list of elements of type struct T, several steps are necessary. Firstly, a component of the list_head type has to be inserted.

```
struct T {
        struct list_head t_list; /* chained struct T */
    ... /* Rest of the structure */
};
```

After an anchor has been defined, elements can be linked together:

```
LIST_HEAD(list);
struct T a, b;
list_add(a, list);
list_add(b, list);
```

How can you access the individual elements in a list, if only their t_list components are linked with each other? To do this, the macro list_entry is used:

```
#define list_entry(ptr, type, member) \
((type *)((char *)(ptr)-(unsigned long)(&((type *)0)->member)))
```

It makes sure that the chained component is "converted" into a pointer in the linked structure. To do this one needs an argument of the list_head type, the type of the linked structure, and the name of the component on which the concatenation is carried out.

```
struct *T elem;
/* gets first element in the list */
elem = list_entry(list.next, struct T, t_list);
/* gets next element after a */
if (a.t_list.next != &list)
  elem = list_entry(a.t_list.next, struct T, t_list);
/* gets element before b */
if (b.t_list.prev != &list)
  elem = list_entry(b.t_list.prev, struct T, t_list);
```

Since list_entry is a macro, notice that the argument ptr points to an element. This is done with a comparison at the beginning of the list. As LIST_HEAD initializes the beginning and the end of the list instead of the anchor, both ends of a list can easily be recognized.

Finally, a function for recognizing an empty list is also available.

```
int list_empty(struct list_head *head)
{
  return head->next == head;
}
```

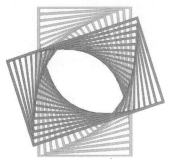

REFERENCES

[Bac86]   Maurice J. Bach. *The Design of the UNIX(R) Operating System*. Prentice Hall International, Inc., London, 1986. *Describes the structure of UNIX System V and how it operates. Together with [LMKQ89] this is the standard literature on Unix operating system implementation.*

[Bac98]   Jean Bacon. *Concurrent Systems*. Addison-Wesley, second edition, 1998. *A good groundwork on parallel systems.*

[BC01]   Daniel P. Bovet and Marco Cesati. *Understanding the Linux Kernel*. O'Reilly & Associates, Inc., 2001. *An excellent book on the Linux kernel 2.2 and the implementation of i386 hardware.*

[Bur95]   Richard A. Burgess. *Developing your own 32-Bit Operating System*. Sams Publishing, 1995. *This book describes the structure and functioning of MMURTL, a multitasking operating system for 80386 systems. The complete source code is included, so that everyone is welcome to experiment.*

[CDM98]   Rémy Card, Eric Dumas, and Franck Mevel. *The Linux Kernel Book*. John Wiley & Sons Ltd., 1998. *The competing work to our book. Rémy Card is the programmer of the standard file system ext2fs for Linux.*

[Cla90]   Ludwig Claßen. *Programmierhandbuch 80386/80486*. Verlag Technik, Berlin, 1990. *A very compact introduction to 80386 programming. There are some references to [CW90]. Available in German only.*

[CO87]   Ludwig Claßen and Ulrich Oefler. *UNIX und C – Ein Anwenderhandbuch*. Verlag Technik, Berlin, 2. Auflage, 1987. *An introduction to Unix and the C programming language. Referring as it does to Unix version 7, it is perhaps not quite up to date, but still readable. Available in German only.*

[Com91]   Douglas E. Comer. *Internetworking With TCP/IP*, Volume I – Principles, Protocols and Architecture. Prentice Hall International, Inc., London, second edition, 1991. *The standard work on TCP/IP. Covers all basic protocols including ARP, TCP, IP, RIP.*

[CS91]   Douglas E. Comer and David L. Stevens. *Internetworking with TCP/IP*, Volume II – Design, Implementation, and Internals. Prentice Hall International, Inc., London, first edition, 1991. *Covers the TCP/IP implementation of the Xinu system. The Xinu system is a free implementation of a Unix-compatible system.*

[CW90]   Ludwig Claßen and Ulrich Wiesner. *Wissensspeicher 80286-Programmierung.* Verlag Technik, Berlin, 1990. *Available in German only.*

[DC85]   S. E. Deering and D. R. Cheriton. *RFC 966 –* host groups: A multicast extension to the internet protocol. December 1985. *Describes the IGMP protocol. For IP multicast packets to be routed efficiently, an exchange of information between the IP routers is required. For this purpose a new protocol was developed, closely modeled on ICMP.*

[Dee89]   S. Deering. *RFC 1112 –* host extensions for ip multicasting, August 1989. *This RFC deals with the extensions and alterations which need to be made in network implementations in order to support IP multicast. In so doing, it only goes into the requirements of individual computers.*

[ELF]   Executable and linkable format (elf). *A description of the ELF binary format. This can be found on many large FTP servers, including (in packet form) on [FTP] in the* file `/pub/os/linux/packages/GCC/ELF.doc.tar.gz`.

[Fei93]   Sidnie Feit. * *TCP/IP – Architecture, Protocols, and Implementation.* McGraw-Hill, Inc., New York, 1993. *One of many books on TCP/IP. A more comprehensive presentation may be found in [Com91].*

[FTP]   `ftp.informatik.hu-berlin.de:/pub/linux`. *The authors' home FTP server. Along with the most important data of other Linux FTP servers, it also contains the PC speaker driver described in this book (in the* `hu-sound/` *directory).*

[Gal95]   Bill O. Gallmeister. *POSIX.4: Programming for the Real World.* O'Reilly & Associates, Inc., 1995. *This book describes the real-time completions of the POSIX standard 1003.1b, better known than POSIX.4. Information on asynchronous IO and POSIX IPC is also available here.*

[GC94]   Berny Goodheart and James Cox. *The Magic Garden Explained.* Prentice Hall International, Inc., 1994. *An up-to-date description of the internals of UNIX System V Release 4.*

[Gir90]   Gintaras R. Gircys. *Understanding and Using COFF.* O'Reilly & Associates, Inc., 1990. *A comprehensive description of the COFF object format. Describes the structure and adaptation more precisely. Since the object format has arisen from the universally known* `a.out` *and there is no appreciable difference between the two, it is also suitable for use as literature for* `a.out`.

[GPL]   Gnu public license. *The GNU Public License specifies the license conditions under which the Linux kernel and most programs included Linux distributions may be used. The wording can be found in the file COPYING of the enclosed CD.*

[HH+96]   Sebastian Hetze, Dirk Hohndel, u.a. *Linux Anwenderhandbuch.* LunetIX Softfair, 6. erweiterte und aktualisierte Auflage, 1996. *A good reference work for the budding Linux user on installing and maintaining the Linux system. Available in German only.*

[Joh95] Michael K. Johnson. *Linux Kernel Hacker's Guide*. Linux Document Project, draft 0.6 edition, 1995. *This should really become the standard work for the Linux kernel. The most recently published version dates from January 1995. For the future, it is rather intended to become a collection of articles. As with all other documentation on the Linux document project, the text of this book is available on all good Linux FTP servers.*

[Knu98] Donald E. Knuth. *The Art of Computer Programming*, Volume 1. O'Reilly & Associates, Inc., third edition, 1998. *The first volume of the most ingenious work ever written on programming.*

[LDP] Linux document project. *In many large software projects there is usually no one who writes the necessary documentation. Luckily, this is not the case with Linux. There soon formed a group of developers who wrote important texts under the name of Linux Document Project. These include the detailed Manual Pages, a Linux installation manual, the Network Administrator's Guide, the Linux Kernel Hacker's Guide, and the Linux Programmer's Guide.*

[Lew91] Donald Lewine. *POSIX Programmer's Guide*. O'Reilly & Associates, Inc., 1991. *Anyone who does not already have the POSIX standard on their desk (and who does?) should at least take a close look at this book.*

[Lio77] John Lions. *Lion's Commentary on UNIX 6th Edition*. 1977. *One of the classical works of the UNIX literature. After having been offered only as a copy for a long time, it is now available as an "official" reprint.*

[LMKQ89] S. J. Leffler, M. K. McKusick, M. J. Karels, and J. S. Quaterman. *The Design and Implementation of the 4.3BSD Unix Operating System*. Addison-Wesley Publishing, Reading, 1989. *In contrast to [Bac86], this concerns the implementation of the BSD variant of Unix. Also a standard work on: "How do I write my own Unix system?." For 4.4 BSD implementation, see [MBKQ96].*

[Max99] Scott Maxwell. *Linux Core Kernel Commentary*. Coriolis Open Press, 1999. *According to [Lio77] this book consists of two parts. First there are about 400 printed sides of original Linux source code. Its operation is described in the second part of about 150 pages.*

[MBKQ96] Marshall Kirk McKusick, Keith Bostic, Michael J. Karels, and John S. Quarterman. *The Design and Implementation of the 4.4 BSD Operating System*. Addison-Wesley Publishing, Reading, 1996. *The successor of [LMKQ89] describes all internals of the newest BSD version.*

[Mes02] Hans-Peter Messmer. *The Indispensable PC Hardware Book Fourth Edition*. Addison-Wesley, London, 2002. *A good, understandable description of standard PC hardware. The fundamental introduction to the thematic of DMA is highly commendable.*

[MM01]   Jim Mauro and Richard McDougall. *Solaris Internals*. Prentice Hall/Sun Microsystems Press, 2001. *This is the ultimate book on the Sun Solaris kernel, a modern commercial Unix implementation.*

[Pos81]   Jon Postel. RFC 793 – transmission control protocol: Protocol specification, September 1981. *This RFC is actually the basis for all implementations of the TCP protocol. If everyone keeps to it, there will be no problems with communication via TCP.*

[PT+91]   Rob Pike, Ken Thomson, et al. Plan 9: The early papers, July 1991. *A very interesting collection of some older works on the experimental Plan 9 operating system. If the authors' names sound familiar, that is because the same people also wrote the first Unix systems 20 years ago. Here one can read how they now regard the Unix concepts. These reports have also been published on the internet and are available on many good FTP servers.*

[Rub98]   Allessandro Rubini. *Linux device drivers*. O'Reilly & Associates, Inc., 1998. *A very good guide for developing device drivers under Linux.*

[Sal94]   Peter H. Salus. *A Quarter Century of Unix*. Addison-Wesley Publishing, Reading, 1994. *A book not about the internals of Unix but about the history of this fascinating operating system.*

[San93]   Michael Santifaller. *TCP/IP und ONC/NFS in Theorie und Praxis*. Addison-Wesley, Bonn, 2., aktualisierte und erweiterte Auflage, 1993. *Introduction to thematics whose emphasis lies in their use.*

[Sch94]   Curt Schimmel. *UNIX Systems for Modern Architectures*. Addison-Wesley Publishing, Reading, 1994. *After a general introduction to the Unix kernel, the author gives a detailed treatment of the problems and possibilities of multiprocessing and caching for Unix systems.*

[SG94]   Avi Silberschatz and Peter Galvin. * Operating System Concepts. Addison-Wesley Publishing, Reading, 1994. *Yet another introduction to the matter.*

[SMP]   Multiprocessor specification. *The Intel multiprocessor specification describes the interaction of several Intel processors in a system. It can be seen under* `http://developer.intel.com/pro/datashts/24201605.pdf`

[Sta94]   Stefan Stapelberg. *UNIX System V.4 für Einsteiger und Fortgeschrittene*. Addison-Wesley, Bonn, 1994. *Availibility in German only.*

[Ste92a]   W. Richard Stevens. *Advanced Programming in the UNIX(R) Environment*. Addison-Wesley Publishing, Reading, 1992. *The ultimate book on programming under Unix. Stevens describes, in over 700 pages, the entire spectrum of system calls from BSD 4.3 through System V Release 4 to the POSIX standard – including the application of system calls – using meaningful examples.*

[Ste92b]   W. Richard Stevens. *Programming* UNIX *Networks*. Coedition Verlage Carl Hanser and Prentice-Hall, München and London, 1992. *Anyone finding the chapter on networks in [Ste92a] too short will find everything about programming Unix networks here. Another very commendable book.*

[Ste94]   W. Richard Stevens. *TCP/IP Illustrated: The Protocols*, Volume 1. Addison-Wesley Publishing, Reading, 1994. *Undoubtedly the leading standard on TCP/IP. Describes the subject matter in exactly the way in which the Unix user encounters it. A set of freely usable tools helps with exploring the network.*

[Ste98]   W. Richard Stevens. *UNIX Network Programming – Interprocess Communications*. Prentice Hall International, Inc., Upper Saddle River, NJ 07458, 1998. *The ultimate book about interprocess communication. It explains everything from System V IPC, the new IPC specification for POSIX, and the communication between POSIX threads.*

[Tan86]   Andrew S. Tanenbaum. *Modern Operating Systems*. Prentice Hall International, Inc., London, 1986. *Does not cover Minix, in contrast to [Tan90]. Describes fundamental principles of the mode of operation of classical and distributed operating systems. These are subsequently explained using, in each case, two concrete examples (MS-DOS, Unix, Amoeba, and Mach). It still remains unclear to us how a description of MS-DOS finds its way into a book called "Modern Operating Systems."*

[Tan89]   Andrew S. Tanenbaum. *Computer Networks*. Prentice Hall International, Inc., London, second edition, 1989. *An overview of how networks operate. Starting with the OSI reference model, the theoretical foundations of the individual layers and their realization in practice are described. A good foundation book, even though it is no longer up to date.*

[Tan90]   Andrew S. Tanenbaum. *Betriebssysteme – Entwurf und Realisierung – Teil 1 Lehrbuch*. Coedition Verlage Carl Hanser and Prentice-Hall, Berlin and London, 1990. *Here Tanenbaum describes the structure and functioning of his Minix system. Minix (Mini Unix) was written by Tanenbaum for educational purposes. It illustrates the concepts of implementing Unix systems very well, but its limitations render it not entirely suitable in practice. Minix was the first Unix system whose source texts could be obtained relatively inexpensively. For this reason it was quite popular with Information Technology students. The development of Linux began under Minix.*

[Val96]   Uresh Valhalla. *UNIX Internals – The New Frontiers*. Prentice Hall, 1996. *A new book about concepts in the development of the Unix operating system.*

[WE96]   Kevin Washburn and Jim Evans. *TCP/IP Second Edition*. Addison-Wesley, London, 1996. *An even more comprehensive introduction to the thematics of TCP/IP. The emphasis lies clearly on the description of the protocols and their application.*

INDEX

The index is intended as a tool for those working with the LINUX kernel. For kernel functions, variables and structures, the file in which the definition can be found is specified in parentheses "( )". Files are specified relative to the root of the LINUX sources (*see* Chapter 2), with the exception of the header files which are located in the include path (thus mainly under /usr/include). In analogy to the include instruction of the C preprocessor, these files are enclosed in angle brackets "< >". The word *static* following a variable or a function indicates that this variable or function is defined locally in the specified file.

If in preprocessor macros the value is a simple number, it is indicated after an equals sign "=". In addition, a file in which the macro is defined is also specified.